German Feminism:
Readings in Politics and Literature

German Feminism: Readings in Politics and Literature

Edited by

EDITH HOSHINO ALTBACH

JEANETTE CLAUSEN

DAGMAR SCHULTZ

NAOMI STEPHAN

State University of New York Press

ALBANY

Published by
State University of New York Press, Albany

©1984 State University of New York

For information, address State University of New York
Press, State University Plaza, Albany, N.Y., 12246

Library of Congress Cataloging in Publication Data

Main entry under title:

German feminism.

1. Feminism—Germany (West and East)—Addresses, essays,
lectures. 2. German prose literature—Germany (West and East) and Austria—
Women authors. 3. German prose literature—20th century.
I. Altbach, Edith Hoshino.
HQ1625.G465 1984   305.4'2'0943   83-17849
ISBN 0-87395-840-3
ISBN 0-87395-841-1 (pbk.)

Contents

Part Three
BODY POLITICS

Part Four
WO/MAN HATING

Part Five
REPORTAGE AND ESSAY

Part Eleven
WOMEN'S STUDIES

A CRITICAL OUTLOOK

Preface

This anthology presents an interplay of two kinds of writing by women in the German language: The new women's prose literature and the working papers from the new German women's movement. The texts—almost sixty in all—are culled from a wide range of commercial, left and feminist presses and journals. While it is not uncommon to find the occasional poem or short story interspersed among the articles and essays in an anthology of feminist writing, in this volume we have sought a more complete merging of literature and politics. This editorial decision was not taken without second thoughts, for the two types of material resisted our initial efforts to assign them to neat, parallel categories reflecting feminist theory and practice. As we worked, however, our conviction grew as to the rightness of our decision.

For one thing, we believe that this intermingling of stories and excerpts from novels together with documents and articles more faithfully presents the range of writing important to well-read and thoughtful feminists. Moreover, the fantastic and realistic tales which make up almost half of this volume may well outlive the other material in their power to evoke a response in us; for the literary texts keep before us the workaday and imaginative world of women—the truth against which feminist impulses and ideas must be measured.

The nonfiction texts, arranged topically, are to be found in sections I, III, VI, VIII, X, and XI. The literary texts (including documentary literature), grouped by tone, mood, or thematic and stylistic elements, are to be found in sections II, IV, V, VII, and IX. The four editors collaborated in the selection of material for this anthology. Edith Hoshino Altbach was responsible for final editing, introductions, and headnotes for sections III, VI, VIII, X, and XI. Jeanette Clausen was responsible for final editing, introductions, and headnotes for sections

I, II, IV, V, VII, and IX. Edith Hoshino Altbach and Jeanette Clausen
prepared the manuscript for publication.

June, 1983
Buffalo, New York
Fort Wayne, Indiana

Introductions

The New German Women's Movement

The international feminist network has brought little news to the United States of the women's movement which emerged in West Germany in the late 1960s (and a few years later in Austria and Switzerland). To be sure, in the late 1960s many a leftist women's study group in the United States studied Friedrich Engels, August Bebel, and Clara Zetkin. However, these authorities were looked to for theoretical and ideological guidance and did not provide an understanding of the historical or contemporary women's movements in Germany. Until this year, no major theoretical work from the current West German movement had been published in the United States.[1] Heinrich Böll and Günter Grass have followings here, but virtually untranslated and unknown until most recently are the realistic and fantastic tales written by women in both Germanys and Austria.[2]

An unspoken anti-German attitude at work? I think it is rather that the general work, the intellectual tour de force translates more successfully than debate and manifesto. And until the late 1970s, the German women's movement had produced little of the former, being of a more activist, practical nature. Thus, Germany remains for most feminists in this country the setting which produced that watchword for women's oppression: *Kinder, Küche, Kirche*. One editor wrote, in the course of declining to publish this anthology, that it was her impression the German movement was "behind" the American and thus of interest only to specialists. This implies that in some international feminist sweepstakes the German movement falls short of the American movement, perhaps in militance or breadth of popular support. Certainly quite a few German women are or were of this opinion. But the American movement has fallen on hard times. This is perhaps a good time to look at a movement with enough parallels to the United States movement to make comparisons in strategy and course instructive.

3

Early Days

On a brief visit to West Berlin in the Fall of 1968, I found no journals or pamphlets to suggest the existence of a women's movement in radical bookstores filled with publications from the student movement, although I had heard that women in and around SDS (Socialist German Students' Federation) were organizing. I found, instead, the "woman question" touched upon in quite a range of publications on culture and sexuality. Among my finds were the four-issue series on "Sexuality and Domination" of the journal *Das Argument*, a thesis-like book by Reimut Reiche *Sexuality and Class Struggle*, and a survey study in the Kinsey tradition *Students—Sexuality* by Hans Giese and Gunter Schmidt.[3]

Drawing on older works by Freud, Wilhelm Reich, Ernst Bloch, Theodor Adorno and Herbert Marcuse, the New Left writers were playing with ideas of manipulation and resistance which at least implied the question of women's liberation. In the book by Giese and Schmidt (a straight-forward empirical study in contrast to the more partisan New Left works), tribute was paid to the World League for Sexual Reform (Weltliga für Sexualreform)—founded in 1928— and its program of demands, at the head of which stood "the political, economic, and sexual emancipation of women." Giese and Schmidt said of these demands that "they are as little fulfilled in 1968 as they were in 1928," thereby acknowledging the continuing relevance of women's liberation. The *Argument* series included a reprint of Ernst Bloch's (a founding member of the World League for Sexual Reform) essay from the 1930s, "The Struggle for the New Woman" ("Kampf ums neue Weib"), which perceptively questioned a feminism based upon the idea of equality alone.

But I sensed the tone taken by one Reinold Thiel to be more typical of the attitude towards women's liberation of the radical man in 1968:

> The women in our society have the same rights and opportunities as do men, but they have one additional option: namely, to be taken care of by a man. . . . The road to emancipation is open. But it is barred by the temptation of taking the more comfortable path of dependence.[4]

Even as he wrote, elsewhere in the city of West Berlin, the Action Council for Women's Liberation (Aktionsrat für die Befreiung der Frauen) was organizing to confront some of the burdens of this "comfortable path of dependence." And in the German Democratic Republic, writers Christa Wolf, Irmtraud Morgner, and Sarah Kirsch had already chosen as their subject the special situation of women in a socialist society where all are relieved of the "shackles" of dependence and "freed" for production.

Chroniclers of the new German women's movement are not agreed as to what constituted its beginning. In society, the falling birth rate and rising divorce rate would later be taken as evidence of women's discontent and rebellion. But a movement demands more tangible beginnings. There are vague reports of women speaking out individually during the 1960s. Gunhild Feigenwinter, later of the Basel *Hexenpresse (Witches' Press)*, is said to have held a one-woman action in 1962, passing out her own leaflets protesting the abortion law in front of the Duisburg train station. However, the first unmistakable sign came in the Spring of 1968, when the Action Council for Women's Liberation was formed in West Berlin.

In September of that year, Helke Sander gave a speech (see Section X) on behalf of the Action Council before the national convention of the SDS in Frankfurt. Sander anticipated some of the themes of the coming women's movement: patriarchy, token women (in German, "alibi-women"), the politics of personal life, the rights and needs of mothers. In political effect the Sander speech can be compared to the speech at the June, 1967 national convention of the American SDS in which women defined themselves as part of the Third World on the basis of their "colonial relationship to men." In tone and substance, the Sander speech is reminiscent of articles written the same year in this country, by Marge Piercy, Marlene Dixon, and Kathy McAfee, and Myrna Wood.

The Aktionsrat, however, had a bit more to bring before the SDS delegates, for the women had, as was well known in the city, organized several store-front day care centers (see Section VIII) and been successful in joining forces with unionized and nonunion nursery and elementary school teachers in the city, as part of a campaign to force changes in the system so that it would meet the needs of mothers, children, and teachers. Sander dared to taunt the delegates with this fact:

> . . . without any help from you . . . people are organizing . . . and in numbers which, were they workers, you would greet as the dawning of a new day.[5]

It is in the nature of things that the tomatoes which one female comrade was provoked to hurl at the male SDS authorities at the close of the speech became as infamous as the speech itself. Most of the radical press treated the "affair" with bemusement. Journalist Ulrike Meinhof (later of the terrorist Baader-Meinhof group), however, skillfully used those very tomatoes as a leitmotif all through her article on the speech, urging the women to organize in their own interest "and leave the men to wash their own tomato-bespattered shirts for once." [6]

However impressive, these early efforts of the Action Council were to be short lived. By 1969, the group had reassembled without the controversial "mother faction," (which had formed into its own new group, Against the Old and for the New) and was doing self-criticism in the SDS organ *SDS info* for having allowed a concentration on children and education to "block their political growth." They blamed these "errors" on their

> . . . situation as petit bourgeois women in a society in which only 33 percent of women are employed . . . only a part in production . . . producing surplus value and experiencing exploitation first hand.[7]

By 1971, when the campaign to abolish the abortion law (Paragraph 218) was in full swing (see Section III), the Frankfurt Old Wives' Council (Weiberrat) and other women's groups which had by then broken away from SDS were left scrambling to keep up with the emerging women's movement. In March of 1971 a tumultuous women's conference—the first national women's conference since the end of the "first" German women's movement—was held in Frankfurt; *then* the women *knew* they had a movement.

Outside Influence

A footnote to the period up until 1970 is the disdain leftist women had for the American women's liberation movement. This attitude grew out of the German New Left's criticism of its American counterpart as lacking in theory, overly spontaneous and politically naive. By 1971, however, the major American, English, and French feminist writings were appearing in German editions.[8]

The increased familiarity with the writings of feminists from other countries has resulted in some interesting critiques. To give one example, Ulrike Prokop authored a book in 1976 with the intriguing title: *The Context of Female Life: On the Limitations of Strategies and the Inappropriateness of Wishes*.[9] In it she criticizes a range of feminist strategies and perspectives. Among her examples are the work of Simone de Beauvoir, Betty Friedan, Kate Millett, Shulamith Firestone, and Germaine Greer. Categorizing these "self-contained" strategies as bureaucratic, technocratic or rhetorical, she actually dispenses with the work of most of the leading strategists and theoreticians the movement had produced up to that point. Her argument is that we understand too little of women's ambivalent and contradictory wishes, poses, fears, and fantasies; too little of the deeper meanings these things may mask, and what subversive or even revolutionary potential such qualities may serve.

A recent retrospective on the origins of the new women's movement in *Emma*, the mass-circulation feminist magazine in West Germany (circulation over 300,000), pointedly placed the spread of American feminist writings *after* the momentum of the German movement was already established. It is true that the immediate model for the campaign against the abortion law came from France (although women in a number of countries mounted similar actions), where in April of 1971, three hundred and forty-three French women signed a statement in a major journal stating that they had had abortions and calling for abortion rights. However, other chroniclers of German feminism acknowledge an early American influence, attributing this to the fact that the United States movement is "tougher, more embittered, pragmatic and determined"—qualities seen as necessary here, where "early capitalist structures, feudalistic conditions, reactionary unions, and strong progressive tendencies" exist side by side.[10] If anything, until the late 1970s, German feminists tended to overestimate the strength of the American movement. A source of envy to German women who came out of the student movement were the links between the American women's liberation movement and the civil rights movement.[11]

Other influences on German feminism have come from England, Italy, and, most recently, again from France—with the work of Julia Kristeva, Hélène Cixous, and Luce Irigaray. It would seem that in the coming phase phase of the German movement, ideas and impulses will be drawn from a wide range of sources, not the least of which will be analysis, history, and literature from their own movement.

Ways and Means

In the 1970s, a young feminist from the United States could go to any major West German city and find much to remind her of home. The first women's centers were opened in 1972, followed by the houses for battered women and a multiplicity of feminist enterprises and projects (see Section VI). A strong and vocal lesbian movement exists, with its own journals, centers, cafes, and bars— much as in the United States. In 1980, a visitor to West Berlin could go on a three-hour guided bus tour, devoted entirely to people and places in the history of the city's lesbian community, going back into the early 1800s. The houses for battered women, perhaps most of all, were quick to spread even into the smaller towns. Moreover, in West Germany, these shelters are products almost exclusively of the women's movement, unlike the situation in the United States, where a variety of community welfare agencies and religious groups are also involved.

Although women's centers and projects might seem to be part of the same mode of organization, they are experienced quite differently. The West German movement, with its highly developed capacity for self-criticism, has produced quite a body of literature on the merits and faults of each form. Those who saw the centers—now mostly defunct—as a unique forum for collective consciousness raising and political action fear that the projects with their specialized functions and diffusion leave the movement without a concentrated power base.[12]

Nevertheless, the projects—health centers, counselling centers, tea and coffee houses, bookstores, facilities serving immigrant women, the shelters—have survived as models for an alternative women's culture. The need for the services the projects provide is undeniable. The two houses for battered women in West Berlin were filled to capacity from the day they opened. But, in the absence of adequate funding, an old question has arisen as to whether the projects can or should continue indefinitely. It is the familiar charge of unknowing cooption and exploitation:

> What function does the social work variant of feminism serve in smoothing over the worst hurts inflicted by a violent patriarchy? [13]

The question of power or the absence of it became acute as the progress thought to have been made in the campaign for abortion rights proved illusory. In 1975 the West German Federal Constitutional Court passed a modified Paragraph 218, allowing abortions to women who meet specified medical or psychological conditions. This was a setback for the women's movement, leading one feminist to call the "218" movement "a children's crusade against the patriarchy." [14]

It was in this climate that the question of political power was debated within the movement. Perhaps, the debate went, feminists should pay more attention to traditional agencies and institutions of power and influence. And, as if in response, in 1979, a new women's party was founded, the Frauenpartei. It is the eighth such founding in the Federal Republic since 1951 and shows every sign of going the way of the others (see article by Hannelore Mabry, Section X).

While the young American feminist would find a familiar subculture awaiting her in Berlin or Frankfurt, an older feminist would certainly note the absence of a national organization such as NOW (The National Organization of Women). While women's professional, labor, and social welfare groups do exist in West Germany, they are rel-

atively nonmilitant, and until recently have had an uneasy relationship with the women's movement—which viewed them as irre-
deemably conservative and antifeminist. Also conspicuous in its
absence is a campaign for an Equal Rights Amendment, for the very
simple reason that in January 1949, the West German Parliament
voted into its constitution Article 3: The Equal Rights Statute. However, the Statute and other equal rights legislation have not provided
women with the necessary legal grounds, in both individual and
class action suits, to combat discrimination on the job, in the health
care system, through the media, to name just a few areas. On a
much smaller scale, there is a move underway in West Germany to
get an anti–sex–discrimination law passed. Supported by women in
traditional organizations as well as some feminists, the campaign is
having a hard struggle, although it has a long way to go before it
matches the United States ERA campaign's record for endurance.

Women's Studies

Women's studies has arrived in West Germany, although not in
the same institutional configuration as in colleges and universities in
the United States. The structure of the German university, in its
conservative, chair-dominated tradition, does not lend itself to the
kind of interdisciplinary women's studies programs and colleges
which have developed in the United States. Feminist teaching and
research have existed since the mid-1970s at the university level in
the Federal Republic but, until about 1980, only within the traditional
departments. Also introduced in the mid-1970s, "Women's Seminars,"
which combine a study of topics of special relevance to women with
collective learning methods and consciousness raising, have proven
very popular. There, the ideas of Paolo Freire on the pedagogy of
the oppressed (albeit fashioned for the Third World) have found a
popular application to women's teaching and learning.[15]
Since 1976, an annual Summer University for Women has been
held at the Free University in West Berlin. With other, more regional
conferences—notably the Women's Forum in the Ruhr in 1978—
these gatherings of academics, students, office workers, and housewives form the women's studies network. The published proceedings
of each Summer University for Women are a sort of yearbook for
the movement. In 1980, a Women's Center for Research, Education,
and Information (FFBIZ) was formed in West Berlin, by both community and university women. The FFBIZ is an autonomous, self-
supporting center, without institutional affiliation. Centers and programs of a sort now exist at a handful of universities (Bielefeld,

Berlin, Hamburg, Dortmund).[16] As yet, there is no German "umbrella" organization similar to our National Women's Studies Association. In West Germany the first institutional home for women's studies lay elsewhere. The *Volkshochschulen* or adult education institutions are unique to Germany, with a long history, dating back to early in the century. Even the smaller towns may have a Volkshochschule, while West Berlin has more than ten. Especially since 1945, and by design, these adult education institutions have had a high enrollment of women, for whom they were to serve both as a training for democracy and a kind of in-service for housewives. These traditional schools, whose curricula for women often resembled home economics courses in the United States at the most conservative period of the 1950s, amazingly, became a vehicle for women's studies. The first "Women's Discussion Groups" at these adult education institutions were begun in the early 1970s, just as the first women's centers appeared (see article by Ingrid Schmidt-Harzbach, Section XI). The effectiveness of this night-school variety of women's studies is an example of how a women's movement may use to its own advantage traditional institutional or organizational networks.

An Old Story

The unresolved conflict between the left, and feminism which surfaced in 1968, has continued to erupt periodically throughout the decade over specific issues. By comparison, in the United States the conflict seems to be experienced on a more theoretical basis. In the United States, two books in particular exemplify the intellectual nature of the conflict: *The Curious Courtship Between Women's Liberation and Socialism* by Batya Weinbaum and *Women and Revolution: A Discussion of the Unhappy Marriage of Marxism and Feminism* edited by Lydia Sargent.[17] Whereas in West Germany, to name just one case, a controversy erupted betwen 1979 and 1981 concerning Netzwerk, a socialist organization founded to give financial aid to progressive model projects. Feminist projects found themselves vying with one another for funding and having to justify their politics before a panel of leftist judges. The whole episode reopened old wounds between the women's movement and the left.

To the outside observer, the alienation of feminists from the left seems more complete in West Germany than in the United States. Rarely does one find the designations "socialist-feminist" or "Marxist-feminist." And the phrase *"autonomous* women's movement" is used constantly, apparently to signal a distinction from the more traditional marxist-leninist groups. An example of this alienation can be found in the call for papers for the first Summer University for Women at the Free University of Berlin in 1976, which welcomed all women

> except those who, under the cloak of a commitment to women, seek to sell an ideology which relegates the oppression of women to a secondary or subordinate status.[18]

German history has a long precedent for the current mutual suspicions between leftist and feminist camps, dating back to the revolutions of 1848, when women were actively involved both on the barricades and in agitational and propaganda work. The militant *Women's Newspaper (Frauen-Zeitung)*, edited by Louise Otto Peters between 1849 and 1852, documents that the women were concerned over the unreliable support of their male comrades, even those on the left. The question was raised as to whether women should organize separately in the revolutionary effort. Louise Otto Peters went on to become a founding leader of the General German Women's Union (Allgemeiner Deutscher Frauenverein) in 1865 and editor, until her death in 1895, of the women's journal *New Paths (Neue Bahnen)*. An intriguing note on this early feminist, whose work and influence are now graduallly being researched, was her probable influence on August Bebel. Apparently Bebel was a frequent visitor to the Peter's home in the early 1860s.

The period between 1860 and 1878 seems to have been relatively free of the conflict between socialists and feminists; the lines had not yet been drawn between them. The 1870s saw the publication of Hedwig Dohm's most important writings: "What the Pastors think of women," 1872; "Jesuitry in the Household," in 1873; "The Scientific Emancipation of Women," 1874; and the "Nature and Rights of Women," in 1876 (in which she called for women's suffrage). The end of the decade saw the publication of Bebel's *The Woman Under Socialism*, in 1879. While not diminishing Bebel's very real contributions, it is important to learn of Dohm's ground-breaking work. (Curiously, Bebel's book makes no reference to Dohm.)

Hedwig Dohm (1833–1919) was one of the most radical and committed of feminists which Germany has produced. She was not an organizer, however. She was Germany's Elizabeth Cady Stanton, without a Susan B. Anthony by her side. Her two main concentrations were women's education and women's suffrage, but her critical eye ranged over all the topics of the day—politics, art, literature, everyday life. In 1902, for example, she wrote "The Anti-Feminists," in the course of which she subjected Friedrich Nietzsche's work to the most devastating ridicule for his attitude toward women.

The antisocialist laws were enacted in 1878, and a decade of repression directed at the left followed. It should be mentioned here that the law on organizations, enacted in 1850, which banned women (along with school pupils and apprentices) from political organizations, was not repealed until 1908. While many socialist leaders were imprisoned or forced into exile, the socialist movement and subculture flourished under siege. Many wage-earning women were drawn to socialism. In 1981, the Social Democratic Party came out in favor of women's suffrage and women wage earners' right to work.[19]

This did not, however, inaugurate an era of cooperation between socialists and feminists. Clara Zetkin had already drawn the class lines on the woman question in her widely read work, *The Question of Women Workers and Women in the Present (Die Arbeiterinnen–und Frauenfrage der Gegenwart)*, 1889. The unbridgeable gap between the "proletarian" and "bourgeois" women's movements was a regular theme in the journal *Equality (Die Gleichheit)*, the official party women's publication of which Zetkin was editor from 1891 to 1916.

While the mainstream of the German women's movement was in fact turning to an emphasis on a sentimental "organized motherliness" and away from political or social reforms, there was a growing radical wing with which socialist women might have rallied. In her journal *Women's Movement (Frauenbewegung)*, published in the early 1890s, Minna Cauer stated that the radical feminists had always acknowledged the contributions of Marx, Engels, and Bebel to women's emancipation but that the struggle must be expanded to encompass psychology, physiology, ethics, and religion. Looking back in 1928, Clara Zetkin did give a slight nod to the "bourgeois" women's movement for its "preparatory work" in the struggle for women's economic and political rights. But she went on to write of the insidious effect of "women's rights dilletantes" on the class consciousness of working women:

> . . . in short, the bourgeois women's movement is a serious, dangerous power of the counter-revolution. With it there can be no compromise, no alliance. It must be beaten down, so that the proletarian world revolution may be victorious.[20]

Lida Gustava Heymann and Anita Augspurg, who alongside with Minna Cauer and Helene Stöcker, were leaders in the radical wing of the women's movement, looked back in despair over the attitude of the socialist women:

> What shortsightedness! Had not the experience of many decades shown that the mass of social democratic men of the world had no intention of putting into practice at home the party program of equal rights? Where he had the opportunity —namely in his own family—the social democratic man

exploited the woman in the same manner as did the men of the middle classes.[21]

And what an unequal contest. The largest socialist women's movement in the world proclaiming as a major foe one of the smallest feminist movements in the world![22] To this day, the scars of that confrontation remain. The leftist legend of the stab in the back it received from the new female voters during the Weimar Republic is still alive, and German feminists today, for their part, have called for an expose of how, in the nineteenth century, the labor movement split the women's movement.

The process of rediscovering and reinterpreting German women's history and the history of German feminism is underway. A different situation with regard to women's history exists across the border in East Germany. There, official tribute is paid to the struggles of the "proletarian" women's movement of the nineteenth century and of the early twentieth century and to the dedication of the central figure in that movement, Clara Zetkin. At least superficially, women in the German Democratic Republic are encouraged to see themselves as belonging to a long, unbroken history of heroic, working-class women.

East and West

The shifting economic, political and cultural relations between East and West Germany have extended to the situation of women. For a generation, policy makers in both countries have, for domestic consumption, looked askance at the status of women across the border. Yes, in the East women have more legal rights, protection against discrimination, and child care services, but in the West women have more freedom of choice, more consumer goods, and better living conditons. These two clauses can just as easily be reversed, depending upon your perspective. Yet, without more than occasional direct contacts and in the absence of common organizations, women in the two Germanys have reached a degree of mutual respect. The old stereotypes fail to inspire the self-satisfaction they once did.

In actuality, it seems clear that by the late 1960s, the women in both societies had made some disquieting conclusions about their lot in life. In the West, this resulted, most visibly, in a revival of feminism. In the East (as well as the West) the classic signs of female discontent, low birth rate and high divorce rate, are the most measurable ones. The more subtle and complex changes in consciousness of women in the German Democratic Republic have become the subject of women writers who survived the pall of socialist realism to produce a body of literature read not only in Eastern Europe but also in West Germany. As Christa Wolf wrote in 1978:

> . . . there are many indications . . . of dissatisfaction among many women in our country: What they have achieved and take for granted is no longer enough. . . . They feel that their new role has already begun to solidify, that they are suddenly no longer able to move in these institutions; their lust for life is great, their hunger for reality insatiable.[23]

In her 1977 film "Redupers," ("The All-Around Reduced Personality" or "Die allseitig reduzierte Persönlichkeit"), Helke Sander treated some of these themes, using in counterpoint scenes from the life in West Berlin of the main character (film maker, single mother, and all-around reduced personality), upbeat pronouncements on East Berlin radio on the status of the all-around well-adjusted personality of GDR womanhood, and telling quotes from Christa Wolf. I think what Sander and other West German feminists value in the work of Wolf and her colleagues is the writer's craft, the sure voice, the sense of political responsibility, and an artistic distance from experience which allows for ambiguities, irony, and fantasy. The experience of being the much-touted linch pin of successive state economic five-year plans seems in some way to have subtly altered their outlook as women writers writing about women. In any case, Christa Wolf, for one, has returned the compliment when she writes of feminists in capitalist countries:

> Deprived of rights, they try to get their sense of self from men; their way to finding themselves is often via a retreat to their own sex; it is necessarily difficult for them to include all of society in their blueprints. And yet, what solidarity among themselves, what struggles to understand their own situation, what spontaneity and inventiveness in their self-help enterprises, what imagination, what abundance. I cannot believe that we in the GDR have nothing to learn from this.[24]

The fact remains that at a time when, in West Germany, "women's novels" and "women's literature" still stood for a kind of mass-produced and predictable "entertainment literature,"[25] in the East, Christa Wolf, Irmtraud Morgner, and others were already publishing some of their best work.[26]

Breaking the Silence

By 1975 the new consciousness among women finally produced a flowering of women's literature in West Germany. An influential

book early in this trend was the novel *Shedding* by Verena Stefan.[27]
The first title from the new feminist publishing house, Frauenoffensive, and the first work of its author, *Shedding* is composed of the
stream of consciousness observations of a young woman fleeing the
urban battle of the sexes for the company of women in the country,
shedding successive layers of her shell of femininity until she reaches
her true metamorphic form. The book was an enormous success.

Within several years a whole shelfful of books had joined *Shedding*
(doubtless, in some cases after languishing in desk drawers, unpub-
lished, for years) with themes of female discontent and revolt: Elisabeth Alexander, *The Woman Who Laughed*, 1975 (see Section IV);
Margot Schroeder, *Take It Like a Woman*, 1975 (see Section VII);
Christa Reinig, *Unmanning*, 1976; Angelika Mechtel, *Dreams of a
Vixen*, 1976 (see Section VII); Brigitte Schwaiger (an Austrian), *How
Does the Salt Get Into the Sea?*, 1977; Jutta Heinrich, *The Gender of
Thoughts*, 1978 (see Section IX). Many of these writers have also
published volumes of poetry, although it is their fiction which receives
the most attention. Groups such as the Meeting of Writing Women
(Treffen schreibender Frauen), began in 1976, have encouraged women
to write and seek publication.

In 1979, an anthology entitled *Overcoming Speechlessness (Überwindung der Sprachlosigkeit)* appeared which presented the most significant essays of feminist cultural self-criticism and, simultaneously,
signalled the close of the early phase of enthusiastic self-discovery.
Whereas the editor, Gabrielle Dietze, affirms that only a women's
movement makes possible "an autonomous female speech," many
of the essays in the book express grave doubts about the so-called
liberated muse. In "The White Fleck on the Feminist Map," Marlies
Gerhardt decries the fact that women still cling to the "Wailing Wall."

> Why are there . . . hardly any female fantasies, . . . pictures
> of that which is not, sketches which make future-music,
> engender future-desire? [28]

Gerhardt decides that perhaps the "angry view of garbage arrange-
ments" still corresponds too closely to our daily reality to allow a
"utopian long view." Poet Ursula Krechel also longs for fantasy,
"which plays tricks and rushes ahead of theory and praxis." Krechel
is resentful of demands placed upon feminist artists by their audience:
"There is already something like a sample catalog of feminist . . .
literary places and objects." As an example of the preference for
tracts over literature, Krechel quotes the 1977 editorial in *Courage* (a
major journal of the women's movement, published in West Berlin)
which intoned: "Leave the poetry, write reports! " [29] Interestingly,
the feminist press, Frauenoffensive, apparently decided against bring-

ing out a *Women's Yearbook '78*, in part because most of the texts
submitted that year were poems, and the editors did not want to
make of the movement a volume of poetry! [30]

As in the United States, the influence of the ideas of Luce Irigaray
and other French feminists writing on female aesthetics can be felt
in much of the literature on women's culture. The code words of
the Imaginary and fantasy are there, although some may find that
the French women's ideas undergo a curious change once translated
into German, becoming more solid and earth-bound, more social.
Gisela von Wysocki, in a beautifully and meticulously fashioned
volume of essays on individual women artists from England, the
United States and Germany—*Frosts of Freedom: Fantasies of Uprising*—
values a women's art which can be read as "dosiers of female
deserters":

> They are descriptions of uprisings, records of transgressions.
> They are the dosiers of female deserters. . . . The unknown
> genealogy of the female steps forth out of the dark. Her
> unclear script, hard to decipher, points to other possibilities of
> life than the neon-script of patriarchy.[31]

At odds with both the "feminist realist" and "psychoanalytic"
schools of literature, the journal *The Black Messenger*, fem. (*Die
Schwarze Botin*) has, since its first issue in 1976, provided independent
and satirical cultural critique to a small audience, some of it directed
against tendencies within the women's movement. The journal has
been especially harsh with what the editors consider the self-pitying,
self-indulgent excesses of certain strains of feminist culture. Brigitte
Classen, one of the editors of the journal, does not share a fascination
for the unknown and indecipherable quality of a female female
language:

> I find that the overcoming of speechlessness lies in the use of
> language upon radical themes, not necessarily in its use in
> failed linguistic self-reflection. To write about language is not
> yet to change it with our wishes. We have always tried to use
> the critical potential of language.[32]

The Home Front

Since 1976, an increasing proportion of West German feminist
publications have concentrated on theory and analysis. A major
portion of this work has concerned "home economics," in the materialist feminist sense linking housework and motherhood with the
world economy. In 1977, the subject of housework and the issue of

wages for housework became a major topic of political controversy in the West German movement, way beyond the more academic and scholarly treatment of these topics in the United States.

For the most part, to be sure, the West German movement follows conventional feminist wisdom concerning housework and motherhood: free women for jobs and careers outside the home, made possible through reforms in child care and household services and in the division of labor by sex. The repercussions of these changes, plus a strong women's movement, will then serve to overcome the patriarchal and capitalist forms of women's oppression.

Much along these lines, the radical and "proletarian" wings of the nineteenth century German women's movement spent much effort in fighting off the repressive *ideology* of the housewife and mother then being inculcated—the now world-renowned *kinder-küche-kirche*. As early as 1869, Hedwig Dohm and Social Democrats Louise Otto Peters and Luise Büchner each protested the Party's invoking of the ideal of man as organized worker and woman as housewife and mother. "Proletarian antifeminism" cherished the same ideals of woman which were becoming so central to the values of the emerging middle classes.[33]

A few years later, Hedwig Dohm scandalized the moderate women's rights movement, socialists and the general public with her satirical piece, "Jesuitry in the Household," which concocted a list of dogmas of the good housewife, culminating in the housewife's oath:

> I, Madam Schulz, believe with all my heart and with all my powers in myself and my kitchen, my nursery, my laundry cellar, . . . and my sewing machine. . . . I believe servant girls to be a worthless race. And I declare any woman who dares to doubt my infallibility or who takes up so-called ideas to be an immoral and repulsive emancipated creature, a blasphemer. For I was, I am, and will always be—a German housewife.[34]

There is, however, a strain in the German movement which turns conventional feminist wisdom on housework and motherhood on its head. The thinking is materialist, polemical, and quite distinctive. Moreover, this position has roots in the "first" German women's movement as well—in the period from 1900–1920. Under the leadership of the Federation for the Protection of Mothers and Sexual Reform (Bund für Mütterschutz und Sexualreform), founded in 1904 and headed from 1905–1910 by Helene Stöcker. Under the banner of the "New Ethics," a new approach emerged on the age-old women's issue.[35]

Elisabeth Busse-Wilson, socialist *and* radical feminist, stated the
new principle of autonomous motherhood in an essay entitled "Modern Anti-Feminism." This wide-ranging work shows a close familiarity
with the writings of Hedwig Dohm, Mathilde Vaerting,[36] and Ellen
Key; it also examines convincingly the hidden antifeminism in the
new progressive youth movement of that time. On the subject of
motherhood:

> . . . love may be a private matter between two persons, but
> the desire for motherhood remains a separate instinct which is
> as valid as sexuality. The individual woman has a right to this
> fulfillment. Furthermore, the privileged position of legitimate
> motherhood is ethically vulnerable. If anything, motherhood in
> and of itself should be elevated to the highest position of
> honor for women.
>   Today the opposite is the case. Here we come up against
> the deepest source of women's inferiority. Motherhood is the
> greatest burden which nature has laid upon women, as
> opposed to men. For in order to secure herself and the child,
> she had to put herself in the protection of the stronger male.
> . . . Through motherhood the woman was first made
> economically dependent upon the man. Her moral dependence
> is only a consequence of this material fact. Even today, in
> order to attain motherhood, she is forced unavoidably to an
> individual man and must always simultaneously become his
> "housewife"—a combination as portentous as it appears
> natural to us. Only when society gives compensation for
> motherhood will the woman be able to free herself of this
> dependence.[37]

The revival of this maternal feminism can be seen today in the
writings of Gunhild Feigenwinter, editor of the former *Hexenpresse
(Witches' Press)*, published in Basel, Switzerland, and which was
infulential in the mid-1970s. In her "Mothers' Manifesto," (1977)
Feigenwinter argues for a perspective that *begins* with the needs of
mothers and children and repudiates a feminist call for "Equality"
that ignores the differences between men and women, thereby in-
suring that the physically stronger will set the competitive standards
in life. Feigenwinter decries the degradation of the primal mother-
child relationship to mere "ideology," and she does not fear the
word "instinct."

> Did I say "mother-instinct"? Forgive me, sisters, I know that
> only the male sexual instinct is permitted as such. As in the
> nineteenth century women were allowed no sexual feeling, so

today, in this peculiar women's movement, mothers must practice emotional asceticism and reveal no feeling.[38]

The work of Hannelore Mabry is another representative of this strain of German feminism. Her work on a "Feminist Theory of Surplus Value" (see Section VIII) retains a few concepts of Marx, while outlining a new theory—one in which, for the first time, the labor of housewife and mother is no longer invisible. There is nothing modest in the proposals of Feigenwinter and Mabry. Feigenwinter states that "on the basis of home-economics we come to a parting of minds: the liberals from the radicals, the idealists from the materialists." [39] If Feigenwinter and Mabry call for a perspective which does not lose sight of the rights of the individual mother or the aggregate labor of the mass of individual women, the recent work of Claudia von Werlhof looks at housework in the broadest possible terms and at the world economy in terms of housework. She says that "housework is that phenomenon most difficult to grasp [and] once we understand housework, we will understand all things." [40]

Building in part upon the earlier historical study by Gisela Bock and Barbara Duden, "Labor of Love—Love as Labor: On the Genesis of Housework in Capitalism," [41] von Werlhof identifies housework as *the* primary capitalist mode of production. The brief appearance of the wage laborer—the proletarian—on the world economic stage is about to end, she says, in the deepening world economic crisis. Here her approach has much in common with recent trends in world system analysis. The economies of the industrialized countries will be "feminized," "housewificized"—become increasingly part-time, temporary, unspecialized, and highly exploited.

> Not the 10 percent of free wage laborers but rather the 90 percent nonwage laborers are the pillars of accumulation and growth. They are the truly exploited, the true "producers," the "norm," in capitalism.[42]

Nor is this anything new. A kind of euro-centrism led to the arrogance which envisioned the model of the free wage laborer spreading out to the "under-developed" Third World from the centers of civilization and modernity. Werlhof, finally, foresees a possible scenario in which this proletarian man accepts the new economic conditions—with all the loss of prestige and security—in exchange for a continued supremacy over women.

All three authors—Feigenwinter, Mabry and von Werlhof—urge women to organize; and all convey the European sense of impending doom, that time is short in which to avert the next and perhaps final conflict. As Werlhof warns, in another context:

By itself, capital is dead. And, vampire-like, only the flow of fresh blood lends it the appearance of life.[43]

War and Peace

West Germany today offers the latest historical setting for the confrontation between feminism and the great questions of war and peace. Historically, this confrontation has placed feminism in tremendous jeopardy. Except for periods of nationalistic frenzy, most women's movements have had, at least implicitly, a strong pacifist, antiwar tendency. Of course, in times of war or the threat of war, women (and, consequently, women's movements) are under extreme pressure to sacrifice for the greater cause—be that in the war effort or in the peace movement. In the prenuclear age, war's end would find women fully preoccupied in restoring to normalcy the devastated or booming postwar economies and the women's movement in dissarray. The West German women's movement has informed itself of the lessons of the past; consequently, the movement's attitude toward the new political configurations of the 1980s is ambivalent.

First of all, this latest phase was preceded, in the late 1970s, by a broad debate within and outside the women's movement on the question of violence. In the women's movement this led to tentative beginnings of a more complex analysis of violence, from rape, to terrorism, to war—the spectrum of violence.

Although women were prominent in the terrorist Red Army Faction (R.A.F.), most spectacularly in the Baader-Meinhof group, their political path lay apart from that of the women's movement. Women in the R.A.F. had chosen a life which seemed to block out all the potential conflicts in women's lives—on the job, on the street, and at home.[44] Moreover, all the conflicts which exist between feminists and the left in general would be heightened with regard to the terrorist movement.

However, in 1977, during the period of outrage and government reprisal following the escalation of terrorist attacks on government officials and the death of the R.A.F. prisoners at Stammheim, the women's movement was forced to clarify its position on "armed resistance." (See article on the "Resistance Group," Section X) In part, this required merely a reiteration of earlier feminist critiques of violence and vanguardism in New Left strategies. (See article by Sibylle Plogstedt, Section X) In two women's congresses held in 1978 (the year of the Russell Tribunals on war crimes) the spectrum of violence, repression, and criminality, in relation to feminist strategy was explored. This discussion remains as yet incomplete, perhaps awaiting a time when a feminist organizational base is in place which would make the options less hypothetical. For now, the feminist exploration of the political spectrum of violence has been subsumed by the global issues of war and peace.

The populist political force which sprang up in West Germany in the late 1970s was made up of many "citizens' initiatives" agitating around a range of ecological and antinuclear issues. Part of a new antinuclear and antiwar movement in Western Europe, the citizens' initiatives are said to be West Germany's first grassroots movement. The "Greens"—an alliance of leftist and environmental groups— have moved ahead of the Free Democratic Party in several state elections and, in the 1983 general election, won seats in the parliament.

Women have worked hard in the rank and file of the new ecology and peace movement. (See article by Delphine Brox-Brochot, Section X) A reflection of this is the fact that the "Greens" portray themselves as a prowoman party. Yet, ominous signs soon developed. At the 1980 Baden-Württemberg Convention of the "Greens," the women saw their platform, with its demand for abortion rights, pass by a small margin, only to be voted down after the Party Chairman called for a recount, first warning the delegates that a vote for abortion could split the "Greens." The year before, when some "Green" women in Bremen gave their support for a birth strike to protest economic and military nuclear policies, they were severely chastised by the organization.

The feminist quarrel with the ecology and peace movement goes beyond the fact that women are underrepresented in the leadership; it goes beyond a critique of what some have called the "male" hierarchical mode of organization. It even goes beyond the lack of support for specific feminist demands. At issue is a fundamental unwillingness of the mainstream of the ecology and peace movement to develop a philosophy and program which reflects the links between the struggle against "the horror of programmed destruction" and the long-standing feminist struggle against "the horror of women's everyday life." [45] Hannelore Mabry, for one, has complained that the "Greens" were only looking at the "symptoms of patriarchy." [46] And, as one activist in the ecology movement has noted: "As we learned from the labor movement, all women's problems will be solved automatically in an ecological society." [47]

As of 1982, questions such as possible Communist influence, the spectre of a new reunified German state outside both United States and Soviet spheres, and a "new German patriotism" were threatening to overshadow any grassroots vitality of the women. However, feminists such as Petra Kelly and Eva Quistorp, in the "Greens," have the hope that the ecology movement will become part of a larger international movement infused with the spirit already shown by countless women in the citizens' initiatives in reclaiming control over reproduction and production.

Conclusion

Many parallels exist between the new German women's movement and the American movement. Both arose at the end of the 1960s or early 1970s, as the generation born after World War II was coming of age. Both movements have concentrated on issues of abortion rights, the range of women's health concerns, sexuality, and alternative women's institutions. The American movement has been more occupied with appeals, and lawsuits, and with lobbying efforts to win rights, concessions, and reforms from government and many public and private institutions.

The American movement is the larger, with more of a sense that it has the tacit if not always open support of ordinary women. German feminists seem more aware of the fragility of their cause, more anxious as to its survival. Yet, it is this very anxiety which perhaps feeds the often bitter nature of internal disputes, which, in turn, threatens the solidarity of the movement. Yet, the German movement as a whole seems to have a dedication to asking the basic questions and drawing out the consequences of any line of thought or action. It is a didactic movement, and apt to create speculation as to what lessons are to be learned and passed on.

Feminist intellectuals in West Germany seem closer to their activist roots or origins. No doubt this is in part due to the fact that the academic community provides less of a forum for feminist scholars in West Germany; whereas in the United States it often seems as if women's studies has supplanted the movement from whence it sprang.

The two areas in which the new German women's movement has made unique contributions are housework and motherhood and, more recently, war and peace. The challenge, will, as always, be to follow up the theoretical and polemical work with practical results or, as the Germans say, to keep head and stomach together. If the women's movement is to figure prominently in the new grassroots and institutional configurations of the 1980s, it will take a massive educational and organizational campaign.

Now, truly, the time has come when, in Christa Wolf's words, the women need blueprints which include all of society. Then German women will have answered the appeal made in 1898 by Minna Cauer: "We call upon our sisters in the Twentieth Century: Complete what we have begun!" [48]

Edith Hoshino Altbach

Notes

A revised version of this essay appeared in *Signs: Journal of Women in Culture and Society.* vol. 9, no. 3 (Spring 1984).

1. Marielouise Janssen-Jurreit, *Sexism: The Male Monopoly on History and Thought* (New York: Farrar, Straus & Giroux, 1982).

2. Christa Wolf, *The Quest for Christa T.* (New York: Farrar, Straus & Giroux, 1970; Wolf, *A Model Childhood* (New York: Farrar, Straus & Giroux, 1980); Wolf, *No Place On Earth* (New York: Farrar, Straus & Giroux, 1982). Verena Stefan, *Shedding* (Houston: Daughters, Inc., 1978).

3. "Sexualität und Herrschaft," *Das Argument* nos.22–24 (1967/1968). Reimut Reiche, *Sexualität und Klassenkampf* (Frankfurt: Verlag Neue Kritik, 1968). Hans Giese and Gunter Schmidt, *Studenten: Sexualität* (Reinbeck bei Hamburg: Rowohlt, 1968).

4. Reinold E. Thiel, "Zum Frauenbild des Films," *Das Argument* no. 24 (March, 1968), 8–9.

5. Helke Sander, "Rede des Aktionsrates zur Befreiung der Frauen bei der 23. Delegiertenkonferenz des SDS im September 1968 in Frankfurt," *Frauenjahrbuch 1* (Frankfurt: Verlag Roter Stern, 1975), p. 13.

6. Ulrike Meinhof, "Die Frauen im SDS oder in Eigener Sache," *konkret* no.12 (1968).

7. "Aktionsrat zur Befreiung der Frau," *SDS info* nos. 26/27 (December, 1969), p. 37.

8. *The Feminine Mystique* (Ger. title, *Der Weiblichkeitswahn*) by Betty Friedan had already been published in German in 1966. Other publication dates of note: Naomi Weisstein, "Psychology Constructs the Female," in *Die Zeit* (1970); Kate Millett, *Sexual Politics (Ger. title, Sexus und Herrschaft)* (1971); Germaine Greer, *The Female Eunuch* (Ger. title, *Der weibliche Eunuch*) (1971); Juliet Mitchell, "Women, the Longest Revolution" (Ger. title, "Frauen, die längste Revolution) (1971); Margaret Benston, "The Political Economy of Women" (Ger. title, "Zur politischen Ökonomie der Frauenemanzipation") (1971); Pamela Allen, "Free Space" (Ger. title, "Der Freiraum") (1972); Mariarosa Dalla Costa and Selma James, "The Power of Women and the Subversion of the Community" (Ger. title, "Die Macht der Frauen und der Umsturz der Gesellschaft") (1973); Phyllis Chesler, *Women and Madness* (Ger. title, *Frauen: Das verrückte Geschlecht?*) (1974); Shulamith Firestone, *The Dialectic of Sex* (Ger. title, *Frauenbefreiung und Sexuelle Revolution*) (1975);

and Eleanor Flexner, *Century of Struggle* (Ger. title, *Hundert Jahre Kampf)* *(1975).*

9. Ulrike Prokop, *Weiblicher Lebenszusammenhang. Von der Beschränktheit der Strategien und der Unangemessenheit der Wünsche* (Frankfurt: Suhrkamp, 1976).

10. Marielouise Janssen-Jurreit, "USA," in: *Frauenprogramm—Gegen Diskriminierung,* ed. Janssen-Jurreit (Reinbek bei Hamburg: Rowohlt, 1979), p. 270.

11. Ursula Linnhoff, *Die neue Frauenbewegung. USA-Europa seit 1968* (Cologne: Kiepenheuer & Witsch, 1974), p. 11.

12. Astrid Osterland, "Tabu Macht," *Emma Sonderband 1* (1980), 56–57.

13. Ursula Krechel, *Selbsterfahrung und Fremdbestimmung: Bericht aus der neuen Frauenbewegung* 4th, revised edition (Darmstadt: Luchterhand, 1980), p. 161.

14. Gunhild Feigenwinter, "Manifest der Mütter," *Die Hexenpresse* no. 5 (1976), p. 40.

15. Sigrid Metz-Göckel, "Feminismus an der Hochschule: Erfahrungen und Überlegungen zur Arbeitsform in Frauenseminaren," in: *Frauenstudium: Zur alternativen Wissenschaftsaneignung von Frauen,* ed. Metz-Göckel (Hamburg: Arbeitsgemeinschaft für Hochschuldidaktik, 1979),47–62. Maria Mies, "Towards a Methodology for Feminist Research," in: *Theories of Women's Studies II,* eds. Gloria Bowles and Renate Duelli-Klein (Berkeley: University of California, Women's Studies, 1981), 25–46. (See Section XI)

16. Renate Duelli-Klein, Maresi Nerad, and Sigrid Metz-Göckel, eds., *Feministische Wissenschaft und Frauenstudium* (Hamburg: Arbeitsgemeinschaft für Hochschuldidaktik, 1982).

17. Batya Weinbaum, *The Curious Courtship Between Women's Liberation and Socialism* (Boston: South End Press, 1978). Lydia Sargent, ed. *Women and Revolution: A Discussion of the Unhappy Marriage Between Marxism and Feminism* (Boston: South End Press, 1981).

18. "Sommeruniversität der Frauen," *Pelagea* no. 12 (1980), p. 27.

19. Jean H. Quataert, *Reluctant Feminists in German Social Democracy, 1885-1917* (Princeton: Princeton University Press, 1979), 232–33.

20. Clara Zetkin, "Die bürgerliche Frauenbewegung," in: Zetkin, *Zur Geschichte der proletarischen Frauenbewegung Deutschlands* (Frankfurt: Verlag Roter Stern, 1971), p. 211. (original edition, Moscow, 1928).

21. Lida Gustava Heymann and Anita Augspurg, *Erlebtes und Erschautes* (Meisenheim, 1972), p. 90.

22. In 1908 *Die Gleichheit* had a circulation of 85,000. The women's suffrage movement in Germany had fewer than 10,000 members at that time.

23. Christa Wolf, "In Berührung," (forward to) Maxie Wander, *Guten Morgen, du Schöne* (Darmstadt: Luchterhand, 1978). (see Section V)

24. Ibid.

25. Barbara Weinmayer, "Frauenromane in der BRD," *kürbiskern* no. 1 (1971), 80–92.

26. Christa Wolf, *Der geteilte Himmel* (Berlin: Aufbau Verlag, 1963), *Nachdenken über Christa Wolf* (Berlin: Aufbau Verlag, 1969); Irmtraud Morgner, *Hochzeit in Konstantinopel* (Berlin: Aufbau Verlag, 1968). (see Section II)

27. Verena Stefan, *Häutungen* (Munich: Frauenoffensive, 1975). (see Section I)

28. Marlies Gerhardt, "Der weisse Fleck auf der feministischen Landkarte," in: *Die Überwindung der Sprachlosigkeit*, ed. Gabriele Dietze (Darmstadt: Luchterhand, 1979), p. 22.

29. Ursula Krechel, "Freie Formen über das unfreie Gedicht in der Mangel," in: *Die Überwindung der Sprachlosigkeit*, ed. Gabriele Dietze (Darmstadt: Luchterhand, 1979), p. 61.

30. Lottemi Doormann, ed., *Keiner schiebt uns weg: Zwischenbilanz der Frauenbewegung in der Bundesrepublik* (Weinheim: Beltz Verlag, 1979), p. 57.

31. Gisela von Wysocki, *Die Fröste der Freiheit: Aufbruchsphantasien* (Frankfurt: Syndikat, 1980), p. 7.

32. Letter from Brigitte Classen to E. S. Hoshino, August 1, 1982.

33. Werner Thönnessen, *Frauenemanzipation: Politik und Literatur der deutschen Sozialdemokratie zur Frauenbewegung 1863-1933* (Frankfurt: Europäische Verlagsanstalt, 1969), p. 5.

34. Margrit Twellmann, *Die deutsche Frauenbewegung: Ihre Anfänge, Quellen 1843-1889* (Meisenheim: Verlag Anton Hain, 1972), 216-18.

35. American socialist feminists admired this movement in Germany—for its outlook combining both materialist and erotic elements. See Mari Jo Buhle, *Women and American Socialism, 1870-1920* (Urbana: University of Illinois Press, 1981), 270-71.

36. Mathilde Vaerting, *Die weibliche Eigenart im Männerstaat und die männliche Eigenart im Frauenstaat* (Karlsruhe: G. Braunsche Hofbuchdruckerei, 1921). English edition: *The Dominant Sex: A Study in the Sociology of Sex Differentiation* (London: Allen & Unwin, 1923).

37. Elisabeth Busse-Wilson, *Die Frau und die Jugendbewegung: Ein Beitrag zur weiblichen Charakterologie und zur Kritik des Antifeminismus* (Hamburg: Freideutscher Jugendverlag Adolf Saal, 1920). 34-35.

38. Feigenwinter, p. 18.

39. Ibid., p. 19.

40. Claudia von Werlhof, "Die Hausfrauisierung der Arbeit," (original title, "Der Proletarier ist tot. Es lebe die Hausfrau?" or, in English, The proletarian is dead. Long live the housewife?) *Courage* vol. 7 (March, 1982), p. 34. (see Section VIII)

41. Gisela Bock and Barbara Duden, "Labor of Love—Love as Labor: On the Genesis of Housework in Capitalism," in: *From Feminism to Liberation*, ed. Edith Hoshino Altbach (Cambridge, Mass.: Schenkman, 1980), 153-92.

42. von Werlhof, op. cit., p. 38.

43. Ibid., p. 42.

44. Margarethe Fabricius-Brand, "Wie emanzipiert sind Terroristinnen? " *Emma* no. 4 (April, 1978), 27-29.

45. Anna Dorothea Brockmann, "Wider die Friedfertigkeit: Gedanken über den kriergerischen Alltag," *Courage* vol. 6 (March, 1981), p. 22.

46. Hannelore Mabry, "Wir sollen bereit sein—dass ich nicht lache! " *Courage* vol. 5 (February, 1980), p. 12.

47. Ulla Terlinden, "Frauen in der Ökologie Bewegung—Ökologie in der Frauenbewegung," *Beiträge zur feministischen Theorie und Praxis* no. 4 (1980), p. 99. (see Section X)

48. Marielouise Janssen-Jurreit, *Sexismus: Über die Abtreibung der Frauen-frage* (Frankfurt: Fischer Taschenbuch, 1979), 303–04.

Literature and Politics

Dear Readers

In composing my introductory remarks to you, I have thought about all the different people you are. Some of you, especially the members of the Coalition of Women in German, are my friends and know as much about the authors and issues in this anthology as I, or more. Many of you, I hope, are teachers and students of German and Women's Studies, for you are the readers we thought most often about in choosing, editing and translating our material. Most of you are probably women, but some will also be men—if not among the wider readership, then the narrower one of promotion committees. Welcome to this book. It is intended for all of you, for different reasons. But all the reasons are pertinent to my topic, literature and politics.

Getting Past Gatekeepers

In 1978, when I believed—erroneously, it turned out—that an earlier version of this anthology was about to be accepted for publication, I wrote in my introductory essay: Of the authors we have selected, only a few are familiar to readers (other than feminist Germanists) outside their own countries. Discouragingly, though not surprisingly, the statement is still true. Except for several of Christa Wolf's works,[1] no book-length work by any author included in our collection has appeared in English translation. Shorter works by German women in English translation are scattered in various anthologies and journal issues; as of this writing there is still only one anthology devoted entirely to translated works by German women.[2] It is in keeping with this state of affairs that it took so long to find

27

a publisher for this anthology—quite apart from the book's merits, or lack of them.

The issue isn't just works in translation, or this particular book, but what gets published and what we study, especially in an academic context. In a recent article, the editor of an international feminist journal discusses what she calls the "gatekeepers" of publishing and "the role played by publication in shaping a discipline, in determining the "fashionable" questions—and answers—which set the parameters in which individuals are encouraged to work, if they wish to be at the centre of the issues in their discipline." [3] Obviously, getting past gatekeepers will be easier for those who "choose" to work within such parameters; for those who don't (or can't) "choose" this, there are the margins, or silence. Reading this, I couldn't help thinking of the gatekeeper in Kafka's parable "Before the Law," who tells the dying man from the country that the door he was never permitted to enter was meant only for him.

Changing what we study requires a substantial amount of determination. Feminist Germanists in the United States have been working actively since the early 1970s to educate, first ourselves, then our students, colleagues, and "the profession" in general about women authors and the women's movement in Germany. We have found ourselves outside the gates of two disciplines: women writers have long been excluded from the field of German Studies; the much newer field of Women's Studies has tended not to acknowledge national literatures other than British and American. [4] A handful of volumes dealing with the vast subject of women and German literature has appeared since the Coalition of Women in German was formed in 1975. [5] The shape of our disciplines has made it difficult even for us—and I include myself—to get beyond notions such as the one Edith Hoshino mentions in her essay—that the contemporary German women's movement is "several years behind" the American one; one also hears it said that there are no really "good" feminist authors in West Germany, that there is no "positive" lesbian writing in German, and so on. The point isn't whether statements like these are valid or not, but how such ideas shape the questions we ask. Instead of agreeing that, well yes, German feminism is "behind" the United States, as some of us have done, I think we should ask: What are the politics of "ahead" and "behind" and what do they have to do with feminism? Similarly, instead of justifying the study of authors and texts not "central" to our disciplines (and not "in demand"), we ask what the implications of these designations are. And rather than railing against gatekeepers (as it may well seem that I have been doing), we should look closely at what happens when those on the margins do get past them.

The authors we've "discovered" (as if they hadn't been there all along) have had to get past gatekeepers too. One of my favorite anecdotes on this subject is Margot Schroeder's experience with the collective "Literature of the Working World" (Werkkreis Literatur der Arbeitswelt) when she was working on her first book, *Take It Like a Woman (Ich stehe meine Frau*, 1975), excerpted here. Schroeder wanted to (and did) write a book about the everyday life of working-class housewives and mothers, but didn't get a contract until she agreed to provide a clear plot line for her narrative. (The daily lives of housewives just don't have much plot.) She did this by devising a "citizens' action" around the issue of playgrounds for her characters' children. Then, contract in hand after several chapters were written, Schroeder gleefully let that "central" focus fade into the background, producing a book that represents, in both content and form, the fragmented and unfocused daily life she knew from her own experience—rather than the model of grass-roots political organizing the collective would have liked.[6] *Take It Like a Woman* went on to become one of the most successful titles in the "Literature of the Working World" series.

Schroeder's book appeared in 1975, at a time when the German women's movement had already called attention to many of the issues she raises in it. As Ulla Bock and Barbara Witych show in their essay "A Female Counter-Public," included here, by the late 1970s women's writing had become "fashionable" enough in the Federal Republic to convince major publishing houses of its marketability. Bock and Witych also mention some consequences of this development: cooptation; dilution of feminist content; competition among feminist and other alternative presses, making their survival even more precarious. Again I am reminded of Kafka's man from the country, who used up all his resources on the first gatekeeper, forgetting the other, more powerful ones beyond the first. The point isn't to reproach those who get past gatekeepers for being myopic (though some of them probably are), but to suggest an image of a complex system whose center and margins aren't easily changed.

The network of gatekeepers has, of course, its roots in the literary and political past in the FRG and the GDR, as elsewhere. In her overview of developments in the GDR since World War II, Patricia Herminghouse aptly calls the cultural heritage shared by East and West "a long-standing philosophical tradition of misogyny" ("Legal Equality and Women's Reality," section I, this volume). No clear break from that tradition can be established for postwar developments in the West.

Looking Back

In commenting on some of the better-known women writers in West Germany and Austria since 1945, I don't wish to give the impression of a continuous progression toward a more "feminist" literature, or even a "more visible female presence." The picture is more complex than that. When we look back, we find large numbers of women writing and publishing—contrary to the impression most of us had from college and graduate school that there were none, or only a very few ("exceptions!"). Though that myth hasn't yet been laid to rest, studies already done or underway will make it harder to maintain in the future.[7] The question of a female presence in German literature thus becomes one of examining the treatment of women writers by literary historians and critics. And the question of a feminist literature changes as we learn more about how women writers saw themselves, and how the lenses they looked through shaped what they saw, or were able to see.

The end of World War II has often been called "year zero" (das Jahr Null) to express the feeling that everything had stopped and had to start over. The country was devastated; it seemed that nothing and no one remained untainted by National Socialism; many prominent German writers had gone into exile and had not yet returned. Many of those who remained had been silenced, either directly, by their being forbidden to publish, or indirectly, by their withdrawing in response to perceived threats ("inner emigration"). Women so silenced were among the first writers to begin publishing again. For example, Luise Rinser (1911–) was imprisoned in 1944, accused of "high treason and undermining the military." Her first publication after the war was her prison diary (*Gefängnistagebuch*, 1946), which documents several months of her internment in a women's prison and gives sensitive descriptions of many of the other women there. Elisabeth Langgässer (1899–1950) was forbidden to publish in 1937 ("Jewish blood" in her family) and was forced to work in a factory during the war. Her first postwar publication was a novel in 1947, about the spiritual trials of a baptized Jew. Marie-Luise Kaschnitz (1901–1974) did not publish between 1937 and 1947, when a volume of her poetry appeared. Each in her own way, these and other women authors began writing about wartime experiences, injustices toward Jews and other groups, resistance efforts—often struggling to find an avenue for hope and renewal through religion. Their major characters are often ordinary women facing extraordinary situations. Their works are widely read, but up to now they have had a secure but secondary "women's place" in literary history.[8]

During West Germany's return to political stability and prosperity—
the well-known "economic miracle" (*Wirtschaftswunder*) of the 1950s—
a new generation of writers began to emerge and with it, new
gatekeepers. Mostly they were writers who had not published before
the war, and virtually all who achieved critical acclaim at the time
were associated, for a while at least, with "Group 47" (*Gruppe 47*,
named after the year it was founded). The goals of Group 47 (not
a formal organization, but a series of annual meetings at which
invited authors read from their works) were to promote a new,
socially conscious, democratic, and responsible German literature—
in the words of its founder, a "democratic elite." Predictably, the
elite that did emerge was predominantly male and middle class. In
the two decades of the Group's existence, only a handful of women
(but over two hundred men) were invited to read at its meetings,
and only two women, both Austrians, received the prestigious Group
47 prize: Ilse Aichinger in 1952 and Ingeborg Bachmann in 1953.
Both Aichinger (1921–) and Bachmann (1926–1973) shared their
male colleagues' concern for criticizing and questioning language and
for exploring formal possibilities for a new literary aesthetic. Their
works from this period, not unlike those of many of the leading
male authors, often have seemingly genderless narrative voices and
depict "timeless" situations; they treat questions of injustice, destructive power, guilt, individual freedom, and others, from a more philosophical perspective (Bachmann, much influenced by Heidegger) or
symbolically.

Those of us who attended graduate school in the United States in
the 1960s knew these two authors' names and had probably read
some of their works. Most of us did not then know about a gen-
erational contemporary of theirs, Ingeborg Drewitz (1923–). In 1951,
Drewitz was the first of that generation to write "KZ-Dramen"
(concentration camp plays)—which were not kindly received by
critics. She also did research on nineteenth-century German women
writers years before the women's movement rekindled a wider interest
in them; she was an early supporter of working-class literature, and
also helped promote the work of other women writers such as poet
Nelly Sachs (1891–1970), besides publishing numerous novels and
stories, many with emancipatory themes.[9] By contrast, the writings
of Aichinger and Bachmann portrayed women characters, when at
all, as ciphers for "the human condition." Their greater visibility at
the time is hardly an accident. Aichinger continues to express her
visions in a more abstract way, often through the fantastic, surreal,
and absurd. Bachmann turned in her later years increasingly to female
subjects and contemporary settings. Her prose works from these years
show her moving more and more toward an explicitly feminist

perspective and incorporating her personal experience into her writing.[10]

Up Against the Wall

Many new women authors entered the literary scene during the 1960s, though the total number of successful women writers was still small as compared to men. That male writers began to perceive the women's talent and energy as threatening, however, is indicated by a remark attributed to Günter Grass in the mid-1960s: "Diese Frauen fangen an, uns an die Wand zu schreiben."—"These women are starting to write us [men] up against the wall." [11] The reaction seems laughable to West German feminists today, considering the absence of a female "counter-public" to support women writers at the time. However, it shows (as if proof were needed) that women who wished to define themselves simply as *writers* didn't have that option. As we would expect, their treatment by critics and publishers only confirms this. For example, Gisela Elsner (1937–   ) has received harsh treatment at the hands of literary critics for her often grotesque depictions of male-female relations and explicit sexual scenes—for writing, as one sympathizer points out, that would most likely be perceived as "uncompromising realism" if done by a man.[12] Another writer, Angelika Mechtel (1943–   ) recalls: "My editor [in 1968] told me 'Your capital is that you're young and female.' Not one word about talent." [13] Authors as diverse as Karin Struck (1947–   ), who wrote passionately if not analytically about mothers and children; Gabriele Wohmann (1932–   ), whose more-distanced treatments of family relationships, marriage and heterosexual relations, child rearing, etc. have often been best sellers; and Helga Novak (1935–   ), admired for her unsentimental, "factual" style, could tell similar stories.[14] It would seem that if anyone was "up against the wall," it was the women. Maybe that is the angle from which we might view their writing as a kind of prelude to feminist literature of the 1970s.

We can see a different kind of prelude to feminist literature in the work of collectives dedicated to recovering and studying working-class literature. Their activity parallels the rise of New Left political activism during the 1960s. Groups such as the Dortmund *Gruppe 61*, of which Angelika Mechtel was a member, and the later collective "Literature of the Working World," mentioned above in connection with Margot Schroeder, reprinted neglected works and supported publication of new titles by working-class authors. They also produced much documentary literature, such as reportages, interviews and protocols. Their work helped provide a context and to some extent a methodology for the numerous documentary collections about women's lives that were published in the 1970s. Despite the fact that many women were active in groups such as these, it wasn't until the early days of the new German women's movement that a collection dealing only with women appeared, Erika Runge's *Women: Efforts Toward Emancipation* (*Frauen: Versuche zur Emanzipation,* 1968).

Developments in postwar West German literature, then, clearly did not favor women writers or "emancipatory" themes. The example of Ingeborg Drewitz suggests that a woman writer's politics were as important a factor as gender in terms of her literary reception. Women who wrote explicitly about female experience probably had an additional handicap. I believe it is accurate to say that none of the writers I have mentioned began her career by thinking of herself as writing "for women" or even "from a woman's perspective" (though some—Drewitz, Bachmann, Mechtel, Rinser—later moved in that direction). The reality of the recent German past was too close and too complex; the myth of equal opportunity was too great; there was no public forum to provide a context for valuing women's experiences specifically or even for acknowledging what now seems obvious, to feminists, at least: that women and men experience the world differently and that experience shapes what we see. Looking back from a 1980s perspective, through the lens of feminism, we have the possibility of redefining literature to include women writers and— eventually—of defining women's literature in a way that does justice to its complexity.

Feminism and Literature

With the above advice in mind, I now turn to the texts we have included in this anthology. First, why did we make the selections we did? It would be nice to be able to say we have chosen a "representative sampling" or "cross section" of authors whose work best illustrates "major tendencies" among women writing in German today. The truth, however, is somewhat different and maybe more interesting. We did look for literary texts that show, in content or form or both, a critical awareness of women's role and status in society, and we were not interested in antifeminist writing. Also, we were not immune to questions of who is considered "important" and what issues are or have been much discussed among German feminists. Of course, we were not able to get permission for everything we wanted to use, and we had limited space. So, our final product reflects these considerations plus one, which was not the least decisive: every literary text chosen for this volume is here because some or all of the co-editors *liked* it well enough to want it included.

(Why do we read literature?) I invite you to examine your own likes and dislikes when you read the literary pieces in this collection.

Second, what do the literary pieces have to do with German feminism? Certainly only a few of the authors could be considered active in the women's movement—Jutta Heinrich, Christa Reinig, Margot Schroeder. Heinrich's novel *The Gender of Thoughts (Das Geschlecht der Gedanken)*, excerpted here, is one of the books Edith Hoshino mentions as languishing in desk drawers unpublished for years. It was published by the feminist press Frauenoffensive in 1978, but Heinrich had taken it to other publishers without success since 1972. In her words: "It was as if the whole world had gotten together and agreed 'Anyone but her.' Nothing, it was impossible, not a poem, not a diary entry, a play, nothing. Not one sentence of mine." [15] The book was a success, and Heinrich has become a frequent guest at women's writing workshops and feminist literary discussion groups. Christa Reinig is a possibly unique example of a writer with an established reputation (she began publishing in the FRG in 1960) whose priorities shifted radically in the mid-1970s. She was influenced by events being debated by feminists at the time, especially the Itzehoe trial (see section VI, this volume) to change both her life and her writing. She came out publicly as a lesbian, has tried to find a less "masculine" way of writing, and often writes for feminist magazines such as *Die Schwarze Botin, Frauenoffensive Journal*, and *Courage*. Margot Schroeder's recent activities include traveling with members of the feminist band *Schneewittchen*, speaking and giving poetry readings on feminism and peace.

But critically conscious writing doesn't only come from avowed feminists. I am reminded of a statement by a Dutch feminist trying to describe the emergence of the women's movement in her country: "It is commonplace to say that feminism 'grew out of the left' . . . Feminism did not grow out of the left, feminism grew out of women's oppression." [16] In the same way, I think that writing that offers a critical interpretation of women's specific situation grows out of women's experience. (Which is not the same as saying that all women will write that way). So, writers such as Elfriede Brüning, Sarah Kirsch, Helga Novak and Irmtraud Morgner, who would have no patience with some of the more polemic debates among feminists, nevertheless "tell it like it is" to be a woman in a patriarchal society.

And despite my previous disclaimer as the the "representative" aspect of our collection, the literary texts do reflect a number of issues much discussed by German feminists. An example is the question of writing as an "emancipatory act" for women, which Brigitte Wartmann analyzes ("Writing as an Attack Against Patriarchy," section I) and the editors of *Die schwarze Botin* so emphatically disdain ("To bleed or not to bleed," section I). Both Sarah Kirsch's story "The Smith of Kosewalk" and Helga Novak's "Palisades" thematize writing; Kirsch's character Hanna finds the quality of her daily life altered by her letter-writing and Novak's unnamed narrator literally uses writing as an act of resistance. Novak's piece is a typical example of her prose style: spare, simple sentences stripped of most syntactic elements such as conjunctions which would explicitly express causality and other connections.

Questions of language and form, and the debate over a female or feminist aesthetic continue to be the subject of intense discussion and sharp disagreement among German feminists. Several authors included here, whether aware of these debates or not, have experimented in various ways to subvert "grammatical silencing techniques" (Mary Daly) and unmask assumptions silently perpetuated by conventional language. Jutta Schutting ("Park Murder") parodies journalistic language that erases the female victim of crime. Elfriede Jelinek ("Women as Lovers") mimics the language of popular culture, abruptly demystifying its clichés about love. Christa Reinig ("The Wolf and the Woman") dissects scholarly language that deletes the real agents of oppression—men—from syntactical structures and from consciousness. Christa Wolf ("The Teacher") explores her memory in a self-interrupting dialogue that fuses her past and present selves by acknowledging and exploring the split into "second and third person." "It is a human being who remembers . . . a human being who has learned to see herself not as an I, but as a you." [17] These (and other) authors confront the problems of language concretely, bypassing the "either/or" polarization so common in theoretical writing, and move forward to claim language for women.

Literary forms for breaking the silence about women's lives also include documentary forms—interviews (Maxie Wander, "Ruth B."), reportage and essay-like first-person accounts (selections from *Dear Colleague* and *From Hand to Mouth*). These pieces are examples of collaborative efforts between interviewer and interviewee, or between editors and writers, to create new possibilities for women's self-expression, especially women we wouldn't otherwise hear from. Women's new literary forms invite reflection on how we fictionalize our lives when speaking or writing about them. The border between fiction and nonfiction no longer seems as clear as many of us used to think.

Not least, our selections show that women writing in German today have a sense of humor (whether the women's movement does or not). Margot Schroeder's self-ironic Charlie Bieber, Irmtraud Morgner's scooter-riding streetcar conductor, Elisabeth Alexander's "Women who laugh," and Christa Reinig's fantasy of mashing all of humanity's genetic material into a ball, for example, show that humor can indeed be a means of turning anger into a fine art.[18]

Or is it art? Where do questions of literary quality fit into a discussion of this diverse collection of prose writing? Again, maybe this is the wrong question for now. I think of the editor of a recent collection of women's writing published by Suhrkamp. He points with satisfaction to the increased ratio of unsolicited female-authored manuscripts received by Suhrkamp, from one in ten some years ago, to equal numbers of manuscripts by women and men in 1980. (Unfortunately, he doesn't tell us how the ratio of female-authored manuscripts *accepted* has changed). He then goes on to assure us that "more and more women are writing, and more and more are writing well . . . . They meet and surpass the standards of their male colleagues, for centuries privileged . . . . Literature is what emerges, not just 'women's literature'." [19] It sounds very much as if he is saying tht women have learned to write like men. Yet "quality" and "good writing" are not eternal universal categories either, and our understanding of them must change as women continue trying to learn to write like themselves—like women. For Christa Wolf, the quality of our experience is the decisive factor: "The need to write in a new way follows, though perhaps at a distance, a new way of being in the world." [20] Margot Schroeder mentions time to write and a degree of distance: "Naked feelings are not literature. They must be clothed in language, but that only happens when thought and feeling become one." [21] And Ruth B., waitress: "Reality is no yardstick for me. I'd rather hang on to my inner dream." Women writing in German today are telling it like it is, unlearning lies, laughing, getting angry, making dreams visible—and pointing to new directions for literature.

Jeanette Clausen

Notes

1. Wolf's novels *The Quest for Christa T.* (1970), *A Model Childhood* (1980) and *No Place on Earth* (1982) are available from Farrar, Straus and Giroux, New York. The first edition of her collected essays is available in English as: *The Reader and the Writer: essays, sketches, memories* (New York: International Publishers, 1977).

2. *German Women Writers of the Twentieth Century*, ed. Elizabeth Rütschi Hermann and Edna Huttenmaier Spitz (New York and Oxford: Pergamon

Press, 1978). A dual-language collection is to appear in 1983: *Frauen im Mittelpunkt/Focus on Women,* ed. Patricia Herminghouse (Suhrkamp/Cambridge, to appear). Short prose and poetry by Sarah Kirsch, Helga Novak, Christa Wolf, Angelika Mechtel and Christa Reinig can be found in English in various issues of the dual-language journal *Dimension.* Prose by Christa Wolf, Verena Stefan, Irmtraud Morgner, and Elisabeth Alexander has appeared in English in issues 13, 15, and 23 of the journal *New German Critique.*

3. Dale Spender, "The gatekeepers: a feminist critique of academic publishing," *Doing Feminist Research,* ed. Helen Roberts (London, Boston and Henley: Routledge and Kegan Paul, 1981), p. 187. Spender is editor of *Women's Studies International Forum,* formerly *Women's Studies International Quarterly.*

4. These issues were the subject of a panel entitled "Gibt es eine weibliche Germanistik?" at the October 1982 Women in German conference. See *Women in German Newsletter* # 29 (Nov. 1982), pp. 4–5.

5. Collections containing articles in English on contemporary German women's writing are: *Beyond the Eternal Feminine: Critical Essays on Women and German Literature,* ed. Susan L. Cocalis and Kay Goodman (Stuttgart: Akademischer Verlag Hans-Dieter Heinz, 1982) S.A.G. 98; *Gestaltet und Gestaltend. Frauen in der deutschen Literatur,* ed. Marianne Burkhard, *Amsterdamer Beiträge zur neueren Germanistik,* Vol. 10, 1980; *Proceedings of the Second Annual Women in German Symposium,* ed. Kay Goodman and Ruth H. Sanders (Oxford, Ohio: Miami University, Sept. 1977).

6. The source for this anecdote is a talk given by Margot Schroeder at the Fifth Annual Women in German conference, October 1980, in Racine, Wisconsin.

7. See *Women in Print I: Opportunities for Women's Studies Research in Language and Literature,* ed. Ellen Messer-Davidow and Joan E. Hartman (Sept. 1982), available from the Modern Language Association, New York.

8. For works in English translation by these writers, see *Women Authors in Translation,* ed. Isabelle de Courtivron and Margery Resnick (Garland Press, 1983).

9. Drewitz' works have not been translated into English. Sources for the information given are: Bärbel Jäschke, "Ingeborg Drewitz," *Neue Literatur der Frauen. Deutschsprachige Autorinnen der Gegenwart,* ed. Heinz Puknus (Munich: Beck, 1980), pp. 69–74, and "Ingeborg Drewitz: Nur als Funktionärin anerkannt," *Frauen schreiben. Ein neues Kapitel deutschsprachiger Literatur* (Hamburg: Verlag Grunder & Jahr AG & Co., 1979), pp. 287–88.

10. For works in English translation by Aichinger and Bachmann, see *Women Authors in Translation,* op. cit.

11. Cited by Inge Nordhoff, "Die schreiben uns noch an die Wand." Beobachtungen beim 5. Treffen Schreibender Frauen in Bremen, in *Keiner schiebt uns weg. Zwischenbilanz der Frauenbewegung in der Bundesrepublik* (Weinheim and Basel: Beltz, 1979), pp. 241–45.

12. Marlies Gerhardt, "Gisela Elsner," in *Neue Literatur der Frauen,* op. cit., pp. 88–94.

13. "Angelika Mechtel: Von Talent Redeten die Männer nicht," in *Frauen schreiben,* op. cit., pp. 284–86.

14. Nina Morris-Farber, "Sociological Implications of Gabriele Wohmann's Critical Reception," and Leslie Adelson, "The Question of a Feminist Aesthetic and Karin Struck's *Klassenliebe*," both in *Beyond the Eternal Feminine*.

15. "Gespräch mit Jutta Heinrich," Protokoll des Lese– und Diskussionsabends im Hannover Frauenzentrum am 25. 10. 78. Typescript, 13 pp., n.d.

16. Petra De Vries, "Feminism in the Netherlands," *Women's Studies International Quarterly* Vol. 4, no. 4 (1981), pp. 389–407.

17. Christa Wolf, *Kindheitsmuster* (Darmstadt and Neuwied: Luchterhand, 1977), p. 9. For a fuller discussion of self-reference in Wolf's writing, see Jeanette Clausen, "The Difficulty of Saying 'I' as Theme and Narrative Technique in the Works of Christa Wolf," *Gestaltet und Gestaltend, op. cit*, pp. 319–33.

18. Mary Kay Blakely, "Dear Gloria," *Pulling Our Own Strings. Feminist Humor and Satire* (Bloomington: Indiana University Press, 1980), p. 12.

19. Siegfried Unseld, "Geleitwort" zu *Im Jahrhundert der Frau. Ein Almanach des Suhrkamp Verlags* (Frankfurt/M.: Suhrkamp, 1980), p. 8.

20. Christa Wolf, "Lesen und Schreiben," in *Lesen und Schreiben. Neue Sammlung* (Darmstadt and Neuwied: Luchterhand, 1980), p. 9.

21. Margot Schroeder, "Begleittext" zu "Spaltungsirre" (poem) in *Frauen, die pfeifen. Verständigungstexte*, ed. Ruth Geiger, Hilke Holinka, Claudia Rosenkranz, Sigrid Weigel (Frankfurt/M.: Suhrkamp, 1978), p. 272.

Part One

Breaking the Silence

To understand German-language literature by women from the 1970s, it is important to be aware of the contexts in which it emerged. Herminghouse's essay in this section surveys developments in the socialist German Democratic Republic, where women authors responded not to a feminist call for "autonomous female self-expression" (as in the West), but to contradictions they saw in a society well on its way toward achieving "equal" participation by women in the labor force while ignoring the double burden for women at home.[1] The bold and imaginative treatment of emancipatory themes by GDR women writers leads Herminghouse to call their work a unique development in German—not only GDR—literary history. Many West German feminists would agree, pointing for example to the relative absence of feminist utopian literature in the German-speaking West. On the other hand, GDR women writers still remain largely silent on many issues—openly debated in the West—that have no "official" existence in their country, for example rape and other violence against women; lesbianism and homosexuality; pornography.

The West German women's movement's early focus on sexuality and women's right to control their bodies inevitably influenced feminist literary experimentation. Discussion of the "emancipatory potential" of women's writing contributed to an impressive burst of first publications. And, much as in the United States and other Western countries, feminist writers and critics analyzed sexism in language and debated the question of a specifically female or feminine aesthetic. In a much-discussed essay of 1976, critic Silvia Bovenschen asked "But what if we no longer view the difference [between women and men] as deficiency, loss, self-effacement and deprivation, but rather as opportunity?"[2] Emphasis on the positive aspects of "difference," dubbed "die neue Weiblichkeit" ("new femaleness/femi-

39

ninity"), elicited much controversy during the second half of the decade, often centering on Verena Stefan's *Shedding*.

Stefan's foreword to *Shedding*, included here, describes her attempt to create a more "feminine" language for describing women's experiences and (especially) sexuality. Response to the book ranged from the incautiously positive—Christa Reinig called it "das Ende der weiblichen Ichlosigkeit" (the end of female "I-lessness")—to outraged accusations of ahistorical, irresponsible and superficial self-contemplation. More balanced perspectives on *Shedding* and "die neue Weiblichkeit" are presented by the Bock/Witych and Wartmann essays in this section, where women's individual efforts to "write themselves" are seen as part of a collective process of increasing awareness. Critics' charges of a too facile (re-)appropriation of "positive" female qualities are not unfounded, but tend to ignore or minimize the importance of process and to obscure the substantive issues (see the Classen/Goettle essay). The essays give a feeling for directions in feminist literature and criticism during the period when most of the literary works in this volume were written.

Notes

1. A convenient source of information on women's rights, employment, status, etc. in the two German states is: Harry G. Shaffer, *Women in the Two Germanies: A Comparative Study of a Socialist and a Non-Socialist Society* (Pergamon 1981).

2. Silvia Bovenschen, "Is There a Feminine Aesthetic?" in *New German Critique* 10 (1977), pp. 111–137 (p. 117); German original "Gibt es eine weibliche Aesthetik?" in *Aesthetik und Kommunikation* 25 (Sept. 1976).

1. Legal Equality and Women's Reality in the German Democratic Republic

Patricia Herminghouse

In this article, American Germanist Patricia Herminghouse outlines three successive stages in GDR literary history: a first stage of "changing consciousness," a transitional one of "arrival," and a third reflecting a "changed consciousness." The stages imply that the feminism of contemporary GDR women writers such as Wolf, Morgner, Wander and Wolter included in this volume grew logically (though not inevitably) out of the context of their particular situation.

Ever since 1949, when Article 7 of its first constitution stated unequivocally "Men and women have equal rights," the German Democratic Republic has insisted upon the integration of women as full and equal participants in the building of a socialist German state. A long-standing philosophical tradition of misogyny, characterized by names such as Arthur Schopenhauer, Friedrich Nietzsche, and Sigmund Freud, has been supplanted by a political heritage rooted in the ideas of Karl Marx and Friedrich Engels, August Bebel, Clara Zetkin, and Rosa Luxemburg. In this tradition it is assumed that woman's position in society is necessarily linked to her position in the production process and that women's emancipation is inextricably bound up with human emancipation in the class struggle. For this reason, there is no "women's movement" in the GDR and writers who are labeled as "feminist" by enthusiastic readers in the West are quick to reject the appellation, viewing "feminism" as a bourgeois attempt to achieve superficial liberation through a battle of the sexes rather than genuine emanicipation through an attack on the material basis of oppression. There is an innocuous women's monthly magazine, *Für Dich* (For You), and a mass women's organization, which is represented in the People's Assembly, but neither could ever be termed a GDR counterpart to institutions of the women's movement in the West.

There has always been a strong female presence in the historical development and literature of the GDR, beginning in the immediate postwar years in the East Sector under Soviet occupation. Here,

41

where there was no Marshall Plan and where wartime losses of the male work force were compounded by emigration to the West, survival, much less reconstruction, would have been impossible without participation by women in unprecedented numbers and in unprecedented fields of labor. Women cleared the rubble of Germany's devastated cities, helped to reestablish homes, local governments, food supplies—and factories. Marx's thesis that major social transformations are impossible without women's involvement was probably less decisive than was sheer economic necessity in bringing about the emphasis that the young state placed not only on women's right to work, but on their duty to work as well. By 1951, "women's committees" had been established in industry to provide for the special needs of working women and to further their integration into the production process. Ten years later, an important party communiqué, "Women—Peace and Socialism," praised women's achievements and contributions to the cause of peace—through their work in building a socialist state which could stand on its own in negotiations with imperialist states. It decreed the establishment of affirmative action programs with goals and quotas to increase systematically the number of women in leadership and management positions in the government and in the workplace. Intensive political and technical training programs were implemented with paid released time and special provisions for women who must interrupt their training for family obligations. Services and consumer goods were called for to ameliorate the double burden of working wives, rather than demanding more radical forms of emancipation in family life. In 1961, 64 percent of the able-bodied women of working age were employed or training for employment. Today the figure approaches 90 percent: fully half the work force of the GDR is female, supported by an impressive array of legal and practical measures encouraging this high employment rate while promoting the nuclear family as the fundamental unit of society. The situation is not without its paradoxes.

The Family Code of 1965, for example, clearly establishes the state's interest in upholding marriage and the family. While declaring the duty of both partners to respect one another's rights to personal and social development, it specifically provides that a woman cannot be hindered in her choice of a profession or in her pursuance of social and political advancement, even if this leads to temporary separation from the family. Nor can she be forced to work unsalaried in the home or in a family business. Immense strides have been made outside the family in establishing free nurseries and kindergartens—often operated by a given enterprise for its own employees—and after-school-care programs for younger children of working parents. Hot lunch programs at minimal cost for both children and workers further attempt to relieve women of some of their traditional domestic duties. The recently revised Labor Code provides six months of maternity leave at full pay for each pregnancy and the right to a year of unpaid leave with no loss of seniority after the birth of a first child, to a year of paid leave after the birth of each subsequent child. Substantial birth stipends as well as monthly allowances for each child are paid to families, with no discrimination in these benefits between wed and unwed mothers. Abortion was legalized in 1972— the GDR, with its severe problems in population maintenance, having been the last of the socialist states to grant this right. But in addition to the generous provisions made for the biologically determined aspects of reproduction, other measures seem merely to perpetuate patriarchal traditions. Thus mothers of two or more children are given a shortened work week and additional days of vacation each year and all women—whether they are mothers or not—are allowed one day off work each month for doing housework. Beneficial as such provisions may be in the real situation of working women, they not only reflect but even reinforce the considerable gap between legal equality and women's reality in the GDR and represent tacit acceptance of the women's claim that, unlike men, they spend an average of thirty-seven hours a week on their domestic "duties" in the realm of reproduction in addition to their real "work" in material production. But women's impatience with the contradictions between their continued exploitation in the family and the sense of self, of social and economic independence which they gain in the workplace, is reflected in an ever-increasing divorce rate, in which most cases are filed by women.

If the family has remained a bastion of conservatism, one might expect more progress towards real equality for women in the ranks of government and party officials who, after all, have set up the legal framework for women's emancipation. Women do comprise about one third of the holders of public office, particularly at the local level, and one third of the party membership. Yet in the powerful Central Committee of the Socialist Unity Party, women are only meagerly represented and only recently was the first woman admitted to its policy-making and administrative organ, the Politbüro. Nor have women ever had more than token representation in the Council of Ministers, the highest body of government. Where power rather than production is at stake, state and party authorities seem curiously unable to define and accept the implications of the equal status for women which they have proclaimed. The consciousness raising which they called for has yet to produce the ultimate political results.

In the GDR, consciousness raising has been considered the "work" of artists, especially writers. At a writers' conference in 1966, Minister of Culture Kurt Hager explained, "The writer's role is that of a leader and planner of the socialist consciousness of the people." The tenets of Socialist Realism expect artists to produce a "correct" view of social reality, not a mere reflection of things as they are, but one which bridges the gap between the real and the ideal by viewing the present from the perspective of the future towards which it is developing. Writers, like everyone else, are expected to serve society with writing that is productive both in its effects on the people for whom it is intended and in its responsiveness to the needs of these readers. In terms of writing by and about women, this meant for several decades the portrayal of positive socialist heroines: women in vital social functions, not entirely dissimilar to the role models Western feminists began seeking in literature in the early stages of the women's movement. Parallel to the development of the GDR, its literature went through several distinct stages, the latest of which is represented by the selections in this anthology.

The first period, in the 1950s, might be termed a period of changing consciousness, in which writers zealously joined the official effort to enlist women into the work of building a new society, primarily in the factory and on the farm, and to make them aware of the opportunities open to them. In this stage, the works of women writers are not distinguishable from those of their male colleagues, since all seem to write very self-consciously from the same official viewpoint about a rather limited segment of society, producing works with a manifesto-like quality and uniformly happy endings. The housewife who finds happiness and fulfillment as a crane operator is almost a stock figure in works of this era, symbolizing as she does the productive potential inherent in a combination of machine technology and womanly attributes of patience and dexterity. Another stock character is the (invariably male) party secretary, a benevolent father figure who looks after her best interests in both personal and professional matters.

The second stage, the literature of the 1960s, reflects both women's advancement to much more important positions and also their attempts to adjust to new social roles with a greater degree of psychological credibility than was depicted in the early works. Although the literature of this period is still perceptibly didactic and can barely dispense with the intercession of the party secretary, it ranges over a wider variety of situations and presents characters who are interesting in their own right as individuals, not merely as representative types in representative situations. New women writers, such as Christa Wolf and Brigitte Reimann, begin to emerge, and the ubiquitous happy ending of earlier works often yields to a more open conclusion that acknowledges the possibility of tragedy when individual needs and values are subordinated to broader societal priorities.

The most recent trends in women's writing may be traced to the 1968 publication of Christa Wolf's *The Quest for Christa T.* (trans. Christopher Middleton; pub. by Farrar, Straus and Giroux, 1970), which relates the attempt to portray a young woman who was not "exemplary," the struggle for a more honest mode of writing grounded in women's own experience: "Just for once, for this once, I want to discover how it is and to tell it like it is: the unexemplary life, a life that can't be used as a model." Expressions such as "the journey toward oneself," "the difficulty of saying 'I' " indicate a woman's search for a way of living and writing which is rooted in authenticity instead of authority, need-oriented rather than goal-oriented, and expressive rather than instrumental. Wolf's description of the attempt to write the female experience, to break the silence of women who had conformed to patriarchal values rather than define themselves on the basis of their own experience and perceptions is at least as significant part of the novel as is the actual story of the life and death of her semi-autobiographical main character, who finally suc-cumbs to leukemia—or, just as plausibly, to alienation. The first edition of the novel had only a very limited circulation in the GDR: Christa T's notion that "fantasy" and "integrity" rather than con-formity were the most important qualities for human survival was ahead of its time, but certainly not without resonance. Women writers in particular began to expand the traditional concept of Socialist Realism to include elements of the fantastic, which is employed for its emancipatory potential: not to escape, but to critique reality. Especially popular have been the so-called sex-change stories, which— usually in a light-hearted vein—imaginatively portray the experiences of an individual who is transformed into a member of the opposite sex in order to unmask sexist standards of behavior. Of the authors represented in this anthology, Wolf, Irmtraud Morgner, and Sarah Kirsch have written such stories.

The exploration of relations between women which began with *Christa T.* also continues, most notably in Morgner's *Life and Ad-ventures of the Trobadora Beatriz as Chronicled by her Minstrel Laura* (1974), the most complex work ever written by a woman in the German language. In this fantastic montage novel, the identities of Laura, a contemporary GDR woman, and her friend the medieval trobadora Beatriz, ultimately merge—as those of Christa T. and her narrator often seem to do in Wolf's novel. A few of the younger writers have produced works that are exclusively about women who

live independently of men, but specifically lesbian themes have yet
to emerge.

The accent on subjectivity, the desire to ground literature in wom-
en's own experiences, is also reflected in so-called "documentary"
literature. Erika Runge, who pioneered this trend in West Germany,
was the first to record East German women's attempts to voice their
own experiences in 1969. Four years later, the poet Sarah Kirsch
produced a much more literary anthology, *The Panther Woman, Five
Unretouched Stories from the Tape Recorder*. But Maxie Wander's 1977
collection is by far the most frank and intimate of those that have
appeared thus far. Wolf's review of that work, included here, is
explicit in its analysis of the significance of that book and indicates
how far women in the GDR have come in the last decade in
challenging and reshaping social relations according to a feminist
vision, much as they may still avoid the term. Ranging from the
heights of the fantastic to the depths of subjective experience, from
the aggressiveness of Morgner to the pensiveness of Wolf, recent
writing by the younger generation of GDR women writers represents
a unique development in German literary history: the first attempt
by women to lead a literary movement which is authentic, experimental, and emancipatory.

2. The Women's Movement and the Construction of a "Female" Counter-Public*

Ulla Bock and Barbara Witych

Political and consciousness-raising activities of the West German women's movement paved the way for a veritable explosion of women's publications by the mid-1970s. This article, condensed from Bock's and Witych's introduction to their comprehensive bibliography Thema: Frau *(Subject: Woman), outlines developments up to 1979. The authors define "women's literature" on a continuum ranging from pamphlets and protocols to belles lettres and scholarly articles. They document the importance of independent and alternative publishing for creating a female market or "counter-public."*

The first written products of the new West German movement were pamphlets, appeals for action, and resolutions; here, women expressed their views in political/agitatorial fashion. The subsequent development of organized women's groups and the later autonomous women's centers brought with it a flood of subjective reports and self-presentations which reflect the multifarious debates but do not usually go beyond their regional area. Topics predominating at this time were the repeal of Paragraph 218; sexuality and relating to one's body; male-female relationships and women's relationships to each other; housework versus paid employment; the situation of mothers. Establishing autonomous women's centers and founding a women's newspaper for wider distribution were the first attempts to gain a broader support base, outside the university milieu, for the "new" women's movement's ideas and goals.

[Much of the movement's energies have been directed toward] the construction of a "female counter-public," i.e., a public defined and supported by women. This is apparent today in a broad spectrum of women's cultural activities (in areas such as film, music, graphic and plastic arts, dance, theater). Publishing houses, printers, book distributors, communication centers, tearooms, coffeehouses, bookstores, counselling centers and the like have emerged, all independently run by women. Precisely those projects which aim to publish

and distribute "women's literature" have acquired a special significance for women's emancipatory efforts.

The first women's press was Frauenoffensive, founded in Munich
in 1976. It grew out of a women's series in Trikont Verlag, initiated
in 1974 by Gisela Erler, a co-founder of Trikont. The best seller
Shedding (1975) by Verena Stefan, who placed part of her royalties
at the press's disposal, made it possible to establish an independent
press. The series had begun by thematizing general problems of
women's oppression, but shifted in 1975–76 to publications concentrating especially on concern with one's body. An additional focus
was analysis of male-dominated research. The spring 1978 program
presented, along with Jutta Heinrich's novel *The Gender of Thoughts*
and Charlotte Perkins Gilman's story *The Yellow Wallpaper,* studies
better classified as anthropology, such as Anne Kent Rush's *Moon,
Moon* and Josefine Schreiber's *Goddesses,* as well as a women's movement "classic," Ti-Grace Atkinson's *Amazon Odyssey.*

The press Frauenpolitik (women's politics) emerged in Münster in
the same year (1976). The women at Frauenpolitik consider themselves part of both the women's movement and the "New Left."
Though their priorities are clearly with the women's movement, this
press differs from other autonomous women's projects such as Frauenoffensive, in its relatively close collaboration with leftist projects,
including ones led predominantly by men. In designing their program,
the women of this press believe it is fundamentally important to
clarify the fact that the "new" women's movement has a tradition
that women can identify with and learn from. Thus, one of their
goals is to make documents from this early history accessible to the
public again. Besides books on "women under fascism" and "women
in the third world," they have published literary texts and also a
book on the subject of male sterilization. It is the only book authored
by a man to appear in a women's press; given the heated controversy
over its publication, it will probably remain the only one for the
time being.

Courage, the first larger feminist magazine for women, also appeared
in 1976. Edited by a Berlin women's collective and initially circulated
only in West Berlin, it was soon available throughout the FRG (circ.
70,000 by Nov. 1978). The first issue of the Cologne magazine edited
by Alice Schwarzer, *Emma—Magazine by Women for Women,* appeared
in February 1977 (initial imprint 300,000). Like *Courage, Emma* is
available at newsstands. Besides these two mass-circulation women's
magazines, there are also a number of smaller ones representing a
variety of mostly more radical trends within the "new" women's
movement.

Belletristic Literature

The developments described thus far show that the principle of personal involvement (Betroffenheit) characterizes "women's literature." This is especially true of the belletristic literature. Encouraged by the women's movement, women writers began to take issue with their social role as woman more intensely than had female authors in the past, and to thematize woman-specific issues in a manner such that their own involvement is more consciously integrated into the work. Here, two factors must be emphasized as essential to so-called belletristic literature. One is the writing process itself, which at the level of individual experience becomes a medium for self-exploration and self-knowledge, and thus may have both an emancipatory and a therapeutic function. A second is that the written texts make possible a collective communication with readers, and of readers with each other. The texts produced by women must be understood as documents of their personal situation as well as of the societal.

Verena Stefan's *Shedding* (Frauenoffensive 1975) is a good example of a book with great appeal for identification. Though West German literary critics initially took no notice of it, word-of-mouth propaganda alone made it a best seller. It was *the* book a new generation of women identified with, eliciting awareness of involvement among them. At the same time, the reception and criticism of this book represented a public debate over the "new" women's movement's ideological production. The book's success—100,000 copies by 1979—opened up the market for "women's literature,": even unknown writers were more readily given a chance to publish. The entire publishing industry began giving more emphasis to "women's literature." Announcements of publications now contain full-page ads with comments like ". . . especially for women readers" (Herder), or "she has long since discovered us" (dtv). Though Brigitte Schwaiger found no German publisher for *How does the Salt get into the Sea?* in 1975 (later published in Austria), ever since this additional successful first work (150,000 copies sold by 1979), there has been an abundance of first publications by women as well as an increase in translations of foreign titles and new editions of historical autobiographies, biographies, letters, and diaries. Examples are the autobiographical *Una donna* (1906) by Sybilla Alaramo and Agnes Smedley's *Daughter of Earth* (1929).

The importance of the radical insertion of one's own life story into the work is matched by the significance of developing utopias in literature. The women's movement is becoming increasingly aware of the role of fantasies in imagining an emancipated life. Recent discussions concerning a "female language" or a "female aesthetic" have been strongly influenced by the French theorists Luce Irigaray and Hélène Cixous, and women writers are making greater use of techniques of fictional representation to express women's fantasies and alternative worlds. Thus, for example, Jutta Heinrich, in *The Gender of Thoughts* (1978), blurs levels of reality and fiction, seeing her first-person narrator as representative of her sex without explicitly treating her own biography. This tendency is not new; however, up to now it has been developed much more consistently in GDR literature and in English-language literature.

Factual and Scholarly Literature

While the literary market in the early stages of the "new" women's movement was heavily subjective, a tendency toward serious analytic and explanatory texts can be observed since about the mid-70s. In the transitional area to this more theoretical and scholarly literature are texts documenting the "context of women's daily life"—protocols, interviews—that are sometimes very close to literary forms (e.g., Maxie Wander's *Guten Morgen, du Schöne,* 1978). Documentary literature about women had begun as early as 1968, with Erika Runge's publication of *Women: Efforts Toward Emancipation.* This form of literature continues in many variations to this day.

While the women in the transcribed protocols and interviews speak for themselves as witnesses of their daily life, engaged feminist women in theoretical and practical fields, investigating the causes and interrelations of women's oppression, take those stated everyday experiences as the starting point for their theory. They consider personal involvement and partisanship necesary preconditions of research, by contrast to the prevailing methodological postulate of value-free research and neutrality with respect to "research objects." Aware involvement emerges through identification with one's own oppressed group. It is a collective process of becoming aware, in which all participants contribute to investigating and clarifying an oppressive situation.*

The search for theoretical explanations guides the current (1979) discussion of the advantages and disadvantages of "institutionalizing the woman question," i.e., whether this means a progressive development within the women's movement. The goal of advancing the

---

* For a fuller discussion of research methods grounded in collective social action projects, see Mies, "Towards a Methodology for Feminist Research," section XI, this volume.

necessary theoretical work in the women's movement has led, for example, to a coalition of women social scientists. Their association, "Social Science Research and Practice for Women," founded in 1978, gives them a framework for scholarly debate, which then appears for public criticism in the journal *Contributions to Feminist Theory and Practice (Beiträge zur feministischen Theorie und Praxis)*. Reciprocal interweaving of theory and practice has helped contribute to a veritable boom in literature on the woman question.

Expansion of the Market for "Women's Literature"

It was pointed out earlier that problems have resulted from the marketing of women's literature. One of these is an increasingly competitive market. The closed season is over on women's presses, whose successes called attention to the market gap. Understandably, many women from the movement are irritated by "having to watch the well-known, financially secure commercial presses start their own women's series two or three years after the small feminist presses, espcially Frauenoffensive, have done the groundwork." The larger presses can shut out financially weaker bidders when buying options on foreign books by women. They can also outdo smaller presses in competition for buyers by producing cheaper books and investing more in advertising. It is more attractive for authors to publish with larger presses in any case. Books from leftist and other small presses are also competition for autonomous women's presses. Thus, assertion by women's presses or printers of their right to exist largely independent of patriarchal institutions and to develop collective work patterns intensifies the problems of being embedded in the capitalist market system. Fundamentally, these women's projects find themselves in contradiction aptly formulated in *Courage* (1978): "It's very difficult to be a women's project which must face market rules and financial exigencies without turning into something different; on the other hand, can our business survive if we don't face them?" The question cannot be answered in detail here. However, it must be clearly understood that the profit-oriented marketing of the women's movement's original ideas and goals leads to depoliticization and watering down. The attractive label "women's emancipation" is used to distribute information that does, of course, modify traditional role-assignments but doesn't fundamentally question them, as the women's movement aims to do. Their demands require revolutionizing society's structure as a whole.

Translated by Jeanette Clausen

Notes

* German original: Ulla Bock and Barbara Witych, "Frauenbewegung und Aufbau einer 'weiblichen' Gegenöffentlichkeit," *Thema Frau: Bibliographie der deutschsprachigen Literatur zur Frauenfrage 1949–1979*, ed. Ulla Bock and Barbara Witych (Bielefeld: AJZ, 1980), xiv–xxxiv. Condensed, translated and reprinted with permission.

3. *Foreword to* Shedding*

Verena Stefan

In working on Shedding, *her first book, Verena Stefan—like many feminist writers—discovered that sexism in language goes far beyond the use of masculine "generic" pronouns. This foreword, in which she describes her struggles to find vocabulary that would not falsify her experiences, was omitted from the English translation (Daughters Press, 1978).*

While writing this book, whose subject matter is long overdue in Germany, I kept bumping into the language at hand, word upon word, concept upon concept. Of course I experienced this all the more intensely because I was writing about sexuality. *All* the customary expressions which refer to coitus—the spoken as well as the written ones—are brutal and denigrate women (i.e., *screw, fuck, thrust, bang, stick it in*). The leftist idiom reflects the existing power structure in much the same way, though perhaps a shade more bluntly. The leftist cock enters the leftist pussy and people (merrily) screw around. But the processes themselves remain unaffected. To say *enter* instead of *penetrate* does not take issue with the fact of the matter. If a woman starts talking about her *pussy*, she is merely adopting the jargon of leftist men. Her vagina, her body, her true self remain to her as inaccessible as before. If she uses these expressions to talk "candidly" about her body and her sexuality, this merely means she is conforming to male attempts at overcoming sexual taboos. So when I write about heterosexuality, I will use the clinical terminology. It is more neutral, less offensive, further removed.

Language fails me the moment I attempt to describe new experiences. Experiences that are supposedly new cannot be considered really new if they are expressed in the same everyday idiom. Articles and books that treat the subject of sexuality without addressing the problem of language are worthless, they serve to maintain the status quo.

I mean to break down the familiar ties. I mean to call into question and set aside all those concepts which shed no light—concepts like relationship, problem-relating, mechanisms, socialization, orgasm, desire, passion—all of them meaningless. They will have to be replaced by new descriptions before a new way of thinking can evolve. Each

53

word must be carefully examined before deciding to use or discard it.

It all starts with the teensy word *man: man* hat, *man* tut, *man* fühlt.[1] *Man* is used to describe conditions, feelings, situations—for human beings in general. Sences that commence "*als frau hat man ja . . .*" ("as a woman one has . . .") are most revealing. *Man* has no meaning for woman. Only as woman can she seek woman. When I wanted to write about sensitivity, experiences, eroticism among women, I could not find the words. This is why I distanced myself from everyday language as much as possible, and why I tried to find new paths via poetry. Natural similes and metaphors come to mind immediately. However, woman as nature seems such a hackneyed cliché, destroyed by the patriarchy, that our own relationship to nature has been severed, and we must examine it anew.

Writing, I encountered language. That may sound odd, yet it is surprising how many people can write without ever entering into touch with language itself. In *Shedding*, I was unable to examine closely each and every word without first paving the way by working through one fragment of my own history. Only now can I begin to concentrate systematically on sexism in language, on feminine language, on a feminine literature; only now can I begin reporting on life among women.

Translated by Johanna Moore and Beth Weckmueller

Notes

* German original: Verena Stefan, *Häutungen* (Munich: Frauenoffensive, 1975), pp. 3–4. Translated and reprinted with permission.

1. "One has, one does, one feels . . ." *Man*, corresponding to English *one* or *they*, is a German "masculine generic" pronoun that has no exact English equivalent.

4. Writing as an Attack Against Patriarchy*

Brigitte Wartmann

This article analyzes ordinary women's efforts to write their experiences in the context of psychoanalytic, feminist, and Marxist theoretical work. The author argues for the potential for a transformation of consciousness via women's self-exploration through and with language, while also cautioning against premature or uncritical appropriation of still unrealizable alternatives. In suggesting that a feminist critique of patriarchy may be achieved through dialectic logic, it is not clear that the author has taken her own advice.

In the struggle to develop strategies for liberation from alien training models, women's "writing" has increasingly acquired a special significance. Embedded in other efforts by feminists to develop resistance to "normal conditions" in a male-defined world, writing should be understood as the expression of an initially quite private struggle for most women. It facilitates the individual's search for a lost self-consciousness; beyond this, a collective cultural destiny can be discerned in women's texts through the multiple variations of individual experience.

Text Production as Blueprint for Transforming Women's Life-Practice

"What am I actually writing for, putting all these strange marks on paper?" asks a woman at the June 1978 "Meeting of Writing Women" in Bremen. "I'm spitting out everything I usually swallow unresistingly, without objecting. Writing: a way to clear out the dirt that has piled up. Scream it all out, spill it out, write it out of me. Become completely empty. And then: I've freed myself and collapse into myself again, dissolve. Passive, unanchored, biding my time; accept, like a sponge. Absorb, bottle up, burst open." [1] Resistance and the experiencing of one's own ego are more laborious, more tedious than women had imagined. Spitting out and collapsing back is an endless process of many small individual efforts toward lib-

55

eration, that can arise only very slowly in the interplay of frustration
and relief. The [written] text captures ideas that would otherwise
soon evaporate in the process of daily life. Like a mirror, it picks
up the image a woman outlines of herself, but it becomes clear that
the image looking back at her isn't identical to the one she wanted
to produce. She observes remains of male thought-patterns in the
desires and strategies her text has captured, still preventing her from
freeing herself from prescribed role models and from "opening up
at last for a melody of her own." [2] The melody of an autonomous
feminist way of life is hard to define and it certainly won't be found
only in literature, independent of other social forms. But literature
can be understood as a place where our dreams of a different life
begin to take shape a little. "A literature which dares more than
that which we already know" [3] is the beginning of a utopia aiming
toward a complete transformation of life. One's own writing can
help liberate dreams from their literary insecurity and give one
courage to fill them with real life.

Connecting women's life-practice to aesthetics has a tradition. In
the bourgeois conception, the role of woman as object of male
adoration is closely linked with aesthetics, defined as a beautiful,
harmonious counter-world to alienated masculine social practice. In
this view, women and art are alike in having been stylized by men
striving for social liberation into harmonious, idealized elements of
a freer life-context. Woman, with her beauty, sensuality and morality
in opposition to man's spiritual and physical work, was equated with
a "metaphysically transfigured nature principle." In this, she was
"simultaneously elevated and degraded," placed "so high and so
low that she could no longer find a place in society's life-context." [4]
An ideologically distorted male "longing for reconciliation with nature, for a nonalienated existence, is projected onto femaleness." [5] It
is directed toward an object of desire that, like nature itself, is not
acknowledged to have independent needs. In recent years women
have had success in resisting this status. However, a contradictory
factor in the real substance of these male projections remains: by
virtue of their exclusion from society's life-contexts, women have
maintained certain abilities that may actually have left them the less-
alienated ones; [they have these abilities] *because* they either could
not find, or could find only with difficulty a place in society's life
and work. When women no longer feel compelled to concentrate
their spontaneity, directness, cheerfulness (results of their social "def-
icit") on men, but begin to make them useful for themselves, there
emerges the possibility to outline a social practice that moves in a
"different melody."

Radical Subjectivity in a Male World

The most varied feminist groups are brought together by their demand for a transformed female life-practice that does not exhaust itself in theories *about* objective social transformations but formulates the necessity to begin the transformation with oneself. This was expressed by the slogan "the personal is political," formulated by women in 1968 to attack the left. "Radical subjectivity" [6] was demanded at one of the first "Meetings of Writing Women" in Munich in 1976. It was to be the point of departure for a transformed female identity—varied though the concepts behind this demand were. "We are fascinated by the sense of personal responsibility, the group feeling, the therapeutic effect of individual writing and above all by our overview of the entire work-process," wrote the editors of a small volume entitled *Werkstatt Schreibender Frauen* (Writing Women's Workshop); the title refers to women "who are nameless in our culture industry." [7] The texts in this volume can be considered exemplary for many others, and deal with women's everyday life, their thoughts, their worries. The intentions underlying these writing initiatives do not have the larger social transformation in view but are the expression of resistance at the microlevel of everyday life. Often this simply means to start taking oneself more seriously and stop meeting expectations as usual; not looking after the children but sitting down at one's desk or getting together with a group.

Blocking women's detachment from patriarchal reality is the fact that general social functions are closed to them anyway; thus, their withdrawal reproduces this status. To reverse social deficits means fighting for general male privileges in male society. The struggle for feelings of self-worth, separated from functioning *for* men, must be taken out of the self-exploratory female sphere as a *social struggle*. Yet it cannot and must not become involved with this struggle's patriarchal rules and goals.

On the other hand, women are forced, for example in the workplace, more and more to adapt to the male cultural model. To satisfy social pressure to compete, they had to acquiesce to male performance norms and learn to work, think, and act like men. The wish "Oh, if I'd only been born a man," expressed in a poem by GDR author Bettina Wegner, is still inside the confines of a culture that has excluded women. Looking enviously at male privileges, longing "to do the same things men do" [8]—these attitudes know no utopia, no vision that the world *could* be understood a new way, ordered in a new way. It is as if it were only a question of giving men and women equal rights and privileges, and the world would be all right. The women trying to comprehend their new life-practice, and thus

also their writing, as a culture-destroying process go farther than
Bettina Wegner, who does not understand that "wanting to do the
same things men do" can be only part of women's emancipatory
strategies.

Writing with the View of Feminist Partisanship

"We want a literature that belongs to 'us,' where we are present,
with our cares, needs and desires." Many women, especially those
who are themselves writers, make this demand the focus of their
new understanding of culture, and thus of literature. It is aimed
toward a new, feminist partisanship in literature. "I was trying to
construct counterworlds in my texts . . . to stimulate the reader in
turn to construct a world that *she* defines" [9] The anticipation of a
reality believed to be impossible is what constitutes the appeal of
feminist literature for many women. Radical dreams produce an erratic
energy capable of causing substantial irritation to a seemingly solidly
joined world view—even when, or precisely when, the dreams seem
irrational and beyond the realms of common sense. Feminist dreams
of a world without men have, first and foremost, that kind of
provocative value.

"Men appear in my texts like natural catastrophes. They are in the
same category as fires, floods and avalanches, among the calamities
that women must deal with, that they founder on, react to, must
reckon with: the anonymous custodians of power. In my texts,
communication, feelings, and exchange of ideas are reserved for
women." [10] What is problematic in such desires and feelings, however,
is their relation to reality. They can lead to a dangerous simplification
without any reference to their anticipatory value; this easily petrifies
into a dogmatic world view that simply sweeps away the formerly
dominant cultural figure by the attributes "fire" and "flood." The
irritation issuing from such statements can petrify into a verbalized
matriarchal fantasy of omnipotence. It thus loses much of its playful,
experimental, imaginative substance and becomes a concrete but
unrealizable desire: a history without men.

Utopias which no longer want to "admit" men run the risk of
cheap partisan solutions which avoid the *structure* of the evil and
obscure the condition of the men themselves who cannot freely
determine their male roles and who are also caught in a system of
thought-patterns they neither chose nor are able to control. If it is
to be logically consistent, a feminine life-practice, and that includes
a feminine way of writing, must strive not for a society without men,
but for a society *without male structures*—and no one knows the
reality of such a utopia.

Work with Language, Working on Language

Women who write demonstrate over and over that the struggle against patriarchal culture must begin with resistance to the foundations of consciousness itself, of language. With their writing, they try to recognize, extinguish and transform their consciousness, which has taken possession of them *through* language. The oppression of "femaleness" is embodied in the normality of usage by the symbolic order prevailing under the conditions of the censoring and controlling authorities of male power (this is shown by the sexual, political, and economic taboos, as well as the ideological ones that patriarchal society has established for women). The exclusion of femaleness from the bourgeois system's rationality corresponds to its exclusion of subjectivity pure and simple. As Sohn-Rethel has shown, there is an intimate connection between the economy of commodity production and the denial of subjective creativity. The form of socialization "comes to people *post festum*, in the "reified' Gestalt of exchange objects as 'values.' In this form, by virtue of their value-properties, things regulate the socially necessary activity of human beings; things tell human beings how each of them is to act. The people obey the things' requirements. That is the quintessence of bourgeois reason." [11] People obey those requirements—of "things"— which are *mediated* via the symbolic order. This order is dual and idealistic. It links *its* progress to the primacy of the spirit—and women are the exploited contrasting background of this spirituality. Witches, for example, were stylized into the antithesis of bourgeois-male reason, seen as "untamed nature" surrendering to "unbridled sensuality;" they were the "worst enemies of rational humanity," [12] and were to be eliminated.

The possibility for a consciousness-transforming practice lies herein: through a transformed usage, to make visible the unconscious, not-yet-exhausted open places hidden in the symbolic order, in language. This struggle with the form of the usual signifying system's usage is the decisive one for women who see their writing as an attack on the solidified forms of patriarchal consciousness.

It is the attempt to remove oneself from the culture as from a skin that Verena Stefan tries to describe in her book *Shedding:* "The imprint seems indelible. To try to erase it one would have to counteract the brainwashing." [13] She reflects her struggle with her own consciousness as a laborious and difficult effort to free herself from conventional thought-patterns, and presents the goal of a transformed life-practice as almost unattainable: "I walk around for days without finding any words, or can't choose between the words I do find. They are all inadequate. It wouldn't be so bad if all I had to do was choose the words and then arrange them in a certain order, construct the phrases and arrange them in a certain pattern, and, having done this, find that everything I wanted to say would be there in black and white. But I must create new words, must be selective, write differently, use concepts in a different way." [14] The struggle with language *may* bring an ideologically hidden usage to light, as long as one begins to go into its ambiguous sense, which does not produce only one truth or right way, not only unmistakable meanings or morals. Through this, a hitherto ignored practice of assigning meaning becomes possible. This is true both for the process of writing and for the reading of a text.

Aesthetic Practice as Life Form

The "effect woman," which turns out to be the forgotten and repressed possibility of a sensually-defined practice, serves as the model for a "logical," unconcrete form of utopia; a *not-real* but still not impossible dream. Julia Kristeva describes it as a utopia that establishes its logic at the level of the *not-said*, that is "outside of time, without before or after, without true or false." [15] When women, with a new consciousness of their female identity, take up the struggle against the male world's limiting dogma, they have taken the first step toward the transformation of patriarchal self-understanding. Seen in this way, female and aesthetic productivity are understandable as a form of *practice* that changes the social *form*.

It is the social task of poetry to connect spirit and sensuality, reason and pleasure. Poetry is the place where the otherwise divergent elements of physicality and spirituality are brought productively together. Bourgeois aesthetic theory has emphasized that this task of poetry is one of its most important characteristics. In his *Lectures on Aesthetics*, Hegel speaks of how spirit and sensuality are joined in art, and postulates a fusing together of the two elements such that "the sensual becomes spiritualized" via the aesthetic, "since the spiritual appears within it as sensualized." [16]

It is logically consistent when writing women's aesthetic practice attempts to bring this immanent element of sensuality strongly to bear, the very element that is lost from scientific textual practice. In the context of women's social reduction to this very sensuality, however, it would then be primarily an act of constituting and self-ascertaining a *different* sensuality to define aesthetic practice. A female physicality that attempts to free itself from these male projections and develop its own needs will irritate the thetically defined bourgeois life-forms by a *practice* that does not adapt to male-rational demands, but draws sensuality into its blueprint. Discovering woman's physicality points to the realization of a pleasurable "life-dream" that produces sensuality *for* itself, not *outside of* itself by killing off its own desires.

Barbara Starett[17] asserts "I dream female," meaning that she intends her poems to change the form, logic, and grammar of rationality that is constituted by excluding the physical. The question is what it means to reflect on the "economy" of the un-logical sensual consciousness—and, finally, what effects it has on text production. In his analysis of the work of dreams, Freud has given a model for production-forms of a nonrational consciousness bound to prevailing symbolic norms.

The forms for processing meaning in dreams, which, according to Freud, produce a formally and substantively over-determined "rebus puzzle," [18] are played out between the levels of their latent thought-material and their *manifest* dream-content.[19] If one applies Freud's ideas on the work of dreams to the thesis that femininity is only the latency, only the "worker behind the scenes" of manifest male power, a strong possibility exists for recognizing and defining a structure of that productivity and transformation which is located *before* logical language, but is nevertheless active; in society, it is represented by the role of women performing concrete but suppressed work.

The displacement of the unconscious, symbolizing work-process in the "thinking" of dreams, i.e., the *un*-logical production of *un*-logical puzzles, is paralleled by the displacement of "living work" in the commodity-production process from its function of *producing* "progress." The "spirit" of the patriarch (God, Father, and Industry), not the concrete activity, is the propelling force of history.

For scientifically motivated feminists it is important to ask to what extent dialectic logic already represents the formal structure of our hoped-for victory over a Western culture that follows a binary logic. It would be equivalent to moving Hegelian dialectics from the head of the father to the feet of a repressed femininity. Marx did this for the economy of capitalist commodity production by defining the role of productive work in the exchange-vaue process and the character of its repression under the dictate of value-form. Thus, it would be a question of doing for the analysis of patriarchal consciousness and its symbolic order what Marx has already achieved for the analysis of capitalist society.

The political strategy of emancipating human productivity from its "logical" commodity-structure in the economic sphere requires a correlate in the sphere of spiritual productivity. Women's textual practice is a form of social labor objectifying itself. Aesthetic production, which can be understood as a means of producing an objective status of subjectivity to oneself as well as together with other women, mobilizes an awareness of the fact that thinking contains a historical progress-function *as* a sign *in* its objective gestalt. Women are trying to work on social progress in the sphere to which they are culturally relegated anyway; that is, in aesthetics, where sensuality as their socially defined domain is combined with rational productivity. They use the marginalization of this sphere as a form of subversion. Attacking the "logocentrism" of the symbolic order of patriarchy is an effort to shift the basis of the culture, an effort that extends beyond the subjective level of writing.

Translated by Jeanette Clausen

Notes

* German original: Brigitte Wartmann, "Schreiben als Angriff auf das Patriarchat," *Literaturmagazin* 11. *Schreiben oder Literatur* (dnb 129, Reinbek 1979), pp. 108–129. Abridged, translated and reprinted with permission. Notes have been renumbered.

1. Inge Buck, Radio Program (Rias I, 2 July 1978), in: *Schreiben*, Sonderheft Treffen Schreibender Frauen (Bremen 1978), p. 48.

2. From a poem by Brigitte Nachreiner.

3. Ursula Krechel, "Freie Formen über das unfreie Gedicht in der Mangel," in *Frauenoffensive* 11 (1978), p. 9.

4. Silvia Bovenschen, *Die imaginierte Weiblichkeit. Exemplarische Untersuchungen zu kulturgeschichtlichen und literarischen Präsentationsformen des Weiblichen* (Frankfurt/M., 1979), p. 31.

5. Ibid, p. 32.

6. Johanna Wördemann, "Schreiben um zu überleben oder Schreiben als Arbeit. Notizen zum Treffen schreibender Frauen in München, Mai 1976," in: *Alternative* 108/109, p. 115.

7. *Werkstatt schreibender Frauen: Vorurteile* (Bern, n.d.).

8. Bettina Wegner, poem "Ach, wenn ich doch als Mann auf diese Welt gekommen wär," in: *Pelagea, Frau und Literatur* (ed. Sozialistischer Frauenbund Westberlin), Heft 10 (n.d.), p. 5–6.

9. Barbara Fiedler, " Über Lyrik," in: *Frauenoffensive, Journal* 11, p. 16.

10. Barbara Fiedler, "Warum ich schreibe," in: *Schreiben*, FrauenliteraturZeitung 1 (1977), p. 31.

11. Alfred Sohn-Rethel, *Geistige und körperliche Arbeit* (Frankfurt/M., 1970), p. 91.

12. Claudia Honegger, "Die Hexen der Neuzeit," in: Honegger, ed., *Die Hexen der Neuzeit. Studien zur Sozialgeschichte eines kulturellen Deutungsmusters* (Frankfurt/M.), p. 102.

13. Verena Stefan, *Shedding* (New York: Daughters Publishing Co., Inc., 1978), p. 66. German original *Häutungen* (Munich: Frauenoffensive, 1975), p. 74.

14. *Shedding*, pp. 105–6. (*Häutungen*, p. 112).

15. Julia Kristeva, *Die Chinesin. Die Rolle der Frau in China* (München 1976), pp. 263–4.

16. G.W.F. Hegel, *Vorlesungen über die Ästhetik I. Werke in zwanzig Bänden* 13 (Frankfurt/M., 1970), p. 61.

17. Barbara Starett, *Ich träume weiblich* (München).

18. Sigmund Freud, *Die Traumdeutung* (Frankfurt/M. and Hamburg, 1964), p. 235.

19. Ibid.

5. To Bleed or not to Bleed
That is the Question*

Brigitte Classen and Gabriele Goettle

By contrast to Wartmann in the preceding article, Classen/Goettle sum-marily dismiss feminist texts focusing on women's sexuality (Schwarzer's The "Little" Difference . . ., excerpted in section III, this volume) and/ or language (Stefan's Shedding*). It should be remembered that they were criticizing the very tendency toward enthusiastic but unreflecting self-exploration that Wartmann cautioned against. In their tongue-in-cheek statement of editorial policy, they advise readers to "strip away old categories of thinking"—an oft-repeated dictum of the "new femaleness."*

Readers with their bleeding hearts set on feeling their way forward in the style of *Shedding* or the "little difference" will soon be asking us to explain our relationship to the women's movement, and our point of view. Let this be done right from the start, to preclude any doubt as to our intentions. Both begin for us at the point where the sticky mucus of female togetherness ends.

Women were ill advised when they started believing that everything women think, say, write and do is useful—if not in fact good—for emancipation from the aspect of a new femaleness. Nothing is easier than elevating stupidity to a golden mean with which all can be equally satisfied. Literary production in the form of diverse books and journals still derives consolation from the enthusings of those who, after centuries of phlegmatic indolence, think one independent step signals victory over deep-seated modes of behavior. Our review of Verena Stefan's *Shedding* (in the first issue of *Courage*) makes clear what we mean. When, in connection with language, someone ex-presses the desire to "get behind" its secrets and explore the male thought structures "embedded" in it, we can of course affirm the moral responsibility of such a venture, but we do not see that the time is ripe for dwelling either on renovating the language or on the need to create female feeling anew. It's bad enough when the image of things is studied instead of the things, but when these images then acquire a utility that makes it impossible to perceive the things any more, the first step toward new disfranchisement has been voluntarily taken. Thus, insistence upon self-exploration and self-affirmation makes the self more and more invisible; *wimmin* don't give a second thought to going with their flow: newly discovered senses (i.e., the new tenderness, body autonomy,) are supposed to take care of thinking, but only take care of themselves. This guarantees that the "new experiences" can't possibly be realized, or that they're only the old ones all over again. Because critical-minded women didn't want to be spoil-sports about the "new female thinking," which alleges to be headed somewhere or other, they've been silent up to now.

Women's insistence upon nonaggression, gentleness, and woman-specific thinking leads to locating conflicts only at points where the solution won't cause a collision with patriarchal power. Women are still on their guard against arousing "false" suspicion which could undermine general credibility. The impression of well-behaved progressiveness and emancipation is rewarded by the provisory conferring of dubious honors on eager baby steps. All right, women hadn't set their sights on the sympathetic good will of men, but they engendered it by relinquishing a clear battle-stance. There must be no uncertainty as to the need to develop a strategy for battle. Up to now there's been little to defend. Doing battle would mean mobilizing forces to gain essential territory. And that also includes making use of what men have thought of, so that we can get beyond it! When women become conscious of their budding potency, their thinking will be sharpened up and they will no longer expose themselves to the arbitrariness of the limits to tolerance within patriarchy, but will appropriate the space that seems useful to them. By contrast, the development of the women's movement so far (with some exceptions) leaves the impression of a costume-change for a tear-jerking performance of a gushing New Femaleness. Stages with beflowered curtains open up onto beflowered women who stand before beflowered backdrops spewing deflowered insipidities, while the women in the audience for their part no longer wish to flower in obscurity, and so forth. This garbage, piled up by the ton, of sentimental feelings, unreflected enthusiasm, and paper-maiché problems inhibits all activity, distorts our view and our movement.

*The Black Messenger** sees herself as a satirist; in this she cannot be reconciled with the object of her satire: she is totally without a sense of humor. She understands satire as a technique for unmasking false and harmful thinking. She assumes her women readers are not

---

* *Die schwarze Botin*—feminist journal edited by the authors.

in a position to get the joke, but to get serious. We do not expect our messages to become the substance of new female feeling. On the contrary, we intend to make absolutely ruthless use of our inclination toward consistency. In this we proceed from the conviction that *The Black Messenger* is more essential to her own existence than those who read her. *The Black Messenger* will perhaps be hard to understand at first, but even harder to misunderstand. We are counting on women's being able to free themselves from that intellectual addiction to trying to iron everything out on pre-formed rational levels, which after all encompass only mediocre thinking. And that *The Black Messenger* won't disintegrate into its subject matter for them, or into the foreignness of its subject matter. Those who think *The Black Messenger* should be free of contradictions and that she owes them proof and documentation for estranging the real must strip away old categories of reading and thinking.

We have no interest whatsoever in aspiring to become some kind of figurehead, just as it is not our intention to try to compete with other women's newspapers. What we do aspire to, and have great interest in, is an unrelenting opposition to those women who want to sell the rest of us down the river, and charge us for it into the bargain.

Translated by Jeanette Clausen

Notes

* German original: Brigitte Classen and Gabriele Goettle, "Schleim oder Nichtschleim, das ist hier die Frage," *Die Schwarze Botin*, No. 1 (Berlin: Verlag Brigitte Classen, 1976), pp. 4–5. Translated and reprinted with permission. Portions of this text have been excerpted.

Part Two

The Way It Is

On the surface, each story in this section is an account of an individual woman's experience, but each also addresses a larger aspect of women's lives in patriarchal society. The authors are all from the GDR. Elfriede Brüning (1910–) and Irmtraud Morgner (1933–) continue to reside and work there, while Helga Novak (1935–) and Sarah Kirsch (1935–) have lived in the West since 1967 and 1977, respectively.

Brüning began publishing fiction in the 1950s, the GDR's period of "changing consciousness," producing numerous didactic novels and stories dealing with problems of employed women and their children. Her story "Heaven on Earth" criticizes supposedly outmoded "bourgeois" behavior and insensitivity toward the elderly. Morgner and Kirsch were, along with Christa Wolf, among the first GDR women writers of a younger generation to achieve recognition outside their country. In "White Easter," a fine example of Morgner's earlier work, her unrelenting eye for contradictions between theory and the reality of women's lives, and her caustic humor, are already apparent. Kirsch, best known for her poetry, writes in a more lyrical voice and addresses contradictions more open-endedly. "The Smith of Kosewalk," an early prose piece, is a complex and compact commentary on life and love in an isolated rural village. Novak's story "Palisades," set in Switzerland, is representative of much of her prose writing. Here, she examines institutional "care" of the emotionally traumatized, showing how it reproduces and magnifies the oppressive treatment of women in society generally. Both Novak's story and the one by Kirsch also invite reflection on writing as a form of self-exploration and/or resistance for women (cf. essays in section I).

6. Heaven on Earth*

Elfriede Brüning

This story follows an upwardly mobile family through twenty years of the GDR, from the difficult early years through the raising of the Berlin Wall (1961) and subsequent readjustment and prosperity. Focusing on a reluctantly self-sacrificing grandmother, Brüning shows how the old woman's hard work in the family business is both essential and invisible— to the family as well as to the larger community. The tragic ending is a departure from Brüning's determined optimism in earlier works.

At exactly 2:30 every afternoon old Mrs. Grimma climbed the stairs to the mansard room the children had fixed up for her on their second floor. Until then she was always busy downstairs in the kitchen. Her day began early. Shortly after 7:00 you would hear the two assistants banging around down in the shop, and if the old woman didn't want to risk running into them unwashed and untidy, she had to sneak downstairs into the bathroom quickly before the younger Grimmas were up and about. Once or twice she hadn't made it and her son Werner had rattled the doorknob impatiently. "Hurry up, Mother." Irma, her daughter-in-law, would be standing right behind him. "We can put a washbasin in Grannie's room for her," she suggested pleasantly. And that very day she dug up an old cast-off washbowl, so now the old woman could wash upstairs in her room. To do this, she had to take a pail of water upstairs every evening and carry the dirty water out again each morning. But, after all, she was used to work and didn't complain. For fifteen years they had lived in this house together, three generations under one roof, and there had never been the slightest problem. "We don't have arguments," the daughter-in-law would assert, "We get along famously,"—flashing her mother-in-law a look which demanded approval. And Frau Grimma would hasten to agree.

Although . . . she hadn't exactly jumped for joy when her son had urged her to give up her own small apartment and move in with them. Werner had been lucky to get the three-bedroom house at a good price and was living there alone with his young wife. With each day they feared the housing authorities would force them to take in roomers. "You can't allow that to happen, Mom!" he

68

begged her. And old Mrs. Grimma understood. Werner had just finished a retraining course in T.V. repair and was recently established in the city. He was in no position to risk having some incompetent person nosing around the shop. Without Werner's regular excursions from the GDR to West Berlin, necessary because of the chronic lack of spare parts, he would never have made a go of it in his new shop, quite apart from developing a booming business. And so Frau Grimma finally stopped resisting, gave up the life she had come to love, departed tearfully from her life-long friend Alma, who had lived next door to her for over twenty years, and moved in with Irma and Werner on the other side of town. At that time she was sixty-five and still very active.

The saying goes that when you're old each year counts double. This had always made the old woman laugh. Age didn't bother her. Having the three of them in the house turned out to be the life of Riley. Of course she did her best to make herself useful; no one could say she didn't earn her board and keep. She kept the rooms and the shop spotless, scrubbed the stairs, got down on her knees to do the linoleum. And simply because she was there, her only child Werner was able to thumb his nose at the housing authorities. In gratitude he had turned over both second-floor rooms to her; his mother would have a bedroom *and* a living room. She felt like she was in heaven. But then one of the rooms had to be given back again, since the family increased. A baby was brought home. Irma knew she would never have a child of her own, but she did so want to be a mother. And so Werner, not wanting to deny his wife anything, went with her to an orphanage and Irma picked out the only little boy worth considering, Wolf-Dieter with his violet-blue eyes and curly hair. Irma could finally fulfill her maternal role and Werner no doubt saw in the tot a future partner, indeed, the one who would inherit his business.

Back then no one could have foreseen how the business would develop. In those days T.V. was still in its infancy. Production lagged pitifully behind demand, and only the privileged with some kind of special coupon could get hold of a set while the majority had to wait months—even years. Werner, who took care of service under warranty, could easily handle all the repairs alone. Then almost over night this changed. All at once there were so many sets around that people could actually buy them instead of just looking. And there was no longer a stigma attached to buying on time. The people jumped at the chance (who could tell how long this would last) and forests of antennae sprang up on all the rooftops. As the only repairman, Werner scarcely had time to change his clothes. Werner hired an assistant and then another one; and Irma provided meals for both of them. But Irma, in trying to give Werner some relief, had unexpectedly been transformed from "just a housewife" into "a working member of the family." She traded her place at the stove for one on the phone. She argued with overdue suppliers, pacified angry customers, took down due dates or scribbled long columns of figures into various colored notebooks. The one marked INTERNAL (which wasn't intended for the auditors) she hastily shoved back into the bottom drawer as soon as she was through using it. With all her new duties Irma began to neglect her maternal role, and Wolf-Dieter, who had experienced parental love for such a short time, became a pampered grandma's boy.

Now, the old woman had done all she could. Honestly. She had kept on scouring the floors, if not quite so thoroughly as before, since Wolf-Dieter was constantly underfoot. She would put Wolf-Dieter on the potty, make her way past the incapacitated T.V. sets to the toilet to empty it, chase Wolf-Dieter down away from the half-open window when she came back (her heart leaped up into her throat for a moment, she was so horrified). She cooked and did the so-called hand laundry, including the three men's work clothes, which none of the commercial laundries around had wanted to take. Then one day when she was so tired she couldn't move, she stayed in bed and Werner decided "We'll have to get help for the housework. Mother can't do it alone any more." (After all she was now over seventy). The Children's Home had just begun to make referrals of some girls, those who had proven themselves to be "adaptable" and "employable," to do housework in private homes—that is, in respectable homes. Werner applied and came back grinning from ear to ear with fifteen-year old Rosa. "From now on Grannie can take it easy," he said to Irma with relief, and Irma told the customers about the good solution they had found and the customers told other customers. Soon everyone in town knew (after all the Grimmas were popular and well-liked because of their repair service). The old woman "had managed to get rid of the housework and now all she had to do was take care of the little boy, how about that . . ."

The old woman, however, was still the first one to get up in the morning. The two employees wanted their breakfast shortly after 7 A.M. As soon as the assistants were back in the shop, Irma and Werner sat down and wanted fresh coffee, they had been waiting for the crusty rolls that Rosa picked up on her way out to the shop. When she arrived in the morning old Mrs. Grimma sent her out again to do the shopping (but naturally not until she'd had a good breakfast)—she turned out to be unsuitable for any other work. Just about that time the bell would ring in the shop. Werner would be off like a shot. "Will you be home on time? " Irma asked every day.

It never seemed to bother her that she didn't get an answer. She wouldn't have heard it anyway, because long before Werner had left she was sitting at the phone haggling over some terribly important T.V. tubes. In the meantime the old woman started preparing the mid-morning snack, which everyone ate on the run. At some point Rosa would come back from shopping, grab something to eat and leave again, this time with a long list of errands. For lunch there were usually five people, excluding Werner, who didn't get another warm meal until evening. With all this activity in the house Wolf-Dieter, the child no one had time for, had gotten bigger and had turned unexpectedly into a tall, lanky roughneck; already the girls were starting to notice him.

In the meantime there had been a crisis, a serious crisis. Werner came home one day as white as a sheet. "Now they're going to do us in," he predicted. A state-owned radio and T.V. shop—with repair service—was to be opened in the downtown area. Werner was beside himself with rage. The fact that "the guys on top" were threatening to take the monopoly from him, Werner Grimma, and put up a state-run shop right under his nose was proof enough for him that the small businessman was going to be liquidated. To stay on top of things he even took out a subscription to the official party news-paper, *Neues Deutschland.* He also had a long talk with Irma, which resulted in a great flurry of activity. Irma ignored the telephone and began to dig around in boxes and trunks and Werner drove day after day to East Berlin to return the spare parts he had only recently "imported" from West Berlin. The old woman watched the comings and goings for a time without comment. "Tell me what on earth is going on here" she pleaded at last, when she couldn't stand the secrecy any longer. Irma wouldn't say a word. Werner looked up for a split second from the papers he was altering. "We're going to cross the border, Grannie" he replied. "You can see they're trying to ruin us," and he tore the receipts intended for the auditors into shreds. For the first time Mrs. Grimma was displeased with her son. "I'm staying here! " she announced. But when she was alone upstairs in her room, she cried her eyes out. What would she do here without the others? No, she would have to go along. There was nothing to be done. When the trip finally got underway that Saturday, they closed the shop early—for "personal reasons." Rosa and the two assistants were sent home. Wolf-Dieter thought it was going to be a happy family outing (and probably still thinks so). It was the twelfth of August, 1961. Their intention was to spend Saturday night with a distant relative in Berlin—Grünau, who had hastily been let in on the plan. The following morning, refreshed and in good spirits from a good night's sleep, they would follow the path of the spare parts which they had previously deposited at the Zoo station. As we know, this was no longer possible. That very night the border was walled up so tight that not even a mouse could get across, let alone young Grimma and his family.

Let bygones be bygones! It was as if there were an unspoken agreement among the family members never to broach this subject again. They were back home, and started over again. The first months were difficult. To Werner's boundless amazement, however, it turned out that he could exist without his business ties to West Berlin. He didn't even need to worry about competition from the state-owned shop. There were still plenty of people who preferred the private shop to the official Government repair service. In addition to their defective T.V. sets, they could also unload all their family gossip on Werner and Irma—not to mention the fact that the waiting period was actually shorter. In an astonishingly short time his business was back to its former status, and everything could have gone on as before.

However, neither Irma nor Werner was the type to be satisfied with their former achievements. As soon as the shop was doing well again they started looking for new projects. They decided to build a vacation trailer. Instead of watching T.V. after work like everyone else, or paying attention to Wolf-Dieter's progress in school—which was urgently in need of attention—they hammered and pounded out in the yard until late at night, not allowing themselves to rest until the trailer was finished. For the next three years they travelled like gypsies through the People's Republics, to Hungary, Bulgaria, and the Soviet Union. Just the two of them, of course, for Wolf-Dieter was in good hands with old Mrs. Grimma. After that they'd had enough of travelling around. They got rid of the trailer for a good price and bought themselves a farmer's cottage on the coast (every independent businessman or skilled repairman had a weekend house, even in those days). The Grimmas' cottage had to be re-modelled and enlarged, and the basic design completely redone. The work dragged out over several years. This time Wolf-Dieter was included too. But as Werner began to realize that the boy had cotton between his ears and wasn't interested in physical labor, his relationship to his adopted son cooled noticeably. "You never know what's going on inside a kid like that," he grumbled to Irma, and Irma understood him at once and added with a sigh, "He's not our flesh and blood." So they started leaving the boy at home again and old Mrs. Grimma was glad she didn't have to sit around the big house alone any more.

It wasn't as if the children hadn't asked her to go along now and then. She'd been allowed to participate at the housewarming and she'd also visited "Irma's Haven" once last summer. At the house-warming party she had helped energetically—even at seventy-five she was still in good shape. She had opened the bottles and poured the wine; later she made coffee and prepared platters of cold cuts and cheese; she actually spent most of the evening in the tiny kitchen. But she had enjoyed all the guests. The vacationers were in the guest room and she, Werner's mother, was supposed to sleep on the couch in the den. But in the evening they sat drinking in front of the fireplace until late and she sat with them, bored and constantly dozing off. In the middle of the night some other people had arrived, friends of friends, hoping they could camp out on the sofa; when they left with long faces to pitch their tent, old Mrs. Grimma felt like crawling into a hole.

No, that wasn't for her. She preferred to say quietly at home, for she needed peace and quiet. She often thought with an aching heart of her old one-bedroom apartment, which was so quiet and away from all the hustle and bustle. Here peace and quiet were impossible because of Wolf-Dieter. He was fifteen now. It was funny but he had managed to select the worst of his classmates as friends and the old woman would have liked nothing better than to throw them all out. How easily their bad example could influence her grandson. When Wolf-Dieter heard these misgivings he laughed them off. She got along best with him when she said nothing at all.

When she was alone she always used the downstairs bathroom. One Sunday she blacked out, staggered, and fell back into the bathtub. When she came to again, she carefully felt all the parts of her body: no, nothing was broken but it was as if her arms and legs were no longer part of her and would not respond. When Irma and Werner arrived home they found her half dead and covered with sweat from so many futile attempts to get back up on her feet. They were terribly upset. "We can't leave Grannie alone any more" Werner said to Irma and there was anger in his voice as well as concern. Their vacation was coming up; just the two of them together in "Irma's Haven" for three long intimate weeks. And they didn't want to be troubled by pangs of conscience. Thus it was decided that Grannie should take a trip.

It turned out to be a nice restful time. Old Mrs. Grimma sat in the garden on the banks of the lazily flowing river Dahme and let herself be pampered to her heart's content by her distant relative, a vigorous woman of sixty. She would have been happy to stay right there. But then the "children" wrote that they were home and she had to pack and be off. At home terrible news awaited her: Werner had sent Wolf-Dieter off to a boarding school. "Now let's see what somebody else can do with him," he said bluntly. In time his mother was able to pry the truth out of him. Wolf-Dieter had been speeding out in the country with a friend on a stolen motorcycle. Along the way they were stopped by a traffic control and at that point the whole story came out. The "friend," who already had several thefts on his record, was arrested. Wolf-Dieter got off lightly. He claimed to know nothing about the theft. "Just imagine," Irma said exasperated, "the police coming to us of all people! When we've never done anything against the law." "You only wanted to abandon the country where you earn your living," thought old Mrs. Grimma, but she was careful not to say it out loud. Her throat felt choked up anyway.

And so the years went by. The old woman would turn eighty this month. Werner wanted to "lift a few" for the occasion. "After all," he maintained cheerfully, "his mother would be eighty only once, and that called for a celebration." With Irma's help he remodeled the ground floor; space had to be made for all the guests. Half the neighborhood was invited in addition to all the friends who lived near "Irma's Haven." When the day finally arrived Mrs. Grimma sat among the well-wishers and felt superfluous. The only people she valued, Wolf-Dieter and her old friend Alma, weren't there. Wolf-Dieter hadn't been heard from and Alma was no longer able to get around on her own. She had not asked her son to pick up Alma. There were just too many other things he had to take care of.

In the fall Rosa announced that she was quitting. She was going to get married and move to a village some fifteen miles away. That evening at dinner Irma and Werner discussed what to do. "Well, if you can persuade your assistants to eat in a restaurant," Irma said energetically, "I'll make out all right alone. It's really no big thing to cook for two, and we can hire a woman to do the heavy cleaning." "They aren't even including me in any more," thought old Mrs. Grimma. She had been there listening to the entire discussion. The children hadn't even bothered to postpone their discussion until she had gone up to bed, to lie there restlessly, unable to sleep. For there were no more evenings spent together in the living room, occasionally even sharing a bottle of wine, as they used to.

Yes, time had certainly changed. Werner had gotten older too. Now and then he discussed with Irma the advisability of cutting back. Their acquisitions began to be a burden. They now owned two cars (the second one was illegally registered in a friend's name), a weekend house, and a sporty sailboat; yet after a week of hard work all Werner felt like doing was hitting the hay. Which was just what he wasn't able to do. Instead he had to drive ninety-five miles across Mecklenburg, up to the coast where the weekend guests were expecting to be waited upon by him and Irma. Did they really need all that? Who were they wearing themselves out for? For Wolf-Dieter, the failure? No, least of all for him. Without giving it much thought, he had recently rejected the idea of learning T.V. repair so he could run his father's business, which he would inherit one day. He didn't give a damn about his inheritance, he had explained laughing. He was now attending technical school, maybe he'd even go to the university—he'd make it on his own! "Can you figure that out? " Irma asked. But Werner couldn't make heads nor tails of it. "Sometimes they send certain ones on to school," was all he could say. It didn't matter. They really didn't need to bother with the boy any longer. But then with whom? They had both been in bed sick last winter while their colleagues in the state-owned shops had gotten fat and sassy, just brimming over with good health. No, they ought to dump some ballast. After all, they did own their home. Of course, some minor alterations would be necessary to meet their new needs.

So Werner and Irma had given their life new meaning, and soon there were remodelling plans scattered all over the house. With one stroke of his pen Werner rearranged the business rooms—the shop and the office as they formerly were—and began to incorporate them into the living quarters. This created an area which "you could make something out of," he beamed. The kitchen and bath could finally be enlarged. Irma insisted on a "powder room," and one room would have to be reserved for Wolf-Dieter in case he happened to come back. "Wolf-Dieter? He still has his room upstairs," Irma interrupted. Werner made a face. He had his own special plans for the mansard rooms, he announced; he was going to put his and Irma's bedroom up there! "How are you going to do that? " Irma asked uncomprehendingly. Okay, the wall between the two rooms would have to be ripped out, Werner began to explain, that way there'd be one big room. Out under the eaves he would build a balcony————. He stopped in the middle of his sentence. Irma looked as if she absolutely wasn't following him. She pointed to the ceiling. "But ———— but————" she stammered helplessly. Werner pulled his chair closer to Irma's. "Listen," he said patiently. "If we're going to plan at all, then we may as well plan big. Grannie won't live forever, after all. She's eighty-two now. Should we make ourselves twice the expense on account of her? Naturally we won't take her to an old folks home the way some people would. As long as Grannie is here we'll both sleep downstairs like we always have. But I don't see any reason why we can't start now with the remodelling."

And that very evening he had a conversation with his mother. That hadn't happened for a good many years. Old Mrs. Grimma was even allowed to sit in the living room with them again. "Naturally it'll be a little hectic," Werner admitted. "But afterward things'll be that much nicer for you. Just imagine all this space. Up to now you've had to be cooped up." "But it was so cozy up there," whispered the old woman. "It'll be cozy again," Werner comforted her. Then he stood up and got busy at the bar, considering the subject closed.

And so the workers moved in the following week. Werner had his connections. Because it would take time to cut back on the business operations, the remodelling work was begun upstairs. Grannie had to move her things out into the hall for the time being. Irma promptly put up a plastic curtain around her bed. On Sunday the younger Grimmas went out to "Irma's Haven." Werner's For Sale Ad had attracted scores of prospective buyers. Having gotten much more than expected from the sale, they came back home Sunday evening in a good mood. Irma tripped over something bundled up on the floor. Werner bent over to look first. Together they carried the slight body back to the bed. The water glass was still on the telephone table, with white particles sticking to its edges. The old woman apparently hadn't had the strength to get herself back into bed. The couple stood speechless for a few minutes next to the lifeless body. Then Irma threw herself in Werner's arms. "We were always so happy together," she sobbed. Werner thought hard for a while. "She must have done it in a deranged moment," he finally said. "She didn't have a reason in the world to do such a thing. Her place with us was really heaven on earth."

Translated by Marjorie Tussing and Jeanette Clausen

Notes

* German original: Elfriede Brüning, "Himmel auf Erden," *Neue Deutsche Literatur*, No. 4 (1974). Translated and reprinted with permission of the author. Portions of this text are excerpted.

7. White Easter*

Irmtraud Morgner

The narrator's stoically humorous account of the birth of her first child brings out contradictions between theory and practice. Statutory non-discrimination of unmarried mothers in the GDR and classes on prepared childbirth bear little relationship to the reality of a difficult labor and insensitive treatment by hospital staff. A leitmotiv of death, suggesting a Pieta scene interrupts the narrator's thoughts throughout the story, considered one of Morgner's best. Other stories by Morgner are included in section VII.

When I reached the transfer-station the contractions were already coming at twenty-minute intervals. The crowd pushed out of the train doors to the exits. I leaned my suitcase against my right calf and waited at the end of the platform, which was built on a bridge. As the train pulled out, the bridge shook and the view of the two platform roofs, which crossed the bridge at a right angle, was no longer obstructed. The roofs were surrounded by a halo of light which lifted them out of the darkness. Between the boarding platforms there were two tracks, to the right and left of them were several more. The wind was sweeping snow from the blooming forsythia bushes growing along the embankment. When the crowd had vanished into the exit tunnels, I carefully picked up my suitcase again and slowly descended the steps to the platform island on the right. A contraction took me by surprise, I headed for the nearest bench, but couldn't get there in time and sat down on my suitcase. The bench was occupied by a man and three women. Remembering the suggestions given us in the course, I stayed seated on my suitcase and recited psychoprophylactic techniques to myself. Although the instructions tell you to go to the clinic without delay in the case of premature rupture of the membrane, the train was late. Then it took its sweet time, the taxi driver didn't go over twenty, and I also had to wait outside the maternity ward and ring several times before a nurse opened the door. I handed her a card certifying that I had taken the class in prepared childbirth and explained my situation. The nurse put the card in her apron pocket, relieved me of my suitcase, and carried it through a warm, conspicuously waxed corridor smelling of Pine-Sol, echoing and overlit. The white walls glared; so did the nurse's crisp apron and pleated hood; she looked freshly washed, starched and antiseptic. In the reception room she made herself a cup of coffee while I got undressed. I locked my clothes in a closet and hoped they soon would no longer fit me. Since I had taken the course and read a lot I was not surprised that I was issued a nightgown but not bathed; I presumed that the gown reached to my thighs. Then I waddled over to a cot; all women in the final stages of pregnancy waddle with their legs wide apart and bellies protruding. Mine had already gone down in size; with the help of a footstool, I climbed up on the bed. The nurse cleared away the coffee cups, handed me a thermometer, took my pulse, pressed a cold metal stethoscope against my hot belly and sat down satisfied behind her desk. There she took down my personal data and inquired about childhood and other diseases, operations, births, miscarriages, abortions, the course of the pregnancy, due date, onset of labor, length of contractions, interval between contractions; I guessed I was dilated three centimeters. The nurse slipped a rubber glove on her right hand and soon said: two centimeters. She curved her lips up into a smile, but I didn't let my disappointment show; the textbooks claim that disappointment lowers your pain threshold. The nurse chalked my name onto a blue slate. It was the width of the wall and about two meters high; data on everyone admitted that day were noted on it in chalk; beside my name was the number twenty-one; the nurse wished me luck on the unique event ahead of me and led me to the labor room. On the way there, walking through the conspicuously waxed, echoing corridor, I wondered where I knew those people from. The man had slumped forward in the corner of the bench, the three women were speaking to one another, you could see their breath. As the rapid transit train for Mahlsdorf pulled in, the women stood up and indicated to the man that he'd have to wake up if he wanted to go along. Then the eldest of the women tapped him on the stomach, arm, and back; finally, she seized him by the shoulder and shook him so hard that his head hit the white enamel sign hanging above the back of the double bench. On the sign was the name of the station in large black letters: East Cross. The door marked "Labor Room" was open, an orderly wheeled a stretcher into the corridor, a woman was lying on it, her hair all matted down. The orderly told the nurse that the head doctor had gotten stuck in the snow with his Mercedes. The nurse said "Boss's patient." I was taken to the small labor room. A room with light-blue tiled walls, two empty beds with bedside tables at the head and small tables behind the foot boards, on the small tables chrome-plated instrument trays, beside them covered basins hanging in metal stands, between the beds a movable partition, across from the milk glass windows a water-boiler and sink, on the facing wall the clock. The clock said seven minutes after midnight when I climbed onto the labor bed. Not one minute later a woman wearing a neck brooch entered and came over to my bed, greeting me with a handshake. I thought she was a midwife; but she turned out to be the head midwife. She shaved me unceremoniously, administered an enema and complained about the unseasonable weather. Then she gave me a thermometer, took my pulse, placed a cold stethoscope on my hot belly and sat down satisfied behind the desk. For there was also a desk in the small labor room. Then she took down my personal data and inquired about childhood and other diseases, operations, births, miscarriages, abortions, the course of the pregnancy, due date, onset of labor, interval between contractions, intensity of contractions. I said, bearable, two centimeters, some men like modest women. The head midwife slipped a rubber glove on her right hand and soon said, "two millimeters." She said my contractions were not serious. She advised me to sleep, so as to conserve energy, and wished me good night. Then she turned off the light and walked out of the room leaving the door open. The door led to the large labor room and adjacent nursery. I rolled over to the side I didn't feel any movement on, a relaxation position, training is training, a labor bed is hard. I shut my eyes tight to conserve my energy. The head doctor had apparently arrived. I kept hearing female voices repeating his official title and a male voice that said "Nice Sunday." Groaning, screams, commands, a baby's crying; I was annoyed that I kept searching my memory for the slot occupied by the man and the three women. The man had a round head with thinning, light-colored hair and a beard. His eyes, spectacles, skin and suit all seemed as pale and inadequate as his hair; at any rate, only his full red beard stood out in the light. The brass-colored sickle divided the figure of the man; someone claimed he had a hammer; the women called for a doctor. Approximately every hour a doctor with a rubber glove came to my bed, every half-hour a nurse with a metal stethoscope and a timer, at least every quarter of an hour I heard the first cry of a baby. About mine I was told only that it was doing well, cephalic presentation. It kicked me in the diaphragm. All the doctors who looked under my covers in the course of this night said they would begin recording my contractions and administer penicillin. The chief-of-staff was expected to make his rounds at eight o'clock. At five the cleaning woman came and said that talk about everything being forgotten as soon as the child was there was hogwash. You wouldn't forget an ordeal like that, she'd been through it six times, there was nothing she didn't know. "Had you taken the course for painless

childbirth," I asked. "God forbid," she said. "Eleven boys so far
tonight; today the lid is off the boy crate; if you hurry, you might
get one. My husband was furious when the first one was a girl. It's
your first, isn't it? " "Yes," I said, "Uh huh," she said, "some men
wouldn't come to visit their wives when they had girls; that's why
the nurses aren't allowed to tell them on the telephone if it's a boy
or a girl. Orders from the chief-of-staff. I've got four sons and two
daughters, what're you hoping for? " "A human being," I said. "And
your husband? " "I want a healthy human being of moderate intelligence," I said. "Some days there are more single women having
babies than married ones," she said. "I got married when I was
eighteen and had the children one right after another; my mother
had eight; when the children were grown and my father dead she
made a good life for herself." We wished each other luck and went
about our work: she mopped and waxed, I breathed according to
instructions. At seven my covers were smoothed out. At quarter to
nine the chief-of-staff appeared with the head doctor, a woman; also
two staff physicians and the head midwife; the interns had to stay
outside. The chief said "record contractions, penicillin" and asked
me if I had seen the art exhibition; we exchanged views on Paula
Modersohn-Becker. After the rounds the head midwife brought me
three pills, a glass of water, a shot of penicillin, a second hand-bell,
and said,' "The things you see. Not long ago a girl came in at night
and you could see the head already; she came with her mother and
mother-in-law and husband, a girl of maybe seventeen. The husband
wasn't much older either and so excited he couldn't speak. I say to
him didn't your wife complain about pains, first stage labor is painful;
most women find it more painful than second stage labor. Surely
your mother-in-law must've known it was time, why're you coming
so late; but he couldn't say anything. We'd hardly gotten her clothes
off and the child was there already; the things you see." In one of
the books I'd read it said a generation would have to be raised
which would never think of the term "birth pain," so the word
would be neither spoken nor written, but replaced by "birth contraction." Of course, a painless or short delivery would not arouse
the interest of gossipy women, who would rather tell each other
dramatic stories about an unusual and complicated birth. But anyone
expecting a child shouldn't listen to those stories to begin with, since
they reinforce the conditioned pain reflex; the station master had
yelled that the station paramedic had been alerted. Everyone who
had been sitting on the other side of the double bench got up
abruptly and picked up their baggage. A human whirlpool formed
in the crowd that poured down from the platform above. Whoever
fell into its current became part of a circular human mass, the center

of which was the man I knew, but from where. His head had slumped so far foward that his brass-red beard was lying on his shirt-front like a bib. Three pills every hour, slowly they began to take effect. The head doctor said, "Let's see if you can do it alone." "And if I can't do it alone? " I asked. "We'll have to take it out," she said. There was a half-wit who helped out at the produce co-op, a forceps delivery; formerly the chances of survival for the fetus were slim when the membrane ruptured prematurely, claims Anne, usually the child was dismembered to save the mother, she said; I was freezing, I remembered that my friend Anne had recommended woolen socks for the labor room; my friend Anne is a nurse, if you're yelling, you aren't working, she said; I resolved to work. That was during the period when there's no work, in medical parlance the dilation stage of labor. The mechanism was working, driven by pills and injections, it was working hard. Five weeks too early. The concept "birth pain" did not enter my mind, my thoughts went outside, Sunday, first Sunday after the first full moon of spring; I thought: Never again. The head midwife said we'd be through in two hours. I can't take two more hours, I thought, out with it, alive or dead, the three women had laid the man on the bench, probably with great effort, his limbs were dangling; when the second stage contractions started the professor appeared with the head doctor, the anesthetist and the head midwife. The head midwife gave the orders, when the contraction came she would raise my head until my chin hit my breast-bone and give the orders, take a breath, now push, three times each; she reprimanded me when I took a breath while pushing, I heard nothing but orders and reprimands and clasped my knees as hard as I could, sometimes my sweaty hands would slip, that was also cause for a reprimand; the contractions were not coming in rapid succession, the cramping hardly let up at all, in the short pauses I shuddered as if I had the chills; the midwife said keep going, God must be a man, she said, a woman would have figured out a better solution for this business, keep going, keep going; injustice must be met with anger, she said, come on, come on, come on, the head is just visible now, you can see it quite well, now very clearly, a head with black hair. I was told to grit my teeth and push to beat hell: fine. Before the ether mask felled the pain giant I counted him out, one, two, three, four, five, six, seven, eight, nine. When I awoke I was laying stretched out in bed, my ankles crossed, a warm wrinkle-free blanket pressing against me. The professor said "All over." "And the afterbirth," I said. "It's all over, congratulations on your son; hey, let her have a look at the little guy." The anesthetist and the head woman doctor congratulated me. The head midwife said "I'm hungry." When my son was brought to me I was shocked, but merely

expressed my surprised at the fact that such little people are produced
in such big bellies. The professor said, "3375 grams is not little." I
saw head and genitals, both disproportionately large—the most important things—then rather red, powdered skin, a squashed ear,
eyebrows, big closed eyelids, lashes, a tin tag with the number
twenty-one stamped on it, hands the size of teaspoons, fingernails,
half moons; I asked "Is everything there?" Since experts were watching me, I decided to touch a leg with my right index-finger tip. It
had a wrinkles on the thigh. The skin on the upper arms was also
wrinkled and it hung loosely everywhere else too, like on puppies.
I stayed in the labor room another two hours and listened to the
crying of the babies; my son gurgled. He was lying in an infant
warmer in the nursery. I lay alone in the small labor room waiting
for a meal. I hadn't eaten for twenty-one hours. Since the midwives
were busy I had to wait a long time. I heard their commands,
groaning, screams, crying, gurgling, two, three hours of that day
passed in which I did not regret being a woman. I remembered that
the man was the owner of the garden plot adjacent to my aunt's.
In the summer he used to live in a garden house with his mother,
his mother's sister and a woman named Mary. Mary had placed his
legs, which were clothed in black corduroy, on the bench in such a
way that knees and ankles were touching. His mother's sister had
folded his hands in the hollow below his chest. The mother talked
insistently to his head, which had a yellow sheen. The eyes of the
carpenter were staring in the direction of the beams of the cross
which formed the roof of the transfer station. I tried hard to comprehend that I had a son.

Translated by Karen Achberger

Notes

* German original: Irmtraud Morgner, "Weisses Ostern," *Hochzeit in Konstantinopel,* Berlin: Aufbau, 1968, pp. 71–77. Translated and reprinted with
permission.

8. The Smith of Kosewalk*

Sarah Kirsch

The setting is a small rural village in the GDR. On one level, the story portrays successful integration of tradition and technology, symbolized by the three-hundred-year-old smithy housing both modern machinery and an antique forge. But the inner life of the blacksmith's daughter, and her limited options for self-realization, are the author's real focus. The gently ironic tone is characteristic of Kirsch's early prose.

In Kosewalk, an out-of-the-way place on the coast, there was a smithy that was still in operation. From the outside it looked as if it hadn't kept pace with the rate of progress in this village: an open fire in the forge glowed through the narrow sooty windowpanes. But once you set foot across the threshold, you were struck by the modern machines. One of them in fact was so tall that the ceiling had been cut through so that its upper half could be accommodated in the second story of the nearly three-hundred-year-old building. For the smith was a man of intelligence as well as of physical strength. He had become a member of the local cooperative. Under his expert hands the most urgently needed replacement parts for harvesting machines took shape. He could build indestructible axles, now and again he shod a horse. He was of average height but when sitting down he seemed a giant, and just as you'd expect from a blacksmith, he would occasionally, on holidays, bend an iron horseshoe straight for the amusement of the villagers. It pleased them even more when he would join their company wearing his good suit, ready to play his accordion for their dancing and singing. He had a gentle baritone voice, and after a few brandies he would sing strange songs. They told of the lives of resistance fighters and of the spirit and beauty of a girl from a far-off land, and the words and melodies were so foreign to this region that everyone assumed the smith had composed these songs himself.

Now this smith had a daughter, a brown-haired girl with big eyes, who did her father's bookkeeping. Because of her skill in stenography she was occasionally asked to write up reports for the chairman of the cooperative. This usually happened in spring around the Day of

83

Readiness.* The previous year, when dictating the annual report to be sent to the county seat, he reported that all the machines were repaired and ready for service and then added that he wanted to marry her. Hanna, for that was her name, almost wrote that down too, so unmindful was she of the speaker. But you can't be serious, she said. Sure, I'm past twenty-five, but I'm not in any hurry. When he heard about it the smith didn't even shake his head, let alone reproach her. He sang one of his songs and said: that's something you don't understand. But his daughter was already out the door, and probably the words hadn't been meant for her anyway.

During the summer he noticed that Hanna was writing his songs down. He asked what for and learned that she had found, in *Magazin*, the address of a volunteer doing time in the army who was looking for a pen pal and that she had written to this man, more out of boredom than curiosity. Several letters had been exchanged; now the songs were keeping the correspondence going, for he sang in an ensemble and wrote that they didn't have enough songs. And he can even read music, she assured her father and added that he wanted to visit her here next year when his military service was over. Writing music down is a good thing, the smith observed and said no more.

Summer came to an end. It was harvest time, and the smith got up early even on Sundays to be able to fill all the orders for the cooperative. He produced all the parts needed for repairs and rebuilt an old bulldozer to run the milking equipment when the electricity went out. The villagers had long since ceased to be amazed at his skill; they were accustomed to his succeeding with whatever he touched. Hanna kept the books, ordered supplies, and continued to help out at the co-op. Once, when the bookkeeper became dangerously ill after a hunting trip, she took over the payroll calculations, handling this work to everyone's satisfaction. The chairman had never repeated his attempt to court Hanna. Because the postman left the mail for the whole village at the co-op he couldn't help noticing that Hanna got a letter every week from a serviceman, and he said to himself that she must be writing just as often to him. Which is the way it was, only the girl rode her bicycle four kilometers in order to put her letters directly into the hands of the post office. It went against her simply to bring them to the co-op office, since mail wasn't picked up regularly there, only when the postman came by

* Day of Readiness *(Tag der Bereitschaft)*: a day in early spring before plowing and planting of fields begin, when farm machinery is inspected to make sure it is properly serviced and ready for use.

to deliver some. So she would have been able to see her letter lying there while she took dictation for a report, and she probably would have delayed sending it off, if not prevented altogether. For she had conflicting feelings about the letters she wrote and those she received. Although she was an open, straightforward person, almost too trusting, she often had misgivings about the rightness of her actions. What would happen if the image of the young soldier that she got from his letters, an image she was helping to create, didn't correspond to reality? She had noticed that letters can be peculiar, independent beings. She wrote things she probably never would have said out loud. And even when she was writing happily about her work, the condition of the crops, and the walks she took alone, she saw clearly that these letters gave her away. But she wondered how she could keep on living without writing. It seemed that this summer had been more beautiful than other ones. When writing about the woods or about a heavy storm which demolished a haybarn, or when describing the harvest celebration and the farmers' conversations, she had the impression that she had never before seen these things so clearly or experienced them so intensely.

As the year drew to a close the soldier's letters grew friendlier and her reservations vanished. Besides telling about his training and performances with the ensemble he found room for a few lines about himself. He told her about his home, described his civilian occupation, and asked her opinion as to how he ought to manage things if he went to technical school after his discharge. From time to time he lost his train of thought in childhood memories and decorated his letters with drawings. One of these showed the girl riding her bicycle through the rain, her clothes clinging to her. At that point Hanna decided it was time to send him a photograph. It was a portrait taken at the studio in the county seat. Her eyes looked a bit vacant; her mouth, which should have smiling, had a defiant expression. Her short boyish hairdo clung to her head as always, thick and bristling out at the temples. The soldier liked the picture very much. He imagined setting her on his motorcycle, putting on his jeans, and taking off over the ridge road in the Thuringian mountains. Or along a road on the coast. The picture met with approval from his comrades, not that this was important to him. He looked at it often, lost it once and found it again, suggested in his next letter to Hanna that they use the familiar *Du*, thought up some affectionate speeches for the one after that, and Hanna followed suit. She was always cheerful these days. When the rainy season came, making it unthinkable to get anywhere by bicycle, she went through the mud on foot to mail her letter, turning down the offer of a ride back in a truck returning from delivering sugar beets to the factory. She was out there when the mud started to freeze, she was on the road when it started to snow, and once she wrote his initials in the snow. She hesitated over adding her own and drawing a heart around the whole thing. She didn't do it, probably didn't want to tempt fate, but knew that she was in love. She planned Christmas presents to surprise him, but his present outdid hers: he sent an engagement ring by registered mail. When he saw it on her finger the smith said: well, that's something! and put more coal on the fire. He neither approved nor disapproved of what Hanna was doing; he sang during the noisiest part of his work, which he had always done. He found himself in a peculiar situation at the co-op. When the farmers asked him what kind of guy his son-in-law was, the smith said a fine-looking person, although he hadn't even seen a picture, for the young soldier hadn't returned Hanna's favor. The chairman of the co-op drank two vodkas with him to the son-in-law's health and so did the postman, who maintained that Hanna had gotten an intellectual, and at that the smith drank with half the village. The tractor drivers, his best customers, danced with Hanna to the accordion which had been joined by a bass violin. They asked Hanna what color his eyes were and if he was a passionate lover, but she, who would have liked to know those things herself, gave no answer.

It was a good year. On New Year's Hanna looked back on a stack of forty-two letters. Soon she was transporting her last letter. By then the trees along the road had new leaves, the smith had whitewashed the smithy, and it was the perfect time for the wedding. Her soldier already had one foot in civilian life but was going to arrive still in uniform, stay two weeks, and on the tenth day they would have the civil ceremony at the county courthouse. Where could they live? Later in the man's home town, but for now above the smithy where the machine's head towered over the furnishings, where you didn't have to turn the lights down low—the open fire on the first floor would serve to illuminate what there was to see.

Now everything was ready and the smith breathed a sigh of relief. He had begun to fear that the couple would have a child before they had seen each other. He took a car to pick the soldier up at the railroad station. At the last minute Hanna had pleaded a report as excuse and gone to the co-op. Indeed, the soldier was a fine-looking person—the smith hadn't been bragging—and a tall one besides, at least six foot five. They drove toward the village talking about the smith's songs. The soldier had brought one of them into wider circulation through his ensemble; however, the soldiers sang it in a major key, whereas Hanna had set down the version she sent in a minor key. The smith didn't object. Rather, his opinion was that almost every song potentially contained both keys and it was up to people to pick the one that suited them. What was sung as major one day might be minor the next, and vice versa. And with these words, singing examples to each other, they arrived in Kosewalk at the smithy, where Hanna came to meet them. Their first meeting was without embarrassment or nervousness. They used each other's first names and Hanna pointed out to him various trees and objects familiar to him from her letters. She liked him. The uniform emphasized his strong, straight build. He had an open face, beautiful long eyelashes that didn't turn up, so that he seemed to be looking through newly sprouted grass. Hanna thought she smelled rain and she had the sensation that her heart moved over from her left side to the right. He's the one, she said to herself and had an urge to write a letter. The soldier moved into the room above the smithy. From the first he felt right at home in Kosewalk, in the smithy, with Hanna. In the morning he came downstairs to the shop. The noise level was rising; he recognized the roar of the machines, the voices of the smith and his customers. When the time came he helped them temper the hot steel in the water bath and was standing in such a cloud of steam that Hanna couldn't find him. They took walks or rode bicycles to the beach. There they would lie in a hollow looking up at the sky, when they weren't swimming or letting themselves be carried by the surf. For the time being there was no great show of affection between them. We have time, thought Hanna. And he found her different from the girls he had known before. He thought special treatment was due her and was content to walk among the dunes with his right arm around her.

So the first five days went by, and the time left before the wedding would have passed in the same pleasant way, had not an utterly new person appeared on the scene at the worst time, when the play was half over. Her name was Christine and she wanted to see how a wedding took shape. Or so she said upon meeting the couple on the beach, while Hanna rejoiced that she had accepted her invitation and while the soldier was thinking he would rather be alone with his fiancee. They walked along looking for fossilized sea-urchins. Christine found one right away, in good condition. She handed it casually to the soldier, saying she had a whole collection of them at home. He put it in his breast pocket and would have forgotten it had the fossil not made itself painfully apparent that evening when he took Hanna in his arms on the stairway to the second floor. He felt its pressure, he felt tired and said so, yet couldn't fall asleep. The light from the fire danced along the ceiling, it was like a red forest. He saw Christine's red dress fluttering among the flame-trees: that was surely the girl from the smith's songs. He rebuked himself for his inconstancy and made himself think about Hanna. The next

day he stayed in the smithy a long time, went to the co-op with
the smith, and was more affectionate with Hanna than before. And
during all this he was plagued by strange thoughts.

On his arrival in the village he had scarcely noticed that Hanna's
figure was rather bulky from her shoulders—which he knew from
the portrait—on down. Now he wanted to find out for sure if he
loved her and would be able to love her for a long time. Hanna
spent the night with him above the smithy. The reflection from the
fire dealt kindly with her, creating a pleasant landscape without any
rough places. The top of the machine, which caused the floor to
vibrate slightly, towered into the shadows. The vibrations spread all
the way to the soles of their feet, driving them to greater and greater
haste. Hanna didn't know if she was laughing or crying and the
soldier too felt in excellent spirits. But when the fire in the smithy
below them went out, he saw no reason to rekindle it. He felt as
helpless as before.

The next day he could be seen sitting on a big rock at the beach
at first by himself. Then Christine appeared. She was in a melancholy
mood and spoke of going away. She turned around to leave, came
up behind him and put her arms around his neck, skinning her
knees on the rock. The soldier cried out and realized it was time to
bare his soul to the smith. The smith was singing his songs in a
minor key. He was up to his ears in work, haying had begun.

He was sharpening the blades from a mower and brandished them
before the soldier's eyes. What the hell, said the smith, a wedding's
a wedding. And he said he would arrange it for him and Hanna's
friend Christine; it would be up to them to get the necessary papers
at the county courthouse.

The soldier was surprised but did what the smith said. A very
beautiful wedding took place. It almost seemed as if no one in
Kosewalk was surprised that the soldier got engaged to Hanna and
married to Christine. Or people didn't show it, out of respect for
the smith. A grand table was set in the Fischerkrug Inn, extending
through the open doors to the outside. Linden branches brushed the
tablecloth and tapped the platters piled with delicious things, among
them a roast wild boar provided by the bookkeeper. Everyone had
come with a good appetite and for a while only the clattering of
knives and forks could be heard. But soon the guests, animated by
drinking, started talking and laughing, in fact, howling. They drank
a toast to the bride's health, the chairman drank to Hanna and her
father, the smith sang two-part harmony with the soldier, and the
dancing started. Hanna was in demand as a dance partner. While
the similarity between her figure and the smith's couldn't be denied,
her movements were nimble and light-footed. At one point when

the smith set down his accordion she left the party and walked straight across the cobblestone street, through the schoolyard, past the church to the smithy. She turned the light on and looked in the spattered mirror hanging over a wash basin so small that the smith had gotten into the habit of washing his hands one at a time. She started the machine, a drop hammer, and laid her left hand on the platform. The valves groaned, the weight rose up into the second story, hung there a moment and came whistling down. The smith, who had followed Hanna, didn't move a muscle. He watched with satisfaction as she braked the machine with her right hand just as the weight was a hair's breadth above her left. It was a trick he often used to do with his gold watch for the amusement of his wife. He came up to Hanna, praised her, and looked at her hand. She was wearing the engagement ring which now had a tiny flattened spot; no one but the smith would have noticed it. They went back to their guests. As they walked the moon came up. The sky was clear. But from the ground there rose a white mist which crept along the earth and covered it as if with white veils.

Translated by Jeanette Clausen

Notes

* German original: Sarah Kirsch, "Der Schmied von Kosewalk," *Die unge-heuren bergehohen Wellen auf See*, Berlin: Eulenspiegel, 1973, pp. 42–57. Translated and reprinted with permission.

9. Palisades
or Time Spent in a Mad House*

Helga Novak

The treatment of women patients in a mental "health" facility is here presented as almost a caricature of sex-role socialization. The narrator's description of details of her stay in the "mad house" and her efforts at resistance create a feeling of authenticity. The simplicity and clarity of presentation unmask structures of oppression. The story is typical of many of Novak's semidocumentary pieces.

The birds twitter. They trill, whistle, scold, scream.
Sister Margret says we rejoice listening to them, because they are attuned to life.
In between them the crows.
Sister Margret comes through the dormitory. She claps her hands together several times and calls out now up! and on your feet! wake up now!
Get up at five A.M.
Get attuned to life.

no no please no shot that makes me stiff the shots are to make me stiff no no anything but a shot to make me stiff

First we crowd around the wash basin six at a time. Hedwig washes up later. She gets out the folding screen from behind the medicine cabinet and sets it up carefully around the wash basin. The screen is so low that everyone can see her dab the washcloth hastily under her arms.

Calendar saying for April 22.
"God resists the proud, but gives grace unto the humble."

Our nightgowns are made of coarse fabric, white. They button in front and are open down the back. When we wash our faces we hold the gowns together over our buttocks with one hand.

Oh you're from Berlin my fiance is from Berlin too I have a fiance
in Berlin at the moment I've lost track of him I lost him like I lost
my handbag with all my papers in it when I didn't know what was
going on see I didn't know what was going on any more then I lost
my handbag and my fiance he's waiting for me in Berlin I'm sure
we'll all meet there some day.

wait	Get up. Get dressed. Make the bed. Set the table.	wait
wait	Get up at five. Wait for breakfast from seven to eight.	wait
wait	Wait for the bread, the butter. For the morning coffee,	wait
wait	gray and thin like silk stockings, wait for the morning	wait
wait	milk. Talk about the weather, the flowers, the trees	wait
wait	in the park. Wait. Wait for the next meal. For the	wait
wait	doctor, for your pill, your walk. Wait for supper, wait	wait
wait	for night. Always wait for night.	wait

No matches allowed. No scissors allowed. No nail file allowed. Before
you came I filed my nails with sandpaper and even that was supervised. No closing the toilet stall door behind you. No lying down
during the day. Walk around. Keep moving. Knit. Write.

The blue jeans incident isn't worth mentioning.
I say Sister Margret, give me my blue jeans back. I can't go around
in this pink dress every day. Sister Margret says it's absolutely out
of the question for you to go around in blue jeans here. It's not
appropriate. Besides, your blue jeans are dirty and we insist on
cleanliness. I say my blue jeans aren't dirty, they're only faded.
Please give them to me. Sister Margret says I've locked the blue
jeans up and there they'll stay until you leave this establishment. I
say if I don't get my blue jeans I'll break into the closet. Sister
Margret says you won't do that. In your own interest. If you haven't
learned obedience by now, you'll learn it here.
I spit in front of Sister Margret's feet.
She laughs and says don't get excited, it's not worth mentioning.
The pink dress is really very pretty. No one else here has such a
pretty dress. I say my dress is too good for this cage.

Calendar saying for April 23.
"Submit yourself to every ordinance of man for the Lord's sake."

Knit. Knit day in and day out. I don't knit. I write. I've been given
permission to write. I don't knit. You knit. She knits. She knits and
she does. You knit. They knit. Knit purl. Knit purl. Purl. Purl. Purl.
Two. Three. Four. In a straight line around the curve. The whole
thing in reverse. March. March. Company halt. Don't get out of line.

An army of stitches in motion. The knitting needles are the bayonets. That's probably why they're locked away at night, so nobody gets hurt.

The bells ring.
All the bells ring, the cowbells too.
And the gong that summons us.
And the bell jingles to dismiss us.
Any one of us everyone someday some time or other.

Where'd you get those earrings? My mother had earrings just like those. Off with them. Take them off. Give them here.
I scream.

Immanuela hangs on my ears. She pulls, won't let go.
I yell. I strike out. She falls down. I fall beside her. My earlobes get hot and swell up.

Mozart's concert aria "So laughs the gentle springtime." That was the day you brought me meat during visiting hours instead of flowers. Dry smoked ham from Graubünden. Aren't you eating right at this place? No, I don't eat that swill. But I crammed the meat you brought me in my mouth the moment you were gone. Meat. Eat meat. When you come back, bring meat and fruit. No flowers.
K 580. "So laughs the gentle springtime."
Please, take part in our projects just this once. Aren't you at all interested in helping your fellow-humans?
Don't stop writing now.
Patterns for baby outfits go from hand to hand. And circular knitting needles. Baby clothes for needy, mentally confused, unhappy expectant mothers.
Have you no heart at all? No pity for others?
Where would I end up if I started knitting after all this. Catch me doing that. What are expectant mothers to me, whether they've lost their minds or not.
Idiotic. Forget that about the meat. I'm getting out. By the next visitors' day I'll be out. Then we'll go out drinking and eat meat. Then we'll take a bottle of vodka to a meadow that's not fenced in. Not do anything. Just sit there. Daydream. Think ourselves far away. No brooding. Either you write or you knit.
Only no flowers. Meat.
"So laughs . . ."

I need a clean shirt from my suitcase. I say Sister Margret, permit me to put a clean shirt on. Sister Margret says your things aren't marked, therefore you may not use them. Mark your shirts, mark all your clothes. Also your compact, toothbrush and toothpaste. Then you may have access to everything. I say I won't be here long enough to make it worth my while to mark all my things. She says then you don't need a clean shirt.

Feeling perfectly blissful. Fell off cloud nine after a short excursion to heaven and landed here. In a building consisting of long corridors. You never understood why I wanted to leave. So many misunderstandings. So many distortions. So many false statements. And the lump in my throat when I saw you again. A wall of thick, clean glass between us. Oh never again listen when you speak. Because it doesn't reach this far.

Calendar saying for April 24.
"Ye slaves, be subject to your masters with all fear, not only to the good and gentle ones, but also to the contrary ones."

Haha.
Pst.

It's deathly quiet. Then the Fräulein Doctor starts practicing softly. Fräulein Doctor is taking private lessons in acting. —e—i—ei—a—i—ai—o—i—oi—.
On visitors' days Fräulein Doctor is often visited by two elderly gentlemen. One of them calls her Mademoiselle, while the other addresses her as Signorina. In reality the Fräulein's name is Dr. Gerda. Gerda must have had a stroke. Her right leg is paralyzed. Her right eye is closed, but the left one is normal. She smiles with this left, open eye. But if she cries, tears stream out of her closed right eye. When we take walks to the park Sister Margret asks us to push Gerda's wheelchair. I wouldn't dream of pushing the wheelchair, least of all uphill. I walk beside Gerda and offer her a cigarette. We both smoke, and her left eye smiles.
I say Gerda, what are you actually here for? Gerda says all my friends died on me all of a sudden, so suddenly, everyone around me dead, one after another, gone. I say well I for example took sleeping pills, not enough, as you see. Gerda laughs. Sister Margret says I must ask you to change the subject. No one here is interested in why someone is with us. I say then why are they all listening to me so attentively? Sister Margret says because it has something to do with outside. But for good reasons, our job here is to radiate

cheerful serenity to one another, via a happy, tension-free approach.
I say then you'd have to do a lot of changing.

Suddenly Gerda starts crying with her closed right eye.
Sister Margret says to me look, that's what you get. Then she says
no crying, we don't cry here. Stop crying! Stop crying at once!
Sister Margret is afraid Gerda might get us started. She takes over
the wheelchair. I offer Gerda another cigarette.
At the top of the hill we meet the men's ward. The men set benches
out for us. They shake our hands and say hello. We talk to them
about the weather, the flowers, the smell of the fresh birch twigs.
Gerda likes talking with the men. She's nice to them. I glide down
the slope and lie in the grass.
How quiet it is.

No talking about our illnesses.
No telling anyone why we're here.
No finding out why the others are.
No better place to learn repression than here.

Christa says she predicted the Israeli Blitzkrieg. And that she took
the wheel away from her uncle because he won't listen. I ask her
why she jumped off the balcony. She says on account of the Vietnam
war. Christa says under no circumstances should I talk to her doctor
about it. I say what do I care about your doctor. She says and
television is corrupt too. Swiss television lies. That's why I went
there and asked them to stop it once and for all. I demanded that
they come over to our side. I say who brought you here? She says
my mother, she's divorced and remarried. She and her new husband
lie to each other too. I begged them not to do it any more but they
denied everything and brought me here. I say but you're still in
school. She says yes, I'm sixteen and now I'm missing so much. I
say you can finish school when you get out. Christa says but don't
tell my doctor, they didn't want me at that school any more. I
pleaded with the teacher to side with us, so he went to my mother
and said in the first place I was in danger and in the second place
a young girl like me had no business getting involved in politics. I
say don't let it drive you crazy just because they all lie. You have
to understand why people do that. Can't you get books that tell
why they lie, why nobody's interested in Vietnam, why you aren't
supposed to get involved in politics. Christa says I don't have any
books like that. I say I'll give you some. While I'm here I can also
talk to you about politics. And give up on your uncle, and television,

and your teacher and your mother. Christa says but they're all so good to me and I'm even in the youth choir.

Given permission to write. Then write, come hell or high water. Write without stopping or be made to knit. Nothing left to write, nothing else to communicate. The activity is all that counts. The representation of writing. Wielding the pencil. The letters count, the words, the pages with writing on. Keep going. Keep on writing. No stopping. Chin up. Sister Margret says if you aren't writing will you please knit. Surely you can at least knit potholders, right? Don't shut the notebook. Don't let your arms drop. Don't prop your head on your hand. I can't knit. I'll be released soon, maybe tomorrow. Why learn to knit now?
Take down the calendar. Read the calendar of the Reformed Swiss Institute. Copy calendar sayings. The point is: write.

Crap.

Sister Margret tosses a ball of yarn onto my notebook. And here's a set of needles. Should you by any remote chance stop writing. Does it absolutely have to be potholders when I never touch pots and pans? But I've seen you eat, hot meals included.
Knit? No, never. Don't stop writing for anything in the world. Rather stop eating first. Not eat a thing any more. Write. Write.

there over there there he goes bumps into the ceiling like a blowfly flies around the angel circles under the ceiling the poor thing is cold because he's not dressed right he's always dragging the big palm tree behind him the heavy beam on his shoulder he circles under the ceiling bumps into it casts shadows the cross casts shadows the angel would like to rest can't lie down go to bed flying flying can't rest he carries the cross around with him on his shoulder so it won't fall on our heads when the angel sweats it rains

Sister Margret has on a black dress made of cotton sateen. She has a white apron on that smells of bleach and feels like wrapping paper. She sits by the radio and knits.

It's pretty bad when they forget to put salt out for the deer.
Anita, you put your flowers out in the hallway at night too.
Listen, a hundred and seven people in the plane crash over Japan.
That's a charming playsuit. After you've finished the light blue one you can do one in pink.

You need size-two needles for these mittens, otherwise they'll be too loose and the poor little mite will freeze. Immanuela, where did you get that necklace? You know you aren't allowed to have necklaces. Take it off right now, you might get caught on something.
Hand in all the needlework, we're going to the park now. Some needles are still missing, don't anyone try to keep their needles on me.
The knitting needles get locked up. Sister Margret crouches down at the sideboard putting away the needlework. She's wearing house slippers that let her toenails peek out in front.

The mobile on the ceiling is made of five walnut shell halves. Each of them has two tiny sails. Five little boats swinging to and fro under the ceiling. They dance in the cross-draft. I watch the boats roll and turn.

Every day we spend three hours in the morning and three hours in the afternoon in the recreation room. Hand-woven cloths on the tables, green hand-woven cushions on the chairs, the floor lamp has a pleated shade covering made of hand-woven fabric.
The floor in the recreation room has been laid with carpet tiles. The windows are barred, and made of brownish glass. The pattern of the bars makes the brownish windowpanes look like bulls-eye glass. Stained-glass pictures have been inserted in some of the squares of the grating. Colorful birds, sitting on the edges of colorful nests. Bars. Haha. Bars. Because I mustn't stop writing. That's why. Keep on. Keep on writing. Don't let up.

Somewhere there's still a square centimeter of stuff I haven't mentioned yet.
Before I forget, the calendar of the Reformed Swiss Institute hangs on the china cupboard. You bet. When I can't think of anything else I copy calendar sayings. Don't by any means let your head sink onto your arms, the notebook, the table. I have a headache. I ask to be allowed to lie down. There's no lying down during the day. A person who lies down will be tempted to brood. There's nothing else to tempt you here. Exercise, fresh air. You'll see how fast your headache disappears.

The doctor says here's a sheet of paper, now write us a nice curriculum vitae. I say hey, I'm not applying for a job here. He says everyone turns in their curriculum vitae to us. I say too bad, I don't have one. He says you don't say, no CV at your age? I say I took it for a ride. He says then go get it back. I say I'm like a new-born babe. The doctor says you know, actually I wanted to be a concert violinist.

Waltz melodies on the radio, then Händel, then Sister Margret turns the noise-box off, then silence reigns. Please, please, a bit more Händel. Is anyone opposed to our turning off the radio? No one's listening anyway, are they? Kiss my ass then, okay, no more Händel. Needles clicking. Gerda practices reading. —o—i—oi—a—u—au—. Ow ow ow ow ow. No bad moods, please, no rage, no angry outbursts. If you have a tantrum you stay in longer. Being disfranchised. Liking it. Laugh, tease, joke, dance, skip. Hug each other. Cuddle up to Sister Margret. Cackle, giggle, radiate cheerful serenity. Tee hee. Sister Margret says pack up, we're going to the yard to play badminton. Oh God thank you for letting my dream come true. Playing badminton. You are so blasé. There's simply no pleasing you. What do you want, anyway? Take a guess. Out. I want out. Then we can talk some more.

Why not stop writing. Why not knit. Have they got me to that point yet? In this joint even the bath towels are knitted. Knitted from the finest cotton yarn. What a luxury. Knitted towels. Who can afford that these days. And why not knit washrags, with red and blue tags. Each of us gets two knitted washrags. The one with the red tag is for above the navel, the one with the blue tag is for below it. But please set up the folding screen. I ask for a tub bath. Sister Margret says I can't promise anything, I say but you did promise. She says we'll see. You may remind me again tomorrow. Anyway you can wash in the dormitory. You can wash yourself all over, every bit. Just don't forget to put up the screen.

Sofia had a visitor. Her cousin was here.
Her cousin brought her a big bunch of tulips. The tulips are red and yellow. They're all the way open already. Lush calyxes are enthroned on the lush stems.
Sofia said please, don't worry about me any more. I have a delightful window seat. I feel really well here. Just look at it. I feel very safe here, I had always dreamed of a window seat like that. No, no. At home I never had such a nice window seat. Ah, these luminous flowers, take them back with you. What am I going to do with flowers on my long trip? They'll only wilt on me. Put them in a vase for me at home. You don't need to worry about me any more. I'm well taken care of. I hadn't counted on such a wonderful window seat when I got on. And now dear, you must go.

The cousin said we have two or three more minutes. Why should
I leave already?
Sofia said but your time, it's valuable. And the train is just about
to leave, too. Now go. I want to get back to my window seat. Isn't
it nice?

The cousin said well, we'll see you again.
Sofia said why?
The cousin said but we don't want to give up hope.
Sofia said which one?
The tulips lay on the table in front of the cousin. Sofia went to the
dormitory and sat down at the window.

At night we hang our clothes on chairs. Everyone hangs their clothes
neatly over a chair. Then we carry the chairs with our clothes out
in the hall and set them in rank and file at the entrance to our
ward. At ten P.M. the hallway door is locked. Nighttime. If anyone
forgot something in their pocket, they can get in tomorrow. Now
it's time to sleep.

A complicated but symmetrically constructed building with enclosed
gardens and a park surrounded by sharply pointed palisades. Inside
the building is dominated by its corridors, widening ones, narrowing
ones, rising, falling ones, and outside by branching gardens and the
park. Floors and hallways are shut off by electric sliding doors that
function by a secret system of numbers.
Outside is the farm owned by the establishment, with milking machines, manure spreader, pigs, and cows. How it clatters, stinks,
rings, tinkles.
And no butter on the bread at suppertime. Dry bread makes cheeks
red.

To think that we can't get to our clothes at night. But where is the
exit? Around which corner? And how far? And how long? And the
numbers to open the doors? And what for, anyway? They'll let me
go all on their own. They'll be glad when I leave.

well what
the right to love
the right to be afraid
the right to make yourself scarce
the right to say to hell with everything
the right to be alone with yourself
to make up your mind

to feel at home with yourself
where else
the right to strike out
the right to wring people's neck or your own
the right to be good
the right to love
what else

The back of the May 1 calendar page.
"What a big decision the Christian woman of today must face. By the laws of modern society women will soon be equal to men in every respect. Because of this many things in their lives have automatically shifted from inner to outer. This contradicts the Creator's intended purpose for women. The hard masculine world needs to be balanced by a gentle and calm spirit. Woman has this spirit, and it is her task to set a standard opposing all the alienating forces in life that threaten us in advertising, fashion trends, so-called public opinion."

So now we'll enjoy a change of pace.
Go to the park.
Up to the knoll where the men's ward is playing cards.
And smoking and rolling dice and walking back and forth.
And greeting us and setting out benches.
Where we do round dances play catch with rubber balls and jump rope.
I lie down in the grass at a distance.
If someone speaks to me I say
get lost, leave me in peace.
And spit at him.

A flock of pure white doves minces across the green meadow.
Sister Margret cries out don't you see, don't you see how beautiful that is?
She shouts for joy. Distracted, the doves fly away.

Translated by Jeanette Clausen

Notes

* German original: Helga Novak, "Palisaden oder Aufenthalt in einem irren Haus," *Aufenthalt in einem irren Haus*, Darmstadt: Luchterhand, 1971, pp. 194–212. Translated and reprinted with permission.

Part Three

Body Politics

As in other countries, the women's movement in Germany began its struggle with the campaign for abortion rights and in self-help projects such as the houses for battered women and women's health centers. Much of the political content of the movement was directed against the violence and coerciveness of heterosexuality. Alice Schwarzer's 1974 best-selling work The "Little Difference" and Its Big Consequences exemplifies this phase of the movement.

By the end of the decade, however, a backlash of sorts could be observed. The struggle against the external enemy, be that men or the health care system, flagged. In some quarters of the women's movement the sexual theories of the early 1970s were seen as a new set of "dictates of femininity" and as an ideology which demanded too high a price of women in denial and loneliness.

Among a small but articulate minority, both in the United States and Germany, this trend has extended to a feminist exploration of sadomasochism. This controversial exploration, in turn, seems to be sparking interest in new approaches to female sexuality, which will avoid prudishness without resorting to patriarchal images of agony and ecstasy. In her report on the 1982 conference on women's sexuality at Barnard College in New York, Sybille Plogstedt, of the journal Emma (West Berlin), recalled Simone de Beauvoir's comment during the sadomasochism discussions in the 1960s: "To side with de Sade too readily is to betray him." Plogstedt adds: "And to side with de Sade while continuing to follow old man Masoch is to betray ourselves."

10. How It All Began
I have had an abortion*

In 1981, the periodical Emma *began a series of retrospective articles on the history of the current West German women's movement. This, the first in the series, chronicles the opening wedge of that movement—the campaign for women's control over reproduction.*

Historically, privileged people have never freely given up their rights. That's why we demand: Women must become a power factor in the battle to be waged! Women must organize, because they must recognize their most basic problems and learn to represent their interests. Applause from the majority. Boos from some. It was late afternoon already when these now-historic utterances resounded over the mike. Sentences with which—fifty years after the death of the first German Women's Movement—the second German Women's Movement was born. Location: the Youth Hostel in Frankfurt on the banks of the Main River. Midwives: about 450 women from forty groups from the entire Federal Republic gathered here for the first Federal Women's Congress.

There were stormy months preceding these statements. And had someone prophesied to these 450 women a year previously that they would be participating in the rebirth of feminism—most among them would have shaken their heads in disbelief. For at that time the concept of feminism was a pejorative term—especially among the ranks of politicized women. After the first protest in the wake of the 1968 Protest Movement, the beginning of the 1970s seemed to have a deadly calm in terms of women.

In search of a photogenic Women's Lib at home, the magazine *Brigitte* complained coquettishly as late as Spring of 1971: "German women don't burn bras and wedding dresses, don't storm any beauty contests and anti-emancipation editorial boards, do not advocate getting rid of marriage and do not compose manifestos for eradicating men. There are no witches, daughters of Lilith, like in the United States not even Dolle Minnas with a sense of humor like in Holland, there are no aggressive magazines. No Anger."

Well, there was anger. More than *Brigitte* and *Kompagnon* liked. It was quickly directed towards the abortion law and the dictates of femininity. The catalyst was the anti-abortion law (Article 218). The background for it was the increasing infamy and schizophrenia of women's new role. At that time, the much-propagated double burden was beginning to peak: Hold down a job on the side and at the same time be the perfect housewife, good mother, smooth lover—that was the new ideal that we were to attain. Only the spark was missing from the powder keg—but who was going to ignite it?

In April of 1971, 343 French women declared openly: "We have had an abortion and we demand the right to free abortions for every woman." The action was initiated by the Paris Women's Movement, the MLF. The Left Newspaper *Le nouvel Observateur* had published their appeal. It was by chance that the movement spread so rapidly to neighboring Germany. Alice Schwarzer, at that time correspondent in Paris and herself active in the MLF, transported the idea to her German sisters. Determined to keep the feminist impetus of the action, she looked for comparable Women's groups and, on the other hand, for an avenue for publication. *Stern*, which had recognized the dramatic aspect of the action, agreed. Thus we had the ticklish, but ultimately successful short mésalliance between the Hamburg men's magazine and the women's project. The women had their forum and the *Stern* its scandal. If *Stern* had actually known whom it was helping, it would surely have kept its hands off the whole thing. The next step was to find women who would participate. Since it soon became clear that there was no women's group like the Parisian one, which could carry the project centrally, Alice pounded on a lot of doors—including those of SPD, DKP and trade union women, but all refused. Argument: "Such a project would only harm us—it doesn't sound serious." Or, "It would only shock the grass roots." However, from the total of four women's groups remaining, three were prepared to go along with it: (1) the "Frauenaktion 70" in Frankfurt—it had arisen out of the Humanistic Union, consisted of largely middle class working women, and had already taken to the streets with the slogan "My belly belongs to me." (2) The Socialist Women's Federation in Berlin, and (3) The "Red Women" of Munich. Piqued, the student-dominated Women's Council of Frankfurt rejected the project, finding it unpolitical and reformist. On that Friday in May, on which Alice submitted the plan to the "Red Women," the group split spontaneously. One part kept to its schoolings; the others jumped at the chance: "We were delighted to be able to do something for once."

Feverish activities began. The three women's groups gathered about one-half of the 374 signatures in less than a month, and the rest snowballed in. One woman told another, friends, colleagues, neighbors decided together. The courage of these women was enormous.

No one can imagine today what it meant to admit to an abortion at all, not to mention a public confession. Thanks to this campaign, the topic of abortion has, to be sure not yet been solved, but has largely lost its taboo. At that time it was simply a monstrosity, which you didn't admit even to your best friend. Contrary to later propaganda, most of the 374 women were anything but of the priveleged class. Among the first 374 only nine were actresses. The rest were secretaries, housewives (a *lot* of housewives), students, workers, white-collar women. The oldest was seventy-seven, the youngest twenty-one. The campaign was daring on all levels: daring in its collaboration with *Stern* and in the personal risk for each woman. But precisely this risk, the resoluteness of the women not to follow the rules which weren't theirs, and the demonstration of their solidarity constituted the action's immense effect. On July 6, 1971, the open confession of the 374 broke the plot of silence. Millions of copies of *Stern* were at the newsstands, with names and faces of well-known and unknown women who declared in common: "We've had an abortion. We don't demand alms from lawmakers and reform in portions! We demand the cancellation of Article 218 and no substitute laws!"

But really revolutionary was the demand to abolish 218 via the demand attached to it that the woman determine her own destiny! These first weeks and months after June 6 were exciting and radicalizing for all who took part. Ute Geissler: "When I signed the document I was very afraid. And then, when this police raid took place a few months later, it became clear that we wouldn't allow ourselves to be intimidated any more." The police actions "by night and fog," like those in Munich where a raid took place, no longer weakened the campaign, but rather strengthened it, brought a wave of sympathy to it, and—a further wave of women seeking help. Thus the women of Project 218 were initially alone—with the thousands of women who needed counselling and abortions. The only way out was to break the law in their own country or travel abroad. The first contacts with foreign countries were made. On November 1971, women took to the street in almost all Western countries for the right to abortion and self-determination of women. In Paris alone, over 4,000 demonstrated.

Translated by Naomi Stephan

Notes

* Originally published as, "Ich habe abgetrieben—Wie es anfing," *Emma* vol. 5 (March, 1981) 22–29. Translated and reprinted with permission. Portions of this text have been excerpted.

11. The Function of Sexuality in the Oppression of Women*

Alice Schwarzer

This major text of the new German women's movement sees in sexuality both the symbol and source of women's oppression. The author, a leading figure in the abortion struggle of 1971, went on to found the feminist journal Emma *in 1977. The book draws on a variety of well-known sources (Alfred C. Kinsey, Simone de Beauvoir, and others) as well as more recent feminist writers such as Anne Koedt and Shulamith Firestone.*

Almost always (in these past years) when I have tried to speak with men about emancipation—quite apart from whether they were friends or colleagues, on the left or the right—these talks would end up with that one "slight difference." Emancipation was all well and good, but that slight difference—we didn't want to get rid of that, too, did we?

Oh no! We would never dare. Most definitely not! There would always be the eternal *petite différence*, of course. Right? And the more progressive the circles in which it was debated, the smaller the difference was—except the consequences remained equally great.

It is time, therefore, to ask ourselves finally what this oft-quoted slight difference consists of. You don't have to look far in this potency-crazed society for said difference.

Actually, it's not very big. In a state of rest, the experts assure us, it's three to three and one-half inches; aroused, another two to three inches.

And in this nubbin resides manhood, the magical power to make women lustful and to rule the world? The nubbin-wearers, at least, seem to be convinced of it. I think it's nothing more than a pretext. Not this *biological* difference, but its ideological consequences must be categorically eliminated. Biology is not destiny. Masculinity and femininity are not nature but culture. In every generation they represent a renewed, forced identification with dominance and subjection. Penises and vaginas don't make us men and women, but power and powerlessness do.

The ideology of the two halves that supposedly complement each other so well has crippled us and created a rift which is seemingly impossible to overcome. Men and women feel differently, think differently, move differently, live differently. Everyone knows only too well how the stigma of masculinity or of femininity branded on our foreheads confines and defines us.

Nothing, neither race nor class, determines human life to the extent that gender does. Here women and men are both victims of their roles—but women are still victims of victims.

The fear, dependence, distrust, and powerlessness experienced by women are enormous. The closer we look, the deeper the rift between the sexes. Only those who dare to bridge this gap will—one distant day—be able to overcome it. Only those who admit existing conditions will be able to make changes. In the long-run, both sexes stand to gain; in the short-run, women stand to lose their chains and men their privileges.

All who speak of equality—in the face of the inequality between the sexes—are compounding their guilt daily. They are not interested in humanizing men and women but rather in maintaining prevailing conditions, from which they themselves profit. The exploitation of women has not diminished in recent decades but has rather become more acute. Women work more than ever before. Only the forms of this exploitation have sometimes become more subtle, more difficult to detect. What is officially understood by the word *emancipation* often means nothing more than that women who were slaves have now become free slaves.

Vaginal Orgasm and Sex Monopoly

What can we say in favor of penetration? Nothing for women, a lot for men. Coitus, which damns women to passivity, is for men the most uncomplicated and comfortable way of practicing sex: They don't have to communicate with women, don't have to stimulate them mentally or physically—passive compliance is enough.

You really can't underestimate the psychological implications for men of this violent act of invasion. *Screwing,* as it is so aptly called in everyday language, is the highest demonstration of male potency! Besides, for many men power is pleasure and that's why penetration is perhaps the most erotic stimulation for them today. (That women, on the other hand, have become largely unable to experience sex as satisfying because of their oppression and the perversion of relations between the sexes, seems to me to be an indication of their physical integrity. They are evidently not prepared for the perverse separation of physical and mental communication which male society openly practices.)

But that alone does not entirely explain the absolute compulsion for sexual norms which are contrary to the needs of one half of humanity (the female half) and which bring with them the enormous burden of contraception. Imagine: The horror of unwanted pregnancies and abortions, the attendant side effects of the pill, and inflammations caused by the diaphragm—all of this—would become superfluous with one blow if women were allowed to experience their sexuality in accordance with their natural needs. Heterosexual penetration would no longer be a form of making love but would be reserved for procreation. Unwanted pregnancies would no longer be possible.

But neither the misery of abortion nor female frigidity was able to shake the dogma of the vaginal orgasm. The reasons for this have to be momentous. My theory: Only the myth of the vaginal orgasm (and of the importance of penetration) insures sexual monopoly of men over women, which, in turn, is the foundation of the public monopoly of male society over women.

In other words: in this society, people are lonely without a love relationship in which they can buy affection and tenderness with sex; thus, women, like men, must resort to sexual relationships. If this sexuality is only possible under the guise of that certain "difference," if heterosexuality is given priority, then women and men must turn to each other. The monopoly is therefore reversible, it would seem. But only apparently. A man without a woman in our society is still a man, but a woman without a man is not a woman. A woman has no existence as an autonomous being—only in relation to a man. Her definition is that of a sexual being. Every attempt at emancipation must come to a deadend sooner or later, as long as every woman is individually subject to a man on a private level. And as long as she has no alternative, she cannot choose her relationships freely. That's the important point: the sexual monopoly of men over women ensures their emotional monopoly (women fall in love only with men, of course), their social monopoly (for social recognition women must depend on marriage or a relationship with a man), and their economic monopoly (women accept gratis work in the home and "additional income" jobs out of love for men).

Thus only the destruction of the male sexual monopoly from the foundation up will cause gender roles to collapse.

Why Compulsory Heterosexuality Is So Political

Categories like heterosexuality and homosexuality are cultural in nature and cannot be justified on a biological basis. The prevailing heterosexuality is a culturally induced, forced heterosexuality. Just how insupportable the concept of a "natural" heterosexuality is was illustrated by Kinsey in his report on "The Sexual Behavior of Women."

In a culture in which procreation is not the primary impulse for human sexuality, homosexuality as well as heterosexuality and a sexuality with one's self would have to be taken for granted as part of the free development of the individual.

There are political reasons for why things are not that way. The only way the male sexual monopoly can be ensured is through a heterosexuality that is elevated to the status of dogma. Its pretext is that "little difference."

When men no longer view the love of women as an automatic privilege, they'll have to put out some effort. That's why they cling so to that little difference of theirs.

In her militant book, *The Dialectic of Sex*, Shulamith Firestone places the question of sexuality in relation to the question of class:

> Just as the end goal of socialist revolution was not only the elimination of the economic class *privilege* but of the economic class *distinction* itself, so the end goal of feminist revolution must be . . . not just the elimination of male *privilege* but of the sex *distinction* itself.[1]

Because this way of thinking regularly elicits fears of castration and hysterical reactions in males and because it is not a common perspective, I want to explain it in my own words once again:

What this means is that people are first and foremost people and only secondarily female and male. Gender would no longer be destiny. Women and men would not be forced into role behavior, and the masculine mystique would be as superfluous as the femininity complex. Sex-specific divisions of labor and exploitation would be suspended. Only biological motherhood would be woman's affair; social motherhood would be men's affair just as much as women's. People would communicate with one another in unlimited ways, sexually and otherwise, according to their individual needs at any given time and regardless of age, race, and gender. (There would be no class system in this liberated society.) A utopia for tomorrow, but also goals and perspectives which we can't lose sight of today. From now on these things must determine what we do.

Translated by Naomi Stephan

Notes

* Originally published as, Alice Schwarzer, *Der "kleine" Unterschied und seine grossen Folgen* Frankfurt: Fischer, 1975, pp. 177–209. (c) S. Fischer Verlag GmbH, Frankfurt am Main 1975. Translated and reprinted with permission. Portions of this text have been excerpted.

1. Shulamith Firestone, *The Dialectic of Sex* New York: William Morrow, 1970, p. 11.

12. Violence and Desire*

Barbara Sichtermann

Whereas recent defenses in this country of feminist involvement with sado-masochism have followed a civil libertarian approach, this article tries to present "s & m" on its own merits. Yet, the author, like others in this newest feminist vanguard, asks us to make the blind dialectical leap from rejecting a culture which eroticizes violence against women to celebrating a liberating pan-sexuality which features violence.

Discussions within the women's movement on rape have indirectly revealed the outlines of a concept of (female) sexuality disturbing in that it leaves out so much. To be sure, the theme itself—rape— invites an emphasis on peace in the experience and forms of sexuality. But we must go beyond this. It is certainly true that a rape violates not only the peace but also the physical integrity of a woman—just as any other severe bodily injury does. It is equally certain that sexuality is more than a simple matching up of bodies, an exchange of affirmations. It seems to me that an implicit connection has been prematurely made: a fiction of cream-puff sexuality, in which two smiling faces and four open arms embrace. The tendency to base the feminist protest against minimizing the crime of rape upon the fiction of a peaceful/female sexuality—under the slogan "when a woman says *no,* she means *no"*—leaves unexplored the boundary between bodily injury and sexuality. It is precisely this boundary which should concern us.

Recently, my friend Esther told me of seeing an antirape film ("Schrei aus der Stille," author: Poirier) with women from her class at an adult education institution. Esther is the instructor of a remedial course which prepares young women, with personal histories which include youth homes and juvenile detention centers, for their secondary school matriculation exams. The film began with a scene showing the rape from the point of view of the woman. In a discussion following the film, Esther asked the women if they had not found the rape scene to be too realistic and too aesthetically presented. Wasn't there the chance that men would be aroused by such a scene. "What do you mean . . . *men?* " said Gaby, one of the women in the course, "that scene was a turn-on for *me!* " "The crazy thing is," concluded Esther, "as soon as she said that I knew: I had had the same reaction. But without Gaby's comment, I would have repressed it, censored it, quite automatically."

Long suspected, there now seems empirical proof that the sexual fantasies of women include images of rape. With the scientific studies, thank goodness, has come a change of interpretation: Rape fantasies are no longer considered evidence of the essential masochism of the female but merely as a graphic vehicle, as metaphor for a dynamic within "normal" sexuality: a flux between flight and pursuit, concealment and dicovery, curiosity and fear, pain and redemption, deception and surprise. All these movements and sensations constitute a ritual, a play or a dance. In the figures of this dance lies the fulfillment of sexuality.

If there is some blurring of the line between desire and bodily harm then there must be, in desire itself, a facet of (potential) harm, of forcefulness, or, to use the classic terminology, nonperverted sexuality must, then, be alloyed with an element of sadism and its complement, masochism. That this is really so, has, it seems to me, long been known. However, the (new) women's movement is avoiding the implications of this knowledge.[1] The movement has restricted itself largely to refuting the thesis of female masochism. This thesis has, so far as I know, never been subjected to a theoretical examination, but it was sufficiently widely broadcast as opinion as to minimize rape as a crime in the public consciousness.

The discussion, such as it is, revolves around the question of categories: Which sex is the sadistic one, which the masochistic? Women are reluctant to be relegated to the role of the long-suffering ones, and rightly so when one considers the systematic justifications that the thesis of female desire for pain has been used to support. Even the next step—claiming for women a share of sadism—has to do with categories. Put simply, there are three possible solutions to the problem: Firstly, sado-masochism can be pushed aside as a perversion and as such granted no place in the discussion of "normal" (female) sexuality; or, secondly, sado-masochism can be projected, by women, onto men, whereby heterosexual men would be categorized as sadists, homosexual men as masochists; or, thirdly, and readers will anticipate that the "correct" answer follows, we can allow ourselves to consider whether sado-masochism—the pleasure in inflicting and undergoing pain—is an element dwelling within "normal" individual sexuality, one element from the figures of the "dance."

When I say that the pleasure of inflicting and enduring pain dwells within "normal" sexuality, I do not mean that we are all frustrated flagellants, but rather that within "normal" sexual pleasure, in orgasm, lies a kind of pain that we must become "normal masochists" to seek and "normal sadists" to inflict. Orgasmic pleasure not only transports the feeling individual into heaven, it also wounds the individual. Here I am not referring to anything new but perhaps to something forgotten: Especially as women, and as part of the generation of the sexual revolution, we are accustomed to expecting from sexuality only the "gratification," the "release from tension," "the happiness," the "fun"—so that we lose sight of the threatening quality. In fact, as feminists, we have gone so far as to categorize any element of "threat" as a male attribute, as something women can and should rid themselves of, for example, through a penis-boycott. It throws light upon the kind of lesbian relationships within the women's movement that this projection was possible. A sexual relationship without "militance," without "pain-pleasure," is something artificial, a non-thing.

Our pseudo-hedonist culture seeks unceasingly to isolate passion from ecstasy, leaving only a safe pleasure in all its purity; thus, sexual delight becomes a light snack, the "dance" becomes the mere parody of a ritual. If the women's movement wants to keep its radicalism, it must stop working to domesticate sexuality. The movement must stop, in other words, giving credence to the idea that a sexual peace would break out as soon as men clear the field or, at the very least, as soon as they learn to respect the peaceful guidelines set by women.

The core of my thesis is that the "pain" exists within pleasure itself, that the wish to cause or suffer pain is not something allotted to one or the other sex but is rather something that threatens any individual who seeks or finds pleasure.

Sexuality is bisexual. That is, it exists in only one form, and, as such, it exists in each of us. We are unisexual, but that signifies much less about us individually as sexual beings than was previously assumed. I do not believe that sexual experience—the "dance"—differs in essence from sex to sex. Except for those sexual functions tied to motherhood, which are reserved for women, sexual excitement and pleasure are the same, no matter what the sex of the body feeling them. It is certainly one of the most evil accomplishments of patriarchy that by its narrow dictates it has so successfully cut off, for men, the path to pleasure through the figure of flight, and, for women, through the figure of venture and risk.

Our culture, which is characterized by a belief that anything and everything is possible, becomes surprisingly dogmatic on the question of opening up sex roles. However, I miss not only fantasy and experiment with regard to expanding traditional roles but also the ability to understand a certain role element in its double meaning and double effect. Our old friend, Freud, was a better dialectician here than we, who fancy ourselves so far advanced. "One might consider," he wrote, "characterizing femininity psychologically by the preference for passive goals." But, to avoid any misunderstanding: "Quite a bit of activity may be required in order to achieve a passive goal." [2]

What does all this have to do with the subject of rape? A rape is only very indirectly a sexual act. It is, as the women's movement has repeatedly and clearly shown, above all a demonstration of power, an attempt to *re*-establish the dominance of men by means of physical violence, in a manner similar to wife-beating. The execution of the act of violence with the sexual organ does not sexualize the act, but shows rather that the rapist hates and wishes to subjugate not only the woman but sexuality as well. Thus, a confusion of rape with the figures of "flight" and "attack" in sexual ritual would be impossible in this context. It is patriarchy which has always claimed for itself the mitigating circumstance of sexual ecstasy. For this cold contempt of women and sexuality it has earned every kick in its soft underbelly. We must define anew and for ourselves the boundary between violence and desire.

It is quite possible for a woman to say *no* when she means *yes*. It is just as possible for a man. Nor would either one need to dissemble; each might mean the *yes* in the *no*. For just as the double-character of sexual pleasure sometimes makes it hard to distinguish *yes* from *no* . . . , so pleasure may be heightened through reversal, deception, and confusion.

Nevertheless, a *no* arising from the circle of desire and fear can never be confused with the cry for help from a rape victim. The fact that patriarchy feels so damned secure in intentionally confusing the two is bitter evidence of the nature of the erotic culture it has created. We can perhaps take comfort from the fact that patriarchy has denounced above all its own sexuality. This leaves men with nothing left to defend. We could really begin anew.

Translated by Edith Hoshino Altbach

Notes

* Originally published as, Barbara Sichtermann, "Gewalt und Lust, der Tanz des sich Vorwagens," *Courage* Vol. 6 (December 1981), pp. 6–9. Translated and reprinted with permission. Portions of this text have been excerpted.

1. This is naturally not true of all feminists. There are exceptions, for example: Mona Winter in: *Kursbuch* 60, Berlin, 1980; Renate Schlesier in: *Weiblich-Männlich*, Berlin, 1980; Maria Wieden, in: *Aesthetik und Kommunikation*, Berlin, 1981.

2. Sigmund Freud, *Gesammelte Werke*, Vol. 15, Frankfurt, p. 123.

Part Four

Wo/Man Hating

In the texts in this section, institutionalized hostility toward women is confronted head-on. The authors probe beneath the surface to uncover unpleasant realities, and experiment with the language of journalism, popular culture, or advertising to unmask its assumptions. Humor and anger are sometimes uneasy companions on these pages.

Gabriele Goettle, coeditor of the critical journal *Die schwarze Botin*, wrote "Operating Procedures . . ." shortly after terrorist Ulrike Meinhof's death in prison. She uses the post-mortem examination as a framework for exploring Meinhof's threat and her usefulness—in death as in life—to the state and to politicos of the Right and Left. Jutta Schutting (1937–) is an Austrian writer who often bases her literary pieces on real events. In "Park Murder" she examines the ideology of newspaper crime reporting, asking whose interests are served by its sensationalism and pseudo-objectivity. Elfriede Jelinek (1946–), also an Austrian, is appalled by what she sees as the mass production of human beings in industrial society. All of her books are experiments in language and form. In her third novel, excerpted here, she focuses on working-class people and the myths of love and a better future that alienate the women from their actual, concrete experiences. West German author Elisabeth Alexander (1932–) often deliberately sets out to shock her readers. In the texts included here, she uses surrealism and parody to express her view of manipulative behavior in marriage and the manipulation of women by advertising.

13. Operating Procedures for Future-Oriented Women*

Gabriele Goettle

This essay begins with the autopsy performed on Ulrike Meinhof as a final "ritual" of revenge taken by the state. But the author also finds unseemly the willingness of those on the Left (as well as the Right) to use her life and death to validate or vindicate their own ideology. Rather than join in the "dissection" this essay looks at how Ulrike Meinhof's dedication to "consistent action" in the fight against injustice forced her from each "safe refuge" in her life—as student, radical, housewife and mother, journalist, and anarchist.

Messrs. Rauschke and Mallack, state court coroners, put on their surgical gloves at eleven o'clock on a Sunday morning and, considering the hour and the weekend tranquility, went to work with astonishing thoroughness. They had been mandated by the state to determine the cause of the deceased woman's death.

The alleged suicide victim's body bore traces of her past life as a woman: a scar from a caesarean section, stretchmarks on breast and abdominal tissue, and other ordinary deformation processes that women are exposed to through pregnancy and childbirth.

The deceased was no stranger to these gentlemen, for she had attained a degree of celebrity appropriate to the violence she personified during her lifetime. Her transgressions against the social system, to which the two gentlemen belong, were of such consequence that she became dangerous to the system. It was no longer a question of suppressing ordinary adolescent recalcitrance. Rather, it was a woman's abnormal criminality, which had become impossible to predict and had to be eliminated. Her arrest enabled the state to block her activities but not to obliterate the myth surrounding her.

The obscene effect of the unclothed body was as great as the contradiction between the lifeless body's unresisting passivity and the myth of the woman's former aggressive violence. The body's lifelessness also revealed its flaws. These flaws, along with the overall abnormal and hostile behavior pattern of her life, legitimize and facilitate righteous civic indignation. What passed through the gentlemen's heads and fingers as they opened up and carved the dead body of this forty-one-year old woman can easily be guessed from their "prejudicial" position as members of the society under attack. While the gentlemen are occupied, let us give some thought to how this woman came to be placed at their disposal. We can dispense with the factual material since it has meanwhile become sufficiently notorious. Nor are we primarily interested in some things she once did for the women's movement, or in whether she ever did anything at all that we could, if need be, feel solidarity with. We have noticed that panic broke out on all sides when she was spoken about, a panic which can be traced to the fact that no one wanted anything to do with her. After her death some people made efforts to sympathize with her as far as their own political understanding would allow ("she had a lot of good qualities too") or—and this behavior was especially popular among leftists—one seized the opportunity to use her death as blatant proof of how "class justice systematically annihilates its opponents." Not for a moment did those making this point neglect to define the substance of their own opposition, setting it apart from other, destructive kinds. Whatever could possibly be dissected out of her arrest and death for the ideologies of various groups has been dissected out. The Right was able to reassure itself of its all-encompassing power that no anarchist movement could undermine. The Left crowds together under the decoratively bleeding Damoclean sword to call attention more impressively to its own endangered existence. For the deceased, consistent action lent the Damoclean sword potential energy, while the leftists in the airless space of their political solitude scarcely even worry about ending their state of suspension.

What is so monstrous about the deceased is that she drew conclusions from the impossibility of appeal and turned to other forms of "taking a stand on things." The magical call to "abolish paragraph 218," the bearing of talismanic posters similarly inscribed, and the notion of the power of the people to decide will necessarily lead at some point to the realization that these activities are absurd in the face of the "public's" interests. To conclude that it might be more effective to remove some of the legislators' procreative equipment as a prophylactic measure may make more sense, but it is precisely this logic that occasions discomfort. For consistent action is laid low by one's having to recognize consequences for oneself. It means giving up all the situations and material things that do still help one to half-way enjoy life; it means isolation and rejection of stabilizing love-relationships. A consistent subject is progressive, and moves farther and farther away from the meaning of concrete reality, because it no longer sees this reality as binding. In so doing, it changes, and is no longer deterred even by imprisonment, loss of health, or death because it has nothing except its consistency.

For the consistent subject, absolute isolation becomes the most problematic thing; it can occur even when there is a group of subjects acting together. Accordingly, solitary confinement would mean only that the prisoner was isolated from the opportunity to act consistently, which would already be enough to kill her.

The point we want to make can have nothing to do with weaseling out of our own fear of consistent action as soon as the thought of it becomes unpleasant. Rather, we are trying to put our finger on the lie which, on the one hand, strangles us in hopeless rage, but on the other hand makes life very much worth living.

For the deceased, it was not possible to come to terms with things in such a way that at least her existence and survival could be ensured in good company and with vociferous verbal protest. As a woman, she rehearsed all the roles prescribed for her. She was lover, student, wife, mother, housewife; she emancipated herself as a journalist, in her marriage bed, from her husband, from motherhood. And everything up to that point remained within the limits on the range of female development. What she did beyond that was not compatible with either her role as a woman or the interests of the German nation. So she was conjectured to have brain tumors and any number of other idiotic things. After her last role, as emancipated leftist, she became herself. As an anarchist who was no longer mother, lover, or leftist, her only possibility for self-realization was via her boundless hatred. Having lost each and every other safe refuge, she pursued self-realization all the way to loss of life. The representatives of the society she had to die of, because she couldn't live in it, cannot forgive her for this dying because it is the subject's final anarchistic step. As they "examine" the dead woman, they have no inkling either that the cause of death should be sought outside of the woman's body or that they themselves represent those who were the cause of death. The two incisive gentlemen wielded their scalpels so diligently that the next coroner could not even find the scar from the C-section on the deceased woman's body.

The autopsy here appears as a ritual of society's revenge. After psychic destruction came death, and the autopsy is the sequel to that destruction, hyena-like, to the point of making the body unrecognizable.

[Translator's note: This article was written on 5 July 1976. The author later added a postscript, citing an article published in a Frankfurt newspaper on 17 August 1976, which suggested that Ulrike Meinhof had not committed suicide but had been sexually assaulted and strangled. Goettle wrote: "Even the murder of Ms. Meinhof during a sexual attack could not make the image of reform-fascism in Germany . . . clearer than it is already." She concluded by quoting an article by Susan Sontag, "Men as Colonizers, Women as Aborigines" (1973), in which Sontag described fascism as the "normal" disposition of political systems in modern industrial society, and as the "natural" realization of patriarchal values.]

Translated by Jeanette Clausen

Notes

* German original: Gabriele Goettle, "Schnittmuster für zukunftsorientierte Frauen," *Die schwarze Botin* no. 1 (1976), pp. 5–8. Translated and reprinted with permission.

14. Park Murder*

Jutta Schutting

In this parody of journalistic writing, Schutting casts a critical eye on the reporting of violent crime. Zealous attention to detail not only masks the incompetence of "experts" and erases the young female victim, but also provides free advertising for a pen manufacturer, seemingly precipitating the merger of two companies. Many of the texts in the collection from which this is taken could be characterized as literary crime stories.

as was already reported in the morning edition, an ink pen with the brand name Altomonte was secured just after 12:40 P.M. in the immediate vicinity of the horribly mutilated body of a seven-year-old schoolgirl discovered behind a bush yesterday noon. The ink pen in question, the latest model in Altomonte's line, is called "Prestige 12c" (color: silver gray), and not, as was mistakenly reported on radio and TV, the model "Prestige 12b" (also silver gray) advertised in the fall catalogue of the aforementioned firm. The police are requesting pertinent information, since there is reason to believe that the murderer lost possession of his ink pen directly before or after the crime.

Park murder—police puzzled

the homicide bureau in charge of the murder case of the girl in ———park is checking reports and calls made by the public in response to an appeal by the police concerning an Altomonte ink pen "Prestige 12c" which was found in the vicinity of the body. (As reported, the body of a gruesomely murdered schoolgirl was discovered behind a bush at the park entrance by passers-by.) The homicide bureau, according to statements made in a press conference held this noon, has not yet made any headway. The reason for this lack of progress is a change in the manufacture and marketing of these two models, for mass production of the now exclusively custom-made "Prestige 12b" will not begin until next year. Furthermore, in the course of Altomonte's democratization policy which was initiated by the Assistant President (see our interview with the company's works council spokesman), the model "Prestige 12c," despite its

120

relatively high price, has become even more popular among the upper-middle-class and upwardly mobile working-class market. (The manager of the Altomonte affiliate nearest the site of the bloody crime confirmed this trend to our correspondent.) The police's work on this case has been complicated by the fact that this new trend towards more luxurious models had not been taken into account earlier. We repeat the appeal made to the public over radio and TV that each of our readers check any prospective tips for accuracy by first consulting the fall catalogue. (Altomonte catalogues can be found in leading stationery stores. We are including reproductions of ten of the most well-known variants in the Altomonte line in a supplement to our morning edition.)

Park Murder—Is our police force incompetent?

homicide's examination of the Altomonte ink pen has thus far not yielded the expected results. (The pen was found by unsuspecting strollers in the vicinity of the now famous schoolgirl who was murdered in an especially brutal manner.) Owing to the characteristic working of the material of the pen (finely hammered silver, editor's note), the fingerprints were said to have smudged. The small scratch on the cap of the ink pen, prematurely interpreted by detectives as evidence of the unfortunate victim's struggle against her murderer (who still roams at large), now seems to have resulted from the snow chains of a truck which had turned around in the park entrance. An ink pen of the same type put at the police's disposal for tests (as our readers know, it is the model "Prestige 12c"), has proven— even in laboratory tests with a vise—to be surprisingly resistant, thanks to its special "temper," as it is called in technical language. Out of sympathy for the poor parents and the patent rights protection law, the results of spectroscopic tests will probably be disclosed only insofar as they are relevant to a solution of the crime.

Park Murder—Results of the Autopsy

directly after the court-appointed coroner had released the corpse of the little schoolgirl for burial, details of the long-awaited examination were announced: thanks to the company's top-secret special processing of the refined platinum tip on the "Prestige 12c" and other Altomonte pens, it cannot even be estimated whether the "Altomonte" has been previously used or if so for how long. A second expert examination supported by comparative data from spectrum tests confirms the "affidavit" of quality affixed to every product released or tested for the market, so that not even the year of manufacture can be ascertained.

Park Murder—Valuable Clues?

as we have just learned, shreds of skin the size of a child's fingernail as well as an impression of a pencil sharpener were discovered by an alert passer-by in the vicinity of the crime committed on the fourteenth of the month. The police are still waiting for test results. The experts are divided over the question as to whether they are dealing with traces of the child's desperate struggle or whether these are shreds of skin from the sex offender. One consultant told our staff member that in his opinion the shreds of skin—if indeed they come from the murderer—pointed to venereal disease. See the following article for details of the burial of the victim.

Park Murder—Parents tried by sorrow

directly after the well-attended burial of the murder victim whose case has enjoyed wide interest (the corpse of a brutally murdered girl was discovered on the fourteenth of this month in the vicinity of the "Prestige" ink pen—editor's note), the new general manager of the firms Altomonte and Rainbow-Goldpheasant (which merged today in a festive ceremony during the noon hour) promised in a moving speech to present the sorrow-laden parents with next fall's new ink pen model "Renommee." Moreover, the director declared on behalf of his famous company that this same firm was prepared to exchange the ink pen "Prestige 12c," which was lost (or found, as the case may be) at the scene of the crime, for a brand new pen, even if the parents couldn't produce proof of a guarantee, and that they were prepared to do so although X-ray control checks of each product excluded the possibility of any defects in material.

Park Murder—A New Lead?

court medical tests of the bright red, dark red, and red-orange veined "shreds of skin" discovered under a park bench in the vicinity of the murder on June fourteenth, in what now has made local history under the name "Altomonte Park," have revealed, as the alert twenty-one-year-old employee who discovered them promptly and correctly surmised, that these "shreds" are paper-thin shavings from the colored pencils "Cherry," "Rose" and "Tangerine" (grade 13/4 hardness, nonsmearing designed for children, from the colored pencil line "Rainbow Palette" made by the well-known firm Gold-pheasant-Altomonte; they were sharpened with a "Precision" pencil-sharpener made by the firm Rainbow-Goldpheasant, now Altomonte-Goldpheasant, Inc.).

Park Murder—Parents Testify

the parents of the victim who was buried in an emotional ceremony (see the noon edition for our report of the burial) concurred in stating that, like most children in her school class, their child had used colored pencils from the "Rainbow Palette" series ever since first grade (please compare the photos on the opposite page; right—at her desk, left—in the bushes). As far as they knew, the parents sobbed, she used only those pencils, and does not yet own—or rather did not own, they continued sobbing, a "Precision" pencil sharpener. In her modest way the child had only once requested a pencil sharpener, and both parents had forgotten to fulfill this last wish. Now they realized why the tot had sometimes wanted to wait till school to sharpen her colored pencils, which, in spite of their durability, naturally had to be sharpened now and then. (The mother of the victim's erstwhile playmate, the well-known painter A.B., confirmed in a phone call to our staff that before her drawing class, the victim used to like to borrow the "Precision" sharpener owned by her little Susie.)

Park Murder—Case about to break?

a comparative examination yesterday of the quietly exhumed victim and her pencil drawing—referred to by the poor father as a "consoling memory" of the autumn days and sunsets shared with her parents—has revealed beyond a doubt that murderer and murderee used the same colored pencils, but sharpened them with two different sharpening instruments. Thus, the wood shavings found under the bench in Altomonte Park, as it is called, point to some preparatory activity. A child psychologist, who provided our staff with a colored drawing by the unfortunate child (see the full-colored reproduction in the next weekend edition), gave a psychological explanation of the particular effect of the colors in the drawing relative to the child's happy disposition, which itself was in turn related to the cheerful illuminative power of the "Rainbow Palette" colored pencils.

Park Murder—Solved

the murderer of the brutally slain schoolgirl was apprehended this past night thanks to the alertness of a salesperson. Unaware of the new cartridge system now used in the Altomonte ink pen of the firm Altomonte-Goldpheasant, the man, as reported in the morning edition, asked for a refill cartridge for the ink pen "Prestige 12c" (and not, as incorrectly reported, "Prestige 12b"). One day previous to the murder, he had stolen the pen from the refectory of the well-known and respected working people's parson.

Park Murderer Cross-examined—Confession!

having gone down in the annals of the police as the "Colored Pencil Murderer," Mr. ———, in custody since yesterday, made the following confession in a preliminary questioning (as we reported in the late evening edition, Mr. ———, who has been feeble-minded since mid-childhood, had a colored pencil, then not yet safe for children, rammed into his head by a schoolmate during a recess scuffle.). While he was sitting on the park bench closest to the bushes where the famous Altomonte pen was secured, he had by chance seen the so gruesomely murdered tot sorting thirty "Rainbow Palette" colored pencils in the order in which they were illustrated on the box cover. When she had the rainbow assembled, he asked to have all the colored pencils shown to him, since as a child he had never owned such beautiful pencils and besides, had had only two kinds of green—in any case not *four* kinds of blue. When he saw that the pencils were not sharpened very well, and when he offered to "Precision" them (to sharpen them, ed. note), she said, however, that she didn't have a "Precision" (pencil sharpener of a well-known firm). He didn't believe her, since her clothes were neither worn nor dirty. In spite of her lie—as he interpreted it—he pulled out his own "Precision" and sharpened one pencil after another, which thereupon had gleamed even more cheerfully. Since he thought each one more beautiful than the last, but knew she wouldn't have been willing to give him even one of them, he used each one several times—first the dark yellow one ("Eggyolk"), then the dark green one ("Pine"), and finally the bright brown one ("Rare Earth"), then the dark brown one ("Humus"), and last of all the bright blue one ("Sky") and the gleaming white one ("Innocence").

Park Murder, The Murderer's Tragedy

in an examination by the psychiatrist, the "Rainbow Murderer" explained that he had thrown away the ink pen "Prestige 12c" (a product of the Altomonte Firm, ed. note!) directly after the "Colored Pencil Murder," since he thought that "only very rich folks" owned "Prestige" pens, and he didn't want to be caught. When he was assured that his victim actually didn't own a "Precision" brand pencil sharpener, he burst into tears and kept repeating his barely intelligible promise that, even though he hadn't broken the points of her colored pencils, he would buy the child a "Precision" sharpener, since they didn't cost much.

Translated by Naomi Stephan

Notes

* German original: Jutta Schutting, "Parkmord," *Parkmord*, Salzburg: Residenz Verlag, 1975, pp. 5–13. Translated and reprinted with permission.

15. take paula, for example*

Elfriede Jelinek

This excerpt from Die Liebhaberinnen *(Women as Lovers) introduces paula, one of the novel's two main female characters. Jelinek concentrates on contradictions between the women's dreams of love and a better future and the grim reality of the "natural cycle" that awaits them. Characteristic of her analytical style are repetition and variation of clichés, and abrupt reversals of conventional logic to unmask the myths: "life" is death; "love" is hatred and contempt.*

take paula, for example

take paula, for example. she's a country girl. country life has kept her in check up to now—just like her sisters erika and renate, who are married. you can write those two off. it's just like they didn't exist. with paula it's a different story; she's the youngest kid and full of life. she's fifteen years old. by now she's old enough to decide for herself what she'd like to be—housewife or salesgirl. salesgirl or housewife. all the girls her age who are as old as she is are old enough to decide for themselves what they'd like to be. grammar school is over, the men in the village are either lumberers or learning a trade as carpenter, electrician, plumber, mason, or working in the factory. or, they're trying their hand as carpenter, electrician, plumber, mason or factory worker and then they'll go into lumbering anyway. the girls will become their wives. forest rangers are higher on the scale. forest rangers are always brought in from outside. there aren't any teachers or clergy, the village hasn't got a church or a school. the grocery store manager has also been brought in from outside, because its a high-powered job requiring brains. three women and girls from the village are regularly employed under him, plus a female trainee from the village. the women stay salesgirls or assistant salesgirls until they marry. once they're married off, their selling days are over, then they've been sold too, and the next salesgirl can take their place and go on selling. the exchange is smooth and fast.

thus a natural cycle has come about over the years: being born, starting work, getting married, stopping work, having a daughter, housewife or salesgirl, usually a housewife. daughter takes over, mother kicks the bucket, daughter's married off, gets out, jumps from the running board, bears the next daughter in turn. the grocery store dispenses the natural cycle of nature. the fruits and vegetables reflect the seasons and human life in its various forms. in the single display table you can see the alert faces of its salesgirls, gathered here to wait for marriage and life. but marriage always comes alone, without life. a married woman will as good as never work in the store, except if her husband happens to be out of work or badly injured. he's always an alcoholic.

his job as lumberer is difficult and dangerous. some men never return alive from it. that's why they really enjoy their lives as long as they're young. from age thirteen on no girl is safe around them. the general competition begins, wild oats are sown, and the whole village reels from the process. the process reverberates throughout the valley.

at the end of their youth the youngbloods take hardworking, thrifty wives. end of youth, beginning of age.

for the woman end of life and beginning of childbearing. whereas the men mature nicely, begin to age and do full justice to alcohol— it's supposed to fortify them and prevent cancer—the death throes of their women often last for years and years—often even long enough for them to witness the death throes of their daughters. the women begin hating their daughters and want them to die as quickly as possible, just like they did. therefore: high time for a husband!

sometimes a daughter doesn't want to die as fast as she should. she'd rather stay on as salesgirl for one or two years and live! yes live! in rare cases she'd even like to be a salesgirl in the county seat where people have different professions such as priest, teacher, factory worker, plumber, carpenter, locksmith, also watchmaker, baker, butcher! and hog farmer! and lots lots more. lots more hope for a life in a nicer future.

but it isn't easy to hang on to a man with a better future. better jobs have more to offer, too. that's why these jobs can pressure you to do it. but, you shouldn't do it anyway, because a better job will demand something even better and then curtains. sometimes an unskilled lumberer will wait. a better job will never wait. hardly any woman's ever returned from that kind of situation except on a visit and with a bastard son minus father.

a dwindling number of these women'll sometimes come to visit, to show ma and pa the kids, and to show how well off they are. her husband behaves, gives her all his money and only drinks a little, the kitchen's real new, the vacuum cleaner's new, the curtains are new, ditto for the corner table, and the t.v.'s new and the new couch is new and the new stove is used, sure, but it's just like new and the floor's scuffed, but polished—just like new, and the daughter's as good as new, but soon she'll be a salesgirl and age rapidly and be used. but why shouldn't the daughter be used up if the mother is used up too? the daughter's got to be used quickly, she really needs using. fork over new and better ones because there are preachers, teachers, factory workers, plumbers, carpenters, locksmiths, watchmakers, butchers! and hog farmers! and many more, etc. all of them constantly need women and make use of them too. but they personally wouldn't want to buy a used woman and then go on using her. nope. that's the tricky part. where do you get unused women if women are constantly being used up? there isn't any prostitution; but there are a lot of illegitimate kids. that woman. she shouldn't have done it, but she did. actually, it was done to her, he really gave it to her good. there she is, she has to do the work herself—even the work the husband normally does, and the kid stays at her grandmother's, who hates both that goddammotherand-kid. used women are seldom taken and then only by the original user. their whole lives they'll have to listen to things like: if i hadn't married you, no one else would have, and you would've had to see where the money for your kid came from. at the last minute i took you anyway, and you can take my money after i've taken out money for booze first. then in exchange i can take you without a fuss as often as i want, but i'm going to watch out nobody lays hands on our daughter illegally and uses her before marriage, so she won't turn out like her mother who got taken BEFOREHAND.

she's going to wait until somebody takes her and then she'll let somebody take her—but only afterwards. if she lets herself get laid before, then she'll be lucky if anyone will want her at all. and our daughter can thank her lucky stars that she's got a father like me.

awful, this slow dying. the man and the women fade away in like manner, the husband still enjoys some variety in the process. he watches his wife like a hawk. he watches her die. from the inside, the wife keeps an eye on her husband, female guests in the summer, her daughter, and the household money, which isn't supposed to be boozed away. and from the outside, the husband watches his wife, the male guests in the summer, the daughter and the household money, so he can siphon some of it off for boozing. each fades out of the other's life. and the daughter can hardly wait to begin the slow process of dying herself. her parents start buying for her death in advance: linen, hand towels, dish towels and a used refrigerator. then at least she'll be dead, but fresh.

and what will become of paula? salesgirl or housewife? above all, please, let's not forget paula! she's at stake here, after all. what's with paula? an early death or a late one? or maybe she won't even get started with life. death right away? can't wait, then it'll be too late, a kid'll be there, and her mother dies straightaway instead of after the wedding. NO! you see, paula'd like to study tailoring. there's never ever been a girl in the village who wanted to STUDY something. no good will come of it. her mother asks: wouldn't you really like to be a salesgirl so you can meet someone or be a housewife when you have already met someone?

her mother says: paula, you've GOT to become a salesgirl or a housewife. paula answers: there's no opening for a salesgirl trainee. her mother says: then stay at home, paula, and be a housewife and help me with the housework and in the barn and wait on your father like i do and wait on your brother too when he comes home from work. why should you have it better than me, i was never anything better than my mother, who was a housewife. back then there was no such thing as salesgirls in our area and my father would've beaten me if there had been any.

. . . .

the bad example of paula goes on

. . . .

like all women, paula dreams of love.

all women, paula too, dream of love.

many of her former school friends, many of her present coworkers dream of it too, only each of them believes firmly that she alone will have it.

during sales as a salesgirl (that top profession) love has the chance and the opportunity to come in a hundred times a day. but all that comes in are housewives with children, never love. the women coming in who did have love once, way back, despise and pity the salesgirls, because they have to work and can't enjoy the beautiful fruits of love, that is, children and the household money that comes from their husbands—the greater part of which usually goes back to him. the protected women despise the unprotected ones.

and the salesgirls hate the housewives back for no longer having to deal with these problems, whereas the salesgirls are in the tough world of competition. instead of glamorous furniture they have to invest in nylons, sweaters and mini-skirts.

yes, it's expensive!

there's a general atmosphere of hatred in the village, which is spreading continually, infesting everything. it'll stop at nothing. the women don't see their common interests, just their differences. those women who have gotten something better because of their physical advantage want to hold on to it and keep it from the others. the others want to take it away from them or something even better. hatred and contempt are everywhere.

the foundation for such hatred and contempt is laid in school. that paula ever hit on the idea of comparing love with flowers, buds, grass and herbs comes from her schooling.

the magazines she likes to read are responsible for her associating love with passion. paula has heard the word sexuality already, but hasn't quite understood it.

that love has solely to do with work is something no one likes to admit. paula can change a baby's diapers and feed it in her sleep. but paula doesn't know how you prevent a pregnancy.

paula could tell you in her sleep that feeling is the only important thing.

paula is waiting to be picked. that's the important thing. it's important to be picked by the right guy.

paula has never learned to chose for herself, to determine anything for herself. paula experiences everything in the passive voice, not in the active voice. the most that paula has learned is that she can say no sometime but you shouldn't say no too often, because otherwise you've said one too many no's, and happiness will pass on by in the future and not call again.

paula sometimes goes dancing when there's a party. at the party paula's sometimes led away into the woods again by a drunk. no one is supposed to see it because it would reduce her market value to absolutely zero.

in the woods, paula will be touched on her breast or even worse between her legs or on her ass.

paula has learned to size up the one who grabs her between the legs: is it someone with a future or without.

is he someone with a future or a work horse?

if he's a work horse he won't figure in on paula's future. paula's brain has learned to work like a computer. here's the result: married, two children.

next step: push him away, yell, screech, which sometimes is followed by the drunken seducer staggering, reeling and falling over.

sometimes he falls over, leaves her alone and sleeps it off.

sometimes the guy in question is brutal and coarse.

succumbing without thinking, to love when it knocks, isn't enough. you've got to consider your later life which occasionally might follow.

you have to consider the future which lies before you.

the future, that's always the other guy, that always comes from some other guy. the future descends on you like hail. love, if at all, like a storm. at worst not at all. the sewing business is up to you.

the sewing business is up to you.

so, when a guy grabs paula, she starts calculating. during it she often experiences an uncalculated loathing. long, long live loathing! but paula suppresses this feeling immediately. let's hope paula for all her enthusiasm won't accidentally suppress love, too!

paula learned quite early to view her body—and what happens to it—as something which happens to somebody else—to an auxiliary body, so to speak, to an auxiliary paula.

all the material from paula's dreams, all the tenderness happens to paula's main body. her father's beatings happen to her auxiliary body. her mother, who never learned to invent an auxiliary body, has to take everything with her main body. that's why it's gotten so used up and worn out so fast.

you have to know how to help yourself. you have to be able to help yourself! if you can't do anything besides work, if you are constantly done to, then you've got to know how to help yourself. when the women speak about their men, they simply say: mine, MINE nothing else. not my husband, just mine. to a stranger you might say: my spouse—to a local you say: mine. paula observes a victorious smile when her mother or sister say: mine. the only opportunity for the loser to have a victorious smile on her lips.

she hopes that she'll be able to say "mine" to someone. paula never says "my work" about her sewing job. paula never says "mine" about her work. not even inwardly. work, that's something separate from you; work is more a duty and happens to your auxiliary body. love is pure joy, a relief, and therefore it happens to your main body.

work, even if you like to do it, is something to be suffered. in spite of all her love of sewing, paula has learned that work is a burden, something which puts love off rather than attracting it.

only a cement mixer can create order in paula's head now. order in all the physical love and in all the spiritual love for actresses, pop singers and t.v. stars.

paula registers things, but they don't filter through. like a sponge which is never wrung out. like a sponge which is soaked, so that anything additional more or less casually runs off. how's paula supposed to learn anything?

through experience, of course.

which is the best teacher.

Translated by Naomi Stephan

Notes

* German original: Elfriede Jelinek, "am beispiel paula," *Die Liebhaberinnen*, Reinbek bei Hamburg: Rowohlt, 1977, pp. 13–26 (excerpts). Translated and reprinted with permission.

16. A Bowlful of Marriage

Elisabeth Alexander

This story is one of many in the collection The Woman Who Laughed *in which Alexander depicts a rancorous battle of the sexes. As the collection's title suggests, the woman generally gets "the last laugh," as here. This text stands out among the others in its use of surrealism, but the pettiness and vindictiveness of the marriage partners and the mocking tone are typical for the author.*

Mister Charles Weddington knew perfectly well that he had a miserable body. And when he stopped to think about it, a miserable mind, too. But did that prevent him from leading his life like a man of esteem?

When he wanted to, he could make his body just small enough to be able to play hide-and-seek in the egg-timer right before breakfast. He enjoyed it when Victoria, the wife betrothed to him by Reverend Homestone, looked for him. He liked diving into the soft sand, and it amused him that he could interrupt the rhythmical flow of the sand. When, again unobserved, he climbed out and dutifully took his seat at the table, promptly opening the paper to the comics, Victoria would nag, because she hadn't seen her Charles until just now.

Obviously, the eggs were too hard again. Here he expressly asked for tender soft-boiled eggs in the morning. And what did Victoria offer him? Hard, solid eggs, which he refused, and did so just as emphatically as his husbandly rights would allow.

Mister Charles Weddington also knew perfectly well that a few points were still missing from the list of rights he was entitled to. Whenever he thought, as he was doing just now at breakfast, about his wealth of rights, he would slurp his cereal down with great pleasure. Victoria had stopped her nagging and dabbed first at one eye, then the other, with her napkin. They had the same breakfast every Sunday. She asked him to pass the marmalade. One more piece of raisin bread and her fat would become overbearing, Charles remarked. Reverend Homestone, with whom she had remained on friendly terms since the day of the wedding, knew how to guide her across the quotidian cliffs of marriage with marvelous delicacy.

The tea had the same aroma as the tea Mister Charles Weddington's grandmother used to make. Victoria was good at brewing tea. She knew just how to handle the water and the right amount of milk to add. She nibbled on the hard eggs, for somebody had to eat them, and Mister Charles Weddington would never offer his services as a garbage can.

At any rate, Reverend Homestone was not of the opinion that Victoria had a miserable body. At least she had a discreet body, and that was what the church needed, discreet bodies. At church, too, Mister Charles Weddington could make his body small enough to be able to slip in amongst the coins without ever getting caught by the sexton's meaty fingers.

Undiminished, Mister Charles Weddington first finished reading his comics before once again becoming really aware that he did have a wife to call his own. it was so aggravating, having to read the comic right under her eyes. Nonetheless he had pulled himself together enough to let out his laughter without embarrassment. What were his comics to Victoria? Let her read that new Bible Reverend Homestone had brought her as Sunday compensation.

By now Victoria had gotten to the point of regarding Mister Charles Weddington as superfluous. But when she stopped to think about it, she had intended ever since their wedding day to regard Mister Charles Weddington as superfluous. Nancy, a distant cousin of the Reverend, came over in the afternoons. Victoria had often wondered how it happened that Reverend Homestone had so many distant cousins. Nancy was the eleventh distant cousin who came over in the afternoon. Sometimes Reverend Homestone came too, but usually he had to go over the latest marriage announcements with one of the daughters of the congregation.

Victoria couldn't get up from the table yet because she had to sit through Mister Charles Weddington's pipe smoking. He always smoked with particular pleasure in her presence when the comics had left him in a good mood. Victoria always thought what a worthless arrangement it was that prohibited her from chopping Mister Charles Weddington's pipe collection to bits. The pipe smoke seemed to affect him adversely, for he started coughing every time he lit up.

Reverend Homestone never subjected her to that kind of insult. He didn't own a single pipe. But with him she experienced enormous cigars whose smell and smoke went pleasantly to her head. And if Mister Charles Weddington had treated his wife with the same consideration he gave to filling his pipe, Victoria wouldn't have had to dab at her eyes so often.

His muscles tensed as he packed his pipe, and Victoria didn't have to tax her imagination much to see him as a new comic strip character.

She thought about Reverend Homestone and poured the rest of the tea into Mister Charles Weddington's thinning hair. Mister Charles Weddington's rage was more astonished than genuine; in his irritation he made his body just small enough to be able to hide in the bowlful of tobacco.

Victoria didn't feel like looking for him, nor did it bother her fingers that the tobacco was so recalcitrant. She packed the bowl of Mister Charles Weddington's Sunday pipe good and solid. Even though she wasn't an experienced pipe smoker, Victoria enjoyed the miserable aroma of Mister Charles Weddington.

Translated by Jeanette Clausen

Notes

* German original: Elisabeth Alexander, "Ein Häufchen Ehe," *Die Frau, die lachte. Bürgerliche Texte,* Düsseldorf: Erb Verlag, 1978 (2nd, revised edition), pp. 14–17. Translated and reprinted with permission.

17. Commercial Message*

Elisabeth Alexander

In this parody of a television commercial, Alexander spells out some assumptions underlying the marketing of "feminist hygiene" products. She claims to have gotten the idea for this piece from an American advertisement for an elbow cream. Here, a critique of sexist ideology comes through more clearly than in other texts in the same collection.

And for you ladies, we have just what you need: a soothing emollient lotion for your navel. Were you unaware that the navel can exude a foul, unappetizing odor? That all too often it comes to play the vexing role of the body's little wastebasket?

The lotion isn't expensive. You can get it at your favorite drugstore; in the near future it's sure to be available at leading department stores as well. You must take care of your navel, you know. Men don't like it when a woman's navel stinks.

Perhaps you've seen to everything else—applied eyeshadow correctly, a subtle yet effective touch of feminine deodorant spray—but under no circumstance can you neglect the navel. The remains of your dirty bath water are likely to settle there, and we can assume that a grain of sperm has inadvertently crept in. You see, all these things contribute to offensive navel odor.

This navel odor is in no way comparable to the smell of a man's sweaty feet, which is a perfectly natural odor. However, failure to use our lotion causes the reeking navel to become an affront. Consider, if you will, that you are only a woman after all, a mere whim of nature, and thus, far more likely to stink.

You realize, of course, that men are so steadfast, so odorless, so flawless. And another thing which makes them special is their highly developed visual craving; their eyes never see enough. Surely you don't want to risk slighting a man's nose by forcing your stinking navel on him! You mustn't do that. You alone have responsibility for men; you carry it around with you in your breasts. And if these breasts fail to penetrate the male subconscious, your ideas will be utterly useless.

For a man wants them odor-free. Your ideas play virtually no role at all. Unless by chance he finds himself obliged to live with them

137

after a number of years, at which time he'll insist on calling them mutual ideas. Though, you may be sure, any conversation with him will end at the first faint hint of criticism you might be forward enough to make. And all this in addition to your susceptibility to offensive odors.

So never, never let yourself stink. And grant him everything. Put what he wants in bed, on his plate, in the closets, on the back seat. And consider well: he's right, he always knows best, and only he knows how much you can stink, and how dangerous your body odor is to his penis. Indeed, it literally forces him to turn to others now and then, others who have applied a tempting lotion to their navels.

The male has no body odor. On him, all these things are natural. All a man needs is soap, toothpaste and shaving equipment. Even after-shave lotions are superfluous. He doesn't really need them.

Smelling bad is permissible, to be sure, but only for the male. Picking one's nose while reading the newspaper or visiting relatives is permissible. But not for you. It looks so unsanitary on a woman. Don't scratch yourself, either. Fortunately, you don't have testicles that itch and need rubbing when you're out on the sidewalk or listening to a lecture on environmental pollution. Even if you suddenly are seized by an anal irritation, please control yourself; leave this scratching to men too, both at home and in public.

And be glad that men aren't embarrassed to relieve you of these distressing necessities. You need aspire only and solely to an odorless love life, be it at the office, in your car, on the lawn or on the beach, anywhere, at home, even watching TV. Speaking of TV, that brings me once again to our soothing emollient navel lotion. Take our advice, do yourself a favor, and buy this well-meaning lotion. Give yourself a lift by living this commercial message. Be a cover girl. Make yourself useful to men by soothing away odor in true videoland style.

One more thing. Please don't delay. Eliminate your disgusting navel right away—tomorrow, or better yet today, now. And don't oppress your aberrant species. Turn your attention instead to safe-guarding your odor complex. Contribute to a prosperous economy through an odor-free navel. And in short, learn to understand the detrimental and asocial effect your reeking navel can have on the public. Buy it now, the soothing emollient lotion for your one and only navel.

Translated by Jeanette Clausen

Notes

* German original: Elisabeth Alexander, "Werbung," *Die Frau, die lachte. Bürgerliche Texte,* Düsseldorf: Erb Verlag, 1978 (2nd, revised edition), pp. 23–25. Translated and reprinted with permission.

Part Five

Reportage and Essay

This section could be considered a dialogue among women who probably would never meet us or each other in real life: women prisoners; foreign workers and other women employed in the FRG; a single mother employed as a waitress in the GDR. An essay by GDR author Christa Wolf gives her perspective on feminism and the changing roles of women in her country.

The texts show some of the different forms documentary literature about women has taken in the two Germanies. Marianne Herzog, radical journalist and former factory worker, based her reports in *From Hand to Mouth* on personal experience and interviews; she speaks for many women workers, in solidarity with them. The collection *Dear Colleague* was a project of the Berlin workshop Werkkreis Literatur der Arbeitswelt (Collective Literature of the Working World), which promotes working-class literature. The texts in *Dear Colleague* were written by the women workers themselves, in collaboration with members of the collective. The piece "A Measure Taken" reads almost like a short story, quite different from the diary-like form of "Christmastime at Findus." Christa Wolf's essay "In Touch" is at once introduction and eulogy to her friend and colleague Maxie Wander, who died before *Guten Morgen, du Schöne* could be published. Wolf's praise of Wander's open-ended, trust-inspiring, yet bold interviewing style is confirmed by the interview with Ruth B. Through Ruth's reactions during the conversation, we see Wander allowing her own involvement in the process to show through, rather than obliterating it.

The efforts of writers such as Wander and Herzog, and groups such as the Berlin workshop, have helped give a voice to women who would otherwise remain silent. The women's stories are interesting in view of Werlhof's essay on the "housewife-ization" of work (section VIII).

141

18. From Hand to Mouth*

Marianne Herzog

Marianne Herzog, formerly of the GDR, worked for some years doing piecework in West German factories. Her aim in From Hand to Mouth *is to radicalize by revealing the hard facts behind the "choices" women are often forced to make. These three texts focus on discriminatory hiring practices of a major West German firm ("Siemens . . ."); the working conditions in women's prisons; and the double burden of Fatima, a Turkish woman. With her, we see Herzog struggling to communicate across language barriers.*

Siemens is Taking on Workers!

Ruth and I and a Turk are sitting on a corner bench. We are sitting wedged between injured workers, women and men. We are sitting in Siemens in Berlin. In front of us the swing door to the medical room slams to and opens. To our right people are called to the doctor by number, always four at a time.

After ten minutes I am dog-tired from the numbing silence, from the noise of the door. The women aren't sitting here for free, they won't achieve their piece-number today, I know that. It takes about fifteen minutes to leave the machine, go downstairs to the medical room, have a new dressing put on or swallow some pills and go back. That time is not paid for.

I light our last cigarette. The Turk notices that we have only one and gives Ruth one of his filter-cigarettes.

It's 8:30 A.M. We got up at 6, the cards from the Labour Exchange say "Appointment 7:30 A.M.". The door next to the medical room has no handle, to get out we would have to ring the bell. This handle-less door now opens. "New employees," shouts a man.

Now it all begins. You are given a red form by the reception clerks and you fill it in at tables and chairs that look like the counters in a post office. You get up and hand in the form and then you are given a book to read from. The letters are tiny, any normal person would use a magnifying glass. If you don't pass the sight test, if you can't read the tiny letters fast enough, then you are out. We are still in. Now put the right hand then the left hand round an appliance and grip. Siemens is measuring the sweat on your hands. The result is expressed in figures which are stamped on our documents.

We are given application forms to fill in and sit down with them at the tables. After ten minutes I hand mine in and am sent back— dashes won't do. I must say whether I have had any convictions or whether I have ever been threatened with any. Whether I have any physical injuries or disabilities. I say no. If they could, I believe that they would breed people even more exploitable than those they have now, people without heads, just with the organs needed by Siemens for production.

The clerk stares at my completed application form. He opens a steel filing cabinet and looks under the letter *H*. Ruth has finished, and comes up to the counter, both clerks examine her application form and establish that she has worked for Siemens in Munich. They check the sweat on her hands again. I am given a pass for the personnel department. Ruth is given another form: which branch of Siemens did she work for in Munich? What work did she do there? Who was the foreman and which shop was it? "Be quick," I say to Ruth, nudging her, "I'll wait for you in the street." I'd prefer to take her with me now.

Outside in the street the ground is frozen, there is a thin layer of ice where there were puddles yesterday. I am hungry. Nobody is about and I wait, it seems endlessly, for Ruth. When she comes she tells me that the clerks want to make inquiries with Siemens in Munich and then write to her. We wonder what we should say to that. Our aim is to be in a factory together— what do we do now? We decide that I should go ahead, we need the money.

We walk some of the way together to the personnel office. It is ten minutes' walk, passing the Siemens buildings: first the manufacturing section, then administration. On the way Ruth goes into a pub, she is cold. I meet the personnel manager and receive a lecture at a small conference table. I would be joining a new department; it would be very clean and orderly there. "There's one thing we can't be doing with," he says. "If you go sick, the firm has nothing more to do with you." A grimace: "Of course, we can all fall ill. A private question—are you pregnant? " "Bastard," I think to myself, and ask what the hourly rate is. "As you come from the metal industry, DM 5.25 an hour." He is lying, it doesn't matter where you've been, the starting wage at Siemens in January 1975 for all women workers is DM 5.25. No, I haven't a tape recorder to take down my conversation with this dealer in human beings. We're looking for work, that's why we're here. A forewoman from the department I'm supposed to work in comes into the room during this conversation and sits down at the conference table. I'm still asking about money: do they pay fares? "No," he says, at first taking me to mean (or pretending to) reimbursement for my ticket today. "You earn more doing piecework," he says, and the forewoman nods, "Piecework, piecework, tell me what that is then." Forewoman: 'The foreman will show you the work now.'

In the shop the foremen and setters stand around as if nothing ever happened here. A foreman takes me around but I don't pay any attention to what he says. I don't recognize anything in any case—no single whole part, only tiny contacts. The women look up, but they look more at what I'm wearing than at my face. I stop by each woman and start counting. I count at five successive machines and at each one repeat the count several times. With four of the women I count to six and in one case to nine. On these jobs the process takes from six to nine seconds—this is why the women are so young here. I see Turks and Germans, none of whom can be over twenty-five.

I hear the foreman say that the work done here is for news broadcasting. I look around me some more. Everything is new in this building; with the naked eye I can't detect a single fault. This must be a pilot development. Something new is being tried out here: in new premises, with new machinery and with particularly young girls. A woman who has been doing piecework for ten years is not in a position to cope with six-second work units. That means ten parts a minute—a hundred parts in ten minutes.

The shop clerks and setters are not in glass cubicles here as they are in other factories. They sit at desks on a platform alongside the workers. I feel that I'm in gaol, in a new and modern one that I've never seen before—I've got to know the old ones. Does the comparison only mean something to me because I've experienced prison? What difference is there between this new building without a blemish, this working-to-the-second with new machines and even magnifying glasses, and a newly built prison—a Köln-Ossendorf or a Frankfurt-Preungesheim? In neither is your life your own. Connections are snapped into fragments, healthy faculties and organs are destroyed.

On the way back I meet Ruth coming towards me, she couldn't wait that long in the pub. We pass a department store and I suggest that she quickly gets a copy made of my employment form, which I have kept all the time in a folder.

Who would believe it? It's January 1975 and piecework, shiftwork, for one of the biggest companies, brings in an hourly wage—after six weeks—of DM 5.31. I still have to go for a medical check. Ruth waits in the cold. I already know I won't go and work there, but

I'm thinking that if there's nothing else and we have no money I shall have to.

What follows is the examination and this you have to have experienced. This I find the most difficult thing of all to describe. Why exactly is that?

At Agfa in Munich I would not say when my last period was, or whether I was pregnant, so I was presumed to be so and not employed. I am too bound up in it to say whether it is the questions themselves which make me lose my temper.

"Is there any mental illness in your family?" the doctor asks. "Any tuberculosis?" "Have you had any serious operations?" "Is there cancer in your family?" You blow into an apparatus, have your teeth examined with a pocket torch—it's a slave market. In the War, I imagine they checked that you had a pair of shins before they enlisted you.

"Do you suffer from phlebitis?" "Do you have gastritis?" "Do you have circulation problems?" His questions indicate what the major illnesses are among working women. Siemens wants to finish you off by itself; it will not employ a woman made ill or worn out by AEG or any other company. The eye test is long and thorough—not for the eyes, not for the workers—the point is: do you see well enough for Siemens? Do you see well enough to produce tiny component parts on piecework? Are your heart and circulation still good enough for piecework? Piecework paid in Berlin in January 1975 at a rate of DM 5:31 an hour.

Women's Work in Prison

I was in prison from December 1971 to December 1973. Reason for arrest: suspected membership of a criminal organization. I was kept in detention for two years awaiting trial. I refused to make a statement. I was kept in solitary confinement for sixteen months. I got to know five prisons in four Federal states.

Prisons belong to the state. Prisoners are given a reward for work rather than a wage. Neither women nor men in prison get social insurance or a pension. Just as in the factories, women in prison get no training.

The first thing I hear about women's work in prison are the shouts and orders over the tannoy: "Get a move on!" and "Washroom women to work!"

Then I see the names of firms written on the cell doors. The woman shut in behind the door works for the firm either in her cell or in the workroom.

When I take exercise in the yard, I can look for a few moments into a hut where women are making plastic bags.

Prisons I've been in: Anrath near Düsseldorf in Nordrhein-Westfalen. It's a convict prison. One hundred and twenty women imprisoned there are in for life or for long terms. Long terms mean from three to ten years. All the women are convicts and convicts are obliged to work—no training is given. Women are forced to work in the laundry for this and other prisons; they are forced to work in the sewing-room for this and other prisons; they are forced to make up plastic bags in a wooden hut in the yard. They are paid DM 1.50 to DM 1.86 a day for eight hours' work.

Some fifteen women in this prison are lent out to a factory. Just as in the concentration camps, they are called "outside detachments." They leave the prison in the morning under guard, spend eight hours in a local factory working apart from the other working women and men and return in the evening under guard.

Another prison, at Mainz in Rheinland-Pfalz. Ten to fifteen women on remand. There is no workroom. Each prisoner works in the cell in which she is locked up. The work is putting rubber bands through air luggage tags at a set rate which is the required piece number for the day. I spent eight months in this prison. During this time there was no other work for the women. Apart from this I saw women slaving in the laundry, cleaning offices, cleaning the prison, cleaning the medical room: they earned DM 1.50 a day.

In the prison in Hamburg there are eighty women on remand. They work in their cells with a quota: they stick hairpins into cards, they pack tassels in bags, they put together curtain rings, they count fountain pen cartridges into boxes, they wrap up tickets for the State Lottery, they thread strings through bags for cotton wool, they make pan covers.

In the sewing-room they make curtains and bed-linen for the prison and for the staff.

There is no training; they get DM 1.80 a day.

In the gaol in Frankfurt, Hesse, there are two hundred women prisoners—juvenile, on remand or serving sentences. They prepare food for this prison and for the men's prison opposite. In the laundry they wash, dry, mangle, sort out and pack linen for this prison and for others. It is heavy work.

In this prison the women sweep, wipe and polish the corridors, hallways, showers, visiting-rooms, and offices.

This housework includes cleaning the buckets. There is no drainage in two wings of the prison. Cleaning the buckets means carrying away the shit, washing and disinfecting the buckets. Cleaning your teeth, washing yourself, washing your clothes, your sweater and your dishes—and bring back fresh water. This too is heavy work.

In the sewing-room the prison linen gets mended.

In a room for making cardboard cartons, the women fold, rivet, stick, sort, and pack various parts of the cartons.

As in Anrath, women here also go out to work in a local factory. In this case it is the Hammer meat-salad factory. For this they get DM 1.80 a day.

I have read in the newspapers that since 1974 Frankfurt has been providing training for fifteen women as zoo-keepers and florists.

In this prison 180 women sew, wash, polish, change buckets, cook, and fold—and these are the facts—for DM 1.80 for an eight-hour day.

Fatima After the Factory

I visited her in her flat in Schöneberg [a district of Berlin] in November. The streetlights are already lit and I stand in the street because no one is in. I wait—she can't fail to come, she has three children to look after. When she arrives it is her walk I recognize first: I have watched her walk away in the factory so often. She kisses me by way of greeting and I ask her, "Are you having a child?" "Yes Maria, it is heavy."

Fatima was overweight even before her pregnancy. She has water in the legs and climbing the stairs up to her flat on the fourth floor makes her breathe heavily. She doesn't move at all in a portly way even though she is so heavy. I always admired that in the factory.

It is cold in the flat. She has two rooms and a kitchen for the five of them and the rent is DM 120. Her husband has built a bath in a recess in the kitchen. While I used to go home dirty at the end of a day in the factory, Fatima would spend a long time in the changing room washing herself thoroughly in warm water.

She gets up at 5 A.M. each day, and it is now 5 P.M. She lights the fire and I carry her shopping into the kitchen. As we move about we pick up bits of children's clothing scattered on the floor. Then we settle into armchairs. Fatima puts her feet up and we eat mandarins which I've got in my pocket. I ask about work. Fatima isn't on piecework any more, she is sticking numbers on vacuum cleaners now. I ask what the others are doing, but she doesn't understand me too well. Basically we get on by her telling me things, and when I don't understand what she says I ask again and she tells me once more. It emerges that for the first three or four months of her pregnancy she stayed on piecework. I'm not sure whether she left it until then to say that she was pregnant or whether she did so straight away and was only given another job later. What does become clear is that she is earning the same wage as she was getting during her last month's piecework. Fatima has been in the factory for two years and has a good average. I ask which of the other women are still there and Fatima tells me which of them have been sacked. She talks at length about Mustafa's wife and is angry when I can't remember her. She too has been sacked.

Then Fatima says that there are now men working on the carousels. This news brings me to my feet. The men came from the deep-freeze department which had been closed down. They would never manage the piece system and would give notice, but then new men would be taken on and trained for it. Having only seen women working at the carousel, rushing about and out of breath, I feel like going to see with my own eyes men assembling parts at it. For a moment this idea has a liberating effect. I wonder how it affects the women sitting in the shop. I only saw women rushed off their feet, but now they'll be seeing men who can't manage the piecework.

We want coffee, but all the crockery has been used so we go to wash up. The kitchen is an icy hole. "Cold, my sweet," says Fatima, and points to two holes in the window pane. These have been made by children opposite shooting at it with a catapult. A piece of plastic covering the holes is blowing about in the draught. Fatima lends me a knitted jacket. We pile up the crockery and throw away the left-overs. Fatima curses her two older sons for not helping. "Yesterday I cleaned everything, Maria. Every day cleaning, Maria. Husband working. I working, cleaning, cooking, washing children, also cleaning shirts, oh Maria!" Wiping the table Fatima finds two cellulose rags stained with blood. To me they look like the swabs left by a doctor after taking a blood test. I tell her this, but Fatima points to a roll of cellulose hanging on the kitchen wall. She's right, it's the same. She tries to work out what has happened to her children. The last she saw of the big ones was at five o'clock this morning. She goes to the dustbin and turns it out. No blood-stains there, so she sweeps it all up again. The water for the washing-up gradually gets hotter. Fatima unpacks her bag and takes out a new glass coffee pot—two similar ones have already been broken—and a thick, heavy bundle of parsley. She shows me how to pack it into the fridge properly so that it will stay fresh for a week. She says that now that she is pregnant her husband does the shopping every day, so she no longer has to carry heavy loads.

Fatima's husband, Cemal, arrives just as we are finishing the washing-up. He greets me as if he knew me and unpacks the several plastic bags he is carrying. Fatima starts to cook a soup of tomatoes, noodles, a Turkish spice I don't know, and beef stock.

Murat, aged six and the youngest son, comes home from kindergarten with a lantern he has made himself. He lights his lantern and switches off the living-room light. Above the sofa there is a large map of Turkey in bright colours. Murat kneels on the sofa holding the lantern high above his head and shows me his home town, deep in the south of Turkey. In between times I go and help Fatima with the cooking. Cemal goes out again to buy a needle for the record player and some Turkish salami. Murat is hungry and opens a tin of sardines and shares them with me before the meal.

The two older ones are not yet home, but since Cemal doesn't eat on his building site, nor Fatima at the factory, they don't wait to start the meal. On the table are slices of white bread, baked by Fatima, a plate of salami and ham, yesterdays' warmed-up spaghetti, and in the middle the pot of soup, in which the dominant colours are red and green. Beside each plate is a bunch of parsley and I watch Fatima to see how you eat it. She draws the whole stem through her mouth, chewing off the leaves till nothing but the bare stem is left.

We don't talk much during the meal because everyone is hungry. Every so often Cemal turns over the small Turkish records, and Murat tells his mother about the kindergarten. He speaks fluent German with a Berlin accent. Whenever he senses that his mother doesn't understand him he switches to Turkish. Next year he goes to school. He was born in Berlin, in a hospital in Schöneberg, and Fatima would like to go there again for her confinement. The hospital was good, but the births have always been difficult and she is afraid of this happening again. In fact that was the first thing we talked about when we were sitting in the armchairs. She didn't want this child but she couldn't tolerate the pill. After the birth of the fourth child she wants a coil fitted to protect her from the "baby doctor."

Fatima has put her feet up again, her eyes look small. Since I am trying to describe her, I think I shall ask her if I can take her photograph. It is Thursday and Fatima has two more days' work—at the moment Saturdays are being worked in preparation for Christmas. Her maternity leave begins in January.

I feel really warm after the hot soup. Murat has brought out toys from under the sofa—aeroplanes and ships. I'd like to stay sitting in the armchair because it feels good. I only go because I know they both have to leave at 5 A.M. Cemal, who works on a building site, has turned on the news to hear the weather report. The first snowfall is forecast for tomorrow.

Notes

* Originally published in English as: Marianne Herzog, *From Hand to Mouth*, trans. Stanley Mitchell (Pelican Books, 1980), pp. 94–98; 64–66; 142–145. Reprinted by permission of Penguin Books Ltd. German original: Marianne Herzog, *Von der Hand in den Mund: Frauen im Akkord* (Berlin: Rotbuch Verlag, 1976), pp. 30–31; 53–56; 105–107.

19. Selections from *Dear Colleague*

the *Berlin Workship,*
Collective Literature of the Working World

Dear Colleague is a collection of first-person accounts by housewives, women in service occupations, and factory workers. The intent was to describe women's work within a socialist framework and explore possibilities for change through collective action. The women were encouraged to write the texts as a means of understanding and gaining a degree of control over their lives as well as to make their situation public. The editors present the author of "A Measure Taken" as a model whose refusal to sign her supervisor's evaluation of her is a mode of resistance other women can emulate. The author of "Christmastime at Findus" concludes her piece with her fantasy of what women in the FRG must do to improve their situation.

A Measure Taken*

Barbara Tedeski, clerk, Munich

I'm next.

Our supervisor, Fräulein Böllig, is calling me now on the intercom to come up front to her office.

Two other employees from the accounting department have already been in her office. Through the wood-trimmed plate glass that separates our section from billing and bookkeeping we could see Fräulein Böllig wordlessly slide a piece of paper across to each of the two women, which they apparently had to read over.

After reading the text, the first woman blushed beet red. Confused, she looked at Fräulein Böllig, who simply sat there on her padded supervisor's chair with a big friendly grin. Bewildered and resigned, the woman shook her head in disbelief, but Fräulein Böllig had already unscrewed the silver cap of her fountain pen and was dangling it under her nose, whereupon the woman shrugged and signed something. Then she quickly left the office after having first taken the toilet key, which is attached to a red pear-shaped wooden block hanging right next to the door in full view of Fräulein Böllig.

151

Maintaining the same friendly silence with which Fräulein Böllig had held the pen out to her, the second employee put the paper down on Fräulein Böllig's desk and returned to our section with proud determination.

Girls, please.

And you don't know what's going on either? someone asks curiously, naively.

No.

If Fräulein Böllig smiled any harder, her face would crack.

The employee who has just returned casts a contemptuous glance at the section leader, and we know Fräulein Kaminzkat is lying. She is most certainly informed about everything that concerns her section. Even though she constantly claims the contrary is true and pretends to know nothing about what Fräulein Böllig is doing "over her head," she generally plays a decisive role in the instigation of certain events.

Fräulein Kaminzkat nods my way encouragingly: All right, you're next.

I push aside the huge pile of labels I'm sorting according to item and warehouse number and leave. My predecessor smirks ironically.

From all departments I can feel the tense stares of my colleagues; the ones in bookkeeping look as if they would be gleefully rubbing their hands under their desks if Fräulein Böllig weren't sitting right across from them.

It's as if they're the audience at a theater, hardly able to wait for the play to begin.

On may way to Fräulein Böllig I wonder about the meaning of all this. Today was St. Nicolaus' Day,[1] not according to the calendar, but because it's what the office calls that day of the year on which Fräulein Böllig calls us in one by one for about twenty minutes down to the conference room. There, the gentlemen from management normally conduct their business discussions or sit at a table with a white cloth having lunch prepared especially for them by the chef.

That's where Fräulein Böllig is sitting now, on the narrow side of the long conference table, in front of her a steno pad full of notes and a glass ashtray overflowing with lipstick-stained cigarette filters; here's where she has a "heart-to-heart talk" with each of us.

Fräulein Böllig began our conference this afternoon by announcing that this was the last straw and that she was willing to grant me one last trial period of six months to prove myself. My work was inexact, slipshod, sloppy, lacking concentration, and in addition I kept the others from working with my constant chatter. And what did I have to say to that?

I didn't have anything to say to that, and my question why all the above had only become clear to her after a year and a half would surely have been rhetorical.

But at the end of the conference, which was conducted solely by Fräulein Böllig, it now turned out that the company nonetheless valued my work enough to give me a raise of ten dollars, which would in effect put me in a higher tax bracket and net me exactly four dollars less at the end of the month.

I am certain that this all must have to do with St. Nicolas's Day.

Fräulein Böllig pushes the piece of paper toward me almost cheerfully. Please read this through.

My suspicions are fairly accurate. The exact text of our conference this afternoon is on the paper; now, in writing as well, I get my deficiencies outlined by Fräulein Böllig.

And now sign it please, Fräulein Böllig says with a friendly smile.

It occurs to me you would really have to be nuts to acknowledge something like that in writing, and I explain to Fräulein Böllig that I'm not about to sign any such thing.

Is that so, Fräulein Böllig says very calmly. But then you realize I am going to have that put in your personnel file. Now give the thing back to me.

I say: No. —At which point Fräulein Böllig lifts her brow in astonishment. I explain to her that I would like to show that "thing" to the management.

Fräulein Böllig's face brightens faintly. Please come outside for a moment.

Out in the hallway she gives me a confidential pat on the shoulder:

Maybe we both should reconsider that business about the personnel file and the manager, hm?

She grins, sly and chummy.

Translated by Judith McAlister-Hermann

Notes

* German original: "Eine Massnahme," *Liebe Kollegin. Texte zur Emanzipation der Frau in der Bundesrepublik,* ed. Britta Noeske, Gabriele Röhrer,, and the West Berlin Workshop of the Werkkreis Literatur der Arbeitswelt (Frankfurt/

M.: Fischer Taschenbuch Verlag, 1973), pp. 53–56. Translated and reprinted with permission.

[1]. In Germany St. Nicolaus comes on December sixth with gifts for good children and switches for the bad ones, who then are warned to change their ways in time for Christmas. (trans. note)

Christmastime at the Findus Company*

Regina Korn,
Essen Workshop

For the first time since my marriage I've got a job, a job in a company that produces frozen foods. It all began with a junk mail ad: "Good fringe benefits, hot meals in our cafeteria, white uniforms, bright but not refrigerated rooms, no piecework, hourly wage: $1.40. You'll find the working conditions agreeable. You would fit in nicely. Would you like to work for us? Permanently or for the holiday season?"

First Day

We're cleaning purple cabbage at a long table, on our feet for eight hours with short breaks. The long hours of standing are hard, but the work goes quickly and I don't mind doing it, since there's no conveyor belt here. I'll stay here.

Second Day

There's no more cabbage now, and so I was assigned to another job. From a chest-high crate I have to unpack fishsticks that are frozen solid together. I often have to use a chisel; the work has to go quickly and it is quite strenuous. By the time I get to the lower layers, I'm hanging in the crate from the waist up, my feet dangling. I won't be able to stand that for long. I get headaches from bending over all the time and I have difficulty breathing. My thyroid gland presses against my windpipe. This evening I'm going to ask to be transferred.

Another Day

Three of us are working together at a fish saw. My job, for eight solid hours, is to lift twenty-four-pound slabs of fish from a wooden pallet up onto the table and remove the paper wrapping. You bend over, heave the heavy fish slab, let it slam down on the table, tear off the paper, turn around, bend over again, heave the next slab, and so it goes, hours on end, twenty-four pounds per slab. After four hours the young woman who packs the sawed-up fish into boxes grabs my arm and says "Come on, let's trade. Nobody can stand an entire shift doing that."

155

Another Day

On the gourmet filet line the nozzle isn't working. The filets all have to be spread with a topping by hand. That's my job. The filets are in aluminum pans which slide by on the conveyor one right after the other and pass under a nozzle, but it only partially spreads the topping. One woman lays the filets into pans and puts them onto the conveyor belt. Two others catch them behind the nozzle and throw them onto my table. But soon it's overflowing. Because I have to go and get the topping from another belt, take the filets out of the pans, spread the topping on them, put the lid on, and put them back on the belt, all by hand. But the belt runs on and on. A new pan sails onto my table every few seconds. They fly over and on top of each other. The topping from the pans underneath is now sticking to the ones above, which means that now I have to wash them off too. My nerves are ready to snap. At least four women should be working here. Take the filets out of the pans, spread them with topping, put them back in the pans, put lids on them, wash them off, and go get more topping from time to time. I'm going to crack any minute now. I ask another woman to help me. She yells at me. I can't help it, tears are rolling down my face. I keep on working. I'm ashamed to be crying. I can't help it. My nerves are so raw from the rush and the tension that I can't calm myself down. And besides that, the rims of the aluminum pans are sharp. Several of my fingers are already cut up. It's impossible to pick them up carefully in this mad rush. On this line we have rubber finger tips in our uniform pockets just in case. I don't know how many hours go by like this. I keep on rushing and the mountain on the table gets higher and higher. I can't control my tears any longer. Everybody is looking at me. I'm embarrassed but I can't help it. I've simply had it. The woman who yelled at me has long since apologized but that's not it at all. I'm not angry at her. I know what's looming over us all. Forty of us are going to be let go before Christmas. Meanwhile nearly all my fingers are cut up. One so badly that blood is seeping out of the finger tip. I have to go to the nurse to have my finger bandaged so I won't spoil the filets. I go back to work at a different line. But my place on the filet line has now been taken over by *three* women.

Another Day

During lunch break I notice a sign on the bulletin board. All the other notices are on white paper but this one is yellow and has been made even more conspicuous by red lines along the sides. I read it over quickly, since the break is short and you have to stand in line for lunch. Relieved, I go on to the cafeteria. No further layoffs. Only those who wish to leave the company before Christmas of their own accord should report to the office. The company's going to keep the others on for the winter. Today the meal, which in my opinion usually tastes pretty good, is especially delicious. After my break I'm back standing at the conveyor. They keep setting the belt to run faster and faster. The little boxes go by faster than we can pack them. We hold them down on the belt or throw them off the line to keep the scales from getting blocked. I protest to the foreman. "The other shift managed thirteen pallets, you will too." We did.

The Next Day

"The shift before you finished sixteen pallets." And so we did too. We women have got self-respect.

The Beginning of December

In the wall behind where we're working there's an opening at least a yard wide through which a conveyor belt passes into our shop from the outer section of the building. Production has been temporarily stopped on this line. The outer section has a double door leading to the outside. It has been open for days because electric carts have to take crates out to shipping and bring in others with raw material. We're standing with our backs directly opposite the opening in the wall. Since production has been shut down in this section, the opening could be closed off. It's freezing cold and there's quite a stiff wind. We can hardly stand it. Our backs cramp up involuntarily. After several hours our necks are so stiff we can barely turn our heads. The belt in front of me runs on. In spite of all this, the work mustn't lag. I talk to the foreman. He can't do anything about it. We stand in the cold, in this draft, for eight hours. What did the ad say? "Bright, but not refrigerated rooms." The women complain: "Just wait and see, we'll all be sick in bed by Christmas." But nobody dares say a word while the foreman is around. I don't give up. I don't know how many times I talk to the foreman. Finally he stuffs paper bags in the opening. But the wind blows them out again. He's really angry with me. "Why don't you take some sick days," he says. But on the fourth day I get a work area which is less drafty. But my coworkers who can't risk being fired don't dare say anything and they remain exposed to the cold air.

Saturday, December 7, 1968

I'm sitting at home reading a notice from the Findus Company that came in the mail: ". . . And so we have no other choice than to thank you for your hard work with us etc., etc. Your last working day will be December 13, 1968." A letter of dismissal, and with only six days' notice. It's obviously a mimeographed form letter. And because the date of dismissal is also mimeographed and not typed in, I know that many of us are being let go. So they're going to do it after all. What a dirty trick they've pulled on us. They used that yellow notice to keep us quiet and thus prevent us women from taking steps to avoid being fired. It's too late to get a temporary job, we can't avoid the disgrace of being fired, and being fired is considered a disgrace, as I soon find out.

They kept us holding our breath with those twenty-five layoffs in October and the following rumor about forty more layoffs to come and got as much out of us as they could. By this process of selection the Findus Company cultivates specimens with no will of their own who have to survive somehow. On Monday I'm going to take another look at that yellow notice. That was my plan, but after the dismissal notices went out, the sign disappeared. I tell my coworkers about the layoffs before work, during work, and in the breaks. I want to find out who else has been given notice. I say "I'm going to the personnel manager and the chairman of the works council; we've been tricked!" It would be more effective if others would come along, but nobody volunteers. "We can't change anything anyway; it's always been like this," the women say. "But that's no reason why it should stay that way," I reply. My appeals are in vain. I go to Herr Giese and demand to know how many people are being let go with me, since the mimeographed letter indicates a large number of people fired. He claims to know nothing. But finally he reveals that there were not quite thirty. Sixteen had volunteered to leave and that wasn't enough. I remind him of the yellow notice on the bulletin board and call the company's procedure an intentional deception. He holds the notice in his hand but won't give it to me and "interprets" it in the following way: they had tried to keep most of the employees on over the winter. I can't get anything else out of him. I can't find out anything else. I go to my lunch break. I see an older employee sitting in the cafeteria crying over her plate. I can't find out why she's crying. She avoids the others and is still crying when she goes back to work.

December 10

I go to the chairman of the works council, Henrichs, and present my complaint. But he knows even less than Giese. He denies that there was any misleading passage in the yellow notice. Since he's defending only the company and hasn't said a word about the employees, I ask him whose side he's on, anyway, and whether he's in the union. He loses his temper, claims he's on everybody's side, including those in the highest positions, and of course he's in the union. Union membership is required in every works council in the FRG. Then I ask him to get a copy of the notice for me so we could discuss the facts, since he denies the existence of the passage I find so important. He promises to do it and says he'll have me called back to his office. Back at work, I hear from my co-workers that the older woman who cried so much yesterday hasn't come back. She had been with the company almost from the very beginning (i.e., almost five years) and has now been fired. After you've been with the company five years, I further discover, you can be retired with a pension. Everybody thinks it's a damned shame to fire a worker right before she could claim retirement benefits. Once more I try to find out who else was fired when I was, once more without success. The women are ashamed. They're afraid of being considered poor or slow workers. If only they would realize how they are hurting their cause. I don't see any fingers pointing at me with contempt. Several of the few male employees tell me they respect me for my efforts.

The Last Days

On the eleventh of December I wait in vain for works council chairman Henrichs to call me in. On the twelfth I go to see him again. He can't remember making any promises, I should go get the yellow notice from Giese myself. There wasn't a word in the yellow notice about keeping anybody on over the winter; that was a malicious lie on my part, just like my claim that he had promised to see me in his office, etc. I should go back to my work. And finally I did go back.

When I tried to see Herr Giese again on December thirteenth, my last day, he wasn't in.

I wasn't given the chance to represent my interests and those of my coworkers in the company. The only thing left for me to do for my colleagues was to write a report to the food workers' union.

Shortly before the holidays a colleague brought me the company Christmas present that I still had coming and told me: "Just think, a week after you left a whole lot of women were let go." On my last day at work another colleague told me that two women from her neighborhood had applied for work at Findus and had been hired for the first of January. She had seen the letters of acceptance herself. So I was correct in my suspicion that the "seasonal" dismissals were a selection procedure. How many people were let go this winter?

Twenty-five in October, twenty-nine of the thirteenth of December, a good number of the twentieth of December. That makes at least sixty, if not more. In my mind I envision sixty women storming the office of the chairman of the works council, sixty women heading toward the personnel office, and sixty reports to the union. Just a dream, but it must not remain a dream. It's the only chance we have to improve our condition.

Translated by Judith McAlister-Hermann

Notes

* German original: "Weihnachtszeit bei Findus," *Liebe Kollegin. Texte zur Emanzipation der Frau in der Bundersrepublik,* ed. Britta Noeske, Gabriele Röhrer, and the West Berlin Workshop of the Werkkreis Literatur der Arbeitswelt (Frankfurt/M.: Fischer Taschenbuch Verlag, 1973), pp. 136–142. Translated and reprinted with permission. Portions of this text have been excerpted.

20. In Touch*

Christa Wolf

"In Touch," the forword to the West German edition of Wander's book, is clearly addressed to GDR readers. Emphasizing that the interviews "document new realities" (wider participation by women in the public sphere; progress toward economic equality), Wolf argues just as emphatically that true liberation is still a long way off. She finds the spirit of a "concretely existing utopia" in the dreams and aspirations of women like Ruth B., whom she quotes several times. This essay was Wolf's first direct commentary on Western feminism; her own feminism has since become more radical

This is a book to which each person will add his own story.* Self-examination begins even while one reads. In the following nights many female readers, I am certain—I'm not so certain about male readers—will privately draft their own personal report—urgent monologues which no one will ever write down. Encouraged by the openness of others, many women probably wish someone were there with them who wanted to listen—as Maxie Wander listened to the women she spoke with.

The spirit which reigns in this book—no: is at work—is the spirit of a concretely existing utopia, without which every reality becomes unlivable for human beings. Doubly present, its effect is to make this collection more than the sum of its parts: Virtually every one of the conversations extends out beyond itself through longing, challenge, life expectations. Collectively—if one sees the book as a coming together of some of the most diverse people in matters of greatest importance—they give an intimation of a community where the rules would be sympthy, self-respect, trust and friendship. Marks of sisterliness, which, it seems to me, appears more frequently than brotherliness. These seventeen protocols only apparently lack an

---

* Christa Wolf and the women she quotes in this essay follow the standard German convention of using masculine pronouns in the so-called generic sense. These masculine generics are preserved in the translation to bring out the conceptual contradiction they present. (Trans. note.)

eighteenth, the author's personal statement; she is very much present, however, and by no means just passively, recording and mediating. She didn't keep out of things, didn't simply draw out intimate information ("intimate" in the positive sense of "confidential," "in close friendship," "sincere") by her ability to ask questions in a personal, direct, intrepid way: If we could collect the things she revealed about herself in these conversations into one volume, we would have the missing eighteenth report. Her talent was establishing openly friendly relations with people; her gift was letting others find out that they are not sentenced to a lifetime of silence.

No one was "interrogated" here, no well-calculated plan carried out; these are women talking with each other, women who need each other, who are discovering themselves and the other person. There is a consumers' attitude among writers, apparent in their often anguished attempts to heal their distorted relationship to themselves, their lack of sensitivity, their loss of immediacy and their coldness through injections of the drug "Reality." The women interviewed here would have said other things, and in other ways, to that kind of reporter.

These texts did not come about as evidence for preconceived opinions; they support no thesis, the familiar "look how emancipated we are" included. They are not based on any sociological, political, or therapeutic theory. Maxie Wander, in no sense authorized to do a survey, was legitimized only by genuine interest and a desire to learn. She did not come to judge, but to see and to hear. Every productive movement creates a sphere of energy which releases new contradictions, of greater import than the old ones; it is this kind of force field which underlies the contributions in this book and makes them exciting, even when they tell about everyday things which everyone thinks they know.

The motto of this book is not that "Touch-me-not" formula of loneliness and retreat from self, dread of disclosure and withdrawal; here there is touching, intimacy, openness, sometimes a disconcerting candor, an inspiring courage to confront oneself. There is a thin line separating self-disclosure and self-exposure, between intimacy and embarrassment, trust and self-abandonment. Walking this line with aplomb is no technical balancing act, no concession to good taste. It is evidence of self-confidence and of a historical situation which gives women from various strata this sovereignity with respect to their most personal experiences which, until very recently, they concealed from themselves and others.

The private is made public: This has nothing to do with exhibi-tionism. But neither can it be taken for granted that no one will take offense. Men will be disconcerted to observe how women free themselves from their traditional "feminine" identity, how they look men over, are able to get along without them, consider "ousting" them, "put them on hold," are more likely to want "spiritual" than physical touching and are amused when "they" give her Marx's collected works as a divorce present. Is it conceivable that some men (numbers aren't important here) experience the women's good spirits, irony and self-irony as shocking, as too much to take? But then, were they so poorly acquainted with their wives? Do they like them better if they fall in a good old-fashioned faint when suddenly confronted by a husband's infidelity? Incidentally, they do this now and again, but then get up again with the clear understanding that the men "need a new mirror."

Losing privileges is never pleasant. Not the least of this book's accomplishments is that it provides authentic evidence of how extensively the private lives and feelings of many women in the GDR have been changed by their being encouraged to participate in public affairs. It's too late now to say "That's not what we meant." It's becoming clear: unrestrained subjectivity can become a criterion for what we call (inaccurately, I believe) "objective reality"—though only when the subject is not restricted to empty self-observation, but is actively involved in social processes. The subject springs forth of its own accord when it is able to contribute to extracting the utmost from the given social relations. It is driven back into itself when it runs into alienated, destructive structures, into insurmountable taboos in crucial areas.

Maxi Wander's book is a stroke of good luck, but it is no accident. Enjoyable activities—such as learning, research, work, and also writing—are not infrequently robbed of pleasure when they must at all costs lead to results. This book was important to the author but to her, working on it was more important. And these texts *have* been worked on. No one must think that a mechanical transcription, raw material is presented here. Maxie Wander has selected, shortened, summarized, reordered, expanded—but never falsified. The texts which came about in this way—antecedents of literature, not subject to its laws and not open to the temptations of self-censure—are particularly well-suited to document new realities. And in so doing, individual contributions approach literary forms.

★   ★   ★

What the prevailing consciousness is unaware of, the unarticulated and inarticulable, is always found among the underprivileged, the marginal figures, those defined as underage, cut off; where deprivation and degradation completely prevent a potential subject from speaking out. Among those who perform the lowest and dullest labor; in prisons, in barracks, in homes for children, adolescents and the elderly; in hospitals and mental institutions. And for a long time this has been so among women, who were virtually speechless. I think it is false to define all women as a "class," as some feminists do; however, if the wives of workers were doubly oppressed, the wives of the ruling classes were robbed of adult status at least—whether they knew it or know it or not. It is striking that those women who were able to wrest their way into the world of literature shortly before and during the century of the French Revolution—frequently through overexpending their energies—so often express themselves in diaries and letters, in poetry, in travel descriptions, in these highly personal and most subjective literary forms based on personal statement, dialogue and direct address; forms in which the writer can move more spontaneously, also more sociably than in the structures of the novel or the drama. Not to mention that the overwhelming—more correctly: overwhelmed—majority of gifted women possessed neither the external prerequisites nor the ability to muster the minimum amount of self-confidence which is, after all, essential for gaining admittance to that institution called "Literature" (something quite different from writing). Instead—in their place—we find these close alliances between artists and educated women in the nineteenth century—alliances of outsiders, kept together by the pressure of isolation which a society inflexibly committed to efficiency forces on those of its members who want to be productive through activity that is not goal-directed, but for pleasure and to develop their own abilities. Loneliness, esotericism, self-doubt, madness, suicide: the story of the lives and deaths of male and female writers, who serve to this day as models, though modified in various ways.

We too cannot satisfy—it's foolish to deny it—the Marxian postulate for a nonalienated existence: "If you take the *human being* as a *human being* and his relation to the world as a human one, then you can only exchange love for love, trust for trust, ect." Yes: economically and legally we are equal to men, largely independent by virtue of equal educational opportunity and the freedom to make our own decisions about pregnancy and birth, no longer separated from the man of our choice by barriers of class or rank. And now we find out (if it's really love we're talking about, not possession or the mutual performing of services) the degree to which the history of class society, the patriarchy, has deformed its objects and what lengths of time will be required for human beings—men and women—to become subjects. Many women still have to play a part so that their love may be given in exchange for the immature desires of many men. ("You have to put on an act for men, otherwise you scare them away.")

Without aiming to, Maxie Wander's book attests to a significant phenomenon: Only when husband and wife no longer argue about the week's wages, about money for terminating a pregnancy, about whether the wife is allowed to "go to work" and who will take care of the children if she does; only when a woman receives the same salary for her work as a man does; when she can present her own case in a court of law; when girls are no longer trained to be "feminine," at least not in the public schools, and a single mother is no longer held in public contempt: only then does woman begin to have significant experiences which concern her not as a human creature of the female sex in general, but as an individual.

The societal contradictions which formerly tended to wear her out, to run her over, now approach her in the more subtle form of personal conflict, and there is no prescribed role-behavior to resolve this. Now she is faced with a multitude of possibilities, also with possible errors and risks. This book provides illustrations of how differently older and younger women are reacting to this situation. The forty-seven-year-old child welfare worker, "Karoline": "what we now take for granted used to be a luxury; our daily bread, being able to buy shoes, simply being treated like a human being. For this reason it can only be *my* social order." "Erika," forty-one-year-old dramaturgical assistant, wonders: "Maybe that's emancipation, when things which would have been catastrophic in those days aren't even a problem any more. That a woman can say: If you won't cooperate I'll do it alone. Although that's not easy."

Although it's not easy, these women are starting to tell the stories of classical tragedy the other way around: "He's equal to me because I could live without him too." Merely exchanging roles doesn't make them happy. "I used to act like a man, exercise male prerogatives"— female Don-Juanism, which has the same result—or the same cause— as its male counterpart: inability to love. Although it's not easy, women are suppressing their acquired need for protection and "taking it like a man;" are discovering that it isn't always their fault if they are sexually unsatisfied; are finding out that women must "understand with their whole body." (We ought to guard carefully this discovery, still very fragile, so precariously established; it might perhaps help us at least to question the remorseless, alienated rationalism of such institutions as science and medicine.) Although it's very difficult, they are finding out that women can also love each other, be physically affectionate with each other. That they are no longer willing to cover up for it when their husbands, big and strong in the outside world, revert to infantile behavior in their arms. And so they are fleeing the "confinement of the bedroom" to which they have been "banished" with their husbands, are refusing to continue putting up with the atrophy of feeling which many men suffer from, having been pressured for generations to adapt to "goal-oriented" modes of behavior; they are rejecting the mothering role and getting divorced.

They pay for their independence with a pain difficult to bear, often with aloneness, always with a heavier workload, usually with a bad conscience toward husband, children, household, profession, the state as Super-man. Only when we—our daughters, grandchildren—no longer have bad consciences will we truly be able to act conscientiously; only then can we help men to perceive that compulsion to submit and to perform which has become for many of them, subject to history, their hotly defended second nature. Only then will men really want to understand their wives. "I haven't met one yet who wanted to find out what I'm really like and why I'm that way."

These women don't see themselves as the adversaries of men— unlike certain women's groups in capitalist countries whose often fanatical manhating is thrown up to them. But how are they to remain calm, in control, and on top of that keep their sense of humor when they are deprived of the most elementary bases for an independent existence? Especially in the absence of a strong labor movement women are driven into sect-like alliances against men, believing it necessary to fight men with the same means that men have used for centuries to fight them. But—luckily—they do not possess these means; they possess a pervasive feeling of powerlessness. Deprived of rights, they try to get their sense of self from men; their way to finding themselves is often via a retreat to their own sex; it is necessarily difficult for them to include all of society in their blueprints. And yet: what solidarity among themselves, what struggles to understand their own situation, what spontaneity and inventiveness in their self-help enterprises, what imagination, what abundance. I cannot believe that we in the GDR have nothing to learn from this.

For there are many indications, not least in this book, of dissatisfaction among many women in our country: What they have achieved and take for granted is no longer enough. Their first concern is no longer what they have, but who they are. They feel that their new role has already begun to solidify, that they are suddenly no longer able to move within these institutions; their lust for life is great, their hunger for reality insatiable. And so, still feeling their way, they brush against the new taboos, for changes are always most urgently pushed forward precisely at the point where they were the most farreaching. Our society made it possible for women to do what men do; to this they have, predictably, raised the question:

What *do* men do? And is that really what I want? It's not only that they are asking critical questions of institutions—the younger ones among them, especially of schools; not only that they rebel against being deprived of responsibility at the work place, which leads to attitudes of resignation: "If a person isn't allowed to see how things fit together then he can't be made responsible and he can't do decent work, either." They are beginning to ponder what their life has made of them, what they have made of their life. "If you train for productivity over a long period, you destroy something important in your personality." "When I'm not working I'm a stranger to myself." "You aren't happy when you're as fragmented as I am." "I'm totally crusted over." In contrast, as resistance to the new mottoes of younger women: "Spontaneity is something crazy men and women are concerned about." And—a Kleistian statement, spoken by a young waitress: "But all of a sudden I feel so alien among people."

These are the words of the minority. To counterattack with other statements one could find would be senseless. This is the way a new feeling toward life and the times is being articulated (also by young men, incidentally). Women, who have matured by coming to terms with real and consequential experiences, are signaling a radical expectation: to be able to live as a whole person, to make use of all their senses and abilities. These expectations are a great challenge for a society which, like all communities of this age, has imposed— to some extent must impose—multiple pressures on its members. Nonetheless, the society itself has, knowingly or not, awakened these expectations; they can no longer be countered with affirmative action plans, day-care centers and child support payments *alone;* nor, I believe, by delegating more women to those committees in which the "important questions" everywhere in this man's world, in our country too, are decided by men. Should women even wish that greater numbers of them be admitted to those hierarchically functional mechanisms? To assume roles which have done so much damage to men over the centuries? Though one does find women like this university lecturer and government delegate ("Lena," forty-three), who tears down the "facade" of such roles, who breaks through the fear of touching: "I reduce the distance systematically until I have the people's confidence. Anyway, I think this whole mystification of authority is a farce which no rational person needs. This contradiction exists for all those in positions of public influence. One will always have conflicts between authoritarian thinking and being oneself."

Hopefully it will be understood how important women's sensitivity for contradictions like these must be for us all. Conditions in our country have enabled women to develop a self-awareness which does not simultaneously imply the will to control, to dominate, or to subjugate, but rather the ability to cooperate. For the first time in their history they are defining their *differentness*—an immense step forward; for the first time they are not only developing creative imagination: They have also developed that clear-headed vision which men believe to be a typically masculine quality.

I am not claiming that women are by nature more immune than men to political delusions or flights from reality. Only this: A specific historical phase has given them the basis for a voice in shaping life-expectations for men. Of course aggression and fear are loosed when one must shatter old images—especially of oneself. But we will have to become accustomed to the fact that women are no longer just seeking equality, but new ways to live. They are countering mere pragmatism and utilitarianism—that self-deceptive "Ratio"—with rational thinking, sensuality, longing for happiness. Ridiculous to believe that humanity could spend increasing portions of its wealth on weapons for mass destruction and simultaneously be happy; to act as if "normal" relations among people could exist anywhere in the world as long as half of humanity is undernourished or dying of starvation. Those are delusions. It seems to me that women, whose new and painfully won relation to reality is precious to them, are more likely than men to be immune to such madness. And therefore that the productive energy of these women means hope. "The big things," says one of the women in this volume, "are not yet in my power, I'm not fooling myself about that."

Two of her comrades enter into dialogue with her. One of them, "Ruth," a twenty-two-year old waitress: "Sometimes I ask myself: what society are we building, anyway? A person has dreams, you know. My dream: people will treat each other like people, and there won't be any more selfishness, no more envy, no suspicion. A community of close friends. So. Someone'll be around to say yes to me then." And the physicist ("Margot," thirty-six) who now feels the need to paint: "I'd paint my vision—the fear, the way human life can degenerate, the way things hollow people out. The way masses of people exist in their concrete cells and no one has access to anyone else . . . isolation again."

We live, men, women and especially the children, between these kinds of alternatives. How can we women be "liberated" as long as all people are not?

Translated by Jeanette Clausen

Notes

* German original: Christa Wolf, "Berührung," *Neue Deutsche Literatur*, no. 2 (1978). Translation based on the abridged version published as the foreword to: Maxie Wander, *Guten Morgen, du Schöne. Frauen in der DDR* (Darmstadt and Neuwied: Luchterhand, 1978), pp. 9–20. Translated and reprinted with permission of the author.

21. Waiting for a Miracle*

Ruth B., twenty-two, waitress,
unmarried, one child.

I think this is my conflict: I live in an age where lots of things are possible for a woman, but I'm a coward. I'm looking for allies first so we can be supportive of each other, because I'm not good for anything by myself. This insane conflict between what's possible and what I'm afraid of is killing me. I lie a lot, but not on purpose; I'm just used to putting on an act. No, wait—I'm also incredibly hard on myself. I didn't use to be like that, I used to hurt other people, not myself. I always became aggressive when things went wrong. I'm in one of those therapy groups now where you can't get away with clever talk. That only works when people are honest with themselves. They say I deceive myself so much because I can't take life the way it is. I always act a lot braver than I am.

I don't usually complain, really. I make everybody think I'm such a great person. At work I soak up my customers' sad tales like a sponge. It never occurs to anybody that I've got my own problems. They dump them all on me. I can't take that for long. You know, for a while I play the clown who can take anything, but all of a sudden I feel . . . I feel so alien among people. Sometimes—sometimes I get on the streetcar or go out to a new restaurant and I get this look on my face, like this . . . I like to imagine what kind of expression actors get on their faces when they're upset or sad. I sit there—it's not an act, I only want someone to notice. But nobody notices. So what. When I'm that way—weak and helpless—I despise myself. You know, there are some people who are never down.

My father's like that, he's never down. He's really above these things. I've never seen my father angry—he's always quiet, never moody. He lives in poetry—I don't know if you can express it like that. He lives with an incredible number of books. Just like my aunt and her birds. Life doesn't have what you find in books, he says.

You'll have to remind me to look for my little boy later. He's all over the place already—just like a man! My neighbor was going to look after him, but she can't handle him either. My father? He lives in my mother's house. I never refer to her as mother. I'm just doing it for you. He lives in his room. Actually it's the room off the garden

170

and it's kind of chilly, but he lives in there with his books. Sometimes his face starts to glow . . . what's wrong—why are you looking at me like that? I can't say it any clearer. Everything depends on the feeling you get. The external conditions you live in don't matter at all. A person can get to that point if he wants to. I'm not at home anywhere either—I don't *want* to be at home anywhere. Least of all in this apartment complex. Do you know how I feel here? I sit in my new armchair in front of the TV and I can picture it all clearly— in every apartment there's somebody sitting in a chair like mine watching TV. They could be talking to each other—they could be, but nobody knows anybody else. That kills me. This guy who lives upstairs, I see him sometimes in the elevator or at the store. He's incredibly good looking and when I'm in bed at night I fantasize about him. But, do you think I've ever said hello to him? At the restaurant I'm not exactly what you'd call tongue tied. But this damn big apartment house, it has an effect on you.

Sometimes—sometimes it seems like I'm not real. Like I mean suddenly my body hasn't got anything to do with me—I'm just observing it. Look at these long skinny fingers of mine—what they can do to men. They're like animals—spiders or something. And when I look at my breasts—look, I don't wear anything under these men's shirts. Look what she hasn't got. Transparent, like mallows— do you know what mallows are? The stupid pill hasn't changed me one bit. Maybe I'd be a real woman if I had real breasts. Well, I think about those kind of things a lot.

How can I explain it all to you? My dad—he's into himself. If you go to his room—he's sixty-six now and doesn't work any more— you can't just start in talking about yourself. It would disturb him, because what you've got to tell him is boring. I have my own chair in his room. It's made of dark green leather, really shabby. I used to sit in it as a child, when I was still small enough to fall through its cracks. That chair really has a nice smell. I've only met one man who smelled like my father, and when I was around him I acted really weird. Of course, he didn't want to find out what was going on with me, he just never showed up again. You always have to put on an act for men, otherwise you scare them away. I never met one guy who was interested in finding out what I'm really like and why I'm that way. They all had one thing in mind with me.

Sure my father knows me. Why do you ask? I can go to him whenever I feel like it. He's got incredible faith in me. But I'll tell you something really strange: When I pick up a book—just touch it—I get a little scared. Sure, I've read books—in school I had to. Right now I think Hesse and Henry Miller are fantastic. Sometimes I devour a book just like that, and then I really see how susceptible

I am to that stuff. Isn't that strange? My dad doesn't mind that I'm
so ignorant or that I read so little. He never makes demands on me.
He's a bookseller by trade, but after the second World War he was
involved in adult education and then he was a Party functionary—
I don't know exactly what his position was. It had something to do
with bookkeeping, but his real interest always lay somewhere else.
    My mother? Forget it, it's not worth it. I don't know what she's
like. I'd like to say she keeps her house clean. But she doesn't even
do that right. The house is falling apart, nothing's in one piece any
more. Well, I'm not about to be a slave to my apartment, you see
that for yourself. But my mother radiates such disgusting optimism,
she's so complacent and self-satisfied; she thrives on her life of chit-
chat, and wining and dining. She really likes to drink, and then she
makes obscene jokes. It's enough for her if the sun shines once a
week. She doesn't make any demands on life. She's never realized
what kind of person lives under the same roof as her. God, that
baby face with brown curls and little brown eyes, everything about
her cute and dumb. A face like that never ages, either. I'm so happy
with my horse face—and my straight black hair. No way do I want
to look like that woman! My father has always treated her like a
baby and spoiled her rotten. He's eighteen years older than she is,
you know. Can't imagine what he saw in her. He's got a couple of
pictures of her hanging in his room. She looks like the Madonna
herself in those pictures. So innocent, unbelievable. Maybe she was
that way once, or she acted like it around him, because he loves
that kind of woman. Now, at any rate, she's a really ordinary person
that I'm ashamed of when she comes to visit me. Once I needled
her and irritated her so much that she said—the gist of it was—I'm
taking money for the things he can't give me. If he went to a
prostitute who'd turn him on, he'd have to pay for that too. I'm
going to buy nice things with that money.
    This money stuff has always revolted me so much. I could never
accept anything from a man. If I sleep with a man it never costs
him a cent. I see red when somebody tries to give me money. I pay
everything out of my own pocket even when I'm up to my ears in
bills. The only thing I accept as a gift is good English tea from the
West.
    You know, I've about had it. Don't ask me for any more details.
If there's one thing I can't stand, it's that American habit of yakking
about everything—it's perverse. I had an American once; he wanted
to get into the farthest corner of my soul after only three days. I
kicked him out even quicker than the others, believe you me. Everything about people has to be "beautiful," has to have style, somehow.
What do you think of when you hear the word "beautiful?"

Well, take Stalin—he was a beautiful man. My mother admired that man a lot. His picture in her bedroom in a gold frame—seriously. When that wasn't appropriate any more, she hid him in her clothes closet. Jeez, I remember how I used to sit there under the open closet door and how sternly Papa Stalin would look down at me. I never had to be afraid of my dad, he never caught on to what I was doing. But I often had a guilty conscience around Stalin.

My poor, poor teachers, they were so absolutely helpless. The more they got upset with me, the worse I behaved. Always the opposite of what I was supposed to! These expectations they hit you with are something else. I think of my childhood as a street full of all kinds of signs with demands and commands written on them. Not one little path to stray onto without a guilty conscience. Sometimes I would have big ideas, I felt like a god, but my teachers would say I hadn't paid attention again and then they'd proceed to drive me nuts with their boring talk. School was an institution of torture. If adults only knew how terribly lonely kids who get into mischief are. The more pigheaded I was the unhappier I felt. Yet sometimes I was insanely happy and the adults don't know that either. I never was that happy again. In your childhood you experience everything in a daze. And the adults continually disrupt everything. That really does kids in. I never gave myself away. Not to anyone. Even now I think women who have no secrets are stupid.

Everything I do is like I'm insane—I read like crazy, love like crazy; then all of a sudden I wanted to go to college, although I hadn't even finished secondary school. Can you imagine me in college? Eventually I almost managed that, too, and then I was satisfied. Only difficult things stimulate me. That's probably why people think I'm crazy. These people who are hung up on reality. They act like it's the only safe side of the river, and you don't dare leave it or you drown. But you have to venture into the water, or the fire. And you just have to overcome your fear. I'm incredibly frightened. If people knew what goes on inside of me at times. Have you ever noticed how people react when they sense a mental breakdown? Then, too, it's really creepy how people can keep on living such dull lives when life is so confusing. Don't they notice that?

That's another conflict: I always want to get away from the safe side of the river. I'd like to try everything. Reality is no yardstick for me—I'd rather hang onto my inner dream. But the people in my therapy group say I always want to be on top of things and never experience any surprises . . . you know what shakes me up? I'll tell you. I'm making myself read the *Lay of the Nibelungs*, which somebody I cared for gave me. I can't get this Brunhilde out of my head. This proud, invincible woman, how Gunther conquers her in bed. Through

Siegfried's trickery, because *he* now had possession of this other woman, Kriemhild. What a dirty rotten trick! It's insane, because something like that could actually happen to you.

Actually, men make me sick. Yet it's incredibly satisfying for me to see them get soft, to lose their cool. First they're so strong and then so weak. I only have contempt for them then. I've lost all my inhibitions. Mentally I'm about ready to walk the streets.

But if you really want to know, I've never had an orgasm. It's true. But when I meet somebody at the restaurant I think of sex right away, because that's what I know. It's my field, know what I mean? As soon as somebody talks about commitment or something weird like that—actually he only has to open his mouth—I have a fit and kick him out. I like married men the best. On the other hand, they're the most boring. Submission—can't stand that word. Has something to do with weakness.

Oh, my kid. He's the whole problem. He's five now and I'm still not a real mother. I impose the, yes, I do it, I impose the strictest obligations on myself. And not one person asks me what a sacrifice that is for me. I almost never wait tables on weekends, although I lose my best tips that way. I forget how young I am just so I can pick my son up from the Center on time. Then we spend all our time together and I see to it that no men come around to visit. But the little guy likes men, because he's surrounded entirely by women at the Center. He's really starved for a father. I'm both mother and father to my son. I don't treat him like a child because it was so terrible for me the way I was treated. I even let him tell me what to do, because he's so practical minded and because, well, because I think it's nice when somebody cares about me.

I can tell you about a dream I had, because it's so typical of my relationship to my son. You know we constantly rebel against our surroundings. Well, I'm really scared that my son is going to be alienated from me by the school system. So I had this dream. We're sitting in a classroom waiting for some mysterious men—school principles or whatever. We're lying fully clothed in a bathtub, my son and I, our legs dangling over the side, just like snotty kids. When one of the gentlemen comes in, I greet him with these words: Your boss has asked me to tell you you're fired. My little boy next to me just about splits a gut laughing and I whisper to him: be quiet, we're only going to be safe when we're rid of all of them!

I know I do everything wrong. I'm not even any good at mothering. And not even animals do *that* wrong. But where am I supposed to get it from? You tell me! I've gotten hard. Sometimes I don't feel anything, I only act like I do. I'd like to go to bed and sleep, just sleep, a long, long hibernation. But I constantly keep going so nobody will catch on. The only place I can stand it is in the city where something's always happening. If I had my way, I'd move to Berlin. It's really pretty out in nature, but I always feel sad there. I'd stay in the city in the summer too, but my little boy can't take it. My interests are completely different from his. And there's not one person who gives me credit for trying anyway.

I'm, I'm . . . completely crusted over. Now I'm crying . . . there, you see. I still . . . still believe—well, in truth, in something that *has* to come. That can't be all there is—these people at the restaurant, sleeping late in the mornings, all these weekends alone with the kid. I like nights the best. You don't have to squeeze into any kind of mold. Men have time for you at night, they're so different than the day after when they've already forgotten about you and are thinking about their wives or their work.

And still, I'm still waiting for a miracle. A woman's *got* to experience something like that once in her life. I hope and hope, and I don't believe in anything any more. I don't believe that orgasms will be a revelation and that's why I resist having one. I'm afraid of being at the mercy of it. Sometimes when I lie awake, you know, I'm so terribly afraid of dying. I'd like to have someone to pray to: Dear I-don't-know-what, let me be a little bit happy some day. I'll pay any price. Sometimes I wonder if I should move in with a woman. There's a woman in our therapy group, and I get along with her great. She's getting a divorce and has a son too. Why shouldn't we live together. Her husband could take over my apartment and everybody would be better off, right?

Now I've got this Chilean—been going with him a week. Intellectually I have nothing against him. But, I've gotten so jumpy again, because he's so trusting. I feel responsible for this guy because he's told me his sad tale and because I've slept with him a couple of times. And not with anyone else in between. It's enough to drive you up the wall. I know perfectly well how it'll turn out. The kid will never get a father. Not with me. Imagine: he'll be fifteen in ten years and I'll be just thirty-two, that's insane.

Oh listen, I'm beyond blaming men. There've been some nice guys who could have lasted with me and the kid. But somehow or other, I don't know, there was always a fly in the ointment. I've thought to myself—they're such different kinds of guys, they all pounce on me because I'm still a nothing. They can see anything they want to in me, I adapt myself to each one. That's really insane. I always made plans right off with the first few guys I had, but never my *own* plans, always theirs. There was this potter, a neat guy, and we already saw ourselves living in a farm house in the mountains doing pottery together. And another guy, half-Portuguese, been living here for ages, wanted of all things to work at the UN in Geneva as an interpreter. So right away I had to learn Portuguese so I could go to Geneva too. We thought it was all actually going to happen. I'm only now beginning to ask myself: Where do *I* fit in in all these stories? What's *mine*, anyway? I haven't the foggiest. I've gotten to know so much life, only I still don't know my own.

I've always looked for models, but all I ever had were people bossing me around. You're doing that wrong, and that too! You're looking at things the wrong way, here, look at X! Just like in school. They never saw what was going on inside of me. And yet I'm not a difficult person, I just won't swallow what people dish out. I'd like to find myself, not somebody else—some little bourgeois type like my stepbrother from my dad's first marriage. They set him up as an example for me, a person without a single independent thought, just out after a lot of money to show off with, to have security. People like that aren't any different from my Grandma in the West. And he has a prominent position, too. Sometimes I ask myself: what society are we building, anyway? A person has dreams, you know. People are born and have a dream. I dream that people will treat each other like people, and there won't be any more selfishness, no more envy, no suspicion. A community of close friends. So. Someone'll be around to say yes to me then.

Translated by Naomi Stephan

Notes

* German original: "Warten auf ein Wunder," Ruth B., 22, Serviererin, ledig, ein Kind. Maxie Wander, *Guten Morgen, du Schöne. Frauen in der DDR.* (Darmstadt and Neuwied: Luchterhand, 1978), pp. 78–87. Translated and reprinted with permission.

Part Six

Sisterhood

This section presents a cross-section of the tangible forms of solidarity or sisterhood generated by the new German women's movement. Primary among these are, of course, the women's centers and projects. Based on principles of self-help and community organizing, these forms of feminist activity are most characteristic of the United States and German movements in particular.

Issues such as women and the legal system and women and the trade unions do not lend themselves as well to the outreach approach of the centers and projects. One might say that there the feminist response has been one of "much sympathy but few deeds," to echo Claudia Pinl's slogan for union policy towards women.

After the founding of the women's movement journals *Courage* and *Emma* in the mid-1970s and the phasing out of the women's centers, the feminist media increasingly took over the protest and support activities previously carried by the centers. This can be seen in the comparison between the *Women's Year Book One* from 1975 which was filled with leaflets and manifestos from women's centers and later yearbooks which contain reports and articles by individual women, reprinted from feminist publications.

22. Aid for Battered Women: The Second Women's House*

Ulrike Pallmert

Most women's projects must find their way through the labyrinth of ordinances and laws which are connected with governmental funding. This article chronicles the struggles of women in West Berlin to establish two shelters for battered women—the earlier of which was West Germany's first such facility. The unspoken exhortation here is to carry on and remain true to the principles of autonomy and self-help with which the work was begun.

The initiative for the creation of a women's shelter in Berlin can be traced back to a women's group which came together in the Winter of 1974/75. In the Summer of 1975, this group began a broad publicity campaign to inform the general public about the situation of women who were being battered by their husbands. This information was picked up by the mass media and also introduced in national parliamentary initiatives. In April of 1976, the television network WDR (West Deutscher Rundfunk) presented "Scream Quietly . . . .," an extensive report on violence against women within the family in West Germany. This documentary also included coverage of types of assistance already available to some abused women: for example, the women's shelters in England.

In January of 1976, the Berlin initiative, "Women's House—Women Helping Women," had already requested money from the National Ministry for Youth, Family and Health. On November 1, 1976, the first women's shelter in West Germany was opened in Berlin. From the beginning, however, this first house was overcrowded. In November of 1978, the first meeting of the initiative group for a second house in Berlin was held. Also in this same year, an initial report on the experiences from the first house was published: *Women Against Male Violence*. In the meantime a report from the professional staff of the first house is in the final stages of production.

In February of 1979, the Organization for Women's Self-Help was formally established. The next step was to find a suitable house to meet the needs of a second shelter. The search was very time-consuming as we received no help from the Berlin Senate, and many landlords did not want to rent space to such a project. In the fall, a massive conflict developed with the Senate office responsible for the project, the Office for Family, Youth and Sport. This involved the proposed financing under the National Social Support Law, whereby the work of the project was to be financed case by case— in other words, for each individual woman who made use of the house. Under this paragraph of the law, only those individuals are eligible for federal support who are unable to help themselves out of a socially undesirable position. The directives are formulated in a very discriminatory manner. Also, by accepting the money, we would have been required to file a report on each woman granted shelter. We chose to deny the Senate this avenue of control, where-upon it threatened to deny us any public funding if we turned down the terms of financing. Differences arose within our group over this issue, eventually leading to the resignation of several women.

By the summer of 1979, the first Berlin women's shelter had become so overcrowded that several staff members publicly announced that they would not assume responsibility for any consequences of this overcrowding. In the meantime, we had found a building which we were able to present to the Senate as a possible second site for a shelter. Through the public attention we had drawn to both the plight of the first house and our on-going work, the situation was ripe for opening the second shelter. After extensive bargaining with the Senate, we were, finally, assured of public monies as soon as the house was opened. By the end of August the first women had already arrived, some of them coming from the first shelter—relieving the situation there somewhat.

The women who come to us have immediate problems. Often it is a question of survival. I am employed as an attorney, mainly in order to provide preliminary legal counseling; most of the legal stuff goes on outside of the shelter. Naturally, however, many areas of work overlap with one another.

As of January 1, 1980, the Senate had agreed to give us six paid positions per year. This sounds like a lot, but in actuality, it represents very little. For one hundred and forty people, women and children included, there are only six paid staff members. This will jeopardize the effectiveness of our work, especially if we remain at this level of funding. As more battered women come to us, we will be limited to acting as wardens. We will be unable to provide even minimal consultation. I do not know how we will keep up with the work. Fortunately we have the women who do volunteer work for us. They are also members of the organization, for we are a women's *self-help* project. The volunteer staff members each come to the house one day a week. They have their specific areas and tasks and are informed by us as to what needs to be done. Of course there is a difference in the dependability of the volunteers as compared to that of staff members with secure, paid positions. There is no need to sweep this under the rug, it is an objective condition that affects all of us. With all of our idealism, even when we work overtime, we are paid for it. The volunteer receives nothing, and this influences her work.

Earlier, I never really knew what it meant to work in a women's shelter. One woman told me how demanding and stressful the work was. After three years she had to quit and try some different kind of work. I have been working now since September, and I can finally understand what she meant. Nevertheless, I am certain that I will continue, in some capacity. The work is so important. Even when it is so draining, you just have to remain strong enough to have something left over to give to it.

Translated by Martina Hildegard

Notes

* Originally published as, Ulrike Pallmert, "Hilfe für misshandelte Frauen— zweites Frauenhaus," in: *Wohin geht die Frauenbewegung?* ed. Gisela Gassen Frankfurt: Fischer Taschenbuch, 1981, pp. 134–150. Translated and reprinted with permission. Portions of this text have been excerpted.

23. Witch Trial in Itzehoe*

This article is made up of material contained in two leaflets put out in August and October of 1974 by the women's center in Frankfurt am Main. This trial, which attracted national publicity, became a rallying cause in the women's movement.

On August 19, 1974, Marion Ihns and Judy Andersen, lesbians, went on trial for murder. They had allegedly hired Denny Pedersen, a Dane, to kill Mrs. Ihn's husband. Pedersen had already been convicted and sentenced to sixteen years by a Danish court. In Itzehoe they are now trying to establish to what degree both women were involved in the planning and carrying out of the murder.

The women have been forced to describe their miserable youths, every rape, their rotten relationships with rotten men, and their most intimate feelings for one another. Because they are in a lesbian relationship they can be packaged as a sexual curiosity and delivered over to a destructive voyeurism without limits. The murder trial serves as a cover for the court to judge the nature of lesbian relationships. The murder trial has become a witch trial. What men have always feared of the women's movement—that it was out to get them, to kill them—is presented here as reality.

Just like the commercial advertisements which display the legs, bust, and teeth of the models for consumption, Marion Ihns and Judy Andersen are made into objects of public spectacle. Their case is used to show all women what men consider to be feminine, what men have made of female sexuality and what punishment exists for those women who reject such a sexuality.

The portrayal of these two women was offered as proof that there are only two kinds of sexual behavior, masculine and feminine. Marion Ihns becomes the feminine woman whom every man wants to rape: a pitiable, weak, brainless victim. Judy Andersen, however, is protrayed as unattractive—and therefore a lesbian; a crane operator who "even professionally looks down on men." She has experienced all her contacts with men as rapes. She is the real enemy who must be destroyed through ridicule and condemnation.

On October 1 both women were condemned to life prison terms. We, the women of the women's center, find this sentence outrageous.

181

Yet all the efforts of the journalists, judges and lawyers have not accomplished one last objective. They cannot disprove the fact that these two women had more than enough reason to turn away from men and to love one another.

When Marion and Judy fell in love with one another they discovered that they had much in common. Both had been raped as children. Marion saw marriage as a way to escape from her family and her past. Instead she jumped from the frying pan into the fire. What did her marriage with Mr. Ihns look like? At first she was glad that her husband did not force her to have sex with him. This lasted only as long as he was impotent. He even accepted the fact that she slept with a friend of his, as long as he could uphold the outward appearance of an intact marriage. At some point Marion realized that her marriage was becoming a hell on earth. In this repressive situation it was impossible for her to extract even a little happiness out of her life. Then Judy and Marion met, and for the first time Marion received real support from someone. The women began a sexual relationship.

When Ihns learned that Marion wanted to leave him for a woman and not for another man, he threatened to kill her. He actually went so far as to try and poison her. In order to restore his damaged male image, Ihns raped his wife up to three times a day.

The only legal way out (i.e., divorce) was also thwarted by Ihns. While Marion was in Denmark visiting Judy, he bombarded them with abuse and blackmail, threatening to take away their (his and Marion's) child. Marion was pulled back and forth between various guilt feelings.

Marion and Judy, as women, could not escape this constant pressure in any way other than by murdering Mr. Ihns. Their right to free themselves of this kind of terrorism caused them to resort to violence. The violence of self-defense! This is why we declare solidarity with Judy and Marion and demand their release!

As women we have learned the following from the trial in Itzehoe: The system of justice protects laws which continue to uphold the dominance of men over women. Otherwise the violence that Judy and Marion had already experienced in their lives would have been taken into account. There is also a different standard of justice for men and for women. When women resort to violent means they are punished much more harshly than are men.

The other solution for dealing with "violent" women is to declare them insane and have them placed in asylums where they can be further broken down. There are 50 percent more women in asylums than men. This is how a society responds to women who fight back in a hopeless situation.

Translated by Martina Hildegard

Notes

* First appeared as: "Hexenprozess in Itzehoe," *Frauenjahrbuch 1* Frankfurt am Main: Verlag Roter Stern, 1975, pp. 219–224. Translated and reprinted with permission. Portions of this text have been excerpted.

24. Pimps on Trial in Bochum Prostitutes Testify*

Ingrid Strobl

The West German women's movement has tried to extend its support to prostitutes—as sisters and working women who receive a wage for honest work, under deplorable conditions. This trial was widely commented upon in the feminist press.

In the Bochum Superior Court three suits have been brought against seven defendants for "exploitative" and "manipulative" procurement, intimidation, blackmail, deprivation of liberty, grievous bodily harm, rape, and slave trading. Two suits in this, "the largest procuring trial in the Ruhr," are being heard by Presiding Judge Krüper and one by a woman, Alheidis Hussmann, forty years old, calm, cool, self-assured. She must be in order to keep her composure in this trial. Most of the witnesses were under eighteen, between fifteen and seventeen when they were forced into prostitution. A small sample of the methods: The pimps put LSD into the girls' beer and then raped them, or they got them drunk, spiking their drinks with Valium, then drove them to an apartment where they raped them, locked them up, and broke them down for prostitution. Beating, whipping, razor blades, knives and boot heels are the order of the day.

Fifty-seven Charges

The Accused: Pale, shy, some of them would attract no attention on the street. The last occupation you would attribute to them is pimp. Another woman from the press shares my horror. "When I went back to Hamburg on the train the first day, I looked around the car and thought, my God, every other man in here could be a pimp." The best looking is also supposed to be the most brutal. A "real sadist." At any rate the other ones fit the usual image of a pimp: open shirt, lots of gold chains and brutal faces.

The Male Presiding Judge: A real comedian. His little jokes evoke particular mirth in the defendants.

The Female Presiding Judge: She finds the situation less humorous. Above all for the witnesses. Therefore she granted their requests and sometimes excluded the public from the proceedings.

The Public: Housewives, old-age pensioners, the usual kibitzers and plenty of the boys from the defendants' milieu. They are very fond of His Honor because he always gives them something to laugh at.

The Prosecutor: Without him the trial would never have come about. He is concerned about the women. "They have to perform a spiritual striptease in this gigantic courtroom, we can't justify that." Prosecutor Romaneck would be happier if the public remained outside during at least some of the witnesses' testimony.

The Witnesses: They know what is in store for them. They are at least safe from the accused, who are in custody, but the latter's friends are free and accustomed to searching out the "girls" and "punishing" them. Some of the witnesses have in the meantime managed to get out, and are living in other cities and working in "straight" jobs.

The Defense Attorneys: They are all assigned counsel, except for one. They find it annoying when the witnesses appear too self-assured. "She knows details that even the average lawyer doesn't know!"

TAZ (Die Tageszeitung): This "leftist" daily paper doesn't know which side to take. Its reporter, G.H., after four days at the trial, still couldn't say: "These are the good guys and those are the bad guys." He/She "cannot side with *the* women against *the* men."

Although it often gives this impression, the trial is not being held as a public festival. And even though it is unique in the Federal Republic, it stands in a wider international and historical context. Prostitutes in Grenoble brought their pimps to court—and won. This example found followers, and the spirit of resistance spread to prostitutes in Belgium, Switzerland, even in Austria. The women's movement has been deeply concerned about the problem of prostitution in recent years. (By the way, not for the first time: The radical feminists of the first women's movement had already made some very unconventional observations on this question around the turn of the century.)

While the witnesses in the Bochum trial didn't step forth as plaintiffs as the Grenoble women did, they did testify, and they did it amidst very real threats to their lives. The defendants have already shown what they can do.

Before the court the roles keep reversing. The witnesses become the accused and the accused amuse themselves royally on the bench: "You can't believe a word she says, she needs more alcohol than a three-liter Mercedes needs gas!" joked one of the pimps over his "ex," to the enthusiasm of the public.

"If I had known it would be like this, I wouldn't have given a word of testimony!" one of the witnesses tells me over a beer. But she will continue to testify, against the other ones as well. I tell her I admire her courage. She shrugs her shoulders.

Translated by Pamela Selwyn

Notes

* Originally appeared as "Zuhälterprozess in Bochum: Prostituierte Sagen Aus!" *EMMA* Vol. 4 (Dec. 1980), pp. 5–7. Translated and reprinted with permission. Portions of this text have been excerpted.

25. Much Sympathy, But Few Deeds: Union Policy Toward Women*

Claudia Pinl

The autonomous German women's movement has shown little interest in working through the trade unions to fight the discrimination against and exploitation of women at the work place. However, this article states the current situation and poses avenues of possible feminist strategy.

The socialist theory of women's emancipation was based on the premise that the inclusion of women into gainful employment was the prerequisite for their emancipation. Capitalism as the great equalizer of all members of the proletariat was also supposed to even out differences between the proletarian man and woman. As equals among equals, women workers together with the men of their class were to take up the struggle against capitalism.

The socialist theory of women's emancipation never really gained a firm footing in the German trade unions. Up to a point, one paid it lip service, but in practice the trade union movement was almost without exception hostile to women—from its origins in the nineteenth century up until 1933. In women's equality, their male colleagues correctly saw an attack on their privileges within the family and at the work place.

After fascism and the war, all antiwoman rhetoric disappeared from the official utterances of union functionaries. But it was not until the economic upswing of the postwar years, when labor became scarce, that the German Trade Union Association (DGB) could bring itself to support women's employment.

Union leaders are great ones for championing women workers when addressing political parties, the parliament, ministries or public boards. But when it comes to setting their own policy, unions are much more reserved with regard to the woman question. That unions are willing and able to represent women's interests in the general political arena can be seen in the case of social policy. There, unions have fought for reforms such as worker protection and pensions which are of benefit to women.

It is quite another matter in the area of union wage policy. In spite of decades of equal rights' rhetoric on the part of trade unions nothing has changed in the wage discrimination against women. The unions' wage policy is aimed at improving the classification for the lower wage groups, so that the special psychological pressures at women's work places are more fully taken into account. In addition, unions have pursued a policy of continually raising the levels of the lower groups, so that in many categories the difference between the lowest paid unskilled work and that of the basic wage—the wage for simple skilled work—is only 80–85 percent. At the same time, however, in many areas, such as metal work and printing, the top levels of the wage pyramid have been extended to create new wage groupings for especially qualified skilled labor. The wage hierarchy, wherein women occupy the lowest rungs, thereby continues to remain in place.

The discrimination in pay scales is set by wage contracts, but it is carried out in the factories. There the employees are divided into wage groups, but it is the premiums, bonuses and benefits which determine what each individual has at the end of the week or month in their account or their paycheck. In this, the employers cannot act on their own accord. The company councils (Betriebsräte) help devise the contracts, especially the breakdown of the different groupings, what is paid for each completed piece of work and what premiums are offered.

The company councils are not organs of the trade unions but made up of representatives of the employees within the company. On the other hand, most council members are active unionists. The chairs of the company councils of large concerns act as honorary function-aries within the union and have a large say in many of the policy determinations of the union. One might assume that they would feel obligated to follow through on the unions' programs. This, however, is not the case. Women are still the weakest groups within the employee power structures. Agreements and compromises between management and company councils, therefore, are often made at the women's expense. In this fashion, many councils—caught up them-selves in patriarchal attitudes—provide, in management's interest, cheap, passive, continually hirable, easily firable female labor.

For decades, female unionists have been appealing for the solidarity of the working men, especially the shop stewards and those in the company councils. At the women's conference of the Association for Metal Workers (IGM) in 1958, one of the delegates said:

> It is not enough to recommend that women fight for their own wage scales and classification . . . the support must

come from the men in the plants and factories. They make up the majority on the wage commissions, and the wage question depends on them and their attitudes. If solidarity was ever necessary, then it is here that it should be demonstrated.

What can we do? Here are some proposals. A politics limited to equal rights cannot completely solve the problem, but, carried out forcefully, it could create better conditions, as in the case of East Germany and Sweden. The hope that through greater female membership and cooperation union policy will become more supportive to women is illusory, as long as there is no pressure from outside the unions. In the long and short run a supportive policy towards women can be accomplished only through women's caucuses; such as those that exist in French, Italian, and British factories, and in some West German sectors (i.e., some radio stations). Nevertheless, to withdraw totally from the unions is still wrong. Even a bad union can provide minimal protection to women as dependent employees.

Translated by Martina Hildegard
and Edith Hoshino Altbach

Notes

* Originally published as, Claudia Pinl, "Viel Trost und wenig Taten: die Frauenpolitik der Gewerkschaften," in *Frauen als bezahlte und unbezahlte Arbeitskräfte. Beiträge zur 2. Berliner Sommeruniversität für Frauen, 1977* Berlin, 1978, pp. 282–289. Translated and reprinted with permission. Portions of this text have been excerpted.

26. Turkish Women in Berlin
An Interview
with Cornelia Mansfeld*

In the wake of the absorption of foreign workers into the West German economy during the 1960s and 1970s, immigrant (largely Turkish) communities have become a part of all major West German cities. Through their work in women's shelters and other projects, German women have come into close contact with Turkish and other immigrant women. This article concentrates on the mutual benefits in consciousness raising when women of the First world and women of the Third world learn from each other.

In Kreuzberg, (one of the subdivisions of West Berlin where a large percentage of Turkish emigrants live), an initiative has been started by Turkish and German women to make connections to the lives Turkish women had in their home villages. The group has a small storefront that functions as a meeting and information center; it is for (Turkish) women only. Counseling is offered, similar to that available at the district counseling center. It also offers German and literacy training courses, and a Sunday breakfast where the women can meet and talk. This is similar to the get-to-gethers among neighborhood women common in Turkish villages, small cities and the migrant quarters of larger cities.

Q. How many women come to the store, how many work there regularly, and how many take advantage of the language and skills training offered?

A. Up to now all of us have only worked in the store during our spare time. This is true for the Turkish women, who are mostly working women and students, as well as for the Germans, who usually began working with Turkish women through social work. For this reason the store's potential has thus far been limited. Nevertheless, the German course is regularly filled with ten women. This course not only has the function of teaching German, but also offers the women another opportunity to discuss their personal situations, through role playing, etc. At this point, even though we have not publicized the existence of the store in the district, we have as many women coming for counseling as we can handle. By the fall of this year we will probably be officially supported and financed. At that time we will be able to broaden the scope of our activities and publicize our services more widely.

I would like to address a problem that is usually left out of discussions on emigrant workers but that I find important. The families of foreign workers are dependent on the earnings they receive from abroad. Even when the wife does twice the work (her own and her husband's), the land cannot produce any more. After all, the reason for the husband's emigration in the first place was that the land could not guarantee the subsistence of the family. As soon as the husband begins earning money in a foreign country, the work of the wife is no longer as highly valued. A division is established between paid and unpaid labor which did not previously exist in the traditional Turkish village. There the husband and wife both worked without pay. The labor of both was necessary for survival and was therefore equally valued and respected. An emigrant who had returned to his village for vacation was asked why he was not helping with the harvest. He replied: "Why should I work? I am on vacation. My wife does not work all year, let her do it." Agrarian production, insofar as it is unpaid, is no longer seen as real work. This reflects the standards in West Germany, where housework is also not valued as real labor.

Q. How did you come upon the idea of working with Turkish women? Do you see the possiblity for going beyond social work to the beginnings of better communications between German and foreign women, both here and in the countries of origin? Perspectives that can be extended to other parts of the women's movement?

A. I had to confront the problems of Turkish women and foreign emigration because of my work. In the office where I worked the clients were mainly Turkish women and their families. I learned a great deal in this period. The first important realization was that in their relations with other women Turkish women are less influenced by fears of competition and isolation than are German women. I remember well at the beginning of the women's movement how hard we German women had to work to break down the barriers between us.

This is not a problem among Turkish women. All of them have intensive experience in living with other women. It is through the process of emigration that this is partially or fully destroyed. Emigration isolates the women from one another. Yet they have still had the home experience and are not as competitive with one another as German women still are today. One reason for this may be that Turkish women frequently cannot choose the man they will marry. The woman, as well as the man, marries according to the parental arrangement. Not love but rather economic considerations come into play: Is the wife a good worker, can the groom pay a suitable bride price? By our criteria this is a limitation of individual freedom, but this limitation actually leaves Turkish women far less emotionally dependent upon their husbands than are German women. Turkish women are psychologically more independent; they draw their psychological strength and stability from the bonds they form with other women—relatives and neighbors. Yet, the women's movement tends to look at Turkish women with pity, seeing them as poor, unfree, oppressed beings. This stems from a limited view of freedom that does not include an analysis of our own lack of freedom.

A political conclusion I have drawn is that Turkish women could tell us German women a great deal. On the other hand, German women could share their experience with small families, isolation, and economic and social dependence. Many Turkish women dream of marrying a man who earns enough for them to be able to stop working. This is understandable in view of their working conditions, but it is not a solution; it is a dead end. In the meantime, German women have learned this lesson.

When German and Turkish women share their experience they can establish that a housewife's existence is no better than that of a woman who works both inside and outside the home. The necessary conclusion is that housework must finally be paid. A dialogue between Turkish and German women, as between any and all women with different life experiences, will strengthen us all.

Translated by Martina Hildegard

Notes

* Originally published as, Cornelia Mansfeld, "Türkische Frauen in Berlin," *Blätter des Informationszentrum Dritte Welt* (August, 1979), pp. 25–29. Translated and reprinted with permission. Portions of this text have been excerpted.

27. The Youth Centers Release Their Children: On the Needs of Young Women to Spend Their Free Time in Freedom*

Monika Savier

During the decade of the 1970s, feminist social workers in West Germany focused on the situation of girls in the youth centers. The goal was to transform the centers into "liberated spaces" where the girls could find relief from the pressures of home and school while being helped toward a stronger and more autonomous self-image and perspective. In this article, the author suggests that perhaps the girls have been developing autonomous forms of resistance which reach far beyond the youth centers.

After having made attempts to gain ground in the youth centers, girls seem to have decided that this cannot be their territory and is not worth the struggle. At least, one can observe that far fewer girls than boys are found in either the state or church run centers. Increasingly, young women prefer to spend their free time in freedom. During the Seventies, "liberated struggle" in the organized centers meant the creation of new forms of communication based on the reigning ideology of "free sexuality." For young women, however, all this accomplished was the entrenchment of their status as sexual objects. Their role as male accessory was made more ideologically acceptable. The day to day forms of sexual violence, now legitimated, helped to break down the resistance of the girls. Perhaps the mothers who forbade their daughters to go to youth centers did so not out of a conservative family orientation but an awareness of the dangers to their daughters.

The strength for resistance can come only from the young women themselves. Perhaps, however, girls have been developing autonomous forms of resistance all along. Perhaps we have just not yet noticed them because we lack the antennae to detect the new styles in the subculture. If this is the case, then the girls have not only freed themselves from the males, but also from the social workers and other authorities!

> We ask ourselves more and more: Is there life before death? Education no longer functions as an institution for bestowing social and career opportunities. Those who work hard do not get apprenticeships or better job opportunities. There is no decent housing for independent young people except that which is forcibly taken and occupied (by squatters). Those who save have nothing today and most likely nothing tomorrow. To live conscious of time means to live in the here and now.*

This consciousness is an incontrovertibly new attitude toward life. With males, however, the need to "get the most out of their situation" is frequently turned into "letting it all hang out." In their opinion there is not much worth getting into which does not involve harming others.

Young women, on the other hand, express their own "no-future feelings" more through the morally unbounded display and adornment of their own bodies. This "frees the self and also shocks people." In the last couple of years they have also taken part in creating collective living quarters for girls or women only, in house occcupations by and for women, and in women's evenings in the basements of occupied houses taken by mixed groups.

Developing a new internal self-awareness has become increasingly a primary goal of social work among young women. However, the new *inner* awareness proposed by social workers seems to be only *half* of what the girls themselves want. They also want to create new *external* images for themselves. Props and elements of personal style may be viewed as creative signs of collective resistance to the outside world. They are actually a step in the right direction, away from the traditional female functions as male accessory. The totality that these women are looking for should not be merely something that makes everyday life more bearable but rather something that can give them a perspective on a life worth living.

Recognizing that the "youth of today" have, through their political activity, finally broken through the current fatalism and that they are acting as our representatives in doing this, some questions remain.

How are the young women in the future going to deal with the legitimization of political violence, for example, in the illegal occu-

---

* From a paper by the Girls-group Froebenstrasse, "We are not brainless and harmless, but, rather, clear-headed and shameless.

pation of housing by squatters? Are they going to rush to catch up with male forms of violence, even to the extent of emulating them? Or is their own experience with such male violence ever-present enough to enable them to develop responses in resistance to the male methods?

This will be the test of the next period. Will they be able to combat the men's style when necessary, while continuing to remain active in bringing about a worthwhile reality?

Edited and Translated by Martina Hildegard

Notes

* Originally published as: Monika Savier, "Das Freizeitheim entlässt seine Kinder: Über das Bedürfnis von Mädchen, ihre Freizeit wieder in Freiheit zu verbringen," *Autonomie aber wie! Mädchen, Alltag, Abenteuer.* ed. Angela McRobbie and Monika Savier. Munich: Frauenoffensive, 1982, pp. 137–150. Translated and reprinted with permission. Portions of this text have been excerpted.

Part Seven

Struggles, Visions, and Dreams

The texts in this section show women trying to get beyond the confining roles prescribed for us. The emphasis is usually more on the struggle than the dream, but the vision of change, though unrealized, demand attention.

Margot Schroeder (1937–), likes her protagonist in *Take It Like a Woman* the mother of two children, portrays a working-class woman trying to implement her feminist convictions in her daily life. Though not strictly speaking an autobiographical work, this first novel portrays some of Schroeder's personal struggles. Angelika Mechtel (1943–), also a West German author sympathetic to the problems of the working class, presents in "Katrin" a more abstract picture of a housewife/mother/part-time employee and the compromises she must make. GDR author Irmtraud Morgner (1933–), always alert to obstacles to women's emancipation, offers a whimsical vision for escape from dreary everyday reality in "The Duel" and a more pointed critique in "Shoes" and "The Rope." Christine Wolter (1939–), also from the GDR, presents in "I have married again" a tongue-in-cheek solution to problems of inequality in marriage. Concluding this section is an excerpt from *Sonja*, the first literary effort of West German academic Judith Offenbach (a pseudonym). Offenbach writes of her relationship with her disabled lover Sonja after the latter's death by suicide. The book is at once a protocol of Judith's mourning, a memorial to Sonja, and an attempt to document the daily life of a lesbian couple.

28. Take It Like a Woman

Margot Schroeder

Charlie Bieber, a Hamburg housewife, mother and part-time grocery clerk, wants to organize the residents in her apartment complex to protest a letter from Mr. Hansen, the landlord, complaining of damage their children did to the lawn. Charlie's neighbor Mrs. Conrad has volunteered to arrange a meeting with Hansen as this excerpt from the novel begins. Charlie's self-ironic humor is characteristic of much of Schroeder's prose writing. Take It Like a Woman *was her first novel.*

And you're washing the crud off the dishes, Charlie. And your sea is a gravy of water, liquid detergent and garbage. You make suds. The sun scowls into the kitchen curtains. Fork-skeletons shine. Glasses twinkle. Boy, is washing dishes great. In the flawlessly scoured lid of this pot you can see your pores shining in wide-angle distortion. You're a clown, Charlie.

I can never talk to you, even after lunch. Says Susanne.

We just did.

The same crap all the time. At school—

What happened at school?

The way he bumps into me, it's on purpose. He said to Kalle, she's got a great body. And his drawings, Charlie. I brought one home from school once. His desk drawer is full of them. He's always drawing during class. Caricatures and like that. Want me to show you?

Maybe later.

I've about had it with that.

Mrs. Conrad was going to call Hansen today.

That again. You're going to go bananas, Charlie.

I'm anxious to know what he's going to say.

I won't see Knüddel tomorrow. They're going on a field trip.

Think he'll give us an appointment? I ask.

School doesn't turn me on at all. When Knüddel's not there, nothing's happening.

We're talking past each other. We wash dishes. I'm sad. The children: here and there a kiss or a kind word. Haven't you lost contact with them since you started working, Charlie? This place is like Grand

Central Station. And now you're starting up this community action, on top of everything else. You talk to your neighbors but you tell your children you don't have time for them. Am I the only one responsible for them? Why doesn't Werner ever have a guilty conscience?

He just says "Your kids." He pushes them off on me. After work because he's tired and on Sundays because he's working on the car. He just doesn't notice. His good-humored way of talking: hey, big girl, hiya, son. Be fair, Charlie, he works his tail off. And what about you? That's different, real different. You're just a housewife, you just work to help out, you're just a mother. That's all, a by-the-way person. What if you wanted a career? Your mother would say: those poor kids. The neighbors would say: that pushy woman.

The more I think about it, the loonier it seems I am. I love the children, I respect myself. I want the children to be something someday. I want to be something someday. I want an equal chance. Is that a crime? Unnatural, that's what it is. The man provides for the family. The woman goes to the dogs. That's natural.

Susanne's doing her homework. The building is quiet. Now and then someone flushes a toilet. A door slams shut. At times like these I become aware of the apartment. Our home. The grease-spattered wallpaper in the kitchen. The shabby carpet in the hallway. The broken latches on the closet doors in the bedroom. The worn out upholstery of the living room furniture. The scratched bathtub.

This feeling: everything's falling apart. This uneasiness: not doing enough. This self-accusation: you're a failure. I sit in the armchair unable to move. You ought to be darning socks, ironing, giving the place a good cleaning. You need a drink, Charlie. But at 3:30 you've got to be at the kindergarten. You can have two, Charlie. Schnaps dilates the blood vessels. Two. How many do salesmen drink on the road? How many do bosses drink with their business partners? How many does Werner drink on the job?

I'm on my way to the kitchen. On the hallway floor I run into Susanne's coat. Taken off and dropped. One sleeve in—one sleeve out.

Susanne, I yell. What's this?

No answer.

Susanne!

She comes out of their room dragging her feet.

Yeah?

What's the reason for this?

For what?

This coat.

Come off it.

She picks it up slowly. Shrugging her shoulders she hangs it up in the closet. One sleeve in—one sleeve out. That's too much for my nerves. I don't slap her, I don't bitch her out. I start to cry.

Come on, forget that meeting with the landlord. Says Susanne.

Lie on the couch and think about Ulli. You're trying to recapture his face. But you can't. As if there were a nylon stocking over it. Still, that weekend at the beach, that love marathon. Do you still remember when I was so drunk, Ulli? I could taste salt water. I remember it perfectly. Haven't forgotten a thing.

You're going to catch cold. You said.

I love the sea. Said I.

And I ran, and I fell and I ran. I threw stones in the surf. I lay down in the sand. I threw wet sand in my face.

Are you crazy? You said.

I laughed. I lay in the sand and laughed. The clear starry night: beautiful, beautiful, beautiful.

You're not free. You said.

Liberate me, I said.

Your nerves are shot. You said.

I got sick. I stood up and ran towards the sea. I threw up running. The wind tore strings of mucus from my fingers. I was cold.

Come on now. You said and wiped off my face with a kleenex.

I'm a slob. Said I.

You're drunk, that's all. You said.

I'm a slob. Said I.

If you say so. You said.

I clung to the sleeve of his jacket.

You can make me a child, why can't you make me a brain? I asked. If you could, Ulli, I'd screw till I was a genius.

You think too much in terms of the individual. You said.

Let's form a collective. Said I.

You loved me madly. Was our love class hatred?

Class hatred, Charlie? What are these categories you always think in when you think about Ulli? There was so much tenderness in your love. Don't kid yourself, Charlie. Have you forgotten how he destroyed every tender moment? His letters: it was great with you, but I'm not really in love with you. You've got to understand. Even love between two people has to be a component of a larger group. Individual happiness is irresponsible in a collective. Why did you ever sign your letters "Yours, Ulli? " And just think, the grass roots you were trying to reach had to look up all those foreign words in your letters in the dictionary. When I used to point that out to you sometimes, you'd laugh. You laughed me right back to Werner.

You're just someplace in between, Charlie. Sitting on thin air, a floating asshole. Get up, you've got to pick up your son.
Six thirty already. Why doesn't that Conrad woman call? Wonder if she got us an appointment. Maybe she was scared to ask Hansen? Even if she was, Conrad's pretty dependable. If only because she doesn't want to make an ass of herself in front of the others. But why doesn't she call back? Susanne, Wulf and I eat supper. Werner's lying on the living room couch sleeping. I'm worried about him. Lately he complains more and more about kidney problems.
What're you thinking, Mommy? Asks Wulf.
Nothing.
Is nothing something?
Nothing's nothing.
Why're you thinking then, if nothing's nothing?
Oh, Wulf.
Mom's tired, Wulf. Susanne says.
She can sleep any old time. Says Wulf.
He bites off pieces of his bread to make it look like a ship. A battleship, Mom. Says he.
What's a battleship, Wulf?
Bang, bang, he says. And points a cannon-shaped piece of bread at me.
Do you know what war means? I ask.
Somebody wins.
Everybody loses. Say I.
You're trying to fool me. When big Tom beats up on me, I've losed.
Lost, Wulf. Why do you think big Tom beats up on you?
Because he's stronger.
Don't you have any friends?
Bernie, Mark and Benno.
Okay, how about if the three of you get together to defend yourself against Tom?
Is that war, Mommy?
What I mean is, if the three of you play next to him, he's not as likely to hit you.
And is that war?
That's how you avoid war. You keep peace.
What's peace?
When you don't beat up on each other.
Wulf nods satisfied. He finishes eating his battleship. I've gotten him fed up. I've explained a cease-fire to him. That's all I know about peace.
You've got patience with Wulf. Says Susanne.
But not with your love life?

Those few minutes when we were washing dishes.
You practically follow me to the john, Susanne.
I have rights too.
You do it, though.
I'm bugging you, huh?
Cut it out.
Seems to disagree with you, Charlie.
The phone rings. Well finally. I light a cigarette. I trip over Susanne's legs. Why's the phone have to be in the bedroom anyway?
Biebers, I say. When I can't see the person I'm talking to my voice starts sounding refined.
This is Mrs. Conrad. Hello, Mrs. Bieber.
Hello.
Have you been waiting with bated breath?
That's putting it mildly. I'm breathless.
Well, I called Mr. Hansen about five o'clock and told him that the families in question were really offended by his letter of complaint. Mrs. Bieber, the man was beside himself. I almost dropped the phone. He yelled that those brats are terrorizing the neighborhood and he was already considering taking them to court for the damage to the lawn.
Huh? Court? I ask.
Yes, just imagine. I tell you, I was appalled. Mr. Hansen, I said, your complaint is far in excess of the minimal damage caused by our kids. I'd advise you to try to take the gophers to court next. Mr. Hansen didn't know what to say to that. After a while he asked if we were willing to assume the cost of repairing the damage. I said we'd have to talk about it. And then he raved on about lack of time, the tenants should be thankful, the Lord knows he's not exploiting anyone, but that's gratitude for you, this development only pays him a small dividend, it's a modest retirement income. I didn't reply to any of that. I only asked him when would be a good time for us to meet. I think I got him with my business-like reaction, Mrs. Bieber. He barked back at me and asked if Friday night at eight would be okay. I was so surprised I agreed right then and there. Please don't tell me you're doing something on Friday.
Hey, even if I had an invitation to a wedding I'd turn it down. Wow, Mrs. Conrad, that was really terrific. I say.
You think so?
I would've blown my cool if he'd barked at me like that.
You can't fight aggression with aggression.
That's what a college education is for. Say I.
I didn't finish my degree.

Still, it's something, Mrs. Conrad. Say, I hope Mrs. Thiede and Mrs. Ludwig can come on Friday evening.

They can. I called them already. They're both coming over tonight. And you're welcome to come too. Do you have time? My husband has a meeting tonight, so we can have the place to ourselves. I think we should get together to discuss what to say to Mr. Hansen on Friday. We'll have to agree among ourselves. Can you come, Mrs. Bieber?

I don't answer right away. I got this whole thing started and now Conrad calls up the others first. Does she want to dump me? Does she want to push me out?

Are you still there? She asks.

I can come. I say.

This day has been incredibly positive. She says. How about eight o'clock? I'll have a little blue-collar drink for you, too.

Thanks, I say. See you later.

I hang up. Do I hate that woman. The only thing marriage did for her was teach her how to say "my husband," and now she wants to get even by summoning the "ladies" to her place. Don't forget, Charlie, it's a new thing for her. Community awareness is in.

Susanne comes into the bedroom.

Boy, are you long-winded.

Get Wulf ready.

What should I do?

Put Wulf to bed.

I have to go to my guitar lesson.

You'll get there late, then.

Are you out of your tree?

I have to go out tonight.

Again?

The meeting with the landlord is Friday. Today we're getting together at Mrs. Conrad's to discuss things.

Hey, Charlie, it worked?

Yeah.

She's pretty cool, that Mrs. Conrad. Never would've guessed it.

I thought you were in a hurry, Susanne?

I'm going, I'm going. How did Conrad manage to pull it off? Oh well, I would've lost my nerve too, Mom. I mean, there's not much in it for you in the long run.

I don't quite follow you. Say I.

The way Mrs. Conrad can express herself and stuff. You're always telling me to go to college. I bet Conrad did.

Get going, Susanne.

Don't drink, Mom. Says she.

Susanne puts Wulf to bed. Werner is still asleep. He smacks his lips
in his sleep. I wonder if his dreams taste good. One more hour,
Charlie. What're you going to do? Are you going to go? Going to
let Conrad buy you off with a couple of drinks? But isn't Susanne
right? Have a few ahead of time and then don't drink at Conrad's.
But why is Susanne right? Haven't you been giving her the impression
all along that you fill in the gaps in your education with schnaps?
Why do you want a drink now? Because you're mad at Conrad?
Because of your bourgeois jealousy? Or is it your inhibitions again?
These damn hang-ups. Your friends at work all say: you think you've
got hang-ups. Werner says: you talk like a steamroller. Your friend
Elke says: I'd just like to have your self-confidence. Of course you've
got confidence in yourself. Now and then you feed it with delusions
of grandeur. Charlie Bieber: unique and irresistible. Of course you're
going to have hang-ups.
You've gone at your neighbors with the same ironic arrogance as
with Werner and the women at work. Those are human beings,
Charlie, not some theoretical proletarians or classical cases of exploited
workers. Do you think of them as copies dittoed off, to be pasted
in a scrapbook on class struggle, maybe even with a dedication?
How do you actually feel about them? Do you think Mrs. Thiede
and Mrs. Conrad are proletarians? But Mrs. Ludwig, now there's
material for you, Charlie. Go ahead and say it: human material.
Have you forgotten why you fell out of love with Ulli? Humans, he
always used to say, are basically a means to an end. Making a big
deal out of love is just so much sentimental eyewash. And this idiot
claims to be struggling for a more humane future. With a brain like
a computer: the new, social, just, gentle human being emerges from
theories, from a test tube.
I pace restlessly back and forth in the living room. When I'm excited,
I develop an abnormal sensitivity to noises. The clock's ticking sounds
like screams. Werner's snoring is like a one-man orgy. Look at that
ashtray again. And the rest of it. Werner lets his cigarette ashes drop
any old place—on the table, the upholstery, the rug. What's the use,
he says, it's too late to change me. Right, Werner, but why doesn't
it ever occur to you to clean up your own mess? That's what the
maid's for, the old lady, Charlie, your personnel department.
Susanne peeks around the door.
I'm leaving now. She says.
Is Wulf in bed?
Where else would he be? He wants you to say goodnight to him.
I will.
You're in a lousy mood today.
You'll be late, Susanne.

Wasn't I supposed to?
Don't be snotty.
Well, it's true.
She leaves without saying goodbye. Do I take advantage of her?
Can't a fourteen-year-old put her brother to bed once in a while?
It's time to go, Charlie, almost eight.
I go into the children's room.
Sleep tight, Wulf. Say I.
Cuddle, Mommy.
He hugs me and strokes my face.
Get in bed with me a minute, Mommy.
I can't right now. I have to go over to Mrs. Conrad's. You remember her.
That old bitch?
Wulf!
Shit, prick, asshole.
He grins at me and repeats it all again slowly:
Shit, prick, asshole.
Fart, piss, shithead. I say.
That wasn't what he expected. He cocks his head and sizes me up for a while.
What did you say that for, Mommy?
And what did you say that for?
Will you tell me a story, Mommy?
There's not time enough now, Wulf.
Just the short one about the giant dog, just that short one.
Tomorrow I'll tell you two instead.
You always say tomorrow.
Really, Wulf.
I give him a kiss. He turns away.
You're not my favoritest woman any more, he says.
I'm sad.

Translated by Jeanette Clausen and Marjorie Tussing

Notes

* German original: Margot Schroeder, *Ich stehe meine Frau* (Frankfurt/M.: Fischer Taschenbuch, 1975), pp. 92–101. (c) 1975 by Fischer Taschenbuch GmbH, Frankfurt/M. and Werkkreis Literatur der Arbeitswelt, Cologne. Translated and reprinted with permission. Portions of this text have been excerpted.

29. *Katrin**

Angelika Mechtel

Mechtel's narrator condenses her married life into a series of poignant short statements, wondering at the end if her daughter's more assertive behavior means hope. Mechtel has published lyric poetry and reportages as well as prose fiction; the dense, concentrated prose of this text is a method she returned to after experiments in other directions.

I've had his children. I've learned my place. I've tried to see him the way I saw my mother see her husband. I've learned to wash diapers, comfort children, and keep order.

Once I learned Latin and mathematics, physics and French. I was an average student. I've let myself be petted and hit. I've hit back. I've learned that he is my superior.

I've watched my body swell out; I've survived the births, told myself: that's part of being a woman. I've convinced myself I wanted to be happy. I've seen him off to work and cooked the meals.

I've seen his fear when I had a fever, and his impatience when the baby screamed.

I've let him send my mother away because she dried diapers on the oven door in our one-room apartment and left the milk on the window sill. I learned that he could say what was on his mind: what are people going to think? I didn't understand a thing. I got used to it.

I've asked what's bothering him. I've listened to him, made his boss welcome, invited his colleagues over.

I've let his mother tell me how things are done. I was nice to her. From her I learned the kind of life he was used to and what his favorite foods were. I adjusted to it. I've let her tell me how she raised her children. I've taught my children to say please and thank you, when to curtsy or bow, to shake hands nicely and sing Christmas songs. I've gotten to know her son. I've been afraid.

I've tried to be understanding and considerate. I've blamed myself. I've always hoped he could also be my big brother. I've never told him so.

I've told him I love him. I've learned tenderness, protected the children when he was angry, learned that he's allowed to be angry.

I've succeeded in explaining this to myself. I didn't despair. I've told myself I'm happy.

I was happy when he buried me in his arms, when he was nice to me. I've been able to comfort him and convince him to take heart. I had wanted a gentle man. I've cried behind closed doors. I knew that depressions are pathological. I've felt isolated. I've told myself to take heart. I've seen my hands start to look like my mother's, told myself that the daily defeats are nothing compared to how much I care. I didn't ask myself questions.

We've survived the beginnings. I've learned to live with his fears. I've awakened him at night when he cried out in a dream, I've said: it's me. I've asked him to tell me his dreams. I've listened. I've learned to be his sister too. I've been told I radiate motherliness. I've thought to myself: you must be warm and soft like a mother animal, you must be a cave. I've loved our children. A haven, I thought. I wanted to be self-disclosing but couldn't. I've felt guilty.

I've imagined that it'll be over some day, we'll grow older and calmer. I've learned that I can't change a man. I haven't depended on it.

I've learned to forget Latin and higher mathematics.

I've encouraged him when he was unemployed, I've learned to organize moves, furnish apartments and manage on our income. I've survived our children's illnesses. I've had dreams.

I've taken pills for headaches, pills for sleeplessness; I've had treatment for back pains and anemia. I was a sleepwalker.

I've learned how to argue and wage trench-wars. I've withdrawn and refused to speak to him. I've gotten furious when he got furious. I've wished the children would grow up fast.

I've given up, slit my wrists, though I didn't want to die. I let him bandage my arm, let him invent an accident to tell the doctor. I've hoped that somebody would ask.

I've asked myself.

We've survived. I've hoped he would succeed professionally. I've fought for two day-care spaces, bribed the director with presents. I've taken the pill. I've told myself: you can't be afraid any more. I've repressed my feelings, I've set limits. I've stopped letting people hurt me.

I've learned typing and shorthand. I've gone to work. I wanted to gain self-confidence. I've brought home money. At Christmas I recovered from a collapsed artery.

I've worked half-days because of the children.

We could afford vacations and make investments. We've gotten ahead. I didn't watch the time. I've said: a ninety-hour week won't kill me.

I haven't given up my hopes, I've buried them. We've built a house, sent the children to high school. We've joined the parents' advisory board. We've gotten involved when something affected us. We've avoided hanging on to memories. I've made concessions, learned to deal with his moods. I haven't gone under. I learned Latin and math again when the children did.

I haven't stopped telling myself that I'm happy. I've been stubborn. I've kept things to myself. I've raised our daughter to be a protester. I've learned to be alone.

Yesterday I saw my daughter with a young man. I told him about it. I said: she's more like you than me. I've asked myself if that's a chance for her.

Translated by Jeanette Clausen

Notes

* German original: Angelika Mechtel, "Katrin," *Die Träume der Füchsin. Erzählungen* (Stuttgart: Deutsche Verlags-Anstalt, 1976), pp. 7–11. Translated and reprinted with permission.

30. The Duel*

Irmtraud Morgner

Scooter riding becomes a means for the narrator to add excitement and fun to her life while realizing the goals of GDR society. This story, published in the same collection as "White Easter" (section II, this volume) shows a more whimsical, light-hearted side of Morgner's earlier work.

I was preoccupied with this decision for years. One evening it was settled. Just before closing time I entered the store and requested a scooter with pneumatic tires. The clerk showed me various models. I requested a specific one. The clerk brought out three more models from the stockroom. I requested the chrome-plated one from the display window, equipped with foam-rubber cushioned seat, hand and foot brakes and a generator-powered headlight at ninety-eight marks seventy. "Display items are not available until we change our window," said the clerk. "When will it be changed? " "In three to four days." "Too late," I said. The clerk inquired as to the date of the birthday. I assured him tht I didn't wish to buy a birthday present. "Then the child can surely wait another three or four days," he said. "Not even one hour," I said. "How old is the child? " he asked. "I'm buying the scooter for myself," I said. The clerk exchanged a glance with the store manager. The latter motioned the other two clerks to the cash register. I stood in front of the register and waved my check. The manager regretted that he could not accept a check. I pointed out that in this case it was a cashiers' check, put it back, and produced four green bills from my purse. The manager expressed his amazement at the amount of cash I carried with me. "Payday," I said. "Where? " he asked. "At the Berlin Transit Authority," I said. "What do you do there, lady? " he asked further. "I'm a conductor, now do I get the scooter or not? " "Conductor," the manager said and exchanged glances with his staff. I shifted my weight to the other leg. A clerk raised his arm ostentatiously, squared it off at the elbow and announced that in five minutes it would be seven o'clock. We compared our watches. We established unanimity. The manager declared his shop closed and asked me to come again tomorrow. I called his attention to the illegality of his premature action, said furthermore that my time didn't grow on trees, and mounted one of the nearby scooters with pneumatic tires, though not a chrome-plated one equipped with a foam-rubber cushioned seat, determined to utilize the remaining four and a half minutes for training purposes. The store was spacious. Its left wing was supported by four columns. I used it as a slalom course. Although I had never in my life been on a scooter with pneumatic tires, I took the curves with confidence. People stood at the display windows. The fingers of my right hand rested on the brake lever. Before each curve I flipped the turn signal out and reduced speed, according to regulations. Each time I rode past the sales staff, I dimmed the headlight and rang the bell. People crowded up to the store windows. The wheels had excellent bearings, one push with my foot and I had momentum for an entire lap. Masses of people thronged to the store windows. The manager seemed to fear for the window panes. He alternately ran to the windows and after me. I was faster. He gesticulated. Mutely. The whole staff gesticulated mutely. Finally, the manager mounted the display case, to save the reputation of the store, as he later put it in his report to the police. He mounted, as I said, the display case, cut the nylon strings holding the chrome-plated scooter, the one equipped with foam-rubber cushioned seat, hand and foot brakes and a generator-powered headlight, and wrote up a cash receipt; I immediately applied the hand and foot brakes and placed that rel-atively good vehicle back among the others of its kind, expressed my thanks, and was handed over the ultimate vehicle for the amount stated on the price tag. Packaged up. I had to promise to carry my dream-wheels, shrouded in several square meters of corrugated card-board and tied up with cords, all the way home.

As a child I had dreamed of wooden scooters. A girl in the building next door owned one with rubber tires that cost seven marks eighty. I used to ride it over the roofs at night. From time to time a scooter with pedals would also appear in my dreams. It was ridden by ladies from Snow White on up. But not even that one had had pneumatic tires. Not to be compared to the one tied up beyond recognition that I was lugging out of the store. Up onto my shoulder. The crowd formed an aisle. I strode through and took the fastest way home, a promise is a promise.

Most of the residents in my building labelled my hobby strange. At first. An internationally known cycle-ball player living in the front building put his hand to his head in disbelief. I boycotted public transportation, which I was entitled to use free of charge, and rode to work daily on my scooter. My health improved. Dr. Lauritz, who had always prescribed exercise for me, was satisfied. When I revealed how I got my exercise, he engaged me in a prolonged conversation about objects that were sitting on his desk. When not at work, I

preferred to get around on pneumatic tires; I rode to the baker, to
the butcher, I did all my errands by scooter, drudgery was transformed
into pleasure. Sometimes I went shopping for my neighbors. Of
course it was difficult to work the handlebars when overfilled shopping bags were hanging on them, but the training I had had the
benefit of assigned a positive moral value to pleasure only when it
was connected with usefulness. I never steered the wrong way; loaded
and yet light, I sped along, winged by this rarely experienced harmony
between morality and pleasure. I rode and rode, taller than usual—
the distance between running board and street measured twelve
centimeters—on pneumatic cushions I bounced across the rough spots
of cobbled, asphalt, or concrete streets. I never got off going uphill,
a slight downgrade already made it unnecessary to push with my
foot. If I did it anyway, I not infrequently overtook streetcars on
stretches which had a speed limit of thirty kilometers per hour. But
then I would also often sit on the foam-rubber cushioned seat
mounted on steel bars above the chrome fender of the rear wheel,
listening to the humming of the generator and enjoying the headwind.
The wind pushed against me, tousled my hair, billowed out my coat,
made my eyes water: I was always the winner. Thus in a short time
I conquered all the streets in the precinct as well as a thrill of life
which, owing to circumstances, had been denied me until then. I
sang its praises whenever an occasion arose. Most adults, as I said,
found it strange. Sympathetic, or possibly glad of the unexpected
diversion, they looked down upon me. At first. The children listened
to me. Everybody laughed. On the fifth day after my purchase, as
I mounted my scooter to go to work, several women and men were
standing in front of the main entrance to the building. When I
returned, a crowd was blocking the gateway. I asked if they would
be so kind, they were so kind, hesitantly, a woman demanded to
know my objective in behaving in such a way. I offered as an
explanation the objective of getting from place to place. They asked
what sense it made. I offered as an explanation the sense of fun.
The crowd looked up at me distrustfully. The next morning a gentle-
man visited me in my apartment and protested "in the name of"
against such provocations, which amounted to ridicule of the sport
of bicycling, that is to say an Olympic event, that is to say the
Olympic idea. I assured him of my loyalty. He assured me that he
would persist. Towards noon, as I was parking my scooter in the
streetcar depot, I was summoned to Company-Physician Lauritz. He
wrote out a referral for me to the psychiatric ward of Charité Hospital.
On the way to the Charité, I noticed that the foot brake was defective.
Since I knew the store was in the vicinity, I took a small detour
and trustingly consulted the expert from whom I had bought the

scooter. The expert immediately exchanged a glance with the manager. The latter motioned the other two clerks to the cash register. I stood in front of the register and explained my concern. When none of the four gentlemen left the endangered cash registered, as they later put it in the police report, to examine the defect, I demonstrated the defect. I placed my right foot on the running board, gave two vigorous pushes with my left, stepped on the brake pedal several times with my left heel, but in vain; I rode two laps through the spacious store, and all the shoppers present were able to verify that the foot brake was not functioning. The manager took down my personal data, handed me a repair slip, and kept the scooter. Shortly thereafter I received the notification that a complaint had been filed against me for gross misdemeanor as well as public nuisance.

At that point I set out for the third time, entered the shop shortly before the lunch break, positioned myself before the manager at a distance of about two meters, announced my terms, relinquished my right to a second, gave him to the count of three, threw back my shoulders, counted, took a deep breath, and laughed him to death.

Translated by Karen R. Achberger

Notes

* German original: Irmtraud Morgner, "Das Duell," *Hochzeit in Konstantinopel* (Berlin: Aufbau, 1968), pp. 11–15. Translated and reprinted with permission.

31. Shoes*

Irmtraud Morgner

Both "Shoes" and the following text, "The Rope," are self-contained stories in Morgner's fantastic montage novel Trobadora Beatriz, *which draws on a wide range of literary traditions to create a complex and visionary picture of women's struggle to enter history. The novel is part one of a planned trilogy; part two,* Amanda: A Witches' Novel, *appeared in 1983. In "Shoes" and "The Rope," two familiar themes of feminist literature, role reversal and a balancing act, are represented symbolically.*

There was a woman, Walli by name, who preferred men of delicate build. It seemed to her that with them love was more entertaining: exchanging roles was simpler. She married a man named Sigmund. He could wear her sweaters, she his shirts. During their honeymoon, they indulged their longing to become the other or to be together all the time by exchanging articles of clothing. This symbolic action together with the odor of the desired body which lingered in the material consoled, reassured and excited them. Later on, the woman discovered the added advantage that even their shoe size was the same. She made good use of it after the birth of their first son, when the joyous excitement of this event was superseded by the demands of her chosen occupation as secretary. She had ended up choosing this occupation after giving up her aspirations to study medicine, for family reasons. Sigmund had earned his high school diploma at the Workers' and Farmers' School at the same time Walli did, with a grade average one point lower than hers. He was studying engineering in Dresden and visited his family in Leipzig almost every weekend. Walli could manage without his help; she was a strong woman. She had carefully completed the Russian section of her comprehensive finals in spite of the onset of labor pains during the test. She had gotten used to work from early on; she came from a farm family. In order to make the separation easier Walli bought herself a pair of brown lace shoes and entrusted them to Sigmund with the request that he wear them occasionally in Dresden. As soon as he had completed his Masters degree, she wanted to apply to the College of Liberal Arts at Karl Marx University to study Slavics. After work, when her son had been picked up from the day-care center, fed and

213

put to bed, and after the housework had been done, she energetically studied books in Russian. When her son was almost three years old, she gave birth to a daughter. Sigmund completed his Masters with a B average and found a position as engineer in Karl-Marx-Stadt. There and on business trips he wore Walli's shoes as long as he felt he wasn't being observed. When he had worn out the soles and run down the heels, Walli took them to the shoe repair and saw to it that only quality material was used, leather if at all possible. She put the study of Slavics out of her head and set herself instead the goal of becoming an elementary school teacher as soon as her daughter, who for health reasons could not be put in a day-care center, was old enough to go to kindergarten. After the birth of her second son, Walli looked forward to the opportunity of putting an end to nearly four years as a housewife and being able to work as a secretary again. Especially since an apartment in Karl-Marx-Stadt became available for the family.

At small evening gatherings in their home, when Sigmund and his colleagues partake liberally of the wine and swap stories of business trips, and their wives reach for the dessert and their knitting, Walli usually puts on the shoes and folds her arms across her chest. Otherwise, when her husband is not wearing them, she keeps the shoes in the living room glass cabinet next to the crystal and china.

Translated by Karen R. Achberger

Notes

* German original: Irmtraud Morgner, "Schuhe." Zweite Fernwehgeschichte der Spielfrau Laura, *Leben und Abenteuer der Trobadora Beatriz nach Zeugnissen ihrer Spielfrau Laura* (Berlin: Aufbau, 1974), pp. 411–413. Translated and reprinted with permission.

32. The Rope*

Irmtraud Morgner

Professor Gurnemann, director of an academic institute for research on the atomic structure of matter, had a woman physicist on his staff. Her name was Vera Hill and she lived in B.; the institute was situated outside the city limits, not easily accessible by public transportation. On a peninsula, whose inhabitants preferred to use bicycles as their means of transportation and who stared at strangers. When the particle accelerator, by now obsolete and a candidate for razing, had finally been built the institute became the center of local gossip. Ever since local women had been employed as lab assistants and reported that the physicists were working with scissors and looking at films, the physicists were accepted as locals. Vera Hill brought the research institute into disrepute again. A group of citizens who had happened to end up in a village tavern after a town meeting late one night drafted a written complaint to the institute director. His office was in a small neo-Gothic brick building which had once been a chocolate factory. When the delegation which was to deliver the document tried to pass through the entrance, the porter flung open the window without a word of greeting. To Vera Hill he was in the habit of saying on such occasions: "Good morning, Dr. Hill." The two delegates were asked to show their identification. The porter read the personal data of the visitors to the director's secretary over the phone. Later he filled out two passes with carbon copies, handed over the documents with a suspicious look and pressed the button, which produced a buzzing tone and opened the wrought-iron gate in front of the entrance to the brick administration building.

★　★　★

When the two men alluded to the scandalous events and handed the director the written accusations, Gurnemann was silent. His suspicion that the institute, now that the giant oaks next to the new addition had been cut down, was once again being accused of producing atom bombs, proved to be erroneous. Regrettably, the ridiculousness of the new rumor appeared to surpass that of the other one many times over and therefore Gurnemann estimated the chances of refuting it to be negligible. At any rate, it would require

215

considerable effort to refute the claim that a female employee of his institute was walking over the village twice each weekday. The delegation asked Gurnemann to devote particular attention to that section of the complaint in which they had described the threat to public morals which the woman's behavior represented. Gurnemann thought of the two-room apartment which Dr. Hill occupied with her son. The son was three years old, the apartment was furnished with two beds, a table, three chairs, a wardrobe, a carpet and bookshelves. Walls not pasted over with wallpaper, but showing bare, palpable stone. Whitewashed. At any rate, Gurnemann considered walking on air to be a ridiculous form of slander.

★   ★   ★

The wealth of written material spread out before Gurnemann cited among other things disorderly conduct, posing a threat to public health and materialist beliefs, causing power blackouts, exerting a harmful influence on youth, and creating a traffic hazard. So much had the professor's attention been occupied by the material that, though he stalled for time by talking, he had not yet come up with an effective argument. That annoyed him and softened his judgment of colleagues who refused to employ women scientists.

★   ★   ★

Professor Gurnemann, no longer able to resist the appeal of the detailed claims, pursed his handsome lips. Best of all he liked the supernatural aspect of the alleged phenomenon. Gurnemann could not help thinking about Vera Hill's mouth, her full, prominent lips with thread-like traces of lipstick in their creases; her skin looked puckered. One religious couple had thought this woman was the Mother Mary and interpreted this as a sign that the village was chosen to be spared in the event of a nuclear holocaust. But even those who complained that she trespassed and violated their privacy, by alleging that Vera Hill might have or in fact had looked into their windows and balconies, as well as those who defended morality, traffic safety and materialism, all the undersigned testified unanimously that Vera Hill crossed the village twice each workday, namely around 7:15 A.M. in a southwesterly direction, and around 6:00 P.M. in a northeasterly direction, and that she did so walking through the air. Statements concerning how high she was or how fast she walked differed. The owner of a fruit orchard claimed in her damage suit that Vera Hill had knocked down yellow plums and cherry branches with her briefcase. A short-circuit on the third day of Christmas around 5:50 P.M., which left the village without power for more than two hours, was also blamed on Vera Hill. The tavernkeeper did not think it proper that black nylon lace and garters should be viewed by morally upright citizens and children. Gurnemann thought of her long legs and slender thighs, put the complaint into a file, had coffee brought in for his visitors and, rubbing his hands nervously, promised that there would be an investigation. The delegates called his attention to the list of seven other institutions to which copies of their complaint had also been sent. Then the professor shook the men's hands and dismissed them. He was severely jolted, for he was afraid of not getting the allocation of hard currency he needed for the purchase of an English computer. Gurnemann left his coffee unfinished, threw an overcoat over his white smock, crossed the courtyard in long strides and pushed open the door of the institute building. It smelled of fused condensers.

★ ★ ★

Frau Hill was located behind a light green door. The door was locked. Gurnemann pounded with both palms, assuming that Vera Hill had earphones on and a tape recorder running. An instrument of knowledge, she termed it, stating that true science and true music were based on the same mental process. In answer to his question, the theoreticians Hinrich and Wander informed Gurnemann that Dr. Hill, in response to a telephone call from the kindergarten, had left the institute approximately half an hour earlier; her son had apparently taken ill. Gurnemann, himself the father of small children, was vacillating between principle and compassion when he asked jokingly by which means she had left the institute. "By air," the theoreticians replied. At that, Gurnemann doubted his reasoning power for a moment. Although he was used to all sorts of things—there were two sleepwalkers among the theoreticians—he had not yet had to deal with air walkers. Filled with dark premonitions, Gurnemann retired to his villa. He spent the rest of the day there in front of the television set. That night he began to think that the rumor was Hill's way of taking revenge and swore to forego extramarital intimacy altogether from then on. The next morning he awoke with a headache, but in a mellower frame of mind for he had recalled the agreeable fact that Hill was one of those rare women who didn't want to get married. He also valued her fanatic devotion to work and her habit of not forcing conclusions but of letting them develop by themselves.

Confident in his belief that the confusion would resolve itself in some rational, natural way, Gurnemann went once again, after a good breakfast, to Vera Hill's office, where much to his delight he actually found her. He said hello. As soon as he took her hand in his, his concern seemed absurd; he became embarrassed and inquired about her son's health and the progress of her postdoctoral research.

Her answers were encouraging. Given concisely, too. If Gurnemann hadn't suddenly been asked about the real reason for his coming, he would have kept it to himself. He stated it in a subordinate clause; the main clause was a compliment. Vera Hill pushed back her bangs by drawing both index fingers over her eyebrows from the center outwards. Even under normal circumstances she seemed to have trouble closing her mouth, although her dental occlusion was normal. It made Gurnemann suspect that she always had something in her cheek, if only her tongue. Thus he took pains to apologize for the absurdity of the allegation and added that naturally neither he nor any other sensible person had believed it even for a minute. "Why? " asked Vera Hill. Gurnemann asked her to help him clear up the matter as efficiently and quickly as possible. He said that an institute such as his was so financially vulnerable that any reduction in the influx of hard currency as a result of some absurdity could inestimably diminish the potential for scientific research. "The absurdities increase the scientific potential," said Vera Hill. "Of the competition," said Gurnemann. "Do you see me as competition? " asked Hill. The question irritated Gurnemann. Vera Hill saw it on his face, and so she explained to him that she would not be able to complete her research by the agreed date without the short-cut on the rope. In contrast to him, she added, she did not have the services of a housewife or live-in maid at her disposal. After work, when she had done the shopping, picked up her son from kindergarten, fixed supper, eaten, drawn pictures of cars and other things on request for her son, when she had bathed him, told him a story and put him to bed, also done the dishes or laundry, or had mended a hole or chopped wood, and had carried up briquets from the basement, she was able, with the aid of the rope trick, to be back at her desk thinking about invariances by 9:00 P.M. Without the trick it would be an hour later. She would also have to get up an hour earlier without the trick. After less than six hours sleep, she explained to Gurnemann, she wasn't capable of coming up with any useful ideas. Gurnemann spoke urgently and at length with her about the unreal nature of her line of transit.

The next day Vera Hill lost her balance on the way home. The lamplighter discovered her shattered body on the lawn in front of the public library.

Translated by Karen R. Achberger

Notes

* German original: Irmtraud Morgner, "Dritte Bitterfelder Frucht: Das Seil," *Leben und Abenteuer der Trobadora Beatriz nach Zeugnissen ihrer Spielfrau Laura* (Berlin: Aufbau, 1974), pp. 595–603. Abridged, translated and reprinted with permission.

33. I Have Married Again*

Christine Wolter

This story is from Wolter's first collection of short stories, Wie ich meine Unschuld verlor *(How I Lost My Innocence/Virginity), in which she explores typical predicaments of women struggling for independence and equality. In "I Have Married Again," she critiques inequality in marriage and presents a logical alternative.*

I have married again. The news surprised my friends, those who know me well. To be exact, no actual wedding ceremony took place; circumstances do not permit it. But our life together conforms to all the principles of a modern marriage, which should be built on mutual affection and respect and should provide for the rearing of children to be well-balanced human beings.

We both did it for the children's sake. I was concerned for Martin, four years old, very bright and very affectionate, too affectionate for my liking, for in the long run I could no longer reconcile my work with his sitting on my lap for hours on end in the belief that the time I spent working at my desk was designed especially for him. Martin had also been slightly neglected; I'm forever forgetting to cut his hair, so that strangers think he's a girl. Rosa brought Ines with her, two years older than Martin, a sweet, loving little girl, an ideal playmate for Martin. Ines needed a family; Rosa was so gentle, she had let her get away with too much sometimes, but that didn't work with me.

I met Rosa by chance; she came from a different background than mine. If I hadn't met Rosa, my life would never have gotten back on a regular track. In my circle of friends, fairly muddled relations prevail; I don't know why that is, either. Perhaps we're all trying to counter the exceptional stress of our professions with an exceptional private life, so exceptional in fact that it's the same all over. Actually you can't call it a circle of friends; that would sound closed off, rigid; it's more like fields that are constantly changing, as you might say in technical language. I had assured these fields that I would never remarry, and everyone had accepted it.

My life with T. had been exemplary. People had envied us. Nobody was aware of what was gradually germinating in between the antique

220

furniture and a few good pictures in the cultured atmosphere of our apartment. From the seeds of discontent there grew, if I may continue the metaphor, an impenetrable hedge. A kind of aversion developed, to use technical language. Was it because we were both at the peak of our productivity and each had to keep on progressing and being creative in our profession? Here I can speak only for myself, for on the whole I prefer to stick to proven facts, to distinguish clearly between hypotheses and established truths; it's in keeping with my character as well as my profession. According to all empirical data, aversion leads to an explosive separation. Possibly it was because our energies were aimed in the same direction. We were congruous in experience, education, talent. T. wanted and was able to do the same things as I. Suddenly T. got in the habit of simply lying in front of the TV and not lifting a finger in the apartment. I couldn't tolerate that in the long run. T. refused to do the laundry even though we had a nice washing machine (I still have it, Rosa was delighted when she saw it), maintaining that a certain amount of creative leisure was indispensable, while uncreative leisure time was unacceptable, particularly at a stage of life which was so significant for professional productivity. T. explained all this to me while lying on the sofa, smoking and growing calmer all the time, as I was pacing the apartment and bumping into pieces of furniture that had never gotten in my way before.

My irritability increased. There were no actual harsh words between us, we were both too matter-of-fact and objective for that. The explosion didn't take place audibly, but it did occur. I knew that T. was working intensely. But did T. really have the right to do nothing but watch TV in the evening or produce small oil-paintings enhanced by montages of parts of toys, remnants from Martin's toy box? The laundry, the straightening up and cleaning, which we previously had shared, was now up to me alone. It wasn't much, but I was sick of it because I had to do it, while T. had managed to slip out of the trap of household duties. I consider physical exercise highly desirable, but I would have preferred to start going to the tennis club again or go bowling.

T. took charge of other things. For instance, T. decided who was to use the car. Imperceptibly I was being excluded from co-ownership and was forgetting my driving skills. T. would make ironic remarks. Every time I drove the car I was supposed to wash it; T. had a lot of ideas to keep me on the run. T. decided which invitations we accepted, which company parties we went to and when I was to stay home. For Martin's sake, T. said. I always had to go along to T.'s boring brigade gatherings in the evening, but when I enjoyed people, it turned out that I had to stay home.

Suddenly T. disappeared. A love affair, people said, very passionate. They felt sorry for me.

I knew better. Relieved I walked through the half-empty apartment and left the windows open for days in order to get rid of the last trace of T.'s abominable cigarettes. Whether or not it was good for T. that we separated, I don't know.

Of course there were also inconveniences for me. First with Martin. Of course Martin needed T. too. And then among our acquaintances. T. had pushed me to the periphery and made me a mere escort; everybody thought of us in combination: I was important only in relation to T., as I noticed, full of anger and dejection. It took a while before I was my old self again.

It was through Rosa that I found my way back to my real self, and it was by chance that I found Rosa. I managed to book a vacation for Martin and me at a mountain resort; it snowed for two days, then we had some sun; I romped around outside with Martin all day. A little girl stood bashfully watching our wild games, came closer step by step, rolled down the hill with us as if by chance, threw a snowball down my neck as if by mistake, and ended up getting her face rubbed with snow. She bawled, ran away, came back. That was Ines, pampered and timid, but still a good child. Ines and her mother were staying in the same vacation lodge as we were. The two of them ate in a different dining room, which suited me just fine since I didn't like vacation friendships. All I needed was fresh air and snowball fights and chases in the snow, I couldn't comfort a lonely woman. Sometimes Rosa would take a walk on the upper meadow path by the hill where we, Martin, Ines, and I, were stomping through the snow. The sled stood abandoned by the side, we didn't need it. We would never have managed to get acquainted had we not one sunny afternoon—Martin and I had eaten a huge amount of cake in the lodge and were just on our way out again— found Ines with her mother and a heavy suitcase in front of the lodge, Ines bawling, her mother at a loss. The taxi had not come. The train was leaving from the county seat in half an hour. I got my car keys. We raced through the icy, only partially sanded curves at fifty miles an hour. I was driving with confidence again. Martin kept his mouth shut like a real pro. Ines, between her tears, was asking all kinds of silly things, talking about fawns and bunnies, pinching Martin and asking every five minutes if we would be able to make the train if I drove so slowly. The train was standing in the station, I pushed Ines, the suitcase, and her mother in. As the train was beginning to pull out, the mother asked me for my address with insistent and gentle eyes, and I mumbled my street and house number.

Driving back to the resort, I thought about what it was that I had liked in the mother and what had seemed gratifying to me during that frantic trip. She hadn't asked questions, hadn't sighed or looked at her watch. She attentively looked straight ahead as if she wanted to help me drive fast and safely. She was too soft on Ines, I saw that too, the child needed a firm word now and then; but the comforting tranquility that emanated from Rosa remained in my memory.

You may have noticed that I haven't mentioned Rosa's outward appearance. It's true: I didn't really see her back then. I remembered only Rosa's tranquility like a soft chord, like the distant tolling of bells which reached us on Sundays in the snowy mountains and made us pause for a moment in our wild snow games. What was that, we would wonder, for already we wouldn't be able to hear it any more. And when Rosa visited me later I had this elusive sensation again.

Ines and Martin have become friends. It's the best thing you can do for two only children.

Utter harmony reigns at home. I am absolutely my old self again. Rosa radiates peace. She takes a lot off my hands, that's true, but she likes doing it, does it of her own accord. In return, I give her the security of a family, my experience. I notice how cheerful I am, how strings of formulas flow from my pen, I no longer smoke, I'm playing tennis again, and I've stopped yelling at Martin.

Coming home each night, I sense the change Rosa has brought us. The children are playing in the living room. Rosa is bustling about the kitchen, it smells wonderfully of fried onions. I put away my briefcase, set the table together with the children, and, while Rosa is putting the final touches on the meal, I'm almost happy to tackle the children's torn pants in the mending basket. By suppertime I manage to sew on at least two knee patches with fast cross-stitches.

Rosa knows me. She enters the room and instantly knows what kind of day I had and whether my calculations were successful. I told her in the beginning that I'm a difficult person. She looked at me, her big eyes gently smiling, and nodded. Where did she get this talent? Her work as store manager certainly isn't easy, but it seems that the daily bustle of people in the store gives her increasingly greater composure and cheerfulness.

We only had a few difficulties in the beginning, when Rosa and Ines were moving in with us. They brought along an immense quantity of odds and ends, powdery boxes of chocolates, a ship in a bottle, two Dutch kitchen clocks, a collection of colored wine glasses, a guinea pig, a whole population of dolls with beds and a kitchen stove. All this was foreign to my cool, symmetrical apartment.

But after only a few weeks this gypsy caravan had become a part of our life. I took the abstract painting "Bird Screams" off the corridor wall, for it now seemed alien to me, and hung up the ship in the bottle.

As I've already told you, our relationship is not legalized. And why should it be, our partnership is so much a matter of course and so good that it doesn't need even the slightest enforcement.

Surprising, actually, that you haven't run into Rosa and me yet. Ever since we've been together we go out frequently, the children manage famously by themselves.

It's amusing to see how people stare at us when we walk into someone's apartment. A few people are there already, a bar is set up, somebody is putting on a record and stops in mid-motion. Rosa's appeal has a peculiar quality—I'm only now becoming aware of it— she's shorter than I, with a full figure and well-developed hips. She loves rare, rich colors, purple, turquoise, orange. I'm somewhat taller, and evenings, after running around all day in my jeans and white smock, I like to wear long dresses that accentuate my small waist and full breasts.

So we walk in, and for a second there's electricity in the air. We stand there, two women obviously in their prime, but more than that; we are not only radiant in the vitality of our still young years, we glow because we are intelligent, self-confident, have both feet firmly in our profession, and are serving society as far as we can.

T., incidentally, didn't like it when I went to parties in my un-obtrusively daring clothes and then stood there like that—for that delightful moment when you can taste the evening on your tongue before it has begun. He claimed that I made a spectacle of myself, that I showed off, which—he contended—was unworthy of a woman and smacked of decadent-bourgeois social games. T. would add that the men undressed me with their eyes. That was nonsense: that was never necessary with my dresses.

At this moment, then, Rosa and I stand side by side; we find out which way the wind is blowing; we look around to see where the people we like are sitting. We enjoy going to Bert's, he's brilliant, witty, and entertaining. All kinds of colleagues show up whenever he announces in the lab: stop on over tomorrow night. At Bert's parties there are good discussions, dancing, and a lot of drinking. The twilight we're standing in doesn't bother us. It comes from the eyes of a few cross-eyed and near-sighted persons. My school-mate Roswitha, who is the director of Berta-von-Suttner High School, says: you always were a little crazy, and then smiles tolerantly.

I admit that I'm beginning to see Rosa's physical attractiveness, too, which I didn't notice when I first met her. Now I see Rosa with different eyes. Could that be a temptation? I don't think so. Rosa is every bit as intelligent as I am, or: I'm as intelligent as Rosa. We have a happy family life. Sometimes I say to her, or she says to me: you know, it's hit me. That can mean several things. But never would it alter the harmony of our partnership. Never would there be distrust, or confessions, or allusions to morals, considerateness and what people will think.

Bert's party is turning out to be fun. The crackling we sensed when we arrived is clinging to our clothes like an electric charge. Some people are receptive to that. Each of us goes her own way, but we're allies. How different from back then, from my evenings with T.! He's here tonight, too, by himself, and we nod to each other.

Later, when I'm sitting with the small group that has formed around Bert—people are dancing behind us—Rosa whirls past.

Hey, you, she says.

Yes?

Do you mind if I don't come home until tomorrow?

You'd have to pick up the children in the afternoon. I have a research meeting. Who is it, anyway?

Rosa shrugs her shoulder in the direction of the corridor, where a tall man is slipping a trench coat over his shoulders. I recognize T.

Rosa's eyes are big and sweet. Do you mind?

I have to laugh.

It's a beautiful evening, Rosa, I say.

Translated by Friedrich Achberger

Notes

* German original: Christine Wolter, "Ich habe wieder geheiratet," *Wie ich meine Unschuld verlor* (Berlin: Aufbau, 1976), pp. 26–35. Translated and reprinted with permission.

34. Sonja*

Judith Offenbach

Sonja, in a wheelchair since her first suicide attempt, and Judith became lovers while both were students in Hamburg, where they shared an apartment for some years. Only a few close friends knew they were lesbians. In this except from the book, Judith reflects on the outsider status of lesbians and recalls some good and bad times she and Sonja shared before the latter's suicide in 1976. The book's subtitle, "Melancholy for the Advanced," is a quote from American lesbian poet Djuna Barnes, the subject of Sonja's never-completed dissertation.

Sunday, May 28th, 1978, Ten Past Twelve At Night

On TV tonight I saw the film "The Lost Honor of Katharina Blum." At the end Katharina Blum shoots the man who had helped her to her lost honor. I, as a lesbian, have no honor to lose in the first place. As long as I was still able to believe I was simply a person I probably thought that I, too, had some kind of honor. But somewhere between seventeen and twenty, as I was slowly beginning to understand that I was not a person but a lesbian, I also noticed that I would only have my honor as long as I disguised myself as a person.

It didn't seem very nice for Katharina Blum to go and shoot her tormentor. The idea would never have occurred to me. Also, it would be much too much work to kill all the people who would not give me my honor to start with.

Once again I feel like dropping out of everything. The university seems like a network of traps. And yet it's clear to me that at this point I am still living in paradise, so to speak. If I should really get an academic job, this network would enclose me ever more tightly. Perhaps for reasons of economy, homosexuals do not shoot their tormentors but rather themselves.

Then, on TV more demonstrations of civil courage. Jane Fonda tells of her four years of unemployment under Nixon, because she had made films against the Vietnam war. But Jane Fonda has money, a rich father. Four years out of work do not mean the destruction

226

of her material existence. For me to show how I feel inside would surely be to endanger my very existence. So, for now, I'll play along.

A few months ago I watched a concert on TV with Christoph Eschenbach as conductor. I believe that he's homosexual, and I sat there feeling slightly revolted, even titilated, as I watched him. If I'm not even any better than my mother, how can I demand humanity of her?

The phenomenon of Jewish and Black self-hate has been quite well researched sociologically. Homosexual self-hate is most likely in a similar category, but it is considerably more complicated. One knows that one is a Jew or a Black from earliest childhood. That one is homosexual, one begins to suspect only in puberty; it becomes an inescapable fact only between the ages of seventeen and twenty, for many even later. In the "formative" years before, one has plenty of time to absorb fully all the prejudices about homosexuality, and it is all the harder to rid oneself of them. I am now thirty-five and still struggling with this. As a homosexual, one does not have the automatic support of a group, unless one exposes oneself as boldly and uncompromisingly as do radical lesbians. One is a life-long lonely solitary combatant, probably more likely to commit suicide than to organize and fight for change.

What I have to tell today about Sonja and me fits in well with this topic. A journalist from the *Sonntagsblatt* was coming to interview Sonja for a portrait series on "naive" painters.

Shortly before her visit, Sonja's car was smashed up. A drunken bum had simply stepped out in front of our car. I thought, this is the end, but Sonja was able to avoid him, and we drove into a tree instead. The car was a wreck, but the guy was only slightly hurt. We were mainly happy and thankful that nothing serious had happened to him; only later did we think about the car. The guy, of course, had no insurance, and Sonja's insurance would not pay for such damages. The repair job would cost 1,500 marks, which we naturally did not have.

We didn't feel like asking Sonja's mother. In 1963, just after Sonja's first suicide attempt, her parents—presumably at the urging of her mother—had drawn up a will which said that Sonja would be disinherited if in the event of the death of one parent she should dare to claim her share.

So, that was our situation when this journalist was expected for the interview. I thought to myself: "It sure won't make a good impression if Sonja is seen to be living with another woman." [So] I disappeared for two hours and wandered around town. When the coast was clear, I came back to the apartment. I had as a precaution placed myself in the consciousness of this journalist, and from that perspective I, Sonja's life's companion, could only consider myself a blemish which one would do better to keep secret.

At that time, 1972, when I disappeared during that interview, was I smart or not? Was Jane Fonda smart when she made her films on Vietnam? She said proudly: "Now I have a job, and Nixon is unemployed."

Sonja related everything to me, hot off the press. The journalist had hardly paid any attention to her painting after learning of the accident. That was, after all, something that went straight to the heart: "Poor, handicapped woman in dire straits through no fault of her own. Her already minimal freedom of movement reduced to zero." She painted a very touching picture in her article. Sonja and I were very sad and bitter that she had not been taken seriously as an artist.

But we were too harsh in our judgment. The article had an almost fairy-tale effect, in that it brought our misfortune to the attention of a good fairy. The phone rang: Mrs. Bille had read the article at breakfast and wanted to help right away. She simply said Sonja should buy a suitable new car and send her the bill. Finally, they arranged that Mrs. Bille would pay to have the old car repaired.

Sunday, June 4th, Ten o'Clock in the Evening

Two days ago a letter came from my mother. She had read the first one-hundred-and-sixty pages of this book. Not a trace of understanding or sympathy for what happened with Sonja and me. "I have no right to judge you," writes my mother, "and I do not judge you." Yet her whole letter is one long judgment—but she does not judge me. How nice for me. One could easily turn schizophrenic from such words. Recently, Susanne told me about the following statement by her mother: "I don't have anything against other women becoming lesbians. But with you I can't tolerate it."

Nineteen seventy-two was my first year of professional activity. Sonja was busy working on further paintings, and I was travelling twice a week to Bremen. At first, the outlook was still quite rosy. To be sure, I had difficulties in getting used to my new work requirements, but I gradually settled in quite well. My colleagues liked me. I would be invited to small get-togethers in the evening, usually staying overnight then, since the last train to Hamburg left at 10:30 P.M.

Sonja began to sense danger. The "Bremen clique" was more suspect in that it lay beyond her sphere of control. And she could not simply declare Bremen out of bounds because our existence, after all, depended upon my being there. In her helpless rage, Sonja fell into drinking again. Her sense of powerlessness was heightened by the fact that I was having some professional success, while she had still not written a single line of her dissertation on Djuna Barnes. Also, she was not able to progress as quickly as she wished in her painting. We had made contact with the most renowned gallery for naive painters in Germany, and the director was quite pleased with the sample of Sonja's work and wanted to present an exhibit of her work in the near future. But for that she would have to complete at least fifteen pictures, and she had only two done. For her, outward success still lay a long way off, while I was returning each time from Bremen vigorous and in the best of spirits.

Soon after, from May 1972 on, I would come home to find Sonja stinking drunk or at the very least unpleasantly tipsy. More than once I would open the apartment door to find her sitting directly in front of it in her own urine and laughing at me. Now she had me in her power again. She would go completely limp in my arms, becoming almost unmaneuverable. And she actually seemed to enjoy that, as if it were exactly what she had intended. I felt only disgust, hate and contempt for her that she would humiliate herself and torture me so.

In this way, the last year and a half of our life together passed: Sonja fell deeper and deeper into self-contempt, because she wasn't "accomplishing" anything and because she drank and was a torment to me. But Sonja never became a real alcoholic, and naturally we had many beautiful experiences as well in this last phase of our relationship. For example, my first vacation in that hot June of 1972— for the first time in my life I had the feeling I had earned the right to be lazy.

The day before vacation started Sonja and I went out to eat at our little pizzeria to celebrate the day. We sat outside on the sidewalk. A wonderful summer evening—we were happy and made plans. Sonja would have most preferred to travel off into the blue horizon, but I had my doubts. I had visions of a broken axel in the Alps, and then the wheel chair, etc. Sonja found my fears irrational, but I was able to convince her that a holiday spent right there in Hamburg could also be quite nice. And so we conquered Hamburg for ourselves during those four weeks.

It was a lovely time. Not a trace of Sonja's drinking—after all she had me all to herself. We took long walks—which we had never allowed ourselves before. We spent two whole days in Hagenbecks zoo alone, which we found delightful because of its wilhelminian grounds. I remember those two days so well because I didn't sweat at all, despite the fact that it was fantastically hot. Since my twelfth year there had hardly been a day when I did not sweat. So, I must have been feeling quite easy and relaxed and happy, and Sonja, too.

Around this time we received some inconsolable letters from Bella, sounding suicidal. Erika had moved out of the apartment they shared. Sonja and I decided to invite Bella to spend the weekend with us in Hamburg from time to time.

In mid-August I had to attend a professional meeting in Lausanne. My parents drove me as far as Offenburg. There I had two hours' time until my train left and wandered around in the old city. I missed Sonja . . . sent her a postcard of an old apothecary shop. She later incorporated this shop into one of her pictures. (Her analyst bought it for four hundred and fifty marks.) For a long time that postcard stood on her desk.

At the time of my trip to Lausanne, Sonja had just four more years to live, one of them with me. The conference lasted a week, during which time I wrote Sonja three letters. I longed for her and felt alone.

In September came the Olympics, which we followed with great excitement on television. And there again: a feeling of closeness with Sonja—we felt the terrorist attack on the Israelis almost as a personal assault that robbed us of an intense harmonious experience.

As I write this, the world championship soccer games are going on in Argentina. I pay hardly any attention. Without Sonja everything has lost its glow. Sonja killed herself, and I go on here with my everyday life. And people are being tortured in Argentina while the world celebrates its soccer festivities there.

Monday, June 5th, 1978, Ten o'Clock in the Evening

I have asked myself *why* Sonja might have felt so threatened by my professional activity in Bremen, by my new roots there. For when one marriage partner gets ahead professionally, the other one need not find that disconcerting. It only becomes disconcerting when that professional position depends upon having the "right" spouse. Already at the beginning of the Nazi period, for example, it was very detrimental for an official to have a Jewish wife—and the Jewish wife must naturally have felt threatened, no matter how sure she was of her husband's love. Would he not one day give in to the pressure? And after my various "affairs," Sonja could not even be sure of my love at that point. And now she saw how I was treated as a "single" person by my Bremen friends. She was never invited along with me—not only for geographical reasons but because I had never told anyone more than that I lived with a poor handicapped woman who often enough and on top of everything else made my life hell. (I sometimes let that much show through—on the one hand, to relieve some of the domestic stress and, on the other hand, to ward off any suspicion of "perversion."

[As for] what lessons are to be drawn from these relationships— I must do everything that might lead to an eventual humanizing in this area. For example, get this book published as quickly as possible. Not everyone will react like my mother did. Surely there are many who are undecided or uninformed, whom one might still be able to reach.

Translated by Edith Hoshino Altbach

Notes

* Originally published as, Judith Offenbach, *Sonja: Eine Melancholie für Fortgeschrittene* Frankfurt: Suhrkamp, 1981, pp. 235–45. (c) Suhrkamp Verlag Frankfurt am Main 1981. All rights reserved. Translated and reprinted with permission. Portions of this text are excerpted.

Part Eight

Motherhood and Housework

More than most women's movements, except perhaps the Italian, the new German movement has attempted to make the needs of mothers and the issue of housework the basis of theoretical and practical work. In order to do this it has been necessary to revise the attitude of a part of the left (see article "Mothers are Political Persons" by Helke Sander) as well as the century-and-a-half-long feminist struggle against the oppressive ideology of women's role as wife and mother.

In keeping with this trend, the Wages for Housework campaign has attracted more credibility in the German movement than in the United States. It is not so very uncommon to see Wages for Housework mentioned in the movement-curriculum vitae of West German feminists. On the other side of this issue, Alice Schwarzer's editorial states the more mainstream feminist position which stresses careers and work outside the home.

The texts by Claudia von Werlhof and Hannelore Mabry are two divergent materialist theoretical treatises within the discussion on motherhood and housework. Along with the work of Barbara Duden and Gisela Bock on the genesis of housework under capitalism* these contributions deserve a place in the international debate.

---

* Barbara Duden and Gisela Bock, "Labor of Love—Love as Labor: On the Genesis of Housework in Capitalism," *From Feminism to Liberation*, Edith Hoshino Altbach, ed. Cambridge, Mass.: Schenkman, 1980, pp. 153–192.

233

35. Is the Guilt Principle Coming Back Through the Back Door? Reform of Marriage and Family Law*

Heike Mundzeck

No other part of society's laws so clearly reveals and perpetuates the condition of women in a given period as marriage and family law. This article reviews the reforms, since 1949, in West German laws concerning the duties and responsibilities of husbands and wives, pointing out areas of real improvement for women as well as new vulnerabilities.

The Married Woman: Statutory Discrimination in the 20th Century— A Look Back

When the Civil Code took effect on January 1, 1900, Wilhelminian Germany came under a patriarchal-hierarchical system of marriage and family law. This was revealed in the husband's legally defined sole power to decide all questions concerning the marital relationship and the children's education. Among other things, this meant that at marriage the husband acquired the sole right to manage property brought into the marriage by the woman and to use income from it for himself. She had no discretionary power (Verfügungsmacht) of any kind over her own property. In addition, he could determine where his family would reside and dictate how his wife should manage the household. In disputes, "paternal power" made it possible for him to decide about the children's education without considering his wife's opinion if hers differed. Also, a married woman could not be gainfully employed without her husband's consent. This is the origin of the husband's right to terminate an employment contract of his wife's even if she herself wished to be or remain employed.

These provisions of marriage and family law remained in effect until after the second World War. Not until the Constitution of May 23, 1949, in Article 3, were equal rights for men and women declared. Article 117 required any contradictory law to be adjusted by March

31, 1953. This was done in only a few cases. Therefore, on April 1, 1953, all laws which contradicted the equal rights principle lost their validity; however, until codification of the equal rights statute on June 18, 1957 there were only provisional replacements for them. The management and usufruct of the wife's property by the husband, for example, was replaced by separate ownership of property *(Güt-ertrennung)*; the husband's sole decision-making power in all conjugal and family matters gave way to the obligation to agree *(Einigungs-pflicht)*.

Not until the (1957) equal rights statute, then, was patriarchal marriage and family law done away with, though still half-heartedly.

Community of earnings *(Zugewinngemeinschaft)* became the new marital property law on July 1, 1958. It means that husband and wife each retain the property they bring into the marriage; the "earnings" realized during marriage, however, i.e., returns received by one or both partners, are split in the case of divorce. The reason: to equalize the (unpaid) housewife's work and the husband's (paid) employment, at least within marriage.

Though the "ideal of a housewife-marriage" continued to exist, the husband's sole decision-making power in all matters concerning conjugal life disappeared in favor of "division of responsibilities" *(Aufgabenteilung)*: the wife was to contribute to the family's support through housework, the husband through his profession. The wife could be gainfully employed, but only "in so far as was consistent with her marital and family obligations." Now the husband could no longer terminate her employment contract, but the woman risked being named the guilty party in divorce if she insisted on being employed and her husband could convince the court that the house-hold and family suffered under his wife's "secondary employment."

The equality statute gave the woman the right to attach her maiden name to the married name. "Paternal power" was replaced by "pa-rental power" : here, the mother and father have "the right and the responsibility to care for the person and property of the child," and to do this "in mutual consent. . . ." When there are differences of opinion, they must try to reach an agreement.

After Three-Quarters of a Century: Reform of Marriage and Family Law—End to all Discrimination against Women?

The reform of family name law *(eheliches Namensrecht)* initiated a lot of intense discussion, but has proven to be less than revolutionary in its actual consequences. Since July 1, 1976 a couple may choose among various options at marriage.

Either the man's or the woman's name can become the married name. The spouse whose birth name is not chosen can place his/ her birth name (or name used at the time of marriage) in front of the married name.

Formerly a woman only had the option of appending her maiden name to the couple's married name (the husband's family name) after marriage. Thus, there has been equalization in name law. However, only two out of every hundred couples presently opt to use the woman's name as their married name; a very few choose a double name. The majority continues as before: the man's surname becomes the married name.

With the reform of marriage and family law in force since July 1, 1977, the statutory "ideal of a housewife-marriage" was given up. It was replaced by consensual arrangement of conjugal life with division of responsibilities in marriage and professionally. Also, the law no longer refers to "husband" or "wife" but only to "spouses." This means that neither partner has separate rights or responsibilities. Management of the household is regulated "in mutual consent," and "both spouses are entitled to be gainfully employed." In this they are to take each other and the interests of the family into consideration.

The "guilt principle" has been replaced by the "irreparable breakdown principle" (Zerrüttungsprinzip). After a divorce each partner provides for her/himself; support is received only by the one "in need." Retirement benefits accumulated during marriage are divided in the case of divorce.

Even the unemployed wife, who is as a rule financially dependent on her husband, can now leave her husband without fear of being left wholly destitute or unprovided for. However, she must prove that she is in need. The law helps her here, for the care and education of children born during marriage, as well as illness or age, are legally recognized grounds for inability to be gainfully employed, and thus substantiate a claim for support. Also, the party who is unable to find appropriate work, who wishes to train or retool, or who is unsuccessful, despite having tried, in providing her/his own independent and sustained support through gainful employment, has a right to support from the other partner.

Thus, the basic principle is that eligibility for support from the other partner exists whenever the need is "conditioned by marriage" (ehebedingt), i.e., a spouse is unable to support her/himself because of having worked within the family up to the time of separation or because of having to continue caring for children afterwards. Usually the party in need of support is the wife and mother, but the principle also applies to the husband. The employed wife with no small children to care for after the divorce must—under the banner of equality—provide for herself alone.

So much for the equal treatment of men and women under the new support law. Things become critical only in practice. For there is already a series of judicial decisions and decrees which show clearly that there are still two standards being applied when one partner leaves the other, and it might look like this: after a twenty-five-year marriage with an average history, Anna F. (forty-nine), housewife and mother of two grown children, leaves her husband and moves in with Hans K. Then she files for divorce and calls upon her husband to pay support. The husband refuses, on the grounds that she now has a new partner to support her. The court agrees with him. On what grounds?

First of all, it must be pointed out that as a nonemployed wife, Anna F. is eligible for support from her husband—even if she wants to divorce him—for the time that they live apart (up until the divorce decree, which determines future support). For the new law requires that certain separation periods be met as a precondition for divorce (one year when both agree to the divorce, three years if one partner is opposed). Thus, from a legal point of view, Anna F. is acting quite correctly in moving out of their shared living quarters.

But now she has moved, not just out of the conjugal apartment, but into her friend's. And of course in so doing she offends "the sensibility of all right and proper-minded citizens," as it is called in legal jargon. Here a woman (who has kept house for her husband for twenty-five years and raised the couple's children) actually breaks out of the marriage without any ado, settles right down into another ready-made nest, and on top of all this demands that her poor husband help finance this reprehensible cohabitation! No, that's really going too far; it is "grossly unreasonable," as the lawyers say. And so Anna F.'s claim for support is "dismissed as unfounded."

Quite apart from the fact that Hans K. is neither obligated to provide support for Anna F., nor necessarily able to, and that Anna F. may not even want him to support her (so as not to fall into a new dependency), this kind of decision makes abundantly clear what feelings have guided the judge's pen. His substantiation states that despite abolition of the guilt principle, the irreparable breakdown principle does not prohibit "considering a spouse's severe matrimonial transgressions, which have unmistakably contributed to the breakdown of the marriage, as grounds for forfeiture (of support) . . . for example if one spouse has 'willfully' broken out of an average marriage and is living in an extramarital relationship with another partner."

There it is again, the offense, punishable according to marriage law, of "malicious abandonment," which prior to July 1, 1977 made it impossible for any economically dependent woman to "break out of" a marriage that had become intolerable to her, because she would have been the "guilty party" and was thus not eligible for support. That is precisely what we wanted to change, for therein lay the discriminatory injustice of the old law. To be sure, a man who abandoned his wife was named the guilty party in divorce, but he did not lose his basis for existence, because he was (as a rule) economically independent. Men have thoroughly exploited this—as judges too will not deny.

Married women can also fall into a trap if they don't keep their eyes open when drawing up marriage contracts. Both the statutory property law, community of earnings, and support compensation can be legally eliminated by a marriage contract. This means that in a divorce each person would keep what he/she brought into the marriage and earned during marriage; neither the property nor retirement benefits accumulated by one or both together would be divided. Since this applies equally to both partners, the legal provision is correct, except that usually the nonemployed housewife and mother is the one affected, being left with no claim to division of property or support compensation in the case of divorce. Some husbands even try to convince their wives to relinquish support for all time, in a marriage contract. Although the majority of lawyers and notaries will reject such contracts, because relinquishing support for the future is legally prohibited, still contracts are conceivable where agreements which for all practical purposes amount to relinquishing support are reached. For this reason women should be on their guard, and examine marriage contracts very carefully to see if they are assured a financially acceptable settlement if financial assistance from the spouse is relinquished.

To be sure, the state wishes to and should interfere in marriage and the family as little as possible. Still, it could fulfill its obligation to inform in a more directed and comprehensive manner, to make clear to every woman and every man the rights and laws that are in force in the area of marriage and the family, and which they should take advantage of. Thus, every couple should be handed an easily readable brochure when the banns [of marriage] are posted. Also conceivable are discussion courses and contract instruction for future married couples, such as have long been available, with great success, for expectant parents. In one particular subject, "Preparation for Marriage and Family," tests are being done with various experimental models to learn how to interest young people not yet engaged in a profession in their future responsibilities from the point of view of equal rights and equal responsibility.

Discrimination—this can be demonstrated over and over—especially affects those who go through life oppressed, dependent, and uninformed. Married women do not have to be any of these. They should not only be acquainted with the laws and take them at their word, but also develop a secure feeling for their own equal value and communicate this to men.

Translated by Jeanette Clausen

Notes

* Originally published as, Heike Mundzeck, "Kommt das Schuldprinzip durch die Hintertür wieder? Reform des Ehe–und Familienrechts," in: *Frauen-Programm: Gegen Diskriminierung*, ed. Marielouise Janssen-Jurreit Reinbek bei Hamburg: Rowohlt, 1979, pp. 196–203. Translated and reprinted with permission. Portions of this text have been excerpted.

36. Mothers are Political Persons

Helke Sander

In 1978 a debate erupted in the pages of the women's journal Courage
concerning the question of how the rights and responsibilities of mothers
fit into feminist political priorities. It also illuminated many aspects of
the uneasy relationship between the women's movement and the left.
The immediate occasion was an article by Meo Hellriegel-Rentzel chron-
icling the marital battles of a well-known leftist, in the midst of a long
prison term for his political activities, and the author of a recently
published book of poetry, with his wife, mother of their two children,
and then in the process of suing him for alimony and child support.[1]
The article sides with the wife, casting her as the victim and her husband
as irresponsible, cruel, and exploitative—a pattern of behavior which
both predated and was not excused by the political persecution he was
undergoing. The author further questioned the male-dominated politics
of the left, which sanction leaving mothers and children in the lurch.
In the following issues of the journal the rest of that year, the letters
columns were filled with readers' reactions to the article. While about
half the letters supported the position taken in the Hellriegel-Rentzel
article, by far the most impassioned letters came from women on the
left who wrote in to express solidarity and support for their comrade.
These letters also condemned a feminist politics which, they claimed,
not only itself draws back from anything involving risk, violence, and
illegality but even turns against a brother who, in their stead, has shown
his open resistance to the state. In response, radical feminist Gunhild
Feigenwinter wrote a letter in which, referring to the wife's intermittant
stays in mental hospitals, she bitterly noted: "So, the man in prison is
revolutionary, while the woman in the clinic is reactionary!" A sizable
proportion of the readers' letters seemed to fall between pro and con,
agreeing that an important issue had been raised—but with the wrong
man. In October of 1978, Courage published this article by Helke Sander
in which she chronicles an earlier confrontation between the left and a
politics of and for mothers—in the Berlin day-care movement of the late
1960s.

The recurring charge in the critiques of Meo Hellriegel-Rentzel's
article is that while she dealt with an important problem, she picked

240

the wrong man and the wrong time. The fact is that from the perspective of mothers, the similarities between opposing political organizations, whether they call themselves bourgeois or revolutionary, often seem more prominent than their differences. . . .

Unlike the situation ten years ago, today there are publications of the women's movement and enough women to insure at least that these statements are no longer obliterated, as was the case for years under leftist censorship.

What Meo Hellriegel-Rentzel is presenting for debate is in essence the very point which initiated what we call the new women's movement: It is the demand for a politics which no longer proceeds *structurally* at the expense of mothers and children. . . . For ten years it has *always* been the wrong time even to attempt to formulate the conflicts women have with the politics of the left (with an equal right to make mistakes)—because there were always more important matters at hand. . . .

In her article Meo Hellriegel-Rentzel is only reviving an old, repeatedly buried, but never quite obliterated debate over a feminist politics which makes the needs of *mothers* the basis of its theoretical and practical work. To illustrate this, I will very briefly describe the work of the Action Council for Women's Liberation. . . .

From its formation in January 1968 until its disbanding two years later, the Action Council developed a political concept based for the first time on the needs of mothers. Certainly many factors contributed to the eventual failure of this effort: One factor was the increasing number of women students without children who joined the Action Council and for whom other aspects of women's oppression took priority. Another factor was the abstract schooling concept of the emerging Socialist Women's Alliance (SFB) which relegated women to their status as a secondary contradiction and resolutely boycotted initiatives toward a feminist politics. At the same time, the SFB, which engaged in endless attacks against the "mothers' faction," had access at the universities to a communication's base which the non-student, working mothers did not have. A third factor was the emerging, extremely antiwoman, dogmatic and Marxist-Leninist cadre groups that had a monopoly over the leftist public arena. Finally, there were but few mothers able to participate actively in carrying out their own politics.

The Action Council developed a political program which began with *self-help* for women who had children—and were thus kept from their studies, careers and/or political work—in an organizational form which provided the mothers with *time* but did not harm the children. At that time there were no communes, except for Kommune I and II.[2] The public kindergartens were overfilled, thousands of children were on waiting lists, and preference was given to children of women who could thereby be integrated into the Berlin economy. . . . Moreover, these kindergartens were not places where one would want to send one's children. The first meeting of the women who later formed the Action Council came about because of this situation, as did the first kinderläden [store-front day-care centers].

These women shared the double burden of the mass of women but they had the advantage, as politically aware persons, that they understood how mothers can be forced into supporting reactionary social policies out of concern for their children. Parallel to this self-help program they devised a strategy for bringing their problems into the arena of public education. They organized the public kindergarten teachers—who soon comprised such a large group within the Action Council that they organized into a separate occupational group. Together with the teachers, they developed a concept which was intended to (and, to a great extent, did) appeal to the mass of women, who would then carry it out.

The content of public education was called into question by the kindergarten teachers, who formulated concrete demands which would be emphasized in a teachers' strike. Most noteworthy was the scant attention given to economic demands, major focus centering upon substantive demands which would benefit the children—such as small class size. At a general meeting in June 1969, approximately five hundred Berlin kindergarten teachers decided in favor of a strike at the end of June. Then, at the last minute, the Economic Wage Assembly (ÖTV) was able to finagle a delay in the strike by promising its support to the unionized but not to the nonunion teachers and asking the former for extra time in order to clarify these questions. This divided the unionized and nonunion teachers and eventually put a halt to the strike. The unions and the senate were reacting in full awareness of the significance of such a strike; the left, on the other hand, would only very gingerly accept the leaflets passed out by the women.

This strike, which had been two years in the making, would have paralyzed a large sector of Berlin's economy, because on that day none of the mothers dependent upon kindergartens closed by the strike would have been able to go to work; and many of these mothers supported the strike. [A successful strike] . . ., according to the strategy worked out by the Action Council, would have laid the groundwork for a determined campaign against light-wage groups and other conditions and practices discriminatory and oppressive to women.

The left putsch

Fixated as it was upon the male industrial worker, the left took no cognizance of the women's total concept. Rather, in a move with putsch-like phases, the left simply took over the *kinderläden* . . . and used them to develop a theory of socialist and antiauthoritarian education often at odds with the ideas developed by the Action Council. This led to confrontations between the Action Council and the newly formed Central Council of Socialist Kinderläden. The education of young children . . . was declared to be an issue for men at precisely that moment when mothers made their first *public* attempts to gain control over the goals and management of their children's education. . . . The confrontations went so far that women from the Action Council were barred from entering some kinderläden when they wanted to discuss these conflicts with parents. . . . Increasingly, those women were forced out, for whom the centers were originally intended as self-help: women with little money, either employed or wanting to pursue their studies—in any case, women who were unable to sit through the long evening meetings. However, in the many publications put out by the men (women had no time) on the kinderläden and on socialist education no mention is made of the substantive disputes between the Action Council and the Central Council, nor is there any indication that the political strategy of the women was ever even discussed by the Central Council.

This pattern continued after the opening of the first *schülerläden* (store front after-school centers) in 1969–likewise the work of women in the Action Council. The scenario was always the same: The women developed a long-term project, allowing time to define and evaluate the tasks at hand; the men started *proletarian schülerläden*, called the children "red panthers," wrote papers and books on their successes, and held university seminars—which the women, not a part of the university context, were not privy to. The women's assessment of the situation was not taken seriously. Far from making claims for an on-going solidarity, the women counted it a success when, after months of effort, the working-class children in the centers no longer beat on each other. The men, on the other hand, debated the formation of a proletarian children's and youth organization—a sham from the start, because it was based upon wishful thinking and not reality. Moreover, these same illusions were to determine the coming phases of "politics"—for example, the completely mistaken assessment of the people's readiness for struggle. However, the revolutionaries did not want to hear this criticism. Rather than admit defeat or the necessity for long-term work, they discarded the old strategies and denounced them as petit-bourgeois; then, a new party or the urban guerilla would be founded. Of relevance here are the doubts, expressed by women and resisted by men, that a socialist revolution was even possible in Germany within two to five years.

There is still no feminist interpretation of the kinderladen movement which was associated with the student movement. Rarely do the documents record the steady chorus of women since 1968; it is as if they and their murmurings had been left out by inept court clerks. This explains their absence. And where women do appear, nobody remembers now that in each and every case having to do with a leftist publication this was preceded by fierce debate over whether or not to print the women's position papers.

The movement had vastly underestimated the time it takes to commit people to a struggle. The ensuring lies, the use of dogmatism to overcome the chaos, . . . and the deaf ear turned to the women's protestations that the issues were really more complex: All this continued during the period when the first men and women went underground, leaving their children behind with relatives. . . . When Horst Mahler (a prominent leftist lawyer who first defended and then joined the terrorist movement and was sentenced to prison— editor's note) now analyzes this politics in retrospect as false and destructive, his analysis becomes false the minute he uses the word *we*. This *we* implies that the left as a whole—women included— made errors in assessing the militance of the people. However, the women whose work I have described never withheld their criticism of the politics of the left. Unlike those in the women's movement today, these women always sought to confront the men and their concept of politics. The women's experience that this was a hopeless task led, then, to their withdrawal—and to the creation of the very women's publications which now permit such discussions as these. In my opinion more effective use should be made of these means of production created by women, to continue to examine the political perspectives of the left, in the interest of converting it to a feminist politics.

Translated by Edith Hoshino Altbach

Notes

* Originally published as, Helke Sander, "Mütter sind politische Personen," *Courage*, vol. 3 (October, 1978), pp. 38–45. Translated and reprinted with permission. Portions of this text have been excerpted.

1. Meo Hellriegel-Rentzel, "Alltagslyrik von P. P. Zahl," *Courage* vol. 3 (June, 1978), pp. 8–11.

2. Kommune I and II were anti-authoritarian experiments in communal living and politics which scandalized and fascinated West Berliners for a couple of years in the late 1960s. Based on the radical youth communes which sprang up in Russia directly after the revolution, Kommune I and II tried to incorporate the ideas of Wilhelm Reich as well.

37. Wages for Housework as a Perspective of the Women's Movement*

Gisela Bock

In 1977 the issue of wages for housework was raised in the German movement. As a political perspective, wages for housework gained wider support there than it did in the United States. Historian Gisela Bock has been one of the most knowledgeable and persuasive proponents of this position in West Germany.

Early in July 1978, in response to a grievance filed by a widow demanding not just 60 percent of her husband's pension but 100 percent ("equality of rights"), the Federal Constitutional Court reached a decision that means a slap in the face not only for the 3.5 million widows in the Federal Republic, but for all women: The housework done by women is, according to the court, just as "valuable" as men's work, but has no claim to a "wage," or to its equivalent in a pension; houseworkers have only the right to "support," and shall have recourse to their husbands for it; men have a right to the unpaid work of women.

Despite counter-strategies and reform strategies, women are continuing to fight. One example among many: In one Berlin region, prostitutes, who take money for a job that other women do for free, succeeded in getting a wage increase. Starting with the early shift, they raised the prices of their services through collective action and managed to keep the money from flowing into the pockets of the pimps, where it normally ends up.

Housework Becomes Visible When it Isn't Done

The demand for payment for housework was already raised in the first women's movement. But it was repressed by the governmental and economic provisions designed to keep women as a reserve work force, shoving them back and forth between housework and the double burden, and conceding qualified positions to a few women so as to use those few to keep all the others quiet. Moreover, it was swallowed up by the male left's very similar prescription for "emancipation," which aimed to get women into "the" arena of production, at the side of "the" working class, thereby overlooking the female houseworkers' production (because of course the left also profited from it). With the rise of the new women's movement, which took place during a boom in women's paid employment, women made public the fact that promises of independence via extradomestic employment were misleading, and not capable of freeing them from their domestic workplace or their comprehensive female role. Their first job, unpaid housework, continued to be "women's business," and in addition, turned up again at their second workplace: in the "female" work of diligent patience on the assembly line; of nurses' self-sacrifice; in the work of secretaries, salesgirls, educators, teachers, social workers. Above all, *un*paid housework turned up again as *under*paid work outside the home: since women's work is worth *nothing* in the home, it is worth *less* outside the home; since a little money means a lot to women, one can get away with palming that little off on them.

Women seized the evil by its roots. Their movement became a movement of rejecting housework, of refusing to let themselves be shunted off into the private sphere, of refusing to see family, the role of femininity and housework as "private," i.e., as nonsocial, nonpublic and nonpolitical, as nonwork. With its slogan "the personal is political," it was only the uppermost tip of an iceberg of women's resistance. From the early 1960s on the birth rate fell and the divorce rate increased: the statistical expression of the rejection of excessive work for children and husbands. The campaign for decriminalization of abortion showed that motherhood means decades of work in which women give more than they get back. The lesbian women's movement and the campaign against rape show that similar things are true concerning work for men. Not by a new theory, but by refusing to do it, did the women's movement declare housework to be work, that is, an activity which involves discontent, monotony, resignation, isolation, desexualization, physical and mental occupational injuries; an activity from which others profit.

The women's movement has not only made housework visible but has also defined it fully for the first time. It is very special work: the female sex is trained, qualified for it, starting with the first day of life; female nature, the essence of woman is supposed to be realized in it; it is to be done for love, and love is its wages. A job that includes female existence in its entirety: physical, emotional and sexual housework; cleaning, cooking, shopping; comforting and smiling and patient listening; sleeping with and getting raped.

The women's movement rejected this work, the equating of work and love. But at precisely this point it reached a boundary: The survival of millions of women continues to depend on this work done for love, on finding access to the income of a man whom they take care of so he will take care of them and their children. The state guarantees this vicious circle of dependency. Women have always revolted against this dependency, and have by no means worked only out of love, but they usually pay a high price: poverty as single mothers, poverty and discrimination as lesbians, overwork because of the double burden, childlessness against their own will, poverty and loneliness in old age, ostracism of prostitutes—in short: new dependency, new housework.

Wages Against Housework

Since the end of the 1960s women have discussed and publicly demanded wages for housework from the state, and since the beginning of the 1970s various countries have had a campaign for wages for housework, especially England, the United States, Canada, Italy, Switzerland, the FRG. The campaign originated as part of the organized women's movement, in centers and groups, but also from the activity and daily struggles of women who had no time, money, or inclination for that form of organization.

With the demand for payment of unpaid women's work we have crossed the above-mentioned boundary reached by the women's movement of the previous decade: that economic dependence of women on men, which prevents them from refusing to work, indeed, often blocks their becoming conscious of their exploitation. It is no accident that the subject of money was taboo for years in consciousness-raising groups, which otherwise dragged the most personal matters relentlessly into the open. Had those who sought refuge in battered women's houses ever had their own money for their work, they wouldn't have needed a shelter, nor would such great numbers of them have had to return to their husbands afterward. *There is one central power relation at the root of power relations in our society (and not just ours): the one between paid and unpaid work, between men and women (and children); there is a corresponding double work ethic—work done for money/work done for love. To define services performed for love as work, to stop taking them for granted and demand payment for them, is an equally central attack on these power relations.*

The very demand for our own money, even before we get it, calls these power relations into question; it also means the ability to reject that work without feeling guilty. (What man can understand the guilt feelings of married women toward "his" money, the counterpart to "female" self-sacrifice? And yet he counts on these feelings when he hopes that she'll spend it "wisely.")

It is the demand by which our nature ends and our struggle begins because just to want wages for housework means to refuse that work as the expression of our nature, and therefore to refuse precisely the female role that capital has invented for us. . . . When we struggle for wages we struggle unambiguously and directly against our social role. In the same way there is a qualitative difference between the struggles of the wage worker and the struggles of the slave for a wage against that slavery. It should be clear, however, that when we struggle for a wage we do not struggle to enter capitalist relations, because we have never been out of them. We struggle to break capital's plan for women. . . .[1]

Once a price tag is placed on housework it can no longer be expected as natural and taken for granted. The new visibility of unpaid women's work has consequences of trememdous significance: It makes clear how this society actually functions. The productivity of unpaid housework is the source of the productivity of all paid work and, therefore, of all profits, but it produces today's and tomorrow's salaried fe/male workers and, in addition, the next generation of women who are supposed to be headed for the same task. But it is not a theoretical question to ask what work actually *is* (the left customarily says, with disarming male logic, that housework isn't productive, since it's not paid; it can't be paid, either, since it's not productive); it is a question of social power. In economics and politics, among both progressives and conservatives, work has been recognized only where it was extradomestic and paid, but women have put a stop to this. They answer the questions "what is productive work? " and "what is housework? " by an analysis of what they are resisting. What women perceive and experience as productive work, as work that brings dependence to them and advantage to others, they demonstrate not by a "theoretical derivation" but by rejecting it—by striking. This was shown most recently by the general strike of women in Iceland in October 1975: when women are not productive, no one is.

The demand is directed toward the state, which for several generations has more and more taken on the role of the female houseworkers' employer. It regulates the labor market, organizes family, social, school, and tax policy, and it knows what it has going for it: Government authorities have calculated that housewives' work is usually worth well over DM 2000 per month—"naturally" not in cash, but as "hypothetical value." It may take a long time to get there, but what's important is this: The wages for housework campaign links up at the points where women have already gotten money from the state and are able to use it to decrease their work. It wasn't called wages because their services for love remained hidden, and because it was in fact usually used to bind women to the incomes of men (i.e., tax exemptions for married couples, marriage loans). These state monies for women (educational support, child support, pensions, public assistance) must be increased, severed from the tie to men's incomes, and the range of those eligible must be expanded. To be sure, these monies—just like the wage hierarchy and piecework systems at extradomestic workplaces—are conceived of as a bonus for efficiency. But it will be the business of women, of their struggles, and their solidarity to make this charity a right, this assistance a wage, this bonus for productivity a means to their autonomy.

Translated by Jeanette Clausen

Notes

* Originally published as, Gisela Bock, "Lohn für Hausarbeit—Perspektive der Frauenbewegung," in Lottemie Doormann, ed. *Keiner schiebt uns weg* Weinheim: Beltz, 1979, pp. 137–145. Translated and reprinted with permission. Portions of this text have been excerpted.

1. Silvia Federici, *Wages Against Housework*, Bristol: Falling Wall Press, 1975.

38. A Salary for Housewives? *

Alice Schwarzer

The debate within the German women's movement over the question of wages for housework took place in the context over continued public concern for the low birth rate in the Federal Republic and concrete proposals of the leading political parties for a housewives' stipend. This article takes both politicians and Wages for Housework adherents to task.

You're a housewife. Every day you clean up after your dear family. For nothing. And now suddenly you're to get money for doing it. $130, maybe even $150 a month, called "housewives' salary," "child-rearing allowance," or whatever. The state is your employer. Sure, you'd be happy about it.

This gift could become reality. Both the SPD [Social Democratic Party] and the CDU [Christian Democratic Union] [1] are deeply concerned about the "baby slump" and "housewives' lack of enthusiasm." The three C's—children, cooking, consuming [2]—must be made palatable again for the rebellious German woman. The CDU is justifiably worried about the sacred institution of the family and the SPD is so upset about women's unwillingness to bear children that they even held a brain-storming session—exclusively male, I assume, the usual thing in such situations. None of that has very much to do with profeminist concerns. On the contrary. For behind it all there is the intention to keep women in line.

Yet it is not only misogynist politicians, but also women who call themselves feminists, who are arguing for housewives' salaries. They are demanding not $130 but $700. And their arguments are different from those of the politicians. Nevertheless their campaign seems just as dangerous to me, because it leads us to the same dead end— only with even grander illusions.

"Wages for Housework" groups first arose in England, Italy, and America and were the work of women from the male-dominated left rather than of feminists. Now there are also similar groups in the Federal Republic. They published a manifesto addressed "To All Governments," which says in part: "We hereby announce that we intend to be paid for our work. We want wages for every dirty toilet, for every painful birth, for every time we're molested and raped, for

251

every cup of coffee and every smile. And if we don't get what we want, then we will simply stop working! "

And so are we to continue to be molested and raped for money? Are we to continue to cook for the lords of creation at home and make coffee for them at work? What cynicism! Instead of fighting against the housewives' ghetto, against painful birth, and against rape—instead of changing that—we're supposed to leave it at that and sell ourselves?

"Money is independence," the manifesto tells us. How simple. But unfortunately reality isn't like that. Sure, having your own money is a basic requirement for any attempt at emancipation, but it is by no means the same thing. Otherwise, prostitutes, for example, would be emancipated women, for they are paid in cash. But they aren't liberated. First, because a precondition for independence is an awareness of how to make use of one's opportunities. Second, because prostitutes, like housewives, continue to be the victims of degrading working *conditions*. That is the decisive issue.

Just as it must be the goal of the class struggle not to gain higher wages for the assembly-line worker, but rather to abolish the division of labor, it is also true that women must fight for the abolition of the housewife's life and not for its improvement. This of course does not mean that we should not continue to seek relief for housewives and mothers here and now.

Simone de Beauvoir, who strictly opposed wages for housework, argues this way: "There is no activity which is in itself degrading. All work is equal in value. Washing windows, why not? That is just as valuable as typing. What is degrading are the conditions in which windows are washed: in isolation, boredom, . . . and in segregation from the community."

What, then, are the real changes worth striving for? These seem to me to be the essential points:

(1) We reject the assumption that women have the major responsibility for house and children, and thus we also reject the double burden women bear.

(2) We demand that men assume half of all household and child-rearing duties.

(3) We demand that much of household and child-care duties be taken over by social institutions: day-care centers, full day schools, and institutional kitchens, etc.

(4) We must change the nature of housework. It must escape from isolation and arbitrariness. There are already timid attempts

being made (e.g., in several "Young Housewives' Clubs," where the women do their major cleaning together, on a rotating schedule).

When women do find the courage to fight, when they do take to the streets, then in my opinion they should not do so on behalf of half-hearted and misleading demands that can boomerang on them.

Translated by Judy McAlister-Hermann

Notes

* Originally published as, Alice Schwarzer, "Hausfrauenlohn?" *Emma* vol. 1 (May, 1977), p. 3. Translated and reprinted by permission. Portions of this text have been excerpted.

1. The SPD and the CDU are the two major political parties in the Federal Republic.

2. The reference is to the new version of the "three K's," kinder, küche, kirche, now revised by substituting Konsum for kirche (church) in our materialistic post-war society.

39. The Proletarian is Dead Long Live the Housewife? *

Claudia von Werlhof

This article by sociologist Claudia von Werlhof identifies housework as the primary mode of capitalist production. She proposes a view of the world economy which has the potential for shaking to their foundations more conventional schools of thought—both Marxian and Keynesian.

Once We Have Understood Housework, We Will Understand the Economy

Housework is more difficult to comprehend than any other phenomenon. Once we have understood housework, we will understand everything. But that presupposes—and there is still a grave deficiency here—that we not view housework too narrowly or use the term in a restricted sense, and that we relate it, indeed apply it to nothing less than the entire economy, the world economy, in fact.

The Relationship Between the World Economic Crisis and War Danger: War Economy

The reason why a truly general theory of society and a corresponding politics are necessary is nothing less than the current onset of a world economic crisis and the impending threat of war. I am more and more astonished that no connection is being made between crisis and war this time around. In any case the topic has not been discussed so far, even in the not exactly minuscule peace movement in the FRG.

The issue is at bottom very simple: if there is a world-wide economic crisis, it will mean economic changes everywhere. But are these achievable without the use of violence? The goal of this economic policy is to accelerate the national economies' processes of adaptation to the world economy.

Meanwhile, the Third World has an "advantage" here, especially since parts of the First World's industrial production were relocated there, making it possible to cut production costs so much that the hard fact is beginning to penetrate in our country too. (Fröbel et al,

1977) But this cost-cutting is achieved, not by means of free wage labor, but by its exact opposite. At issue is an unfree, "femalized" form of wage labor that means no job permanence; the lowest wages, longest working hours and most monotonous work; no trade unions, no qualification opportunities, no promotions, no rights and no social security benefits. The first to succeed in introducing this kind of working conditions in our country would also be the first to become competitive and make profits again.

The "Pillar" of Capitalist Production, the Proletarian, is Disappearing.

I think we are witnessing the historical moment at which the "pillar" of capitalist production, the free wage laborer or proletarian, is disappearing, never to be seen again. We are dealing with the very worker who has served, ever since the nineteenth century, as the "classic" figure of capital's exploited victim and hence also the one subjectively qualified to revolutionize society—at least in the opinion of the left. But nonleftists also basically had this worker in mind, though they did not call him proletarian, but middle class, or "silent majority." For the proletarian or free wage laborer is not just the factory worker, but actually everyone who earns his living primarily through a wage (or salary), hence even the white-collar worker and civil servant. This type of wage laborer represents a kind of majority in our country; he was the base of society, of democracy; he was the voter, the "free, equal, and fraternal" citizen; civil and human rights were meant for him; he was the allegedly enfranchised and equal partner in contract with his employer; he was protected by law against arbitrary action and violence, enjoyed social security, had a permanent (if not life-long) job in a factory or office; he was free to organize in a union, and he received a wage sufficient to maintain him and his family at an average standard of living: the citizen, the "human being," the member of society, the free individual.

The "Vision of the Future" is Vanishing, Which Leads to General Perplexity.

All theories of progress and modernization—left, right, and center— were unanimous in the assumption that this type of *Homo faber* should and would increase: the free wage laborer represented the "vision of the future" for all those "not yet" working for wages, in fact, for all the rest of humanity. This is the so-called proletarianization thesis, the favorite of the leftists. Others call it the expansion of the middle classes, but mean ultimately the same thing. So-called women's emancipation is also based on the expectation that women will become the very same kind of "equal," quasi-sex-neutral wage laborers, and the socialist countries claim to be emancipated or to have emancipated women because many more women do wage labor there than here. By comparison, the so-called Third World came out the worst, for it was "not yet" at that point, was lagging behind, under-developed, precisely because it had so few wage laborers. And now there is to be an end to this very wage laborer? Many people still cling to the belief that it might turn out to be a mere temporary phase of cyclical unemployment, but then eventually . . . etc. But I think they are gradually realizing that this isn't so.

The Proletarian as Minority Phenomenon and the Discovery of the "Informal Sector"

The proletarian wage laborer is a minority phenomenon in a particular phase of capitalism, restricted to a few areas of the earth. Only a small percentage of today's world population belongs to this category, which never was larger. The "prototype" of the free wage laborer, the white male urban industrial worker over twenty-one years old, (James) is even rarer. In fact, 80 to 90 percent of the world population consists essentially of women, peasants, craftsmen, small retailers, and similar wage laborers who cannot be called "free" or proletarian. Actually, this fact should long since have been given the attention it is now gradually receiving.

What Kind of Mode of Production is Capitalism? Conquest, "The Guilt Question," and "Integration"

The consensus is that capitalism originated in and spread from Europe through the achievements of Europeans; that it is a progressive mode of production and functions through the interplay or contra-diction between wage labor, i.e., free wage labor, and capital; its results are progress, growth, interest, profits, and accumulation; in the political sphere the results are the purported ideals of equality, freedom, fraternity—in short, of democracy. This capitalism and its political form, the democratic state, is put forward as the "vision of the future" for the rest of the world.

To me, this understanding of capitalism is nothing less than the glorification of the "white man" as the creator of culture, civilization, and humanity: the white male as the human being per se.

It is high time to free ourselves from thinking of this image as positive. For as such it has nothing to do with reality; it is ahistorical, racist, supremacist, imperialistic or colonialistic, and of course to top it off, sexist.

With almost incredible tenacity, people perpetuate ever-new var-iations of the thesis that capitalism actually materialized only in

Europe and the United States, that what one finds elsewhere are pre-, post- or noncapitalist modes of production, or else peripherally capitalist or deformed capitalist modes of production. (von Werlhof, 1978) This is a way of blaming the victims. For the concomitant conditions of such modes of production are correspondingly characterized as traditional, backward, primitive, archaic, or not yet developed. The people living under these conditions are considered—in contrast to us, of course—stupid, lazy, apathetic, obstructive, conservative, narrow-minded, ignorant, passive—but also emotional, dangerous, rude, close to nature, bestial, violent, insidious, or unbridled. These clichés are familiar to us women. They are applied to us just as to the Third World.

Everything is Vice Versa: the "Pillar" of Accumulation and the Vision of the "Future" Turn out to be the Third World and the Housewife

But let us return to economy in the narrower sense. The women at least will have noticed by now what this is all leading up to: I am headed toward the meaning of housework and everything related to it—yesterday, today, and tomorrow. Women's work is very easy to compare to work in the Third World. Everything is the reverse of what it seemed: The pillars of accumulation and growth are not the 10 percent free wage laborers, but the 90 percent unfree nonwage laborers; they are the truly exploited, the real "producers," the "norm," the general condition of the human being under capitalism. And to his horror, all this is now very concretely threatening the proletarian. The Third World is coming to us. It shows us the "vision of the future" and the real character of our mode of production. More explicitly; our economy will also be "femalized," "feminized," "marginalized," "naturalized" or "housewificized"—there is just one thing it will not be: proletarianized.

The Housewife as the Proletarian's Opposite and the Continuum Between the Two Prototypes: Housework as the Model of Work

Now the key word has appeared: housewife. My thesis is that the principles of the organization of housework will determine our future and not, as previously assumed, the principles of the organization of proletarian wage labor. The housewife is the exact opposite of the proletarian. Let us begin by seeing it as a contrast between black and white. In principle, you can imagine it to be any woman, for all women are housewives under capitalism whether they want to be or not. Thus, I am by no means interested in glorifying the housewife, as is usually done with the proletarian. What I am arguing for is to perceive housewives from a different perspective, with new eyes. First, let us look through the lens of the contrast between the proletarian and the "just a housewife;" both rare, nevertheless typical, prototypical inventions of capitalism (Bock/Duden; Kittler). This economic love-match is a very rare phenomenon, not only worldwide but in our country also, at least in terms of a life-long union. At present it is about to become extinct. All the same, it has become the ideal type which all people the world over should and must aspire to, even if they never achieve it. It is the Western, white, middle-class nuclear family, propagated ever since the nineteenth century and nowadays, by a gigantic propaganda campaign, being lauded even in the slums of Calcutta where there is certainly nobody with a chance to reach this exalted ideal.

We already defined the proletarian or free wage laborer. The woman who comes with it is the life-long full-time housewife. The word "life-long" already indicates that she is actually in jail. (The *house*wife as *home*wife). The cage may be gilded a bit, but that does not change its character. And no one can change it through pure voluntarism, neither husband nor wife. Both may also be quite satisfied with the situation, for they may not know of any alternatives—and above all, they do not have any. Moreover, their relative economic security depends on their staying together. They are a kind of "Siamese twin" of our economy.

The proletarian is apparently free, equal, and fraternal. The housewife is the reverse: she is very concretely unfree, and in a double sense: she is not free to choose or change the location and type of her work or workplace, but is bound to home, husband and children; nor is she free from all the means of production, in possession only of her mere labor-power, as is true in a certain sense of the proletarian, because she has something no man has, and which is treated as a means of production in our society, her child-bearing capacity. Moreover, she "has" her husband as "breadwinner."

Besides that, she is not equal: formally, of course, we now have equality of rights, but even where these rights actually function, their effects are for the most part harmful to women (e.g., in divorce law), simply because women are in fact unequal as long as they are housewives. Equality of rights for women is—by analogy to the pretense of equality between proletarians and capitalists, i.e., alleged class-neutrality—only the illusion of alleged sex-neutrality in capitalism. Voting and other rights of legal-age adults have of course been granted them, but specific areas of law are clearly split along sex lines, e.g., marriage law. Thus, rape in marriage is not a punishable offense; tolerating it belongs, so to speak, among the one-sided marital obligations of the wife.

Moreover, the inequality is primarily a social one. It is based on the fact that the husband has "the queen of commodities" (Marx), the money in his pocket, while the wife is not paid for her work. Her husband must provide her only with "board and lodging," which he must also do for a slave. Working hours, working conditions, vacations, time off, and so on are not regulated in the housewife's case; the marriage contract is not comparable to an employment contract. There is no right to strike, no fraternal or sisterly housewives' organization; they are individualized and atomized. They do not have social security on the basis of their work as housewives, nor are they protected by law from arbitrary action or violence (cf. houses for battered women). Nobody oversees the observance of human rights in the home; there it is a "private matter," supposedly not the public's business, even when her very physical safety is not guaranteed.

The wife is supposed to serve her husband and above all, obey. He can sue her if she doesn't. In short, the housewife is a life-long, round-the-clock, unpaid worker at the disposal of her husband; more than this, her whole person is at his disposal, inside and out; her sexuality and child-bearing capacity, her psyche and feelings. She is at once slave and bondswoman, compelled to do all the work her husband and children "need," including expressing love even when she feels none. Her work is done for love and love becomes work (Bock/Duden). It may not always be intolerable, but often enough it is and, above all, it is impossible to prevent it from becoming so. This absolute contrast means, e.g., that one need not look to the Third World to find a typical absence of human rights or "homogenous" conditions of work and life.

I believe that the extremely different working conditions of the free wage laborer and the housewife form the two end-poles on a continuum of capitalist conditions of work and relations of production, and that reality lies between the two—now tending more toward free wage labor, now more toward unfree, unpaid housework. All the various conditions of work in the world can be found here, including those usually categorized as third world, precapitalist, or postcapitalist. Slave-work today, unfree forms of wage labor, home-industry, peasant production: all lie on this continuum of capitalist production, which looks more and more like a slide sloping down toward housework. All have one thing in common: market dependence and dependence on money generally—more precisely, on a wage. All the people in the world are in principle dependent on a wage, because they no longer have or control any means of production worth mentioning, as land, machinery, know-how, etc., with which they could survive. Conditions which seem to correspond to precapitalist societies are also located on this continuum. In capitalism they are all united in the work of the housewife: forced labor, serfdom, slavery and unfree wage labor.

This is why all other work can be understood only from below, from the point of view of housework and not from the other way around, from the point of view of wage labor. Basically housework, not wage labor, is the "model" of work in capitalism. In capitalism all people are of course potentially wage laborers, but in reality they are more like "housewives," an industrial reserve army, a relative surplus population, i.e., relative in their relationship to available wage labor.

Only very few housewives are "just" housewives. Almost all women and men are wage laborers, for part of their lives or intermittently, or they sell homemade products outside the home (especially in the Third World). But the female wage laborer (or the unfree male wage laborer) never resembles the free wage laborer. All the conditions of femalized or directly female wage labor point rather toward the houseworklike character of this work, so that it is better understood as paid housework than as free wage labor. (Understood in this sense, wages for housework is nothing new, nor is it a "revolutionary" demand). The wage labor of women is organized and treated as an extension of their housework and moreover, is correspondingly badly paid for this reason. Therefore women are unequal to men outside the home in much the same way as inside it. That is why all women are housewives and are always treated as if they were. This sexism also provides the model for racism: a wage laborer of color is simply never a free wage laborer and isn't treated like one even if he is one. That is why there is no race-neutrality in capitalism either.

Sexual Division, Hierarchization and Devaluation of Labor: The Model of International Division of Labor

As Ivan Illich says, we are dealing with an unprecedented "degradation of women." Such a devaluation of women's work especially, and along with it, of women's lives and the female sex, such a rigid subordination of women, standardized world-wide, touching all spheres of women's lives and thence men's too, was unknown to all pre-capitalist forms of sexual division of labor, including the exploitive ones. It is important to understand this, because in our country both women and men believe they are better off now than before, just as many people in the Third World still believe in the progress the white man has allegedly brought them.

In this they too are victims of the suppression of history. Three hundred years of witch-persecution, parallelling the colonization of the world, were necessary to wrest the women's power, economy, and knowledge from them (as was done to people of color), to erase what was left of their consciousness of it from their brains and feelings, and—continued in their upbringing at home—to "socialize them anew, from birth on, from generation to generation, from day to day, to force them into what they are today: housewives and the "underdeveloped." The housewife—like the "underdeveloped"—is the artificial product, the end result of an unimaginably violent development upon which our whole economy, legal system, government, science, art, and politics have been built; this includes the family, private property, and all modern institutions as well.

This "model" is a best-selling export world wide, and not only today. The treatment of the colonies, the enforcement of an international division of labor following the pattern of sexual division of labor (viz. the division into white wage laborers here and colored, "femalized," nonwage laborers there) were practiced, rehearsed, and forced through—by fire and sword, of course. The Third World as "witch" in those days, and the "total housewife," the "world housewife" today, including Third World men. The relation between husband and wife is repeated in the relationship between the First and Third World.

The Why of the Division: Child-Bearing Capacity and Female vs. Male Capacity for Work

We know that women's work is generally considered (commensurate to its pay) to be worthless, unproductive, or even parasitic, and socially not necessary; it is even viewed as a "natural process" and not as work at all. (von Werlhof, 1981)

Proof that it is so treated lies in the following figures (United Nations): taking the world as a whole, women perform two-thirds of all work, but receive only one-tenth of the world income and control only one-one-hundredth of the world's means of production. Obviously, a similar opinion prevails concerning the Third World's total work contribution in relation to that of the First World (like that of agriculture in relation to industry). Again, everything is exactly reversed.

The housewife has "specialized" in human beings, the wage laborer in things. That is the "secret" of why housework as a "model" of organized work will not disappear along with (free) wage labor, and that is the decisive qualitative difference between the two. In the truest sense of the word, woman is the ground upon which the wage laborer stands. He is defined as human being, she as "nature." The "true essence," so to speak, of this division and its starting point is nothing other than women's natural monopoly, namely their child-bearing capacity. In no mode of production throughout history is the capacity to give birth, the prerequisite for producing human beings, as central as in ours. The reason is that our celebrated surplus value, the goal of capitalist production, can be extracted only from living human beings. The more human beings, the more surplus value can in principle be produced. That is the so-called general law of accumulation and/or "population law" of capitalism, which turns women into child-bearing machines and is responsible for the so-called population "explosion."

Machines cannot produce a surplus, they can only imitate human labor. For capital accumulation and profit, human beings are irreplaceable simply because they are alive. Capital per se is dead. Only its vampire-like sucking of fresh blood makes it appear to be living.

The production of human beings in a society like ours is, however, not only the most important, permanently necessary and most difficult task, it is also particularly frustrating, because human beings are continually being degraded, robbed, and exploited. Women's capacity for work is the most general and the most comprehensive imaginable, because it includes and mobilizes the whole person. And producing this capacity did not "cost" anything; no formal training is necessary for it, or even conceivable. Women's "lack of qualifications" is in reality superqualification. Not only wage labor but accumulation as a whole is based on its cost-free production and appropriation.

The dream of all capitalists is therefore not the generalization of wage labor, but the generalization of housework. There is no cheaper, more productive and more fruitful human labor, and it can also be enforced without a whip. I believe that the restructuring of our economy will involve an attempt to reeducate men and to force women's work-capacity on them, as far as possible. For the wage laborer does too little and knows too little. He can do only what he is paid for and what was agreed upon by contract. He does no more than that and has absolutely no idea how human beings are produced. He functions like a robot, an appendage of the machine; de-emotionalized, he avoids and sabotages every effort to press still more life out of him.

Perspectives: "Femalization" of the Proletarian and New Forms of the Division of Labor

The importing of fresh "guest-workers"—who, because of their use-value orientation and peasant background, are closer to women's work-capacity than are other workers—is done for these reasons, just as in the reverse situation, namely the utilizing of cheap, young, female labor through the transfer of industries to the Third World. Business has begun the process, laying off free wage-laborers and increasingly using unfree, "housewificized," "naturalized" wage laborers; illegal, "black," "borrowed," imported and part-time workers, among them many women: This will go on until the men too are ready to get down off their equal and free proletarian high horse and accept similar working conditions.

They will only acquiesce in exchange for the continued supremacy over women. Thus there is the danger that men will again play along, just as they once accepted the housewife as compensation for the (by no means popular) introduction of wage labor—at the cost of women. Will they make the same mistake again? Surely they see where all this has led—in any case, not to men's happiness.

An alternative is possible only if we, women and men, succeed in permanently regaining not just wages but much more, namely the means of production: our bodies and our children, our houses and our land, our knowledge and creativity, and the results of our labor. We want all this without having to dangle like puppets, so we can work for our own, autonomous existence. However, for that we will need not only no more proletarians, but no more housewives either.

Notes

* Originally published as Claudia von Werlhof, "Hausfrauisierung der Arbeit," *Courage* vol. 7 (March, 1982), pp. 34–43. Translated and reprinted with permission. Portions of this text have been excerpted.

Sources

Gisela Bock and Barbara Duden, "Arbeit aus Liebe—Liebe als Arbeit: Zur Entstehung der Hausarbeit im Kapitalismus," in: Dokumentationsgruppe der Berliner Sommeruniversität für Frauen 1976, eds., *Frauen und Wissenschaft*. Berlin, 1977, pp. 118–199. English translation of a shorter version: "Labor of Love—Love as Labor: On the Genesis of Housework in Capitalism," in: Edith Hoshino Altbach, ed., *From Feminism to Liberation*. Cambridge, Mass.: Schenkman, 1980, pp. 153–192.

F. Fröbel, "The Current Development of the World-Economy: Reproduction of Labor and Accumulation of Capital on a World Scale," *Review* vol. V, no. 4 (Spring, 1982), pp. 507–555.

F. Fröbel, J. Heinrichs, and O. Kreye, *Die neue internationale Arbeitsteilung.* Reinbek bei Hamburg: Rowohlt, 1977.

Ivan Illich, *Shadow-Work, Man.* Cuernavaca, 1980.

Selma James, "Sex, Race and Working Class Power," in: Selma James, *Sex, Race and Class.* London, 1975, pp. 9–19.

G. Kittler, *Hausarbeit: Die Geschichte einer "Naturressource"* Munich, 1980.

Claudia v. Werlhof, "Frauenarbeit: Der blinde Fleck in der Kritik der Politischen Ökonomie," *Beiträge zur feministischen Theorie und Praxis* 1 (1978), pp. 18–32.

———. "Frauen und Dritte Welt als 'Natur' des Kapitals, Oder Ökonomie auf die Füsse gestellt," in: Dauber and Simpfendörfer, eds., *Eigener Haushalt und bewohnter Erdkreis.* Wuppertal, 1981, pp. 287–314.

40. The Feminist Theory of Surplus Value*

Hannelore Mabry

In this excerpt from a longer work, Hannelore Mabry postulates a feminist theory of surplus value which concentrates on the productive labor stolen (above all) from women. As all feminist critics of Marx must, the author homes in on his coupling of productive labor and wage labor. What is significant here is that Mabry never loses sight of the labor of the individual mother or the aggregate labor of women, mothers, and "social" fathers and does not fall into a mere explication of texts.

The concepts fashioned for "Historical and Dialectic Materialism," [1] based extensively upon Hegel's dialectical method, cannot be taken over naively into *feminist political economy*. This conceptual instrument was developed by Marx in order to uncover a quite specific relation *within the capitalist system*. After all, Marx's three-volume major work is called *Capital* and not, say, *Patriarchy*. He never occupied himself with a theory of patriarchy. Of interest to him were not the "visible" relations of dependence and possibilities for exploitation—those which are, so to speak, given by an unjust Nature—but rather the "invisible" relations. Sexual molestation, looting and pillage, slavery, torture, murder, and extortion were for him obviously archaic forms of exploitation not in need of further "unveiling." His research interests were concentrated on the supposedly "hidden" modes of exploitation, for example, wage labor, which obscures the appropriation of *unpaid* labor time.

It has always irritated me that feminist theoreticians uncritically take up the language of Marxists. This affected, academically superior form of expression itself conceals anew the true connections and relations of exploitation. This intellectual dependence is the result primarily of the predominantly academic and/or Marxist past of the authors and spokespersons of the new women's movement. And, unfortunately, there are not yet universities at which feminist political economy and philosophy are taught.

We, however, forego the intellectual magic which still radiates from some of Marx's abstract concepts. We believe it is time to redirect these concepts toward an analysis of patriarchy. Marx wanted to lend his intellectual powers to the exploited, after all, and not to the exploiters. We fulfill his intentions—at least in our opinion—when we examine him critically. Therefore we want to test some Marxist concepts and their theoretical ramifications to see if they adequately represent, explain, and measure economic exploitation.

Central to the feminist rejection of the Marxist theory of surplus value remains the fact that Marx did not occupy himself with exploitation and oppression *within the wage-laborer's family or within the working class.* He maintained the unity and homogeneity of family as well as of class, based upon a supposed common position with regard to the possession or nonpossession of the means of production. However, neither in the family nor in the working class has there ever been a single class position. Women and especially mothers have never been able to offer their labor power "freely" and "equally" in the market as a single man may.

In Marxian theory, however, both the mother and the single male worker—indeed the individual him or herself (the commodity labor power)—disappears once again in the end. The individual is transformed dialectically into "a sum of the necessary means of subsistence"—i.e., individuals produce and reproduce themselves through the individual consumption of the working class. So simple is their birth and upbringing.

Yet Marx was fully aware of the *double* enslavement, the absence of freedom of the married wage-earning woman. The failings of his political economic analysis show themselves through a critical reading. These theoretical contradictions should actually set feminists to thinking. But, fascinated by Marx's method of examining a social relation on the basis of societal contradictions, *Marxist* "feminists" wind up, inadvertently, in the position of smoothing over and rendering harmless these contradictions (as in the question of housework being "unproductive" labor—H. Mabry). The great master can surely only have erred in detail! For if, namely, housework and the upbringing of children are *productive* labor—as we will show and deduce—then the whole theory of surplus value as well as class analysis would have to be fundamentally, reopened. It would no longer be so simple to draw the Marxian theoretical compass out of one's pocket.

We, in any case, have come to completely different conclusions than did Marx: Namely, that *the most productive laborers* for "capitalist" and for all "patriarchal" social systems are mothers and *social fathers,* i.e., fathers who perform half or all of the housework and child care.

The amount of surplus labor, e.g., *surplus value,* which women transfer to the possessor or buyer of their labor power can be very graphically proven with the Feminist Theory of Surplus Value.² No longer abstractly and non-sex-specifically, both the paid unproductive and the unpaid productive work performed for "Capital" and for the "Patriarchy" is measured. The Feminist Theory of Surplus Value encompasses every labor power, differentiates between women's and men's work, and permits us to speak of the exploitation inside and outside of the working class family. Each hour of labor (paid or unpaid) which is performed for others is entered into this model. For the first time, housework and women's work in the Third World are included in the "average worker of society" or, in bourgeois terminology, in the "total economic calculations" or in the "Gross Social Product." The woman and mother as labor power no longer remain "invisible" as up to now in all works of patriarchal economics.

The so-called social product of a country is created by the aggregate labor time (labor power) spent by women and men in and outside the home. The contradiction between the collective fabrication and the "private"—in our case, primarily patriarchal—appropriation of the product has been raised through the demand for wages for housework and child care.

The fight for reimbursement of housework is a social revolution and not a technical occurence. Marx would certainly never have claimed that a change in the relations of production (for example, from bonded labor to wage labor) did not affect a change in consciousness in the class concerned (of peasants, laborers, blacks, or women). The trivializing of this struggle by vulgar Marxists shows all too plainly how little they understand of Marx's "true" essence, of his political ethic. Marx saw in capitalism the "connecting link" which has its function between feudalism and socialism. In this sense we can consider the reimbursement of housework also as a connecting link to a family form no longer patriarchal in structure.

In our feminist analysis we will retain some basic Marxist concepts, for they appear to us especially meaningful in describing relations of exploitation. Expressions used by Marx in the theory of surplus value illuminate the state of affairs—for example, the concept "productive" labor. Productive labor is in every case social labor, by which not the producer but rather the owner of the labor power stands to gain: "To be a productive laborer is, thus, not good luck but ill luck." ³

And it is precisely in this sense that we consider housework and child care also to be "productive" labor, productive for "capital" and for every man living with a woman who takes care of the household (regardless of whether she is grandmother, mother, wife, girl friend, or daughter). As stated, we are in agreement with Marx concerning the division of labor and the evaluation of human labor power "as such": only human labor power can produce surplus value and economic growth.

Up until this point our viewpoint overlaps with the Marxian, but here our paths already diverge. While Marx gives all his attention to the production of commodities and the mode of their exchange on the part of the producer (since in his opinion, the transfer of surplus product, surplus value, takes place only in the exchange and not in the use—consumption—of commodities), feminists are beginning to analyze the processes in economic life in which commodities (every kind of product, including human labor power) is *wrested from the immediate producers through coercion, theft—in short, through use of force*. Included are, thus, all cases in which the actual producer is not even able to appear in person, as seller, in the public market of exchange, for the reason that his or her product has already been confiscated, "expropriated." Usually this occurs through a combination of "lawful" and "unlawful" means.

Marx noted the relations of domination and enslavement, already in place prior to the capitalist mode of production and continuing to exist alongside and within the latter, but he did not analyze them in his political economy. In the end, this omission was his undoing: His theory of surplus value loses sight of the exploited object and the exploiting subject—individuals. "Being" no longer determines consciousness, but rather the new "world spirit"—capital—determines "being."

In the theory of surplus value Marx did not succeed in creating a meaningful bond between Hegel's dialectic and historical materialism: He did not discover the "rational core within the mystical shell." The true nature of exploitation, the extraction by the more powerful of unpaid labor time (a theft instead of an exchange!), is again mystified in the relations of capital. The narrowing down of enforced labor, of productive labor—exploited labor power—to wage labor was a theoretical dead end.

Productive and wage labor are not identical, for the following reasons. One, wage labor, "in itself," *can* but need not necessarily contain exploited labor power. Wage labor, "in itself," means, simply, labor which is paid with a form of money. For example, wage labor would be relieved of its exploitative character in a world economic system which, firstly, used money solely as a calculation standard, means of exchange, and value reserve, without the function of interest and, secondly, paid a uniform wage for each hour of labor performed, according to prevailing productivity (by world standards) and according to internationally set labor times. This humane uniform wage—which has yet to be envisioned or computed by any patriarchal system—would be the first socially and politically meaningful payment for human labor. However, we are farther than ever from that point.

Two, although not defined as wage labor, slave labor, bonded labor, and all housework and raising of children were always productive labor, if the owner of this labor power profitted from it— be it through surplus labor, be it through the sparing of one's own labor power. Every labor power must be thus by feminist definition ranked as *productive labor* if it is paid off with less than the unified wage per labor hour, adjusted according to universal productivity.[4] (see reason number one)

The error in definition regarding wage labor (and productive labor) escaped Marx because of the total coupling of wage labor to the capitalist system. Had he been able to broaden the analysis of wage labor through the evidence provided by the present "socialist" states (which have already completed the socialization of land, capital, and machine), then he most likely would have judged his one-sided interpretation of wage labor to be in need of correction. The "economic concealment" of exploitation (within wage labor) has after all not been eradicated in the present day socialist countries.

While under capitalism the so-called "multis," the banks, and the state rule over appropriation and expropriation, in the "socialist" states this is reserved for the ruling bodies of party and government. Nowhere and at no time has the redistribution, the expropriation of surplus value, in agreement with the actual producers, occurred! The method by which the surplus product, the surplus value, is seized— legally or illegally—from the immediate producers functions as of old in a very simple way. Marx calls it the "natural division of labor." More precisely, "natural" means, for us, according to the "rights" of the mighty. Capital is for us too sex neutral as a concept— it tells us too little. As the perpetrators we see the owners of capital, of the land, of machines—people, usually men.

The individual mother, the individual wage-earning woman, has hardly any idea of the value or size of the surplus product, produced by her, but, in the nature of things, soon taken from her. What use the thief or buyer of her labor power makes of the "spoils"—the surplus value wrought by her—she can at best glimpse now and then in the case of her house patriarch. She is unable to observe, follow and spy upon "capital," or the "party," or the "state." Even if she wished to do so, she does not have the "free time"—to say nothing of inadequate or mis-education. In comparison with her house patriarch, she often does find that he gets more interesting work, with more chance for advancement and better pay, than does she herself, the better to insure his old age. If there are children, invalids, or aged in the household, he spends less time on them than she; thus he has a shorter work day. And if one day she no longer can or wants to live with her house patriarch then she notices too late, all too late, that this social and economic arrangement amounted to her sexual, intellectual, and economic exploitation. An "unequal exchange" of labor time has taken place. For both the archaic and highly specialized forms of exploitation rest on one and the same principle: Either directly or indirectly, the weaker, the more dependent are robbed of their surplus product, their surplus value!

Our feminist theory of surplus value concentrates—as we have seen—on the unpaid labor time, the productive labor stolen from us. This raises the problem of measuring and valuing individual labor time. This was also of concern to Marx, for

> the wage form thus extinguishes every trace of the division of the working-day into necessary labor and surplus labor. All labor appears as paid labor. In [feudal labor] . . . the labor of the worker for himself, and his compulsory labor for his lord, differ in space and time in the clearest possible way. In slave labor, even that part of the working day in which the slave is only replacing the value of his own means of existence, in which, therefore, in fact, he works for himself alone, appears as labor for his master. All his work appears as unpaid labor. In wage labor, on the contrary, even surplus labor, or unpaid labor, appears as paid. There the property relation conceals the labor of the slave for himself; here the money relation conceals the unrequited labor of the wage laborer.[5]

In the abstract, the distinction between slave and wage labor is slight: In both relations of production, the relationship between "necessary" and "surplus" labor can only be determined through analysis. The housewife and mother performs slave labor for the house patriarch and receives in return food and lodging (her means of subsistence). How large the surplus product might be or that part of his "provider's wage," of his total income which the house patriarch reserves for himself and does not pay out as a housewife's wage, remains in the dark with Marxists.

As stated, Marx did not take up that portion which the slave owner exacts from the *productive* labor of the slaves because he wanted to distill out only the surplus value concealed *in the exchange of commodities*. He demystified the world of commodities as a world of "congealed labor power" in which a part of labor power remains unpaid: the surplus value. He did not analyze the individual labor wage but rather the relation between capital and labor power "in themselves." Nor did he compare individual labor wages or question the patriarchal ranking of jobs according to their supposed worth.

(For society? Hardly, otherwise garbage disposal would be valued above the high-paid construction of nuclear weapons!). Marx merely accuses the capitalist system of not paying for a part of the labor power performed by the producers—that part which does not appear on the wage card but can only be found in the exchange value of the commodity.

Here Marx was mistaken. In taking this leap of dialectical abstraction he concealed anew the actual material relations—the economic exploitation of over 60 percent of the laboring world population! Marx's most elementary purpose, the one which permeates all his work, was devoted to the emancipation of the individual, his liberation from archaic as well as capitalist relations of domination and servitude. But he missed his goal and exposed, at the most, only 40 percent of the exploitation—in terms of the whole of society.

In order to represent surplus value he used the formula m over c plus v, in which $m=$surplus value, $c=$constant capital (money, machines, raw materials), and $v=$variable capital (labor power, wage sum). For the rate of surplus value he used the following derivation, among others:[6] surplus value over value of labor power equals surplus value over necessary value: and surplus value over value of labor power equals unpaid labor over paid labor. Wherein *labor* is always understood as *labor power*. In this last formula we see that the abstract transference of exploitation onto the commodity was and is completely unnecessary. The whole purpose is, after all, to uncover and analyze the exploitation of human labor power, i.e., expended labor *time*. Economic exploitation rests today, as it always has, in the final analysis, upon the division of labor and upon the variable valuation of individual labor time and of aggregate labor. The *qualitative* aspect is the wage differences per labor hour, and the *quantitative* aspect is the differences in the total quantum of labor performed by the individual per year. The actually expended labor time "disappears" in the commodity; no one knows how many work hours by how many producers in all are "objectified" in the end product. For hidden in the price of the commodity is not only the wage paid but also the fixed costs (constant capital) and the old-age, accident, sickness, and unemployment insurance; taxes; and profit of the entrepreneur. The jump to commodity price, to exchange of commodity, thus only obscures the exploitation of human labor power, labor time, and most especially the division into paid and unpaid labor time.

Basically, in all the world there is no payment for housework and child rearing, whether women (or, in the minority, men, as well) perform this work, in addition to employment outside the home or as so-called full-time housewives. Neither group is paid nor receives social security for this labor time. The full-time housewives receive for this slave labor, to be sure, the minimum for subsistence from their patriarch, or, in some cases, receive it as social assistance from the state. In terms of time those most exploited are women and mothers who perform both wage labor and slave labor. Thus, for both groups, of either sex, the payment for housework and child rearing is just as important as it is for those who are full-time housewives.

All in all, the women's question proves itself to be a question of children, the sick, and the aged, as well. Children also have fathers; old people also have sons. But the sons and fathers have stuck the women and mothers almost exclusively with this work and up to now have done little or nothing politically to reduce the work day outside the home to five hours for women and men, in order to truly share in the housework. *Without a simultaneous reduction by law of the work day to five hours for both sexes,* all so-called liberation of women for work outside the home means the increased exploitation of the women and a steady expansion of the political and economic power of patriarchy. For this reason, patriarchs of both capitalism and "socialism" are equally interested in the increased employment of women.

Therefore, all women and mothers—and, finally, all fathers!—must fight for a feminist social order and reject all cooperation in the patriarchal left and right. Only when men take up the struggle over housework for their own liberation, only when they *extend* the "provider's wage" to those women with a double and triple burden and *restrict* it to those men who in fact perform the labor of housework and child-rearing, yes, only when they join with us to abolish patriarchal surplus value, only then will we once again be in the same boat with men. Women and mothers did not split the labor movement, but, rather, the male workers have from the beginning betrayed and plundered women and mothers—*because for them, too, the patriarchal right of the mighty prevailed!*

Only when both sexes, in equal portions, perform housework and social labor as well as *political* work outside the home will we create more humane conditions on this earth. For the quality, the content, of my labor determines my social consciousness. Due to their mode of labor and production alone, women tend to overvalue the subjective, the individual and men the "objective," the theoretical and technical. The polarization of work spheres led not only to the economic exploitation of women by men, to the alienation of the sexes in the sexual, emotional, and intellectual realm, but also to the loss of basic human qualities: Communication, understanding, and love cannot flourish under sex-specific modes of production and reproduction. Only when housework and social labor are equally divided and paid according to the time spent will we (and then very willingly, with men) take the next step: to struggle for a humane, unified wage which reflects world productivity levels for all people. As long as some live at the expense of others there can be no peace and no meaningful human relationships. The sexual enslavement of women must be abolished, and the patriarch liberated to become a human being—through his daily work with those weaker and more dependent—so that both will have a different attitude toward violence and war. If we do not overcome patriarchy in the family, in kindergartens, and in schools, we will not overcome it in factories, in parties and in the state. If we do not conquer the patriarchy in and around us, it will conquer us.

Up until now there has been little demand for inquiry into economic and political strategy by feminists—unfortunately. Let us hope for a change in this trend and that the first step—individual and subjective attempts toward emancipation—is followed by the second step: the creation of a common political concept of emancipation and the formation of an autonomous Feminist Party as well as an autonomous Feminist Union.

Translated by Edith Hoshino Altbach

Notes

* Originally published as, Hannelore Mabry, "Die feministische Mehrwerttheorie," *Der Feminist* No. 12 (1981), pp. 8–14. Translated and reprinted with permission. Portions of this text are excerpted.

1. This refers to terms such as *capital, commodity society, proletariat, value of labor power, exchange value, use value, average laborer of society,* or Marx's adaptation and concretization of the paired category: "productive" and "unproductive" labor.

2. Hannelore Mabry, "Mit Oder Ohne Marx zum Feminismus?" *Der Feminist,* No. 3 (1977). ("With or Without Marx To Feminism?") This out-of-print essay has been reprinted in its essential parts in *Der Feminist,* No. 12 (1981). In late 1982 it will be published again, in its entirety, in the collection Hannelore Mabry, *Nicht alle Wege führen zum Feminismus. (Not All Roads Lead to Feminism)*

3. Karl Marx, *Capital,* Vol. I, p. 532.

4. Hannelore Mabry, "Die Unruhe über unsere feministische Klassenanalyse beginnt gerade erst," ("The Unrest over our Feminist Class Analysis Is Just Beginning"), *Der Feminist*, No. 4 (1977).

5. Karl Marx, *Capital* Vol. I, p. 562.

6. *Marx*, p. 556.

Part Nine

Our Pasts, Our Future

"The past is not dead, it is not even past." These words, the opening sentence of GDR author Christa Wolf's *A Model Childhood*, summarize the perspective of the authors in this section. Each in her own way, they approach the task of recognizing the tangible presence of the past in our lives now, and of using that knowledge to think about the future. A concern for maintaining such awareness in an increasingly technological and reifying world is apparent in all the texts.

The Gender of Thoughts, by Jutta Heinrich (1940–), is unique among the many first novels by West German women that appeared during the 1970s. Rather than incorporating elements from her own autobiography, Heinrich attempted to represent a process of psychic deformation during girlhood, so that the book's narrator becomes, in the author's words, "a distorted mirror of the structures of power and powerlessness." Christa Reinig (1926–), who left the GDR for the West in 1964, stands out among writers of an older generation because of the radical shift in her writing and her politics in the mid-1970s. Describing her 1976 novel *Entmannung (Unmanning)* as "my path into the women's movement," she has since published numerous stories, poems and essays that show her moving more and more toward a separatist position—evident in the texts included here. From Christa Wolf (1929–), the most widely known of the women writing in German today, we include a small section of *A Model Childhood*, her most autobiographical work. Wolf chooses a multi-layered, self-interrupting narrative form to represent a more complex reality: memories of her childhood during the Third Reich; events during the time of writing; dreams; conversations; philosophical speculations and other discourses are juxtaposed, merging different levels of time and reality.

41. The Gender of Thoughts*

Jutta Heinrich

In this book, Heinrich wanted to depict a female consciousness that women would both identify with and feel repelled by—a split she considers characteristic of woman's psyche in patriarchy. The beginning of the novel (first excerpt) presents childhood impressions of grotesquely unequal power relations between the sexes. For Heinrich, this is expressed most definitively and violently in sexual relations. In "The Dream," which takes place after the father's death, we see images from early experiences continuing to dominate the adult woman's consciousness.

In the first years of my life I gave my parents names which never faded from within me but kept growing with me as I grew. To my mother, a delicate woman the colors of water, I gave the name Little Ant. My father was The Horse.

I have never left the world of horses or the world of ants—and as far back as I can remember, there have been only the three of us; my father, my mother and I.

For me, every kind of thinking—thinking ahead, thinking back— is to slip back into my beginning, where I was born: I, a tree without roots, its branches and fruits beneath the earth.

My mother became my father, my father my mother, and I am not I.

Just as my parents' names were irreconcilably disproportionate, so was their entire relationship. And it was only because I was timid and uncommunicative that I never once addressed either of them by their respective names.

They told me I had been born in a clinic, which I cannot believe, for I imagine myself suffering even to this day from the shock of being brought violently into the world in our vine-covered house under the wooden stairway, the stairs to the second floor.

I don't know how old I was at birth; I was older, at any rate, for life outside the womb seemed just as terrifying as I had experienced it all along: here and there a suffocating pitch-dark breadbox.

My mother's heart was surely nothing but a riverbed for tears, and I am certain she often screamed, forced her weeping down inside past her throat to her belly, for I came into the world with big ears, and had sensitive hearing, alert and suspicious, the hearing of a life that has ended.

Year by year my mother grew quieter and more sensible, for ever since my birth she understood in duplicate why she should be pushed around and despised.

Once, some time or other shortly before my father came home, as we were both crouching under the wooden stairway to avoid him, my mother made the following statement: "Don't forget, once again a useless being has only given birth to another useless being."

I never heard another statement of such clarity and length from my mother, and that was the first time I consciously heard anything said about my sex, and thus about what I was. For at other times I could only get a feeling of all the things I lacked compared to the sex Father possessed.

So my parents had me baptized Connie, because for them this name represented a combination of both sexes, and my father wouldn't have to be constantly reminded that I would never be anything but a girl.

From that day on, when I found out for certain, I grew helpless and experienced pain, for I couldn't accept the idea that I would be nothing but a Little Ant when I grew up.

In spite of everything the first years of my life were the most bearable, for I couldn't be interrogated.

To be sure, the looks my father gave me during those wordless periods inoculated me so thoroughly that I learned once and for all, beyond any doubt, to be silent and endure his harsh orders, to be on his side.

Because I couldn't let go of his life, for his seemed more desirable, I made myself an ally of the powerful. But my father tolerated me only during sentimental moments or possessive rages, so that I constantly lived in anticipation of his affection, and for this I betrayed my mother, my love for her.

And so it came about that I could give her only the fickle attention of one slave for another.

Because I had to betray my mother I was resolved to suffer with her at night.

The Nights

My parents' bedroom began right next to my bed. My wooden bed, wall-to-wall with theirs, transmitted every move made in that sinister room to me.

My room was long and bare, with several unused bedframes piled high with clean bedding. All I had was the moon which, once having climbed to the bottom window, never let go of me. It would shine along the windowpanes one by one only to stop mercilessly just across from me, dazzling me all through the long night and bathing me in chalk-white light.

Burrowing into my pillows, white on white, the moon became my father, a bilious atmospheric mass which drank up my life and so, many times, I felt myself to be a shadow getting out of bed in the morning, sickle shaped or balloonlike.

Now and then it happened that my eyes fell shut and I had to fight sleep because nothing was stirring in the next room, but then—like a revolving stone—I suddenly heard the doorhandle being pressed down. My mother's hand groped for the light switch and I took her fear upon me as if our beings had been exchanged, felt my body glide over to her in a paroxysm of fear.

I heard her footsteps proceed to the middle of the room, heard the rustling of her dress and underwear and, when her hurrying hands hurriedly lowered her clothing, hurriedly brushing her body, when she sought refuge in bed, rubbing her feet together several times, I found myself wide awake, as if my mother had installed an alarm system in my sleep.

Seconds later she extinguished the light by pulling a cord hanging above her head, and I pressed myself close to the wall, to her body, carried on my dialogue with her, for I knew she would beg my forgiveness.

The older I grew the more I forgave her, resolved to grow strong and steady, perhaps like Father, to protect people like her.

In those seconds of silence, of unbroken solidarity, I felt myself growing larger; yet her room conveyed only sadness to me, as if I could never reach her or catch up to her no matter how fast I grew, and as if she were already giving me away to Others. But the moment the clinking of bottles could be heard I knew I had to be on my guard, and sometimes I was thankful at last to be able to await the ineluctable shock. Then I endured noises one after the other, a countdown before the explosion: my father arranged bottles in the bar, carefully turned the key in the lock, piled newspapers onto a stack, coughed irritably, emptied the ashtray, put out the light, opened the living room door and came thundering on wooden feet through the hallway to their bedroom; with one blow of his hand he opened the door, left it open and disappeared in the bathroom for what seemed an eternity.

My ears conveyed her to me as she lay on the operating table and waited while water roared in the bath, cups clattered in their holder, the toothbrush was tossed aside, while he coughed phlegm out of his throat one last time, then footsteps approached the bedroom.

Stiff and motionless—breathing shallowly—I awaited their ghastly ritual.

Only after many years did I realize what an unheard-of instrument my ears had become. Like a wiretap, like a seismograph; not the slightest sound escaped them, whether flesh upon flesh, breath on breath, eyelids straining open, joints cracking, fingers groping, stroking, pinching.

And during all this I was able to exclude every unessential sound, such as the sighing of the evergreens in front of our house, the constant rustling of the vines, rain, or the wind gathering along the garden wall.

Though I never once pressed my ears to the wall, my parents were connected to my head; images overcame me like apparitions, falling incessantly into my ears, over my head, before my eyes.

It is through my ears that I know my father came naked from the bathroom, that he paused in the doorway as the light flashed on, flung the door to with a crash behind him; that he forced my mother, as he glared at her, to experience those seconds of fright as masculinity.

After an exchange of glances which soldered their eyes together and assured him she was only a foolish woman, he strode to her bed and flushed her body from its place of concealment.

I felt it distinctly as my mother covered her private places with her hands, heard the trembling of her hands which, like her feet, sounded like parchment.

After a few moments my father dropped the blanket again and turned his back on my mother; examining himself in the mirror, he burst out laughing, roaring and howling at her, at me, both of us. His back shook with satisfaction; every single hair on his body stood on end, like stilettos.

He flung himself in bed, yanked the lamp cord, and I knew he was swelling out again in the darkness, a deluge inundating my mother.

Then silence fell, the silence of a violent death.

This strange alliance with my mother lasted until about my eighth year.

Then began a creeping, trailing, something moving toward me from every crack and cranny. At last my mother answered, and although I could endure the crawling sensation on my skin only with difficulty, I never scratched so as not to interfere with her victory march over my father.

Swarms of ants marched across our beds, gathered in my father's bed, occupied his clammy skin.

My father lay unsuspecting, defenseless, all night long, as his skin was perforated through and through, thousands of times.

The Dream

At one intersection several taxis were parked. I inquired about Father, but was unable to describe him. The taxi drivers made fun of me, and at that point they all looked so much alike that I couldn't have described a single one of them, either.

But when I gave the name of the city they became aggressively friendly; each of them pressed to be the one to take me to the City of Horses. I was surprised at the reversal and the rise in value my most secret fear seemed to have undergone. Illuminated and guilt ridden to think I had apparently been mistaken about Father just as about Mother, I gave myself over to one of the drivers, as if he were to take me to the city to make a public appearance. After an endless drive we arrived; the city was of such clinical purity and technical perfection that I thought my heart would stop beating and I would be hooked up to an iron lung. The further we penetrated into the heart of the city the glassier and steelier the outgrowth of marble-cement-concrete-steel giants became. They proliferated into ever higher heights and deeper depths so that neither sky nor clouds could be seen; only a haze, which consumed the light, hung over the city like a crown. The driver deposited me directly into the maw of the huge buildings. The blinding brown walls fused with all the walls and pursued me through the cavernous streets; my heartbeat became the ticking of a clock marking time until it too must stop and become pristine matter.

I could see no person or thing that reminded me of Father or Mother, for my eyes were nothing but a hydrometer which registered movement above the earth's surface by violent reflexes of the pupils. On all sides there were ominous posters, branded into the atmosphere, with the words: "The City of Horses. The Happy City."

On the streets thousands of people hastened along, a leathery smile etched on their faces, enclosed in glass. And they moved cautiously so the glass would not shatter and cause their artificial circulation to come into contact with a human one. Every few hours cars with loudspeakers cruised in circles; newspapers were dispensed and banners hung up. All they had to proclaim was threatening unemployment, a deadly failure of technology to keep pace with human needs, or terror and violence from other cities and countries. The news reports came over the city like a war and then there would be a fresh assault on everything available for purchase, because incessant, mechanical consumption was a last possibility for maintaining this round-the-clock technology at full employment.

Then the city had its gag forced into its mouth again, the barred gates of speechlessness closed; no one could take notice of me, so deeply were they engulfed in the misery of happiness. And they went on endlessly and aimlessly just as I did—breathing with and in the iron lung.

Suddenly all the streets terminated in an arena as dark as night. I escaped into it, fell into one of the countless rows of seats which were gradually filling with people. Before me a black curtain was pulled shut across an immense wall, apparently concealing a stage. The auditorium filled with that same choked silence that made the city like a coffin. A few people hurried to and fro like the hands of a clock, locking all the entrances and exits; the darkness was replaced by a thin light shimmering through from behind the curtain.

Soon after it had gotten dark many people went to sleep. After a while the curtain was drawn; on the vast stage there was only a black steel table covered by a black plastic cloth, nothing else. A naked man came out of a steel chamber, bowed and went to the table; all at once I realized that it was my father. He acknowledged me with a gesture, but I was unable to utter a sound because the gag was still so deep in my throat.

Standing next to the table, naked and glistening with oil, he introduced himself and his art. After giving his name and mine, he said he was the first man to perform this trick, and that it was in complete accord with the technology of the outside world. I sprang to my feet intending to make a sign to him with my hand, for I was still unable to call out, but then everything happened with such frantic speed that my eyes had difficulty following the events.

In one elegant pounce he sprang onto the table and stood up straight, then bent over backward several times testing his agility. He did a flying somersault backward, then forward, tensed his body suddenly and with a lightning-quick arching motion bent all the way over backward so his head touched his feet. He was breathing powerfully in and out now; he paused with his mouth at his feet and then, after he had taken another loud deep breath, his feet disappeared into his mouth. He twisted his head once more with his toes in his mouth and then a shudder passed through his body like an electric current racing through a high voltage cable. He began breathing in and out again and within seconds he had swallowed up his body by inhaling, as in a series of implosions, from his feet up along his legs up his back.

I put my fist in my mouth in horror and heard him inhale once more just as only his neck and mouth were still visible. And before the sound of his inhaling had subsided there was nothing left of him but a drop of sweat on the plastic cloth.

A few people roared "bravo! " and applauded, while I, with a last mute cry, plunged out of the arena and fled from the sea of city light.

A wasteland opened up ahead of me; in a gray-blue haze lights flickered and rose beckoning out of the plain, then faded almost away.

I was glad to hear someone calling, and walked into the haze, into the wavering lights. Signposts loomed up out of the landscape here and there with the words "To the City of Horses" and arrows pointing in the direction I was coming from. Then, set apart in a hollow, a single house surrounded by smoke. The earth covered with withered grass smoldered softly, crackling, fanned by the wind from the knoll which protected the house from behind.

The wind carried sounds of quarrelling wrapped in a cloud of smoke from the house toward me. Doors were flung open and slammed shut again. Ahead of me someone opened all the windows; several candles in the house were extinguished and others flared up wildly. Now I clearly discerned my mother's voice. I had never heard her yelling like that, and she never used to take out her rage on rooms or objects. After a violent torrent of words the windows were unfastened and thrown to the ground. Then Mother appeared standing exhausted in the doorway and stormed back into the house running wildly this way and that. I was overjoyed to have found my mother and covered the stretch of walk separating us at a run. She saw me coming but her anger was unabated. I reached out to her, for she pretended not to see me; she had already taken off her shoes and was holding them in her hand so she could leap across the scorched areas. She was not to be stopped, but propelled herself out of the house with as much energy as if she herself were about to burst into flame. I called to her and wept because the enormous strangeness inside me hurt so terribly. Seeing her bothered me so much that it seemed I had only seen photographs of her all these years, and that I was physically facing her for the first time just now, in this glowing wasteland.

Already on her way, she turned around and called to me: "Oh yes—you want to find Father . . . go ahead, go in, go . . . he's sitting inside with his globe of the world between his legs and his colonies in his head, in his heart . . . playing King of the Ants, grieving to himself because the City doesn't need Horses like him! "

She said all this in a tone of voice which I couldn't recognize as either for me or against me. I felt myself pulled back and forth between childhood and adulthood. Was she not, at that moment, spreading the entire landscape of the past out before me and thereby explaining to me why she had forgotten his grave?

But then, when she simply vanished, taking all the evidence with her into the wall of smoke, she left me hollowed out, a child again. I, who had spent my life carrying buried inside me the things I had seen through the keyholes, a silent secret. For they all let me believe I could only become an adult through keyholes, and that some day, behind the maze of keyholes, the world would lie open before me of its own accord.

Translated by Jeanette Clausen

Notes

* German original: Jutta Heinrich, *Das Geschlecht der Gedanken* (Munich: Frauenoffensive, 1978), pp. 7–9, 10–13, and 122–128. Translated and reprinted with permission.

42. The Widows*

Christa Reinig

With her characteristic bluntness and distinctive sense of human, Reinig sets out to imagine a world without men. Her vision is no happy matriarchal utopia, but a realistic picture of a technological world stopped dead in its tracks, due to women's (forced) dependence on male expertise. For a different perspective on this story, see Plogstedt, "Has Violence Arrived in the Women's Movement?" (section X, this volume).

The cell nucleus of a woman consists of two female halves. The cell nucleus of a man consists of a female and a male half. If we could compress all of mankind's chromosomes together into a ball, the men would be half contained in the total mass of female genetic material, but the other half, their own male genetic material, would drop out of womankind.

As a result, any virus strain that infects women can infect men too. However, there could conceivably be a virus strain that threatens only men and lets women alone, that is, if the virus has specialized in attacking the male half of the cell nucleus. Then the men would be down and the women would stay on their feet—they'd have to.

Let's imagine the consequences this kind of virus would have. At first the women wouldn't even react when their husbands started whining and crawling back to bed. Nor would they think anything of it when their neighbor said "My husband doesn't feel good either." Then all of a sudden every single lamp and light would be extinguished as if by a blow with an axe. The whole country's electricity is off. Because the workers and crew at the power plants are men.

There'd be planes in the air that could never land, not even American planes that had a female copilot. Because the men in the control towers are men. On account of women's inferior—beg pardon!—different qualifications, each and every strategic position in industry and technology has to be occupied by a man. Though there is a female Minister of Family Policy.

There'd be ships on the sea that would never get anywhere. Because the seamen's hierarchy tolerates female taxpayers whose money can be steered toward building new ships; it doesn't tolerate female helmspeople to steer the ships. Though there is a female Minister of Health.

Amazing how many emancipated women there are in the health care system. But they're mostly lowly bedpan-bearers. There are just enough female doctors to doctor up their male colleagues. No female medical power could help the masses of men and counteract the disease.

Trucks stand still on the highways. The drivers have pushed the door handles down and fallen out. Women who had enough penis envy to get a driver's license get out of their Opel Cadets or VW Rabbits into the semitractor cabs and rumble heavily into town with the one– and two-trailer rigs.

In reality, women couldn't handle that. And they can't shake the feeling that they're doing something illegal. But the children have to be fed, and the daily bread is in these trucks lined up at traffic lights that no longer signal anything.

Since women can't think logically, they waste a lot of time dialing dead telephones trying to summon male rescuers. Then more time passes while the women congregate at the elevator, hoping and praying that in some mysterious way it will still work.

Finally the women get to work. They try transporting the men down the stairwells of the highrise apartments. They get as far as the seventh floor. Then the fifth floor shouts up to them that everything's blocked up down there. There are thirty-six men to take to the hospital at once. Some of them die on the steps on the way. The women climb across them and go back to their apartments, not out of hard-heartedness, but in despair.

There's one woman-specific activity that's ideally suited to the abilities of female workers: looking out the window. The women open their windows and look down. Then they do the right thing. They throw their husbands and bosses out of their living room or office windows onto the street. The truck-driver women, who are really into the swim of it now, walk by on patrol and collect the bodies from the sidewalk.

Where there are men there are construction projects, and where there are construction sites there are mixers and cement. Women are highly talented construction assistants. Now their talent is needed. They stack the dead men in the construction sites and cement them in.

Now that the men have collapsed in their death-throes the subway will never run again, so subway tunnels can serve to accommodate the masses of the dead. In this way millions of corpses can be disposed of in no time without danger of polluting the air with smoke or contaminating the environment with chemicals.

From time to time the women are seized by fear and trembling, but they soon shake it off again. Sure, there are no men left to befriend and protect them, but there are none to slaughter or rape them either. The corpses of the dead men disseminate an atmosphere of peace and security that the bodies of the living men never could.

Women who learned karate so they'd know how to ram rapists in the groin with their elbow now wish they'd learned to do emergency technical repairs. Because women who know something about technology are the head honchos now. We'll pretend that they worship the principles of a feminist democracy.

Toward evening all work inevitably has to be stopped. The women light candles or makeshift oil lamps. They gather together. A feeling of embitterment spreads through the crowd. It seems to the women like an unmotivated act of revenge for the men to have left their widows in such a state of ignorance and incompetence, bewilderment and helplessness. But then, since the men aren't really to blame for their own demise, the mood of annoyance is tinged with humor. The women get more and more cheerful.

Some women walk through a park alone at night for the first time in their lives. The bare, cold, cavernous streets of the mammoth cities aren't really as ominous as they appear. A gigantic light goes on. Many women recognize it from television when those men went up there: it's the moon.

We won't conceal the fact that some fighting and looting goes on. But the troublemakers are people like yourself, and strength is met with strength. No overpowering enemy squashes you flat to the ground. The possibility of resisting makes the women resolute, and they send the female rabble-rousers into well-deserved retirement.

The next morning the exodus begins, out of the city to the country where the food grows in the ground and the water-bucket doesn't have to be hoisted up twelve stories.

A few female medical students have stayed behind and are going over the day's agenda. They're ready to dissect a man. But the women have done a thorough job. Where's a man for the dissecting room? They go to the clinic. The women doctors and the cleaning women are scrubbing the floors together. They point their fingers at the ground.

The students go to the basement. The pallbearers are just leaning their stretchers, which turned into biers along the way, against the wall. They shrug their shoulders and leave. Closing time!

The students walk down the streets. Coming toward them is a troop of housewives. They're unemployed, and in the best mood. They're still wearing the remains of their pink blouses, but they've thrown away their high heels. Their feet are caked with plaster.

Their hair is disheveled and covered with white dust. They're handing a bottle back and forth, and they're real loud.

Actually, these women are in such a state of nervous collapse, physical exhaustion, and drunkenness that any one of these conditions could knock them over. But all three together keep their bodies suspended, like three poles leaned together to hold up a tent.

The students address these homemakers, now turned bricklayers, and state their absurd request: they're in urgent need of a male cadaver.

The women's colossal survival effort has distanced them from the cause of their misery: that everything has changed so much from one day to the next because there are no men. The students' question sobers the bricklayers up, and seeing their sobriety, the students undergo an awakening. They wake up to a different world.

The bricklayers walk back a ways with the students to the entrance of a subway station. The entrance has been walled up without a crack. The plaster isn't dry yet. A woman slaps her palm on the bricks she has just mortared in and says "Do you know where we can get something to eat? "

Yes. Now that's the problem.

Translated by Jeanette Clausen

Notes

* German original: Christa Reinig, "Die Witwen," *Der Wolf und die Witwen* (Düsseldorf: Eremiten-Presse, 1979; Munich: Frauenoffensive, 1981), pp. 7–12. Translated and reprinted with permission.

43. The Wolf and the Woman*

Christa Reinig

In this essay, Reinig provides an example of how women must rewrite history, cutting through glib academic explanations that mask the real problems facing women, and all of humanity. Especially interesting is her analysis of scholarly language, which favors the passive voice and other syntactic constructions that delete or hide the real agents of oppression. Both this text and the preceding one, "The Widows," were first published in the journal Die schwarze Botin.

Psychoanalysts have succeeded in curing the oedipus complex. Modern-day sons no longer aspire to sleep with their mothers and kill their fathers. Now they aspire to sleep with their fathers and kill their mothers.

Every year there are as many women murdered the world over as there were Jews in the Third Reich, and for the same reason: because as men see it, female life is life unworthy of living. If men would go ahead and eat the women they slaughter every day, they could solve their nutritional problems better. To men, women are even lower than animals. Maybe that's the reason why we don't end up in the meat grinder.

I am a member of the lesbian nation. Even if I didn't want to, I'd have to be. I'm not a German any more. I've left the German nation because channel 1 of German television has a series called "The Wolf and the Woman." First the male animal, then the female human.

It's Sunday morning and I'm considering whether I'm still willing to share this planet with male beings at all, when Bavarian Broadcasting's program "This World of Ours" comes on. Today's contribution is by Wilhelm Höck, entitled "Only an Imperfect Animal—On the Psychology of the Witch Craze and Male Power."

Well, that's worth listening to, for lately it's been claimed there was no such thing as witch persecution in the sense of a collective extermination action by men against women. It's been proven that an occasional man was also burned at the stake by the inquisition. The author seems to be representing a woman's point of view in the extreme. A man starting with the black pieces! I'm curious to see how a man will play our game.

288

The very first blow goes to Sigmund Freud. Our worthy champion of women declares that there's only a small difference between the Malleus maleficarum and Freud's theories of femininity. He accuses Freud of *basically never departing from the witch persecution position.* Outstanding!

Still, I'm left with an uncomfortable feeling. The author's opening play is to assert that men are afraid of women, which is where their perverse behavior toward women comes from. Now then. It happens to me from time to time that some man or other takes a swing at me. The reason usually is that I'm walking on the same side of the street. The man unloads en passant, you might say—and in an immense burst of strength released in me by fear I'm supposed to hit back at the overwhelming power of these muscles and bones and pounds and decimeters. I can't believe that a man who attacks me on the street does it because he's afraid of me and feels a need to defend himself.

I suppress my discomfort and let the friend to woman speak on. There's so little men could say that I'd agree with. I don't want to be petty about it.

Suddenly the speaker says: . . . *would they present themselves to men of influence . . .*

Women who present themselves to men, what that means in men's imagination is a piece of female crud with her blouse unbuttoned, running her tongue back and forth between her lips. The context is as follows:

. . . *and only after women in all cultures had become identified with nature, as they still are, would they present themselves to men of influence to have evil, the satanic projected onto them and combatted in them.*

That's a false picture if there ever was one. No woman would ever have dreamed of presenting herself to men as evil for them to combat. More correctly: It seemed obvious to project evil and the satanic onto women. Or: This led to evil and the satanic being projected onto women. Or: So it happened that men of influence projected evil and the satanic onto women. *Men of influence* are the subject, whom the author has displaced from the syntax of the sentence. Among all these linguistic possibilities he has chosen the one that expresses active participation by the women in their own mass murder.

The notion of women presenting themselves for mass annihilation makes me furious with the author's subconscious. But I'm like the kindly god at the gates of Sodom and Gomorrha. If there's even one single fair-minded man, I'm willing to spare womankind's enemies.

The friend to woman continues: *But as we have said, it took another century for woman-hating to develop its full force. First they destroyed, tortured and burned only old, ugly women, the Hansel-and-Gretel witches, so to speak. Not until the Reformation and the Renaissance were firmly established do we find, for example, a Darmstadt landgrave writing to his envoy at the Augsburg assembly: Since we have now had well-nigh all the old ones put to death and disposed of, it is time for the young ones.*

What the landgrave is saying is unmistakable. The well-to-do, influential widows have been eliminated and dispossessed. The direct goal of the inquisition is achieved—preventing women from accumulating wealth and political power in society. But they've got that torture device now. What the friend to woman is saying, on the other hand, is ambiguous: Would he have had no objection if the inquisition liquidated "only" old, ugly women?

One can take the view that they only gradually came to believe that evil was hidden and embodied not necessarily in ugliness, but rather in the beautiful and desirable. What threatened salvation was no longer witchcraft as the practice of magic, but the seductive, the beautiful, which the art of the period had begun to celebrate absolutely.

And how do I know that the witch persecutions were about beauty and ugliness, magic and sorcery, or even about God and the devil? Because the inquisitors said so and because it was tortured out of their victims? Is it possible for women's rights advocates to see that everything men say about women must be fundamentally questioned, even when a tortured woman agrees with an accuser's testimony? No, I don't believe the author any more.

To overstate the matter, it could be that the witch hunts burned the very beauty incarnate which Renaissance painting had just placed into flattering bright light, and in which the reality of this world was embodied in an exemplary fashion.

And it could not be. For beauty is the economy of a care-free existence, and the hierarchy of the female population, like every hierarchy, consisted of a few on top and a lot down below. The majority of the young witches were members of women's guilds and female trade unions. They were unkempt working people. And precisely that was their undoing. The male population took the inquisition as a welcome occasion to eliminate competition from female laborers and wage-earners.

With the revaluation of secular beauty in the Renaissance, a crisis was reached not only in medieval thought, rooted in the hereafter, but also by its representatives, men. Not that the men saw their intellectual primacy endangered. In view of woman's natural worldliness, it was not so much the spiritual, speculative potency of men that was challenged, but the secular.

And that's an out-and-out lie. Here the author is doing exactly what he accused Freud of: basically not departing from the witch-persecution position. What men thoroughly and single-mindedly annihilated was the spiritual and mental power of women in the Middle Ages, women's intellect. And what they exempted were the women who posed as *natural-worldly* in order to save their lives.

Sex-difference became a psychic problem the moment nature gained autonomy. Sexuality, which had been more or less taken for granted in the Middle Ages, became a threat. Now it was time to diabolize female superiority. The texts of witch-persecution literature make it only too plain that sex-envy was a basic motif of theoretical woman hating as well as of its practice.

For understandable reasons, the texts of witch persecution literature do not make plain the fact that there were female poets and thinkers, painters and sculptors whose works also consisted of flammable material, just like the bodies of their creators, and that it was the women's culture which aroused the persecutor's envy to such a high degree. Only the synagogue and ecclesia at the Strassburg cathedral, a work by sculptress Sabina von Steinbach, could withstand the annihilating fire of the envious.

The speaker shouts lustily: *Satan's lure! Scum of Paradise! Poison for the hungry! Fountain of sin! Night-owls! Concubines! Fille de Joie! Sirens!*

All synonyms for "woman" in philosophical literature. The counter-argument, objectively understated:

And naturally they didn't notice that with curses like these they quite successfully blinded themselves to their own carnal desires by repressing them and transforming them into aggression and bloodthirstiness.

At the beginning I thought there might be a woman's voice in the chorus of speakers. But it's like a trial for a sex murder where female police officers, criminologists, and jurors are excluded because one can't expect these delicate women to help make decisions when they are expected to be among those affected.

It is no accident that only in the Late Middle Ages, which justified the witch-craze in Scholasticism, was the counter-image developed: the ideal of the Blessed Virgin, Mother of God, who until then had not played a significant role in theology or folk religion. The emphasis on Mary's purity and the diabolizing of pleasure in the image of the witch are correlated by psychological necessity in the history of civilization.

In the language of men I would be a horse's ass, i.e., simply the genital area of a sensitive creature, if I didn't give the enemy his due. At this point I feel I have learned something. I have always wondered why womankind is most deeply insulted and debased in the very countries where male pilgrims hoist their Mother-Mary banners the highest. I'm pleased to be able to thank the author for this.

The sexually free person is not as docilely harnessed into the perform-ance processes. He knows a pleasure other than that of productivity: the pleasure of being one with nature, not only of subjugating nature.

With this observation the author could become an honorary mem-ber of certain women's groups who are preparing for the great age of leisure after the overthrow of male dominance. How I regret that I must contradict him here. The men will leave us a waterless planet where even the surface of the ocean is in flames and all the raving forces of their ruined technology rage about unchecked. Our sexuality will be liberated, our bodies will belong to us. But our time won't belong to us. We'll be harnessed into the rat race to save what's left of nature. Not nice.

Finally the author arrives at a central theme of witch persecution, the male doctors' demand for monopoly and the extermination of female doctors.

The incipient witch craze threw witches and midwives into the same pot.

The author doesn't do this. He wants to rehabilitate the midwives and relegate the witches to the liability column. If you want to rehabilitate the women who burned, you have to put witches and midwives in one pot.

The paradox is disastrous. The very era which consciously turned toward nature set everything in motion to subjugate it, to make it into a commodity, to annihilate it, from execution by burning for the imperfect animal woman to the modern destruction of the human environment under the banner of organized production and growth-obsessed addiction to performance.

Here we have the male counterpart to the *women presenting them-selves,* in that the men do not present themselves in this sentence. According to this syntax there are no men who subjugate women and nature, make them commodities, annihilate them. Instead, a criminal subject named *era* is to blame for everything, it did these heinous deeds.

The author concludes:

The witch craze is the radicalized and technocratic machination of a man's world which repressed its own imperfection and is incapable of reconciling reason and the pleasure principle.

I am not justice. I am partisanship. I can see that the author wanted the best for the nine million women who burned. But I can't honor it. My problem isn't that men can't reconcile reason and the pleasure principle. My problem is that the men here and now don't see me as a rational being. They relegate me to the sphere of the pleasure principle and reduce me to my flammable flesh. The fair-minded man who set out to save the imperfect animal has branded me as imperfect animal. My murderers withdraw the charges. They acquit me and keep on murdering me.

Translated by Jeanette Clausen

Notes

* German original: Christa Reinig, "Der Wolf und die Frau," *Der Wolf und die Witwen* (Düsseldorf: Eremiten-Presse, 1979; Munich: Frauenoffensive, 1981), pp. 13–21. Translated and reprinted with permission.

44. The Teacher*

Christa Wolf

Interwoven with Wolf's narration of events from her childhood are episodes from her 1971 visit to Gorzów Wielkoposki, Poland (formerly the German city Landsberg), accompanied by her husband H., brother Lutz, and daughter Lenka (their fictional names). This chapter excerpt centers around a teacher much admired by the adolescent Nelly Jordan (Wolf's name for her childhood self). The unusual narrative form, in which the author addresses herself while writing as "you," allows her to explore separations and continuities she feels between the distant and the recent past, her present concerns and those of a new generation (Lenka).

It probably wasn't long after this incident that Charlotte and Bruno Jordan agreed that their children should no longer sleep in the same room. The event Nelly had been waiting months for had come about, which she then (hypocritically!) reported to her mother, as if she didn't know what to make of it, whereupon her mother put an arm around her shoulders and called her "my big girl;" now she had to take even greater care of herself and always keep especially clean. Nelly was barely thirteen, and Charlotte thought it was "all too soon;" this is what she told the maid Annemarie, who repeated it to Nelly and to Aunt Lucy. The next day, Nelly was not allowed to climb the ladder in the store, to arrange loaves of bread on the uppermost shelf. It gave her a feeling of satisfaction: everything was following its proper course.

As a result, Frau Kruse—who lived in a second, smaller apartment, next to Hermann and Auguste Menzel in the upper story of the Jordan house for twenty-five marks a month, one room and a kitchen— had to be given notice; the landlord, Bruno Jordan, had other plans for his living space. Frau Kruse considered his request unacceptable in times of war, and cited the dreadful living conditions our soldiers encountered in the East (seven children in one room), in a letter obviously drafted by her son, who was deferred because of war-essential work (and, incidentally, enjoyed ample living space himself), whereupon Bruno Jordan objected to a comparison between his children and Russian and Polish children. Frau Kruse moved. Nelly had a room of her own, with a table covered with black oilcloth,

294

on which she was able to do her homework while from her window she looked out over the whole town, the river, and the plains. The former Kruse kitchen became a storage room for scarce food items, chocolate among others.

Normally, this room was locked, but Nelly was able to get hold of the key; her specialty was milk chocolate, and she grew more and more brazen about swiping it. Lying in bed, reading, eating chocolate. Calling down: Yes yes! When her mother called up from the stairwell: Lights out! She'd turn her light off for a few minutes, then veil it with a scarf and go on reading until one, two o'clock in the morning sometimes, which prompted customers who'd occasionally walk past the house late at night to question the light in her window. That just happened that once, last night, Nelly said when questioned. An exception, really. It won't happen again.

Did her brother, Lutz, remember who it was who briefed him about the facts of life, or had his memory acted in keeping with his boast: that he had none?

You were all tired around noon. Lutz proposed to drive over to "the other side," since, according to experience, the heat worsened in a city, due to its absorption by stone, until around 3:00 P.M. Across the bridge, into the outskirts. Both of you had to admit: no other part of the former town of L. was as unknown to you as this one. In the past, the expression "across the bridge" made you think of people who worked in rope or burlap factories. The poor lived "across the bridge," in little old houses which leaned against each other, or else in badly constructed tenements. In the spring, the cellars were flooded. Their children didn't go to the same schools as you, they didn't bathe at the same spots in the river, but outside the supervised bathing area, where there were sand bars and eddies, and where they established intimate friendships with raftsmen and barge captains, STRAUCH & SONS read a faded sign on the brick wall of a factory building. Strauch, Lutz said pensively, Strauch, wasn't that . . .

Yes, Strauch was Dr. Juliane Strauch's father or grandfather—one of the richest businessmen in town, who had donated the statue for the fountain in the marketplace that the people used to call "Strauch-Marie," after him. But nothing more about Fräulein Strauch, Ph.D., at least not yet. Meanwhile—as you slowly drive through the narrow streets on the other bank of the Warta, which you're seeing again for the first time—you remind your brother who taught him the facts of life. Vaguely, he says, now that you mention it, I seem to remember something. Lenka thought such valiant sisterly efforts deserved a little more gratitude.

At an unexpected spot you suddenly came out on the riverbank, a gently sloping shady grass incline. Let's stop here for a while, Lenka said.

Even you were surprised by the view. The river starts in on its broad sweep at this spot, widens toward the east, and disappears in the underbrush of its embankments. And beyond the river, the skyline of the town—curving railroad tracks, warehouses, the church, residential buildings, they way it's shown on the postcards at the newsstand. In the foreground, the modern concrete overpass, built high into the air, that leads to the bathing area.

And it is now, in front of this view which you yourself hardly expected, which surprised even you, it is now of all times, that they, Lenka and H., think they understand. Yes, they said, it made sense. There really was something to it. A town on a river, one could remember this. They remembered poetry, they quoted lines: "Behind the fields, far / behind the meadows / the stream . . ."

The two of you, Lutz and yourself, are silent. . . .

Lenka, with the infallible sense all children have of their parents' moods, lay on her old windbreaker, her head close to your shoulder; she fell asleep instantly. You watched two children, a boy and a girl, climb the high steps of the new overpass to the bathing area, hand in hand, counting the steps in Polish. You counted along with them, in German, up to a figure you don't remember. Then, suddenly—quite some time had probably passed—three figures came walking toward you in an uncertain kind of weather, on an unknown gray street, three people who had absolutely no relation to each other, as you keenly felt: Vera Pryzbilla and Walpurga Dorting, two girls of your former class, with whom you had never been friendly, and between them your old friend Jossel. Absorbed in calm conversation, they came toward you, they saw you, but seemed to have no desire to explain to you why and how they, of all people, who couldn't possibly know each other, had come together at this point.

The officer awakened you with a soft call. With polite but determined gestures he made you understand that it was forbidden to camp on the embankment. You, in turn, gestured that you hadn't seen the sign—you couldn't have read it, but you would have understood its meaning—and that you were ready to obey by rapidly departing.

A few passersby and residents of nearby houses watched the incident with dispassionate interest. The two children—a boy and a girl—were still, or perhaps again, climbing the stairs. Barely half an hour had gone by. The officer saluted and started his motorcycle, which had a sidecar. *Bye bye,* Lenka said, nice of you not to have come sooner.

What next? The school, you said. Böhmstrasse. Do you know the
way? In my sleep.

It was in your sleep that the two girls, Vera and Walpurga—who
had been friends since Walpurga's belated arrival in Nelly's class—
had ferreted out your friend Jossel, whom they couldn't have known
during their lifetime. What could this mean? Not to mention other
incongruities: the two girls still looked like sixteen-year-olds—Vera
was wearing her pony tail, Walpurga her long loose hair—but Jossel
had been the age he would be today. And the intimacy of the three,
which distorted the true situation, Jossel having been your friend for
years, whereas the other two—God only knew where they might
be!—had never been close to Nelly, and hadn't the faintest knowledge
of Jossel's existence. However, had he met you at that time, when
you three were sixteen (in this respect your dream was correct) and
he was a young man, without his beard, without the expression in
his eyes, an expression that isn't easily definable: "lost" seems to
come closest; back then, when he, the Viennese Jew, had been caught
in France and shipped off to Buchenwald. Had Jossel come to your
town at that time—which would, of course, have been unthinkable—
he might possibly have walked down a random street with Vera
Pryzbilla, the Baptist, and her girlfriend Walpurga, the daughter of
a Christian missionary (who had lived in Korea for years and spoke
fluent but incomprehensible English that even their English teacher
couldn't understand), rather than with Nelly. If it had been the
dream's intention to point out this upsetting fact, it had fulfilled its
purpose. Recall the guards from the gates of consciousness. . . .

Nelly must have been barely twelve when she joined the candidates
for leadership who served not in the school classrooms but in a
special "home": three, four bare rooms under the roof of the former
welfare building, which is still standing. There had to be initiation
ceremonies, stricter rules, in order to learn the duties of a model for
others. They certainly must have had an impact on Nelly. But not
one of these assumptions—which are almost certainties—evokes an
image, a quotable sentence. Only one image and one sentence have
been preserved about this time in her life, both, however, with the
utmost precision: in front of the door of her school library, Nelly
runs into Dr. Juliane Strauch, who is in charge of the library; Nelly
is startled, as she always is when she runs into Fräulein Stauch
(although she secretly hopes for these encounters); she gives the
Hitler salute, which is, however, not returned; instead, the teacher
places an arm on Nelly's shoulder and honors her with a sentence:
Well done, girl! Of course I hadn't expected anything less of you.

If somebody were to say that Nelly could have gone through much
less trouble than playing a role in the Hitler Youth, in order to hear

this sentence, that somebody would be right. As for Juliane Strauch, her German and history teacher, called Julia, your memory couldn't be more exact. Her face, her figure, her walk and behavior have been preserved within you for twenty-nine years, whereas the memory of the period during which she was so important has become rather shredded. As though she had attracted Nelly's concentrated attention to herself alone. (Perhaps one shouldn't draw any hasty conclusions from these observations, least of all analogies. But might it not be true that, except for the particular laws of memory formation during childhood, a slower, perhaps more thorough rhythm of living furnishes a better condition for the development of those sections of the brain which store events than the continuously increasing haste with which persons, objects, and events drift past us, which we're almost embarrassed to call "life" ?)

Well, whatever. You don't exactly want to claim that you're able to describe Nelly's first meeting with Julia Strauch—it probably was a brief passing on the school stairs—but you can vouch for the truthful description of their last meeting. After that, there were only brief encounters in the Hermann Göring gymnasium, and in the large dance hall of the Weinberg Inn, places which served to accommodate refugees from the East in January 1945. As the leader of the National Socialist Women's Organization, Dr. Juliane Strauch played an important role in the care of those refugees, while Nelly was charged with auxiliary tasks, which will be described in due course.

The winter of 1944–45 was cold from the start, and it was coldest in the pale, bare streets around Schlageterplatz, swept by the wind that blew unimpeded through two rows of symmetrically aligned houses. Nelly felt cold in her confirmation coat, while she paced up and down in front of Julia's house, counting the minutes until the clock struck four. She was angry with herself for feeling so disconsolate. But she knew herself: shortly before the fulfillment of something she had wished for long and hard, her happy anticipation collapsed—an inherent weakness of hers, which forced her to develop and refine her talents at pretending.

Nelly felt embarrassed as she rang Julia's bell, but fortunately the instant the steps approached the other side of the door, the old excitement sprang up again inside Nelly, stimulated by a simple method; she rehearsed her glowing fantasies about an invitation to Julia's house. Because one obviously didn't go to Julia's house without having been invited.

Of course Julia wouldn't think of embarrassing Nelly with an apologetic remark about the dry oatmeal cookies, the thin tea, or the barely heated room. Julia was able to radiate relaxation in any

situation, an ability which made her inviolable and not only superior—the word would be too weak—but sublime. It cost her nothing
to counter the unavoidable fits of laughter of her fourteen-and fifteen-
year-old students with the seemingly amused remark: I don't see
what's so funny, unless it's me.

Her greatest achievement must have been the considerable, though
undetectable, effort with which she probably tried to bridge the wide
gap that separated her outward appearance from that of the ideal
German woman, a phenomenon she never tired of extolling. Not
only was she short, but she had black hair and markedly Slavic
features, which the biology books defined as "flat." She was, moreover, the only female intellectual Nelly knew in her youth (disre-
garding Professor Lehmann, the wife of a man who was probably
Jewish) and she had not felt it necessary to get married and contribute
children to the German nation. She did, however, insist that she be
addressed as "Frau Doktor," rather than as Fräulein. After a certain
age a woman had earned the right to be addressed with the honorable
title "Frau." In history class she occasionally remarked that a consequence of European history—the result of an unfortunate godfor-
saken mixture of the noblest blood with the vilest—was that pure
Germanic thinking and feeling could often be found in persons whose
exterior appearance didn't permit such an assumption; in short, that
a Germanic soul was hidden inside such persons.

Such sentences, which you hestitate to commit to paper because
they might easily sound invented, were quite natural to Julia. As a
matter of course, she also said in confidential conversations that
Germany had to make use of all her assets now, including her youth,
to win the decisive battle against her enemies. Lately, however, she
had been noticing signs of unruly behavior in her class—which was
precisely what she'd wanted to discuss with Nelly—transgressions
against the basic rules of discipline: the formation of small cliques.

Nelly had to agree with Julia, unreservedly, on every point, the
way she always agreed with Julia. But can the colorless word "agree"
do justice to something that was more of an alliance, a deep affinity,
although also a form of captivity, as far as Nelly was concerned?
Nelly's first experience of love was that of captivity. . . .

Unlike most of the other teachers, Julia used the exit that was
reserved for students of the lower grades. She mostly stayed in her
library, rather than in the teachers' room, and kept her distance from
the other teachers, who certainly respected her but were hardly fond
of her. People who can't conceal the fact that they consider themselves
more perfect than others are rarely popular. But Nelly, devastated
like everyone else by the unbridgeable gap between Julia's perfection
and her own shortcomings, Nelly would stand outside the school

(ostensibly waiting for a girlfriend, her school bag on the low wall
that ran along the grass), hoping to be singled out by a glance or
a greeting from Julia.

"Devotion" was one of Julia's favorite words. In that respect, at
least, Nelly felt able to meet Julia's demands. Among the women
she knew, not one led a life Nelly would have wished or might
have imagined for herself: except Julia. (Julia! Julia! Charlotte would
say. If Julia asked you to jump out the window, you'd jump, right?)
Nelly listened for the sounds that came from Julia's kitchen, sounds
of somebody being busy in there. Was it true that Julia had an older
sister who kept house for her? Julia made no attempt to explain the
sounds.

The question was not whether she demanded more of Nelly than
of the others: that went without saying, since Nelly had no trouble
excelling in German composition or in history reports, which Julia
graded more severely than those of the others: that was perfectly
all right. Minor extra tasks could be interpreted as proofs of confidence
and marks of distinction: she often let Nelly arrange a class outing,
or asked her to tutor a boy who had every reason to fear that he
might flunk his secondary-school entrance exam.

It was, of course, a high point of confidence when Julia, who was
responsible for the celebration of Hitler's birthday in the auditorium,
entrusted Nelly with the recitation of the main poem: "When need
rises / like a flood up to a nation's chin, / the Lord / picks the
ablest / from among the wealth of men at his disposal. / With his
own hand / pushes him / mercilessly, it seems / into the lightless
abyss, / deals him / fatal wounds / and burdens his heart / with
a pain more bitter than that of all his brothers."

Lenka said: What a memory. I can't remember a poem for longer
than a year. A test shows that she's right. Only fragments, even of
the most popular Goethe poems. However, an indestructible store
of scullery-maid ditties and horror ballads from early childhood, also
Spanish songs from old records, which can't be played on the new
turntable; also Morgenstern and Ringelnatz.

(She can lie around for days, listening to music. Is that how you
want to finish off the year? you ask her. Leave me alone, she says.
The last year hasn't been good. You mean your laziness? I mean
that I'm beginning to get accustomed. To what? To everything being
pseudo, me too, in the end. Pseudo-people, a pseudo-life. Or haven't
you noticed? Or maybe I'm not normal? Or are the people who
don't even think about it right? I sometimes feel that another piece
of me is dying off. And who's to blame? Nobody but me?

A fear for her surges up inside you, a new kind of fear. Writing
should be different, you think, totally different.)

Like every lover, Nelly pines for irrefutable proof of requited love, a proof that shouldn't be linked to merit. It happened that Julia held a class for Nelly all by herself, and it was one of the most extraordinary events of her school years: they discussed the Nordic hero legends, whose spotlighted figures are steeped in blood but never guided by base motivation, and unrepenting Hagen, the darkly tragic knight, the truest of the true, who dips his sword into the blood of his master's enemies, whose dying song Julia knows by heart and recites: "Accursed be the female race / all treachery and lying / 'tis for two wenches' smooth white faces / that Burgundy lies dying! / And should the world's great treasure / Siegfried once more appear, / into his back with pleasure / I'd plant once more my spear."

Finally, at the end of the class, Julia looked Nelly full in the face, and Nelly concealed what she had understood: Julia hated being a woman. And Nelly had to admit that that was not at all the way she felt herself.

At the end of a chain of thoughts that had too many links to enumerate them, you see a picture: Nelly in the so-called parlor, at one end of the sofa, absorbed in forbidden *Schwarze Korps*, which she could read around 4:00 P.M. without the risk of getting caught. In it she reads a report about institutions called "Wells of Life" (you learn many years later that one of its branches was in Thomas Mann's former house in Munich): houses in which tall blond blue-eyed SS men are brought together with brides of similar background for the purpose of producing a racially pure child, whom the mother then offers to the Führer as a gift, as the *Schwarze Korps* approvingly stressed. (Not a word that the same organization was engaged in large-scale child theft in the countries occupied by the German Army.) You clearly remember that the author of the report sharply or mockingly attacked the outmoded prejudices that found fault with the above conduct, conduct worthy of idealistic German men and women.

It shall be truthfully said that, after reading the article, Nelly sat with the paper across her knees, clearly thinking: No, not that.

It was one of those rare, precious, and inexplicable instances when Nelly found herself in conscious opposition to the required convictions she would have liked to share. As so often, it was a feeling of guilt that engraved the incident in her memory. How could she have known that bearing guilt was, under the prevailing conditions, a necessary requirement for inner freedom? There she sat, a thirteen-year-old girl wedged between her mother's warnings not to "throw herself away" and the *Schwarze Korps'* request for unconditional submission for the sake of the Führer. Anything connected with her sex was complicated to the point of being unbearable. She had read a novel about the Thirty Years' War in which a girl, Christine Torstenson, intentionally infected herself with the plague, in order to enter and infect the enemy camp by "giving herself." Not that, Nelly had thought at the end of the novel, filled with admiration and fear. She ran into the kitchen, to stir oats, sugar, milk, and cocoa into a sweep pap which she spooned into herself while staring out the window with unfocused eyes, the paper on her knees.

In the schoolyard (which you entered on July 10, 1971, walking past the red brick school building on the right, through the wrought-iron gate, which was unlocked, as it had always been) Julia used to follow a habitual track when it was her turn to supervise recess. She'd march with long strides, her hands behind her back, in her flat shoes with the worn-down heels, her stockings darned way up her calves. Her attentive eyes were everywhere. There were no fights during her recesses, nor did she have to reprimand anyone for forbidden ball playing, snowball throwing, or improper conduct. Sometimes she'd motion a student to step up to her, and ask her about her private life. . . . Nelly didn't want to be one of the many who were never given the honor of being addressed. She therefore stood by herself, so that, when the bell rang for class, and the courtyard emptied out, Julia would take up her position at the school door and catch Nelly, who'd be going in among the last; she'd lightly lay a hand on Nelly's upper arm, and climb the ten steps to the schoolhouse with her; she'd even stop outside the door to the library and talk with her about the class's failure in the most recent composition.

Not that that failure had been Nelly's: that wasn't to be expected in German composition, Julia didn't even hint at that. But why was it that so many wrote fluently about "a nation hemmed in" or about "the Nordic spirit in the poetry of antiquity," but were totally unable to deal with a subject as easy as "the first snow"? Nelly couldn't say, and she wouldn't have expressed her assumption: that it was a lot more difficult to write about personal matters than about general familiar everyday notions. She remembered clearly: while describing the particular Sunday on which the first snow had fallen that year, she never forgot for a second for whom she was writing. A touch of deceit permeated every line; she had described her family as just a trifle too idyllic and herself as just a trifle too virtuous: exactly the way she thought Julia wished to see her. (The deceit, and the fact that she remained conscious of it, as much as her longing for truthfulness, was this perhaps some form of salvation? A vestige of independence, which she was able to resume later?)

In order to win Julia over—or to deceive her, which seemed to amount to the same thing—she had to refrain from blunt maneuvers and ensnare the demanding teacher, who was not easily flattered, in a web of the sublest weave: looks, gestures, words, lines that lay within a hair's breadth of her true emotions, without ever fully blending with them.

That probably was the reason why Nelly—after the highpoints of exaltation, when Julia had placed a hand on her shoulder in parting, and nodded in her famous fashion—why Nelly collapsed on the stairs to her classroom and felt overcome by a sadness which frightened her and which she refused to acknowledge. It wasn't right that moments of the greatest bliss always ended in emptiness—not to say in disappointment: a word that didn't come to her mind. She'd drop into her seat, show no interest in Fräulein Woyssmann's English exercises, and didn't care what grades she'd be given for her translation; she'd huddle with her friend Hella over a sheet of paper and play Hangman.

It was about this time that Charlotte Jordan noticed that her daughter was tearing her cuticles to shreds, which she naturally, although unsuccessfully, forbade.

You didn't enter the schoolyard proper. You went no farther than the corner of the house, that's when you spotted the superintendent. No one entered the schoolyard during vacation time—unless there was a war on, when students of the upper grades were appointed air-raid wardens for a week, when four of you slept on cots in a classroom and cooked your meals in the school kitchen. Dora, the only girl who knew how to cook, had taught them how to make dumplings, which they had eaten over there, behind the linden trees. Julia, the chief warden, had sat at the head of the crude plank table and praised the dumplings. It must have been a hot summer. They had made a mistake about the quantity of dough, the remaining dumplings were surreptitiously drowned in the Cladow, during the night, despite the huge poster in the kitchen: "Fight Waste! "

In the daytime, air raids were still few and far between. In the evenings they'd sit in the dark, under the linden trees, and sing whatever Julia asked for: "High fir trees point to the stars," "No finer land than our land." Julia asked what they all wanted to be. Dora thought she'd like to be a nurse; Hella wanted to take over her father's bookstore; Marga, who had been evacuated from Berlin, hoped to use her talent for drawing. Nelly said: Teacher. Julia nodded. For a long time Nelly had waited for an opportunity to show her teacher her desire to emulate her. Now she had done so, but at the same time she feared that Julia might think her pushy.

Notes

* Reprinted by permission of Farrar, Straus & Giroux, Inc. Excerpt from chapter 10 of: Christa Wolf, *A Model Childhood*, trans. Ursule Molinaro and Hedwig Rappolt (New York: Farrar, Straus & Giroux, 1980), pp. 213–226. German original: Christa Wolf, *Kindheitsmuster* (Berlin and Weimar: Aufbau, 1976), pp. 280–297.

Part Ten

Feminist Strategy

The texts in this section provide a sampling of the development of feminist strategy in the new German movement.

The kinderläden or store-front day care centers which Helke Sander proposed as a concrete strategy worthy of support from the SDS were in actuality a prelude to the women's self-help projects yet to come. Interestingly, Sander's justification for a strategy concentrating on mothers—"because [their] readiness [for] solidarity and politicization [is] greatest"—reminds us of the hard-working time Sander spent in the German New Left where one was trained to analyze a group's readiness for struggle."

The article on the lesbian action center chronicles the difficulties encountered in forging a coherent strategy when a group must, of necessity, spend much of its energy in providing support and compensation for its members. Moreover, as this article shows, because the center was also the sole arena for political power available to the women, factional disputes took on the tone of power struggles.

It boggles the imagination that since 1950, eight separate women's political parties have been founded in West Germany. Unlike the situation in the United States, there is a long tradition in Europe for multiple national opposition parties—which explains in part the proliferation of women's parties in the Federal Republic. Hannelore Mabry prescribes years of "canal work" before the political base will exist able to support a true women's party and women's trade union.

The other texts in this section all have to do, in one way or another, with the questions of war, peace, and ecology, and their implications for feminist strategy in our time. The on-going discussion of the spectrum of violence has been a distinctive contribution of the new German women's movement. As yet, however, no clear-cut

305

strategies have emerged. Indeed, in her "Critical Outlook" at the end of this volume, Dagmar Schultz implies that this lack may be one reason why so many young women in the movement seem to be turning to spirituality and magic.

45. Speech by the Action Council for Women's Liberation*

Helke Sander

This speech was held at the twenty-third national conference of the Socialist German Students' Federation (SDS) in Frankfurt, West Germany in September, 1968. At the conclusion of the speech one female comrade hurled tomatoes at the SDS authorities. This was an early signal for a new German women's movement.

Dear Comrades,

I am speaking on behalf of the Action Council for Women's Liberation. The Berlin chapter of SDS has given me a delegate seat-even though only a few of us are members. We are here because we know that we can only carry out our work in conjunction with other progressive organizations, and, in our opinion, today SDS is the only one that counts as such.

The precondition for joint work is, however, that the organization comprehends the specific problems women face. This means that years of stifled conflicts must finally be articulated. We are thereby broadening the confrontation between the antiauthoritarians and the CP faction, putting ourselves at once against both camps. We already have both camps against us, in practice even if not on theoretical grounds. We demand that our problems be discussed substantively here. It is no longer enough that women are occasionally allowed to say a few words to which, as good antiauthoritarians, you listen—and then go on with the order of the day.

We maintain that the SDS in its internal organization is a reflection of broader social relations. A certain sphere of life is separated from the social and placed under taboo by giving it the name "private life." In this SDS is no different from the unions or the existing political parties. The tactic allows the specific exploited situation of women to be repressed, enabling the men to retain their old identity as bestowed under patriarchy. Women are granted the freedom to speak, but no one investigates the causes as to why women do not hold up well, why they are passive, why they are in the position of carrying out the organization's policies but not of determining them. The repression becomes complete when a point is made of those few activist women who have reached a certain position within the organization. No one asks what sacrifices the women had to make to get where they are. Also overlooked is the required conformity to an achievement principle from which men suffer as well and which, in fact, they are trying to abolish. Such a concept of emancipation seeks only equality amidst injustice, using the very same competitive and achievement-oriented means which we have rejected.

The division between private and social life forces the woman to work out these conflicts individually and in isolation. She is still trained for private life, for the family, which in turn is dependent upon the same conditions of production which we are combatting. The role training, the instilled sense of inferiority and the contradiction between her own expectations and the claims of society produce in her the guilty feeling of never satisfying the demands placed upon her. She must choose between alternatives which in each instance mean a foregoing of vital needs.

Women are seeking their identity. They cannot achieve this by participating in campaigns which do not touch upon their immediate conflicts. That would be false emancipation. Women can only find their own identity when the social conflicts which have been relegated to private life are articulated; only then will women join together and be politicized. Most women are unpolitical because politics has always been one-sidedly defined and never included their own needs. They, therefore, persisted in their authoritarian appeal to law and order because they did not recognize the explosive nature of their demands on the system.

The most easily politicized groups are women with children. They harbor the most aggression and are the least speechless. The women who today are able to become university students do not have so much the bourgeois emancipation movement to thank for that but rather economic necessities. When these privileged women have children they are then forced into a pattern of behavior which they thought they had already overcome, thanks to their emancipation. Their studies are suspended or put off; intellectual growth stops or is sharply reduced due to the demands of husband and child. In addition there is a sense of insecurity because they were not able to make the choice between blue stocking and housewife—either of building a career with all the sacrifice of happiness entailed or of being a woman whose purpose is consumption. Those privileged women have experienced the falsehood of the bourgeois way to emancipation; they recognize that they cannot liberate themselves by means of competitive struggle, that the achievement principle has become the major factor within personal relationships and that the way to emancipation lies in the method by which one strives for it.

By the time these women have children—if not before—they notice that all their privileges are worth nothing. They are then uniquely able to throw light upon society's garbage heap, which is tantamount to bringing the class struggle into the marriage and into personal relationships. There the man assumes the objective role of the exploiter or class enemy, a role which he subjectively rejects because it is of course in turn forced upon him by an achievement oriented society which imposes a specific role behavior.

The consequences which the Action Council for Women's Liberation has drawn from all this are as follows.

We cannot solve, individually, the social oppression of women. Nor can we wait until after the revolution, because a solely economic and political revolution does not suspend the repression of private life—as proven in all socialist countries.

We are working for conditions of life which suspend the competitive relationship between man and woman. This is only possible through a transformation of production relations and thereby of power relations—which will allow a democratic society to be created.

Because the readiness for solidarity and politicization is greatest among women with children, and because they feel the pressure the most, we have up until now concentrated in our practical work on their conflicts. This does not mean that we do not take seriously the problems of women students without children; nor does it mean that we overlook the class-specific mechanisms of oppression in the face of the common features of all women's oppression.

When our initial efforts at working on these conflicts with and within SDS failed, we withdrew and began to work on our own. When we started out six months ago, most comrades reacted with ridicule. Today, they blame us for withdrawing; they try to show us that our theories are all wrong; they try to shout us down, saying we considered men unnecessary for women's liberation and other inanities which we have never claimed. They boast that they too are oppressed—which we already know. Only, we no longer see why we should submit passively to *their* oppression, with which they oppress *us*. It is because we believe that emancipation is only possible on a societal basis that we are here. We must establish for once that society is comprised of somewhat more women than men, and it is high time that the appropriate demands were put forward and made a part of future planning. Should the SDS fail in a leap forward in this matter, we would of course be forced into a power struggle—which we would rather avoid. (For us it would be a waste of energy.) For we will win this power struggle, because we are historically in the right.

The helplessness and arrogance with which we appear before you today is not much fun. We are helpless in that we actually expect that progressive men will realize the explosive relevance of our conflict. The arrogance comes from seeing what blinders you have over your eyes, for, without any help from you, people are organizing, whom you never even considered, and that in numbers which, were they workers, you would greet as the dawning of a new day. . . .

In our self-chosen isolation, therefore, we did the following: We concentrated our work on women and children because they are the worst off. Consequently, for the first time, we are taking seriously the social injunction that women should rear the children. But, we refuse to rear our children according to the repressive and competitive principles which we perceive as the basis for the preservation of the capitalist system.

We want to attempt to develop models of a utopian society within the existing one. Our own needs must find a place in this society. Thus, our concentration on education is not an alibi for our own suppressed emancipation but rather the precondition for resolving our own conflicts. . . .

If the SDS considers itself an organization which wants to set in motion emancipatory processes within the existing society, so that a revolution may be even possible, then it must draw consequences for its politics from our work.

Comrades, if you are not ready for this discussion—which must be a substantive one—then we must draw the conclusion that the SDS is nothing more than an inflated mass of counter-revolutionary dough.

We comrades (fem.) will then draw our own conclusions.

Translated by Edith Hoshino Altbach

Notes

* Originally published as, Helke Sander, "Rede des Aktionsrates zur Befreiung der Frauen," *Frauenjahrbuch 1* Frankfurt am Main: Verlag Roter Stern, 1975, pp. 10–15. Translated and reprinted with permission. Portions of this text have been excerpted.

46. The Lesbian Action Center, West Berlin: the Formation of Group Solidarity*

Monika Kühn

All women's centers go through distinct phases during their lifespans, with internal dissension sometimes seeming to loom larger than common goals or the enemy at large. This brief summary of changes within the West Berlin Lesbian Action Center shows how the interplay of factions affects group solidarity and how, in one instance, the most radical, separatist stance may prove to be an obstacle to political effectiveness.

When the Lesbian Action Center (LAC) was founded in the Spring of 1972, it was the first German lesbian organization which consciously went beyond integrative approaches and thought of itself as a group transcending politics and societal issues. Starting the project were a few lesbians who could no longer tolerate being isolated socially or being sequestered in lesbian bars. All of the women were attracted primarily by the need to address their own perplexing problems of being lesbian.

For about a year or so we organized discussion groups and ran projects, focusing on theory and self-help. We also spoke to other lesbians through leaflets and talks in lesbian bars. After the first year, there were a series of outreach projects. We felt the need to take our anger, which had long been building up in us, out into the public. We did this by acting provocatively *as lesbians* and venting our anger about the discrimination we had experienced.

Our first public projects were spontaneous reactions to outside attacks, for example, reactions to a series of articles in *Bildzeitung* [a mass-circulation illustrated magazine], "Crimes of Lesbian Women." In spite of our differing expectations and goals we were united by a strong emotional commitment which enabled us collectively to carry out our public projects.

But it became increasingly clear to us that it's not enough to plunge into projects when we lack a uniform base in terms of politics or purpose outside of our own vulnerability. We felt that it was necessary to back out of the public sphere since differing political perspectives were developing as a result of our experiences and fluctuations in group membership.

Characteristic of the Lesbian Action Center since its founding has been the separation into two areas of concentration. While the first was primarily concerned with communication and undertaking projects, the other grouping pushed for connecting theory and practice, politics and pleasure. The latter group met regularly to discuss theoretical topics such as the relationship between capitalism, patriarchy and women's oppression, family ideology, the exclusion of homosexual women. Another emphasis of this group was on joint projects and social events. Debates ensued as to how "political" the Action Center should be, which work we should carry out in public, and, above all, how to reach isolated lesbians. In many cases, the debate took place in a confrontational manner and blocked our growth instead of promoting it.

These "differences of opinion" dragged on for a long time. It became clear that the conflicting functions of the center—on the one hand as loosely structured support group and, on the other hand, as closely organized work group with specific political content and goals—caused us to stagnate. Diverse attempts to master the situation failed—most theoretical groups functioned poorly or quickly turned into consciousness-raising groups. Clearly, the need for reducing anxiety, especially in the area of private problems, took precedence for many women and had to be satisfied before effective theoretical work could follow.

There are currently three distinct divisions in the LAC. First, the women who call themselves "radical lesbians." "Radical lesbians" see the source of all oppression resulting from the differences between the sexes. They interpret capitalism, then, as a phenomenon of male domination. The goal seems to be a counter culture called "Lesbian Nation," a place where women live exclusively and where they exert all their energies for women only. Radical lesbianism means the total, uncompromising rejection of men in every area. For some, this includes boycotting the struggle of heterosexual women against oppression stemming from heterosexuality. Moreover, radical lesbians refuse to accept theories which they have not experienced on an emotional level. Most theories are for them an expression of male dominance, and they consider them a solidification of that dominance.

Opposite this group is another which includes patriarchal as well as capitalist structures in their struggle against their oppression as lesbians. These women think a struggle on both levels is necessary. Their battle is directed against men in those areas where men discriminate against and oppress them—for example, against judges who uphold "male law," when they protect rapists and insult raped women. Or against men who attack them on the street. At the same time they wage a battle against capitalist exploitation and oppression on all levels. It's important to note that these women don't let themselves be used as appendages of male dominated groups, preferring to work on their own as separate women's groups with their specific interests. They are correct in stating that they cannot wait for others, i.e., men, to fight for them. Instead they take matters into their own hands.

The goal of this group in the LAC is to remove predetermined sex roles and to create an egalitarian society which is presently still a utopian idea.

Next to these two divisions there are women in the center—mostly new members—who feel they belong to neither group. They may agree on some points with one of the factions or remove themselves from larger discussions of policy.

Because of internal conflict, it has proven very difficult to work out a comprehensive political strategy within the LAC, one which goes beyond the individual and social-psychological level. One obstacle to the formation of common goals and strategy has been the increasing "radicalization" of one faction which operates on a verbal rather than action level. This perspective within the LAC which sees as "radical" an uncompromising hatred of men and exclusive involvement with lesbians is partially detrimental to lesbians themselves. Women are given little chance to argue and grow. Such dogmatic-sectarian tendencies bring with them the danger of isolation and loss of political power vis a vis areas of society which go beyond the specific oppression lesbians experience directly. If the consciousness of their own "radicalism" is backed up, in addition, by an elitist consciousness, then this radicalism can have a destructive effect in two directions: It prevents a focused struggle against the causes of our oppression, and it brings rivalry and animosity into the group by its absolute claim to the truth. Only a minority stand behind this understanding of "radicalism."

[We must go beyond a] radical lesbianism which has as its goal the retreat into a pure women's culture. This can free lesbians for a time from strong social pressures; however, it has almost no effect in overcoming the patriarchal-capitalist social structures which oppress us.

Notes

* Originally, Monika Kühn, "Das Lesbische Aktionszentrum West-Berlin: Solidarisierungsprozesse bei Lesbierinnen," Diplomarbeit, Pädagogische Hochschule Berlin, 1975, pp. 76–99. Translated and reprinted with permission. Portions of this text have been excerpted.

47. Manifesto of the "Green" Women*

Delphine Brox-Brochot

On December 12, 1979, Representative Delphine Brox-Brochot presented the citizens of Bremen with a statement from women of the "Green" which formed part of the ecology coalition's opposition statement to the state government. In order to get a hearing, Delphine had to force the speaker for the "Greens," Peter Willers, from the podium. To the rumblings of the chairman, she read the women's manifesto, in spite of the fact that the microphone had been turned off.

Speaking as a man, Peter Willers has presented his concept of an ecological politics. But for him to go into the specific concerns of women in the "Greens," strikes me as presumptuous. I consider it essential that a small "Green" women's manifesto be heard in these holy chambers presided over by manly figures. If I am not mistaken, eighty-three men and seventeen women sit in this parliament. How do you gentlemen view us women? As flowers? As a refreshing sight in a place where men speak of important matters? And just what are the matters at hand?

In the meantime, man has actually landed on the moon—an admirable feat. The feminists cheered: "Let him stay there!" We "Green" women, on the other hand, believe that men belong to our environment. In order to rescue that environment for our children we want to confront this man, this adventurer and moon explorer. A female cosmonaut from a so-called socialist republic doesn't justify this energy-wasting enterprise for us at a time when three-fourths of the earth's population is suffering from malnutrition.

Our inability to solve immediate problems may tempt us into escape—to the moon, into careerism, escape into ideologies, into alcohol or other drugs. But one group cannot escape completely: women, society's potential mothers, who must give birth to children, willingly or unwillingly, in this polluted world of ours.

Who are these women? Blue collar workers (3.5 million, in the Federal Republic) and white collar workers (3 million) who don't get the same wages as men in the same jobs and have in addition the double burden of family and housework: academics, who are perhaps in a more equal position; housewives, looked down on by their gainfully employed sisters and by the whole society, very probably because they work without pay in a world which measures the right to existence in terms of money.

Seeing no place for their children in a world where rearmament is the order of the day, where East and West speak of a ten to twelve-fold "world overkill," women have chosen their own forms of protest.

Many women have voiced their thoughts and fears (now that more children than ever before are being born with birth defects) in passive resistance. You can see this in sinking birth rates. Others call for active and intensive resistance, in the interest of the unborn, for they do not want to give up motherhood forever and must still represent the interests of the children and young people now living. They demand a world in which chemical technology is controlled and limited, where water is drinkable again, and air healthy, the soil and its fruits as free as possible from pesticides and chemicals, and where the first and best baby food—mother's milk—is not contaminated by lead, DDT or iodine. The call for a birth strike is certainly blackmail, and the birth-strikers know that it hits the state's nerve center. The ability to give birth is women's only source of power, and they will not shrink from using it now. You gentlemen may gather from this how seriously women take this protest.

We are women who recognize our diversity and want to press for resistance against the rule of technology. We don't find our identity in men's success and are no longer prepared to be corrupted by helping men to climb up the ladder—as skilled workers, engineers, trade unionists, academics or legislators—over the ruins of our own lives.

Gentlemen of the Bremen Parliament, the women's shelter in our city is filled with children and battered wives. Gentlemen, you cut their funds because the women wanted to manage it autonomously. In the beautiful modern apartment buildings, women are suffering from high-rise psychosis. In hospitals patients feel as if they are in super modern repair shops and are denied a dignified death.

We don't want our children to go through education mills that try to teach facts and abstract thinking under the pressure to achieve. We want smaller schools that are easier to oversee, where children receive a real education and an ecological consciousness. The university, where creativity and critical thinking cannot develop, is not a place for emancipation but rather for miseducation. I won't continue the chorus of woe.

I call on all women to seek the way out of their isolation. We women have common problems which we shall solve together. For example, many of us came together in the Fall with our children in

Gorleben, where dangerous atomic waste is being reprocessed for storage, and planted daffodils—women's symbol of peace. Gorleben will bloom at Easter. If necessary we will become more radical, and perhaps we women, with the help of male converts, will put an end to the nuclear program and to irrational economic growth which have become a tower of Babel. And once again it will be a pleasure to be productive, in self-determination, for the good of humanity, which will then have found its way home.

Translated by Pamela Selwyn

Notes

* Originally published as, Delphine Brox-Brochot, "Manifest der 'Grünen Frauen'," *Courage* vol. 5 (February, 1980), pp. 13–17. Translated and reprinted with permission. Portions of this text have been excerpted.

48. Women
   in the Ecology Movement—
   Ecology
   in the Women's Movement

Ulla Terlinden

The extent to which the West German women's movement has taken up the issues of ecology and war and peace is quite striking to the outside observer. In this article, the author implies a unique, almost symbiotic bond between women and the ecology movement. As the author foresaw, the increasing legitimacy and electoral success of the "Greens" and the Alternative List political coalitions have diminished women's special place in the ecology movement.

The Female Concept of the Environment

The female concept of nature is determined by the form and content of housework. Housework is necessary for the reproduction of society; in its microstructure each single household provides for the preservation and care of human life. In housework human dependence on the natural environment is immediately apparent. Nutrition and health are integral features of the female concept of ecology. Along with the care and maintenance of human life goes the care and maintenance of the environment, for the exploitation and destruction of the ecology also means the destruction of human life. This connection, which men in the ecology movement have yet to work out, is clear to women. Another element in their closeness to nature is women's capacity to give birth. In pregnancy and childbirth the continuity between human beings and nature is fully realized. Because women are raised for these social functions they are kept away from all technical matters from an early age. Technology is always associated with the male. In general, male socialization is oriented towards things and female socialization towards people. Correspondingly, women's relations with the environment are different from men's.

Ecological and Female Forms of Organization

Alongside the concrete parallels between women and the ecology movement there are parallels in organizational structure. Basically, the women's movement and the ecology movement display similar patterns of organization. To be sure, this can be explained in part by referring to conditions affecting all social movements in a highly organized and institutionalized society.[1] Nevertheless, I contend that specific analogies can be made between the two movements. In the ecology movement, not complex systems but simple, observable phenomena determine the exchange between human beings and nature. Decentralization, self-help, self-management and self-determination at the grassroots level are the determining democratic organizing principles in an ecological society; hierarchy, specialization and complexity are rejected. The ecology movement attempts to remain true to these principles in its organizational structure. Flexibility is an essential requirement. The emphasis is on spontaneity and direct and concrete political tactics.

The potential for an active and highly informed membership is exceptionally great in comparison to established organizations. Leadership and managerial functions are performed by those who put in the most effort and time. In addition, empirical studies show a high level of consensus among members.[2] The negative aspects of such modes of organization have been raised, for example in connection with the citizens' action groups of Baden-Alsace. Here we find warnings of the danger of disintegration. "The main reason for this is the loose organizational structure of most of these groups, as well as the fact that they neither have nor want any professional functionaries. The membership turnover is rather high. Many activists work very hard for a while, then slow down and gladly give up their duties to others. In the citizens' action groups more influence (power) generally means more work. Thus to a certain extent, the high turnover in membership acts as a structural hindrance to the accumulation of power."[3]

Similar patterns of organization can be seen in political activism among women. Housework requires of women a broad range of knowledge and ability. The nature of the work itself determines its organization.[4] The work at hand must be dealt with in its entirety. "Typically, housework is seen ideally as all-embracing, functionally nonspecific and diffusely organized. The worker must possess a high degree of personal synthesis, initiative, intuition and flexibility."[5]

The structural features of housework, which largely define female socialization and the daily life of women, also shape women's preferences with regard to forms of organized political involvement. Thus women are capable of an expressive, noninstrumental attitude, an orientation not toward long-term goals in complex goal-systems but toward immediate affective reward. Their action is more directed towards people than things.[6] Women do not favor strictly formalized, technocratic organizational frameworks but prefer open, informal ones such as prevail in the ecology movement. The ecology movement actually seems ideally suited for women. Spontaneity, concrete work for visible goals, personal contact among group members, high levels of consensus as well as flexibility and self-initiative are among the organizational features familiar to women.

The Situation of Women in the "Greens"

Unfortunately there are no studies specifically addressing the connection between women and the ecology movement. In studies of environmental groups in general, women are almost ignored as activists or sympathizers, so that a detailed survey of the number and relative importance of women members is impossible. This probably says something about the situation of women in these groups. The data available show clearly at least that those active in citizens' action groups are primarily male.

Even a quick survey shows that while women seem to be more strongly represented in the ecology movement than in other political organizations, even there they are in the minority and have little authority. The objectives of the ecology movement—preservation of the natural environment and conservation of natural resources—find much support among women. This is expressed in many appeals and articles, as well as in the many ecology groups in the women's movement. In recent years ecology-minded women in the women's movement have changed their focus somewhat. At first they were primarily concerned with health and nutrition, corresponding to their areas of competence as women. This area, while still important for women today, has been supplemented by the issue of energy, particularly the opposition to nuclear power plants. The potential for reproductive catastrophes is especially apparent to women because the physical and psychological burden for children genetically damaged by radioactivity would fall upon women above all. By 1975 a women's initiative existed to fight the planned nuclear power plant in Wyhl.

For women, the threat to personal life often forms the point of departure for their perspective on the environment. Women's closeness to the issue of environmental protection is also expressed in slogans and buttons referring to mother and child as symbols of life. In conjunction with the founding of the "Greens," a special "Women's

Program" is now being discussed.[7] To be sure, recommendations for the improvement of women's situation are limited to well-worn demands. Here women do not appear as experts in the debate. As do the "progressive" or "prowoman" wings of the established parties, the "Greens" demand equal opportunity for women in training and employment as well as recognition and social security coverage for "services in the household and child rearing" and the improvement of protection for mothers and fair pension payments. The section "Children" calls for "appropriate home economics and pedagogical training and a salary for child rearing" and the possibility for working parents "to take care of their sick children with full or compensatory pay."

On the whole, women have shown great commitment to the campaign for environmental protection, and we can assume that many more women sympathize with the ecology movement's objectives. So why, we might ask, aren't more women organized in the "Greens" or publicly visible in important positions? Even the presence of a few women in "top positions" in the ecology movement cannot obscure the dominance of men. It is my belief that organizational and structural factors limit women's participation. Not the political content but rather the form in which it is represented is decisive for the situation of women in the "Greens" and the Alternative List groups.

A few examples may provide some insight into these circumstances and serve to document my thesis. As noted above, a "women's" initiative first arose in Wyhl over the installation of a nuclear power plant. The women's group came about in reaction to the role and function of women in "mixed" citizens action groups, where their activities were limited to marginal service work, typing minutes, collecting newspaper clippings and "eroticizing" the atmosphere. When women made substantive suggestions they met with little response. Women from the University of Freiburg who were involved in the fight against the planned nuclear power plant write: "We noticed that such initiatives have absolutely nothing to do with what interested these women. In retrospect it became clear to us how male-dominated the organizations were. Women had open, emotional discussions; the men gave long pathetic speeches. Women expressed personal involvement; the men demonstrated their strength or their resignation." [8] I find that this shows clearly that conflicting ways of organizing the common struggle induced the women to form an autonomous group.

In press reports of the "Greens" and Alternative List campaigns women are also seldom mentioned. Women as spokespersons for environmental initiatives are rare. Regionally or at the national level, the picture is much the same. "At the forefront stands the good cause, which must be supported. The general sentiment seems to be that this good cause must not be blocked or boycotted merely because people are insisting on equality or objecting to discrimination. We are all pulling together, aren't we?" [9] The draft program for the founding of a national ecological party makes not one reference to patriarchal social structures. Rather, we read under "Women's Program:" "The exemplary involvement of women in the citizens' action groups is a signal. Among the "Greens," too, political consciousness and positions are determined by women as well as men, significantly more so than in other parties. This tendency will increase to the extent that women are prepared to take on more political responsibility." [10]

As we learned from the [socialist] labor movement, all of women's problems will automatically be solved in an ecological society. The goal of a society organized along ecological and grassroots democratic principles dominated everybody's thinking to such an extent that much less thought was given to the ways and means of striving for that goal. The more the ecology movement conforms to existing structures, becomes institutionalized, the less involved women will become in matters of orientation and organization.

Translated by Pamela Selwyn

Notes

* Originally published as, Ulla Terlinden, "Frauen in der Ökologiebewegung/ Ökologie in der Frauenbewegung," *Beiträge zur feministischen Theorie und Praxis* no. 4 (1980), pp. 94–100. Translated and reprinted with permission. Portions of this text have been excerpted.

1. See Otthein Ramstedt, *Soziale Bewegungen* Frankfurt, 1978.

2. See Walter Andritzky and Ulla Wahl-Terlinden, *Mitwirkung von Bürgerinitiativen an der Umweltpolitik* Berlin, 1978.

3. See Wolfgang Sternstein, "Zur Organisationsstruktur der badisch-elsässischen Bürgerinitiativen," *Gewaltfreie Aktion* no. 33/34 (1977).

4. This description is not intended as a positive evaluation of housework. One could also point to monotony, dissipation of energy and work as a never-ending rat race.

5. Ilona Ostner, *Beruf und Hausarbeit* Frankfurt, 1978, p. 133.

6. Elena Gianini Belotti, *Was geschieht mit kleinen Mädchen?* Munich, 1975.

7. See "Grüne Frauen im Dilemma," *Courage* vol. 5 (February, 1980).

8. Frauenkollektiv Freiburg, "Frauen erklären Atom und Blei den Krieg," *Frauenoffensive Journal* no. 2 (1975).

9. "Wie grün sind uns die Grünen?" *Emma* vol. 2 (October, 1978).

10. "Frauenprogramm der Grünen," *Courage* vol. 5 (February, 1980).

49. The New Women's Movement and the Party and Trade Union Question*

Hannelore Mabry

The question of a women's party became one focus of the 1979 Summer University for Women in West Berlin. That year had seen the eighth founding of a women's party in West Germany since WW II. This is a short excerpt from a paper, presented at a session of the 1979 Summer University, that is largely critical of the effectiveness of women's parties in the existing political context.

This year we can speak of a certain turning point in the discussion of a women's or a feminist party. For ten years, this question fell on deaf ears, particularly within the women's movement. At the 1978 Summer University it was still not possible to discuss the meaning and purpose of a Feminist Party. This demand was met with whistles and boos rather than arguments. The women had facilely and without reflection taken over the antiparliamentary and anarchist positions of the student movement. They did this despite the fact that the new women's movement had arisen in the Federal Republic in part as a protest against the patronizing attitudes and oppression practiced by patriarchal "comrades" in the extra-parliamentary opposition.

But women neglected, at least in the beginning, to apply their experiences to the political positions of the student "left." Women did not consider whether these extra- and antiparliamentary positions also represented an adequate political theory and strategy for the solution of the "woman problem." The deficiency of analysis was and is astounding, considering that the women's movement continues to draw most of its strength from among students, journalists, and academics in the social sciences. Neither housewives nor workers nor employees, not to speak of farmers or women over thirty-five, are proportionately represented in the movement or determine its orientation and political goals.

The fact that in the last decade only a limited minority of women could be won over to the feminist cause is only partially due to the way in which the movement represented itself. The causes for the limited resonance among the so-called broad masses of women lie in the ever-greater sexual division of labor. The ever-increasing specialization and differentiation of the working world leads in the end to political idiocy and a total avoidance of politics on the part of the majority of the population—especially of women and mothers. The political inferiority of women is no accidental or minor by-product of the workings of the patriarchy. Rather, it is one of the mainstays, a prerequisite and condition for the maintenance of the system.

The Longing for Emancipation Begins with Comparison

The only people who can fight for equality are those who are able to compare themselves with other individuals or groups. Those who view the social order as natural or divinely ordained do not feel the need to criticize or change the existing order.

This year, the Summer University for Women poses the question "Autonomy or Institution? " What does the "or" mean? It seems to me that the political autonomy of the movement is essential and can only take root and develop if we institutionalize ourselves.

The question of whether women need an autonomous political organization hinges upon whether women start comparing current values and practices with those of earlier times, in other countries, and, above all, with those that hold true for men. Why are women paid less for the same work?

In order to remove the discrimination against women in the job market, we need not only professional organizations and the right to vote, more than anything else we also need, in the words of Käthe Schirmacher (1865–1930), "the raising of women's expectations." [1]

The factors which ensure women's exclusion from the political arena cannot be read in the stars or the coffee grounds. Psychoanalysis, dream interpretation and studies of myths, "women's" intuition or "body language" cannot help much either. In order to abolish the twentieth-century patriarchy we need other allies than mother goddesses or amazon armies.

The extent of political prejudice, the ignorance with which historical facts and political experience are presented in the new women's movement is frightening. Nothing can be achieved with blind activism.

The Historical Aspect

After World War I, when women had won the right to vote in most European countries, the leaders and a section of the membership of the women's organizations entered the existing parties of the left and right-wing patriarchy. They believed that they could in that way further the so-called woman question or solve it through their influence on legislation. The experiment failed. After about ten years the evidence was clear. Women had not succeeded in attaining real political influence in any of the patriarchal parties nor could they put through laws not sponsored by men. To this day, they have never achieved more than an "alibi function." While most women learned to live with this alibi function or with an individual career achieved at the expense of the woman question, a minority sought a way out of this dilemma. The calls for both a women's party and list of candidates were loud.

The first and only true women's party was founded in 1915 or 1916 in the United States. Europeans only succeeded in establishing isolated, short-lived women's trade unions. Basically, American women were and are far ahead of us in praxis (organization and strategy). Our feminist presses would do us a great favor by finally translating Inez Haynes Irwin's book *Story of the Woman's Party* (New York, 1921) and bringing it out in a German edition. The founder, Quaker Alice Paul, was one of the most capable and radical feminists, who not only went to prison for women's emancipation but also worked as an excellent organizer for decades! That women achieved the right to vote after World War I owes much to the tireless work by the Women's Party. And from the beginning, these women agitated to keep the women's movement out of men's political parties.

Unfortunately, however, the majority did not and does not listen to these vocies, whether in the United States or in Germany. At the end of the 1920s, women faced the same situation everywhere. In no party had they increased their influence or raised the number of their elected or executive positions. The leading women's rights activists had betrayed their own idea of the "cultural task of women" by their entry and total integration into the ideological and organizational institutions of the patriarchy. They wanted more power within the patriarchal system, but they did not question it as a system.

Even after the collapse of the tyranny of National Socialism, women did not grapple with their past. The majority of women continued to subordinate their own lives and those of their children to the male power struggle. Women had survived, although of course not all of them. Many had lost their homes and "breadwinners" as well.

Now they were the "women of the rubble" (Trümmerfrauen) for the nation, hauling away the debris with their bare hands—while the rulers were back at their desks, leading the state from above. Women tried to survive somehow, as always.

They knew nothing of a political alternative. Even the terms "women's movement" or "feminism" meant nothing anymore. Their history had been obliterated. Where could the sex that appears neither in history books, nor in the everyday centers of power and influence have found a starting point?

I would like to list briefly the attempts up until now, in the Federal Republic, to found a women's party:

1951—Allgemeine Frauenpartei (General Women's Party)

1951—Deutsche Frauenpartei (German Women's Party)

1953—Die Partei der Frauen (The Women's Party)

1970—Erste Frauenpartei (First Women's Party)

1970—Unabhängige Deutsche Frauenpartei (Independent German Women's Party)

1975—Deutsche Frauenbewegung (German Women's Movement)

1975—Demokratische Frauenbewegung Deutschlands (Democratic Women's Movement of Germany)

1979—Frauenpartei (Women's Party)

In other countries feminist parties were also founded in the 1970s: in Norway (1970), in Belgium (1972), in France (1974), in Denmark (1977/1978), in Israel and Turkey, and in Canada and Spain (1979).

It cannot be denied that except for the first two women's parties, which merged in 1953 after two years to form Die Partei der Frauen, almost all the others either perished or vegetated after a relatively short time, either because of splits or personal and ideological power struggles. To date, none of the eight women's parties in West Germany has been able to sustain an on-going organization, and the most recent premature birth does not seem any more viable than its predecessors. All of the party foundings were the work of lone wolves. The women brought very limited experience and knowledge with them. None of the founders had the backing of prominent individuals or strong pressure groups. Of the approximately ten party founders whom I have met, only one of them (the Norwegian Gori Gunwald) had anything resembling charisma—that is, strong personal magnetism, oratorical brilliance, agitational abilities or the political power born of conviction. Yet, regardless of this, these attempts were still doomed to failure. In the political field, the ground has been so cultivated and depleted by patriarchs and inadequately fertilized by feminists, that the seed of a feminist party cannot yet take root.

So what is to be done?

The Practical Aspect

Reduced to a common denominator, I would say: read a lot.[2] Reading, however, is only one aspect. Practice is also indispensable: becoming active in a political women's group or taking part in the activities of other groups, or forming your own group. Other goals are the dismantling of widespread prejudices and illusions and the evaluation and reordering of individual life experiences within a political group process. Developing historical and factual knowledge, self-assurance in public, strategic and procedural practices, and defining the goals and demands essential for feminism—these are things we must all learn when we become politically active. We must bring our work into the public eye and be prepared for the long-term "canal work," in spite of internal and external frustrations.

As regards our political context, we must carefully consider who can be won over as coalition partners. We should call to account women who still invest their money, time and labor in patriarchal institutions (churches, parties, trade unions) and try to convince them that in so doing they harm the cause of women because they awaken hopes which lead women into dead ends and withdrawal from the women's movement.

We must also appeal to the few female celebrities in science, art, or the mass media to stand up for feminism. If they fear the consequences, they can begin by practicing solidarity "in the background." Money is also needed! And we should not ignore the so-called democrats, socialists and "progressives" of the male sex. They should all prove just how serious they are about the abolition of the patriarchy. We are prepared to work with anyone who supports our political program, male or female, old or young, heterosexual or homosexual, housewife or professional, student or pensioner. We want to abolish the system of violence, nonviolently.

Translated by Pamela Selwyn

Notes

* Originally published as, Hannelore Mabry, "Die neue Frauenbewegung und die Partei—und Gewerkschaftsfrage," *Autonomie oder Institution: Über die*

Leidenschaft und Macht von Frauen. Beiträge zur 4. Sommer-Universität der Frauen, 1979 Berlin, 1981, pp. 218–233. Translated and reprinted with permission. Portions of this text have been excerpted.

1. Käthe Schirmacher "Wie und in welchem Masse lässt sich die Wertung der Frauenarbeit steigern?" (1909) in: *Frauenarbeit und Beruf* ed. Brinker-Gabler (Fischer, 1979), p. 203.

2. For example the thirteen issues of *Frauenforum* and the nine numbers of *Der Feminist* because we can study in them the nearly ten-year-old effort to construct a political feminist organization (long-term goal, our own party and trade union)—both the individual successes and the reasons for divisions and failures.

50. A Eulogy to the Resistance Group of the Berlin Women's Center

Anonymous

While it is true that terrorist groups had chosen a political path completely apart from the women's movement, by force of circumstance the West German women's movement has had to come to terms with violence as a strategy and not only as it affects women as victims.

In October 1977, during the Schleyer kidnapping[1] and the heightened state repression, a group of Frankfurt women summoned all women to "invent happiness":

> preamble: we, the mothers, the daughters, the women of this country, demand to be released from this nation which brings forth only unhappiness. The gravity of the situation precludes any further escalation of gravity. Therefore we seize the right to laughter. Step out of line and dance, dance . . . .

At first I experienced this appeal as liberating because it was directed against an orientation toward "public theatrics" and encouraged me to continue developing our women's politics autonomously instead of merely reacting to the destruction of people in prison. But then my doubts returned. I did not feel like such an outsider. On the contrary, since we are struggling for our self-identity in this society, the power of the state affects us women too.

Even before state terror peaked during the "German Autumn," I thought we had to confront the new antisubversives laws because in my opinion they were directed against *all* subversive movements, among which I include the women's movement. The women's movement, however, has never taken a collective stance regarding the legitimization of repression. For example, we did not see the political censorship of a left-wing print shop as a possible danger for our own presses. Is this because a women's press does not print [such] things and therefore is not as threatened, or do we in the women's movement simply avoid such questions?

It appeared to me that a response to state repression was seen as a matter for "the" Left, while the women's movement dealt more with structural, everyday violence. I wanted no part of this separation, which is fatal for both sides. Rather, I wanted to learn how to defend myself against state repression within the context of women's circumstances, without pushing aside the question of my oppression as a woman in everyday life.

The Resistance Group Is Formed

In this context a meeting was held at the women's center [in late 1977] to discuss two separate women's conferences planned for 1978: "Women and Repression," in Frankfurt, and "Women and Violence," in Cologne. The discussion evolved around the intersecting points between everyday, structural violence, and the violence emanating from the state, as they relate to women. We recommended that the two conferences be merged, and a group was formed to begin the conceptual work in preparation for such a conference. This preparatory group later became the resistance group.

Women's Solidarity with the Political Prisoners of the RAF?

We tried in the resistance group to clarify our position on the political prisoners. Specifically, we criticized the letters to Irmgard Möller [the surviving RAF prisoner at Stammheim] from the Bochum women's center. Criticized in the sense that at least one letter arose quite facilely from woman-to-woman solidarity, totally ignoring the fact that Irmgard Möller had consciously pursued a different politics from our own. For us it is important to deal with her politics, that is, with the armed struggle of the RAF (Red Army Faction). [The following are some of the main points] from a paper which grew out of this debate within the women's center:

Broad sections of West German society . . . are not ready or able to resist West German imperialism. Especially the working class has assumed a mentality of *worker aristocracy* and *chauvinism* in relation to Third World Peoples. Thus, there is no basis for mass resistance on which the armed groups could build a movement or to which they could appeal.

The very social structures which rob these sectors of society of their desire and will to resist are not, however, taken seriously. For years armed praxis has neither recognized nor confronted the everyday structures of so-called imperialist power and violence, but rather has been fixated upon the state-institutional level.

The issue for women is not whether the "guerillas" are practicing consistent feminist politics, or whether we should ask them if they would please carry out a "woman-oriented" action for us. . . . What we *are* talking about is whether grounds exist for a *real relationship of solidarity* between the armed groups and the women's movement.

There is a hierarchy of sorts in which the development of a feminist health center or self-protection on the street evoke a weary smile when compared to an attack upon the Federal Constitutional Court.

In our efforts to keep the characteristic of equality of rights alive in the many forms of resistance we have developed, in our attempts to defend ourselves against patriarchal power structures present in everyday life, and in our recognition that herein lies our strength, we find ourselves in a big, fat contradiction to armed struggle.

To the extent that we do not want to submit to the everyday power structures, to "woman's lot," the authoritarian state is embodied not just in the person of . . . [government officials] but also in the person of our own husbands, boyfriends, comrades, colleagues, bosses . . . in medicine, in advertising, at the Social Security office, at the university, at the supermarket, in the bar, on the street . . . .

Positions presented in this paper were not fully shared by all members of the resistance group. Some of us objected to the fact that in the paper armed struggle is equated with the RAF's strategy alone, thereby losing sight of other groups practicing armed struggle (such as the revolutionary cells) which do focus much more on social contradictions within the Federal Republic. Additionally, the paper discusses the solidarity question only from the standpoint of the disagreement with the RAF's political positions, without considering the fact that people are rotting in prison. In the end, we were unable to develop our own form of solidarity, and thus we did not compose a letter to Irmgard Möller.

Women's Struggle and Illegality

Then we tried to relate the question of armed struggle and illegality more closely to our own actions in the women's movement. In this connection, we discussed [a recent] article which said, in effect, "We women have had it up to here with the patriarchy!" "How you flip out is your own affair, whether you leave your macho lover or reach for the gun . . . ." Yet, a hierarchical order is implicit: Reaching for the gun is *the* break with female socialization.

In response to this we looked into the conventional concept of militancy. Why is an action by "Red Zora" (which looted several sex shops in Cologne) more "militant" than a "little" action which all women can perform in everyday life? Can you actually say that Red Zora is more militant than the Frankfurt women who travel to Holland for abortions? Aren't we measuring militancy by the degree of force and illegality? But militancy should only be judged by what the action achieves, circumstances permitting, and not by the means employed. To simply equate militancy with the use of violence is to reproduce the societally defined notion of violence.

Through the concept of militancy we began to focus more on the illegality of certain women's actions. A difference between the Frankfurt women's abortion bus charters and Red Zora lies in their relations to the public. The Frankfurt women could "go public" because their action stood in direct connection to the broad movement against Paragraph 218 [the abortion law]. This could not be criminalized so easily. It is questionable, for example, whether the [bomb] attack on the Supreme Court in Karlsruhe [by Red Zora] could have expected the same solidarity, although it was also directed against Paragraph 218. Certainly it remained unclear whether we should make the degree of popular support anticipated a guideline for an action. We found that deciding how to "go public" with an illegal action was difficult, with the exception of the Frankfurt action (abortion trips).

During Walpurgis Night 1977 [2] our attack on sex shops was a collective one, and besides there had just been demonstrations against violence towards women. Thus there was a broader context for the shop attacks. Red Zora's action (trashing sex shops), on the other hand, was an isolated one, out of which no other actions against pornography and rape have arisen lately. It seems as if Red Zora wanted to send a signal to get a weary women's movement moving again. Behind this lies a certain avant-garde expectation.

Legality or Legalism of the Women's Movement

We focused on two questions regarding the women's movement's unclarified relationship to legality: does the women's movement practice within a legal framework because it is important for us to reach many women on this basis and thus have *terra firma* under our feet? Or does the women's movement cling to legality, resulting in its feeling not concretely affected by the many facets of repression? If, for example, further actions by Red Zora were published in the women's press, would that lead to the criminalizing, by association, of the women's press? Likewise, it is not at all clear to us on what level the conflict legal/illegal is played out in a project such as the women's shelter. This is a complicated issue involving, among other things, the extent to which such projects, which work within a legal framework, are able and willing to jeopardize their autonomy and their public reputation. This is a vicious circle, which we must discuss further.

In the group we were not able to define the connection between structural violence against women and state repression. Rather, in our discussions we often simply assumed that such a connection existed and that we must express it in our actions.

To find the intersecting points between the two kinds of violence we probably should have worked more theoretically; for example, by focusing on economic crises, countermovements and state repression in their relationship to women. For me, the concept "structural violence against women" became increasingly hazy. We often used structural violence and everyday violence synonymously, as if the difference between structural and state violence was that between latent/private and overt/public phenomena. Instead, we should have understood structural violence as that which limits or prevents women's self-determination. Then we would have been able to discuss issues such as women's unemployment, unpaid housework, thus moving the concept of structural violence away from the exclusive sphere of the private. At the same time we could have broadened our notion of violence against persons, beyond the perspective of rape on the one side, and prison on the other.

Despite this vagueness, I learned much from the group. Without it I probably would have fallen back onto a traditional concept of politics, oriented only towards publicly visible violence practiced by the state. This was at least partly the case at the Women and Repression conference in Frankfurt: There we were urged to set aside our women's politics and become absorbed into the Left's struggle against repression. This is the concept of women's politics as the luxury of peaceful times.

Translated by Pamela Selwyn
and Edith Hoshino Altbach

Notes

* Originally published as: "Ein Nachruf auf die Widerstandsgruppe im FZ," *Tango Feminista* (July, 1978), pp. 24–29. Translated and reprinted with permission. Portions of this text have been excerpted.

1. Schleyer was the President of the Association of Employers. He was kidnapped and killed by a terrorist group.

2. Walpurgis Night demonstrations have been staged for several years to protest violence against women, much like the "Take Back the Night" marches in the United States.

51. Has Violence Arrived in the Women's Movement? *

Sibylle Plogstedt

In a reflective, at times retrospective essay, this long-time radical and feminist questions the recent willingness on the part of women to entertain fantasies of violence. She refers, among others, to the story by Christa Reinig, in this volume, "The Widows."

The period since 1979 has seen a growing debate within the women's movement over ecology, nuclear power stations and nuclear weapons. As a result of this and the threat of imminent war, many women have changed their evaluation of the resistance required. Now, with our time running out, it no longer seems enough to build, via our women's projects, bastions against the world of men or to deny the state our children through the long-term strategy of a birthstrike. We seek something more in the way of resistance—in the form of house-occupations (squatter take-overs) never before attempted by women. But even a house occupied by women is only an island.

Enter, the utopias of a world without men, of war waged by women against men. In "The Widows," [1] Christa Reinig proposes that "there could conceivably be a virus strain that threatens only men and lets women alone, that is, if the virus specialized in attacking only the male half of the cell nucleus. Then the men would be laid low, and the women would stay on their feet—they'd have to." The world would be transformed.

In her novel *Wanderland*,[2] Sally Miller Gearhart sees nature in alliance with women. Men become as if paralyzed as soon as they leave the city. They lose the power to beat up or to rape women. . . . As fantasies, I find this alliance with nature, the viral attack, and the paralysis of men highly disturbing. In an age of viruses and sophisticated germ warfare, Christa Reinig comes very close to real violence.

It would be very easy to relegate these utopias to the realm of fantasy. Then we would not have to deal with the threat of violence in these texts and could go on with our utopia-discussion groups at the university and with our man-hating discussions at lesbian meetings. However, utopias were never mere fantasy. They always contained an element of reality.

This is most evident in the book by Francoise d'Eaubonne, *Feminism and "Terrorism."* [3] In a passage referring to the murders [of R.A.F. members] in Stammheim [prison], the author writes:

Is it not better for a woman to be beaten to death by a prison guard at Stammheim than to be humiliated by the blows of a husband's fists? Is it not better to endure insults before a court of law which one can denounce as "Nazi pigs! " than to endure in silence the insults of an employer? And is it not better, ultimately, to meet death having fought back than to die in resignation and defeat? If we must die, then better with weapon in hand.

The position taken by Francoise d'Eaubonne was a controversial one within the French women's movement. The German edition of *Feminism and "Terrorism"* contains a kind of dialogue between the author and French feminist Evelyne LeGarrec. LeGarrec: "The identity of fighter and revolutionary provides no security for women. And armed struggle is not the highest stage of feminism." D'Eaubonne: "When will we know for sure that armed struggle is not the only answer at this stage of degeneracy. How much time do we still have to make our choice, Evelyne? "

The editorial staff of *Courage* has been engaged in an on-going dispute over whether or not to print an article by Francoise d'Eaubonne. All are agreed on the tone and substance of the text itself: It is horrible, brutal, fascist—from the gas piped into the police barracks, to the flower which blooms again, nourished by the bloodshed. Has violence arrived in the women's movement? How many have lost patience with the gradual changes brought about, day-by-day, through the work of the women's movement? How many share the criticism of Red Zora [a women's group practicing "armed resistance"]—that the women's movement will only regain its radicalism through the organization of counter-violence?

Up until now, Red Zora has had little influence on the women's movement. Thus, we did not find it necessary to take a stand on the issue of women guerillas. Before now, criticisms of the social work aspect of the women's movement and its failure to take radical positions have not led to a call for armed struggle. Has this changed?

Throwing stones is no liberation for me. Whenever I threw them during the student movement, I had the feeling I was violating something within myself. At that time, I felt this to be a kind of liberation—identifying with the stone as it flew through the glass, as if one were close behind, being thrown into the battle (not understanding that the real struggle was with one's self).

Not for me the fine distinctions between violence against things and violence against persons. My rage was not directed against things. I struck a policeman in the face at the 1967 anti-Shah demonstration. Retaliation. Helpless rage. At a protest in Moabit courthouse, I jumped a policeman from behind, as he was beating a woman. Proud of my quick reaction, I was also frightened by it. It was not clear to me where the violence in me was coming from. I did not understand it; I only knew that I could not control this violence but that I would have to learn to do so.

Violence, at first limited to stone-throwing, was justified repeatedly: Only pressure from below would bring change. We looked about for more effective weapons. Violence against those who had incited to violence.

The revolution was being rehearsed on a small scale. The great, Vietnamese revolution formed the background for the attacks on Amerika-Haus [an American cultural and international public relation's center in Berlin]. For more revolution, more discipline would be required. As if it were all just a question of organization.

When I returned from Prague, after spending a year and a half (1968–1969) working in the Czech student movement and serving time in a Prague jail for my political activities, the left in West Germany had changed. In the absence of a mass movement, hopes centered on violence—as the most effective form of resistance. Our game of provocation had become violent. Was that what we wanted?

In 1980, when the first apartment houses were occupied and barricades were again raised on the Ku'damm, the call went out for the activists of the 1968 movement. Where were they? Why were they not joining the actions against the police? Perhaps this is an answer: I was only able to throw stones as long as I confused this with my own liberation. In stone throwing there is no continuity of liberation. I cannot throw stones at age thirty-five as I could at age eighteen. Skirmishes with the police are no longer a strategy for changing society. The dynamic of violence lies elsewhere.

I have changed my position. I know—in 1976 I agreed with the eulogy spoken at Ulrike Meinhof's [a leader of the Baader-Meinhof gang] graveside: "Ulrike was . . . the most influential woman since Rosa Luxemburg." My criticism of her political choice was only a vague one at the time; "The conclusions she drew may have been incorrect." (*Courage*, 0/1976). In that same year, however, I did voice specific criticism of the Irish women in their peace campaign. To be against violence in Ireland seemed to me a pacification in keeping with British colonialism. (*Courage*, 2/1976)

Since then, I have given a lot of thought to my relation to violence. I do not believe that we can build a new society on the basis of violence—neither a socialist nor a feminist society. In exercising violence . . . we ourselves are changed. Having once committted violence, it becomes easier to do so again. As women we would betray our inbred peaceableness. Would that be progress?

So, now men—the almighty enemy—are to be forced up against the wall? Have we been so weakened, so blinded that we have forgotten that our goal concerns the *function* of men in the family and other social institutions and in the state? We must abolish these functions, not the individual man. If some women believe that the physical annihilation of men will usher in a happy, harmonious society, then I know nothing good can come of all this. I would not like to live in a women's society based upon violence. I want dominance for women, but not through violence.

Translated by Edith Hoshino Altbach

Notes

* Originally published as, "Ist die Gewalt in der Frauenbewegung angekommen? " *Courage* Vol. 6 (September, 1981), pp. 30–35. Translated and reprinted with permission.

1. Christa Reinig, "Die Witwen," in: *Der Wolf und die Witwen: Erzählungen und Essays* Dusseldorf: Eremiten Presse, 1980. See this volume, Section IX.

2. Sally Miller Gearhart, *Wanderland* Munich: Frauenoffensive, 1981. (English title: *Wanderground*)

3. Francoise d'Eaubonne, *Feminismus und "Terror"* Munich: Trikont, 1978 (German edition).

Part Eleven

Women's Studies

The German women's movement is mindful that the student movement of the 1960s had begun its "long march through the institutions"
in the universities. In this section, authors Metz-Göckel and Mies
are quite aware that *their* movement had its origins not within the
elite enclave of the university but in a broad-based social struggle.

It is of particular interest to note that the women's studies movement in West Germany began not in the universities at all but rather
in the numerous neighborhood and town *Volkschochschulen*—adult
education night-schools. Ingrid Schmidt-Harzbach chronicles the
spread of women's discussion groups at these institutions beginning
in 1972. Perhaps a parallel in the United States is the fact that
women's studies programs tended to spring up first at second and
third rank institutions rather than at the elite universities.

In West Germany, women's studies appeared at the university level
in 1974/75 with the proliferation of "Women's Seminars." Sigrid
Metz-Göckel shows that the stress in these interdisciplinary courses
was not so much upon curriculum as on a new feminist pedagogy
based upon consciousness raising of all concerned. While there is
no West German equivalent to the United States National Women's
Studies Association, since 1976—with the exception of 1981—the
annual Summer University for Women at the Free University of
Berlin has provided a useful forum. Together with more regional
women's conferences—notably the Women's Forum in the Ruhr
(Dortmund)—these meetings allow the exchange of information and
research in the absence of a more formal women's studies network.

Since the late 1970s, university-level women's studies has increased
its academic legitimacy, but an influential text by Maria Mies included
here outlines the strong radical intent of German women's studies
to transform scientific methodology itself.

52. Women's Discussion Groups at Adult Education Institutions in Berlin*

Ingrid Schmidt-Harzbach

This study is based on the results of a survey conducted between July 1978 and May 1979, involving instructors (18 in-depth interviews) and participants (30 in-depth interviews) in women's forums at 10 Berlin Institutions of Adult Education, as well as on the author's personal experience as instructor of women's discussion groups since 1975.

Continuing Education for Women: On the historical Development of Women's Work in Adult Education, 1945–1972

In connection with the Western Allies' re-education policy, adult education after 1945 was oriented to the political education of adults according to the principle of "education by fellow-citizens." This meant, for example, to illuminate the socio-political origins of German fascism; the object was political education as a productive counter-measure. As it was then conceived, this included primarily information on the functioning of a middle-class democratic system, such as how laws originate, or the functioning of individual constitutional agencies, etc. In this conception of political education, oriented toward the middle classes, opposing societal interests between classes and social groups faded into the background.

Women—who were to be recruited into adult education work in increased numbers, to do justice to the high enrollment of women in the courses—were also included in this conception of "education by fellow-citizens": in their roles as homemakers, wives and mothers. "She must comprehend her husband, understand his interests; she must be able to direct the physical, intellectual and psychic education of her children." The aim was to restrict women's political activity to small, manageable areas. However, at this point in time there was still an emphasis on the significance of addressing women personally in the work of political education, and doing so within debate groups and work teams. In this connection, the (female) adult education personnel were convinced of the importance of education specifically

342

for women. Through this women's curriculum, participants were to become "qualified," in the subject matter and personally, to make a self-assured appearance. Contrary to concepts of women's continuing education that have been developed today in the context of the autonomous women's movement, the adult education instructors then saw the women's curriculum as preparation for participation in "mixed courses." Thus, there is talk of "getting women to speak and perform together with men." Distancing on the part of adult education instructors from the development of a "battle-stance with respect to men" makes clear that the goals they envisioned still corresponded to received sex-specific ideals, to the extent that the "logic of men" was to be opposed by a "logic of the heart." [1]

A turning point in adult education for women appears at the beginning of the 1960s, in connection with the need for women in the work force and the ensuing discussion of women's double role and double burden based on increased employment of married women and mothers. Almost all 1960s publications on women's issues thematize this problem, especially from the perspective of the effect of women's extradomestic work on the family. The contradictory demands on women and their double discrimination are thus masked, and a kind of "life plan for the modern woman" worked out by means of various "coping strategies"—part-time work, discontinuity in extradomestic employment. The primary emphasis was on alleviating the worst consequences.

The actual difficulties of the double burden do not come to light as long as the situation is considered unchangeable. Accordingly, in the course of mandated 1960s research, models were developed which supposedly took into account women's changed situation—doing housework while being gainfully employed—but at the same time saw the discontinuity in women's extradomestic employment as an unchangeable quantity. The best-known of the models that emerged during this period is the "Three-Phase Model" of Alva Myrdal and Viola Klein. The first phase consists of education and a first paid-job, followed by a second phase in which women devote themselves exclusively to their family until the children are grown. This is followed by the third phase, re-entry into extradomestic work activity. The first training courses directed specifically toward vocational reintegration of women were established in the mid-1960s.

The assumption that women had a "double role" necessitated a new definition of sex roles: The concession to paid employment for women was accompanied by an appeal to men to take over family duties to a certain extent.

The new concept of partnership, which was touted as progressive but in reality denied the actual needs of the women affected, was also propagated by adult education. Thus, one of the theoreticians of adult education explains in a 1969 position paper on research on women that it must be a basic task of adult education to strengthen women's self-awareness. "Strengthening this self-confidence is one of the functions of adult education courses, which in this way make a direct contribution to continuing vocational training." On the one hand, the goal was to stabilize the self-awareness of women; at the same time the capacity of the female labor force for flexibility and mobility in the job market stood in the foreground of the policy for continuing education. Ideologically, this relationship was justified by the educational policy demand for life-long learning. The traditional sex-specific division of work in family and society was thereby not placed in question. That explains coinciding course offerings: courses to impart qualifications for entering paid employment and parallel courses aimed at qualifying women as marriage partners. A high priority in vocational continuing education was to place the greatest emphasis on the economic aspects precisely in domestic science courses.

Thus we find, in "Suggested Models of Household Management," published by the Pedagogy Department of the German Adult Education Association in 1972: "At a time when work is becoming more scientific, specialized, and interdependent, domestic science must also be seen in a wider context."

Consumer issues, problems of the invasion of technology into the home and of the household as a family organization are mentioned as thematic emphases. The intent here is supposedly to take into account a "changed structure and function of the family" and the "changing role-awareness of family members." The fact that women are solely responsible for the household is not problematized. The guiding principle is formulated as "a people-serving rationalization of the work necessary to maintain the household." According to estimates by the German Adult Education Association, about two-thirds of the course offerings deal with how to work with textiles, and one-third with the kitchen.

The titles are usually like this: "A Change of Pace for the Daily Menu," "Help, I'm Getting Too Fat," "Table Settings—Table Manners—Table Talk," "Make Neatness Count! " "Crocheting the Newest Look," "Tailoring: Mini—Midi—Maxi."

Among the topics under "Living," for example, the following course objective is formulated for a course on textiles in the household: "Participants should become aware of the influence that carpets, curtains, slipcovers, quilts, etc. have on the atmosphere of rooms, and how to make use of this in furnishing an apartment."

Sample questions are: Why do we put carpets on floors and curtains at windows? Is the desire for a maximum amount of natural light compatible with the use of curtains? Are carpets and quilted coverlets a luxury? What requirements should we look for in the quality of upholstered furniture?

The ideal image shaping these courses was the housewife as "an aware consumer." To be sure, the courses offer women a possibility of ongoing training for the household in the sense of professional training; however, housework is not recognized as real work. Moreover the familiar sex-specific division of labor remains untouched.

In the 1970s, in connection with deliberations on how to realize the emancipatory educational goals of adult education, women's problems were dealt with in the framework of "target-group work," which begins by placing the participants' interests at the forefront. From this perspective, adult education programming "to help the housewife" was criticized; it was pointed out that the solidification of the traditional female role was not compatible with the educational mission of continuing education. For this reason, courses were requested for blue-collar working women and housewives in working-class households, because they were seen as the most seriously disadvantaged.

Discussion of the role of women in target-group work was a first step in the development of women's forums. Even more important were the social consequences of the image of women that had recently emerged through the sex-wave and the new femininity craze. This notion, shaped by a consumer mentality, forced women not just to live and work under multiple burdens, but on top of that to be particularly beautiful objects.

With its increased marketing of the female body and the resulting image of the "sexually emancipated woman," the sex-wave and its profusion of ambivalent demands led to women's beginning to resist, first as individuals, then in small discussion groups, and then in the first women's groups of the autonomous women's movement.

If women up to this point had felt a more abstract need for education, in trying to break out of their female role, forget their isolation, abstract from their daily life in order to be better able to participate in discussions about the world outside, there was now a shift toward thematizing the isolation itself, with the common goal of finding a way out of it.

This development stands out clearly when we trace the origins of the first women's forum in Berlin.

From Mothers' Courses to Matriarchy: On the Historical Development of Women's Forums in Berlin, 1972–1979.

The first autonomous women's forum in Berlin: the first women's discussion group at an adult education institution in Berlin was formed in Autumn 1972; it had no connection whatever with the women's center on Hornstrasse founded in the same year. It was probably typical of the situation at that time that the initiative for the first women's forum in Berlin actually came from the Director of one of the Adult Education Institutions. The leader of this first discussion group introduced the course with the assistance of her husband, an adult education instructor, as mediator. Its background was her experience of total dependency on her husband and child—without any connection to the women's movement. Gesine Strempel states: "So I introduced that course. All alone and with the experiences I had had as a woman with an advanced education—master's degree, free-lance radio work—sitting at home because she couldn't pursue her profession with a small child and living in complete dependency on her husband. I had absolutely no idea what the women's movement was about in those days."

At their very first meeting Gesine realized that she was in the same situation as the other women, whether they had advanced degrees or not.

Like the women enrolled in the course, she was trying to assert herself about sharing housework and her own sexual needs, and had to overcome taboos similar to theirs. The women became radicalized from one meeting to the next. At first they stayed in their classroom until the custodian threw them out. They had their first group experiences being thrown out of a bar, for it was then still extraordinary for a group of women to go to a bar "alone." Then the women began to use the intimate *du* with each other—that, too, was not automatic in those days. For these women—housewives, secretaries, salesgirls, typists—it was truly a big step to organize women's celebrations together, before the days of the big women's festivals in Berlin. Today, Gesine S. is of the opinion that the participants of the first women's forum were probably becoming more radicalized in their private lives than was she herself. This radicalism was soon to show itself over the question of excluding men from the course.

For the first two semesters the courses were publicized as "Women's Forum—For Men Too." The idea "For Women Only" would not have occurred to them back then, according to Gesine, out of concern for legitimacy and a sense of democracy reflecting the attitude: If someone signs up, he has the right to come and have his say. However, all the women noticed that some women behaved differently; e.g., did not talk when their husbands were present. They also discussed the discriminatory tricks the men used to try to keep the women from taking the courses. The men were quick to sense the threat posed by the women's course, and their reactions ranged from a paternal "sure, go get emancipated" to outraged phone calls to the adult education director. The women responded by suggesting that the men form a group, too, stop complaining and do something themselves. Ultimately, however, they agreed to exclude men from the course altogether.

From that point on, men were no longer admitted as guest speakers, either.

The euphoric mood the women experienced in their consciousness raising was also communicated to me in interviews with the participants from those days. "I looked forward to that evening all week. It was really a key experience for me—being together with women for the first time and experiencing it as something positive. Before that I had difficulty approaching women; I was very much fixated on men." And Gesine: "The fact that the courses sparked so many things, that they were a great success, had nothing to do with our great personalities—plenty of women were just as great—it was because these women were pressure cookers, it really bowled me over. They could have done that course all by themselves."

From this conversation group the women's group Artemis was founded. In October 1975, Artemis participated in the activities of the women's center against Paragraph 218. Not until 1977 did the group dissolve. However, the women remain in contact, as friends, and have developed some common activities. Some went back and completed their secondary education and are going on for further training; others are now working in women's projects. Only since the Spring of 1975 have women's courses been offered by feminists at other Berlin Adult Education Institutions. In 1976 a general presentation was successfully organized by all the women's courses and with the women's center's theater group on the theme "Violence Against Women." Today there is a wide spectrum of women's courses offered at the twelve Adult Education Institutions in Berlin.

Translated by Jeanette Clausen

Notes

* Originally published as, Ingrid Schmidt-Harzbach, "Weiterbildung für Frauen: Frauengesprächskreise an Berliner Volkschochschulen," Munich: Deutsches Jugendinstitut, 1980, pp. 1–11. Translated and reprinted with permission.

1. But the efforts of the women employed in adult education to get a woman appointed as their representative to the state adult education commission, in the framework of realizing their constitutionally guaranteed equality, were frustrated by the male hegemony in the institution. The societal origins of this male dominance, however, were neither recognized nor sought.

53. Feminism at the University: Experiences and Reflections Concerning the Work-Pattern in Women's Seminars*

Sigrid Metz-Göckel

Influenced by Paolo Freire's Pedagogy of the Oppressed *(trans. M. B. Ramos, Herder & Herder, 1970), Metz-Göckel proposes a "pedogogy based on involvement" (Betroffenheit) for women's studies. While many of the points she makes are familiar to women's studies practitioners in the United States, her discussion of students' reactions to the women's seminars does give insight into feminist education at a West German university.*

Unlike the student movement of the 1960s, the impulses for conscious action by women for women in higher education come from outside: from the broad-based movement against Paragraph 218, from women's concern with the obvious discrimination at their industrial workplace and in the reproductive sphere, from the women's shelter movement and the lesbian movement. The student movement's critical universities have a sequel, in another form and with a different makeup, in the Summer University for women in Berlin and the First Women's Forum in the Ruhr, with this difference: The First Women's Forum succeeded, where the critical universities did not, in drawing in the working-class population.

Feminism at the University

Women's topics are ghetto-topics when they are discussed only by women with women. This objection (of ghetto-building) comes especially from men, but also from many successful women. In the traditional view, working on women's topics is likely to mean being devalued, pushed aside into the women's corner. Up to now, the woman who wanted a scholarly career wisely kept her distance from radical work on women's topics.

That has changed recently. Women's seminars and women's groups in the academic disciplines are consciously taking the situation of women and their involvement as their starting point. From there, they first try to develop an alternative among themselves, with each other. The quality of self-exploration and of the collective process of becoming aware, work on suppressed topics, the consensual re-definition of values and projects cannot (in my experience) be experienced or worked out with men as long as their mere presence has a censoring effect. Men still claim to be the experts on women's issues. The demand (and I do mean demand) for joint activities, for joint problem-solving steps usually comes from the men who think they know better how women should be liberated, and treated. The commonality of life-conditions for male and female is a concept which anticipates a possible future still to be created, through struggle. Women's solidarity among themselves is a prerequisite for it, and in a patriarchal society this is even harder to "work out" than the solidarity of the working class against their employers.

A Pedogogy Based on Involvement

In his pedagogy of the oppressed, Paolo Freire (1978) outlines a teaching method for the rural population of the Third World which proceeds from the contradictions in oppressed people's thinking, acting, and feeling: their situation is imprinted by their internalization of the oppressor, who embodies for them the ideal of a human being in the possibilities he has. Perceiving oppression is obstructed by the fact that the oppressed are "immersed" in the oppression and continue to accept the model of the oppressor as a model for their liberation. In his pedagogy, Freire gives an example of how a "sympathetic" educational project with the oppressed initiates the process of becoming politically aware.

The reference to a pedagogy of the oppressed is meant to give uninitiated readers insight into what is being attempted in women's seminars and women's groups. It is by no means as harmonious and free of contradictions as it may have sounded up to this point. The concrete meaning of a pedagogy based on involvement in higher education for women or in women's education outside the university is to work on seeing the contradictions in women's daily life as changeable. Women have disparate and yet mutually dependent experiences in their familial workplace and at the work-place in the sphere of production/performance. When women come together, they share these experiences and thus integrate their contradictory impressions and achievements. What they want from education or training is conceived in terms of appropriating their experiences, clarifying the contradictions, establishing commonalities, and is directed toward a life plan in which family and professional work can be connected.

This goal limits their spectrum of choice in curriculum and career. Therefore, higher education presently means something decidedly different for women than for men. Since women do not aim exclusively for an instrumental professional life, a scholarly profession remains a problematic choice.

Women's Seminars: A New Learning Situation

In women's seminars there is analysis of woman-specific topics or of topics from a woman's perspective, but the actual women as people are also a topic of the seminars, both on the content level and the relational level. The *goal* is self-definition by the women, independent of relationships to their men, and application of women's capacity for relating to the women themselves. This sounds simple, perhaps even trivial. In point of fact it must be learned, and can be learned only when women change their situations in a practical way. The theory must then be developed from this practice.

The Background of Personal Experience: The Private is Political

I got the courage to offer and continue supporting women's seminars at the university or the teacher training college through a housewives' discussion group in a village at the outskirts of the city. Seeing the way the group carried out their collective task of learning through sharing experiences of the seemingly private was new to me. In this women's group I learned how collective processes of learning, establishing internal solidarity and boundary maintenance, can be connected with lots of energetic assistance in dealing with everyday problems. These included battle strategies (e.g. a "go-in" at the youth welfare office) which were taken out of the reproductive sphere into the public.

In the course of the discussion group's experiences and its battles at various levels it became apparent that the step toward "politicization" came easier than changing the everyday relationships the women lived and worked in. Action was taken on the collective housework projects (shared housekeeping and mending days), but the search for houses where families (with or without a husband) could live communally dominated discussion for a long time, then came to nothing. It is far more difficult to change the conditions and structure of family life in the emancipatory interest of women than to effect a politicization in the middle-class sense of participation and engagement, which is abstract by comparison. Since most family women have either an uncompleted education or an obsolete one, the family's guarantee of existence is implicit in woman's economic dependence.

My experiences of a life partly shared with women from the nonacademic world made clear to me that women from the female "subproletariat" and intellectual women share an interest, despite their class differences, in a socialist transformation of society in which sex-based division of labor is removed in the reproductive sphere also. There is no place where the transformation has been implemented with women's interests in mind.

Psychic Reproduction and Thematic Work

At the level of interaction modes, women's seminars aim to eliminate competition among the women (including competition for men) and to promote self-awareness as women. The formal and informal patterns of social interaction in [traditional] seminars are organized on the basis of hierarchical structures: instructor-student, expert-layperson, professional-undergraduate. These are parallelled by learning processes which even scholars treat as reified commodity-processes, detached from the concrete, living human beings and their practice. Knowledge and skills are transmitted and tested.

Women's forms of social interaction among themselves are imprinted by these contradictions. On the one hand, women are hampered by their experiences of oppression; on the other hand, they have acquired "qualifications" of their own, despite or because of their special position in the reproductive sphere. Since women must always relate to men, formally or informally, and must also qualify themselves via men—for the qualifications scene is exclusively male-defined—a women's seminar is always clearly a step or process of boundary-making. Consequently, many women react with anxiety and disorientation. This is also a reason for what often seems from outside to be a thoroughly anarchical structure, and for the resignative results of women's seminars.

When women students and instructors in these seminars work on a topic in their double role as woman and student or instructor, the conceptual learning process is controlled by their individual and collective experiences and reciprocal validation.

In my estimation, this explains the high value placed on the autonomous small study groups in women's seminars: In these groups the women talk about themselves, and meet listeners who have a similar or different storehouse of experiences, and with whom they are doing something collectively. On the basis of psychic reproduction and understanding, a collective identity emerges. On the other hand, the women's psychic reproduction among themselves is by no means without its problems. Emancipation causes anxiety and, unlike male-female relationships, the relations of women among themselves, especially mother-daughter relationships, are still largely unexplored by the social sciences.

The Work-Pattern in Women's Seminars

The pattern of working and communicating among women is more oriented toward concrete persons and their needs, more strongly collective and authentic. In contrast to the "academic style" in traditional seminars, oral presentations are strikingly cautious, tentative, and linked to people. The radicality of this has obstructed cognitive progress in the seminars because no pre-formed thinking, no authorities, no empty words were tolerated.

I wish tentatively to characterize the seminars' manner of working: It connects feeling and cognition. It is process-oriented. It develops an inductive conceptual process and aims for collective advancement in thinking. Thematic exposition is (as yet) relatively vague and imprecise.

Feelings and Cognition. Women students in these seminars often argue on the basis of feelings they have. At first glance this seems paradoxical. Feelings have no place in scholarship, or if so, only as the objects of cognition, not as a medium for it. Women often say things like: "I have the feeling I'm not included here or that this way isn't right." "I don't feel comfortable here." "I can't do anything with what you just said." "I can't put myself into it," and so on. Women often say "I got a lot out of the last group meeting" (or the weekend retreat, or the women's seminar). But when questioned further, they do not define or communicate this comfortable impression more precisely.

It seems that women's alternative learning situations and thought processes have a basically transitory and open-ended nature which can be captured only at opportune moments, and these are very rare. Since many women relate their own and others' statements very strongly to themselves as people, obtaining the necessary distance from their own thought-processes is already a step toward alienation; they are more likely to consider this step worth taking for career reasons than of their own volition.

Process-Oriented and Result-Oriented Thinking. Women have few possibilities to identify with the products of their work. On the other hand, women (but not only women) resist the reified nature of learning processes.

A continual subject of discussion in the seminars is the question of what form their conclusions should take. The women students either do not believe they have any, or consciously refuse to reify their processes of appropriating knowledge, to generalize, theorize about and publish them. In all my seminar and group meetings with women I am struck again and again by this vague process/relational way of thinking: The atmosphere of the group discussion is important, the impression of having learned something for oneself is important, dealing with the concrete persons present and their statements is important—but the participants resist recording their fleeting learning experiences. A written product causes discomfort. On the other hand, the transitoriness of their study group process also causes frustration: Even though they feel comfortable, they express criticism of the unsatisfactory conclusions.

Perhaps the reason is that women's personal experience of involvement, which is always one of the topics, cannot be captured as a generalization after so short a time, and/or the abstraction must remain linked to the experiences.

Some Contradictions between Small-Group Work and Plenum in (Women's) Seminars

The pedagogical function of the plenum in all seminar types is still relatively poorly understood. Previous criticism of the plenum was based on learning-intensity and learning-organizational factors. In the women's seminars, antagonism between the plenum and small-group work becomes especially clear. Here, some criticisms of the plenum are picked up and analyzed.

"The plenum is ineffective—work gets done only in the small groups. In the vast majority of cases, the plenum is beside the point, a waste of time, devoid of content for most of the women." (result-orientation vs. process-orientation).

Thesis: The plenum is held because and although the women participating have nothing to say to each other. Nevertheless, they stay together because it is assumed that women should and want to have something to say to each other.

"The plenum can't get organized—in the small group it happens spontaneously." If a seminar is structured by a principle of autonomous study groups, the autonomy mandate requires the plenum to be the supraindividual conclusion of the study groups. (organizational form as substantive problem).

Thesis: The plenum raises expectations of collectivity. But under authoritarian structures it becomes an expression of the instructor's individuality; under other structural conditions the plenum is initially chaotic.

"The plenum has no content of its own—in the small group we talk about ourselves."

In the plenum, procedures are discussed, relationships talked about, but little of substance is presented. The plenum usually represents a metalevel for the study group. Here, the content of the small group's conclusions seems trivial. Reflection of the relational level also takes place on a metalevel in the plenum report: e.g., "In our group we shared our experiences." But these experiences are not named as "content." (Content level and relational level diverge.)

Thesis: There is no immediacy in the plenum. It produces only mediated reactions about content or procedures as content.

"The plenum is frustrating and chaotic. In the small group either there is a "leader" or else everyone talks."

The plenum is the unconscious expression of the respective individual consciousness. The participants behave realistically in the plenum; they do not appropriate it, but put up with it or stay away. The plenum is based on a latent authority structure and individual aggression structures. The strongest will assert themselves (power structure).

Thesis: The relationships of study groups and plenum corresponds (by way of analogy) to the differing qualities of family and social experiences.

"The plenum has an alienated atmosphere, it blocks you. But the small group is stimulating and warm."

In contrast to the discussion structures and patterns of interaction in small groups, the plenum is not a place for self-presentation or stimulating reflection for most women. The plenum addresses different feelings than does the small group. It releases more anxiety and contains many opportunities to withdraw.

Thesis: The plenum demands more self-awareness and aggressivity for self-assertion than the small group.

For these reasons women students as a rule feel more comfortable in small groups. Consequences of large groups are greater vulnerability to criticism and nonacceptance, and less commitment to the individual. These observations allow these conclusions: The plenum organizes a different kind of learning process. It is itself a result of the separation of the private from the public sphere, a consequence of the division of labor even in learning processes.

Translated by Jeanette Clausen

Notes

* Originally published as, Sigrid Metz-Göckel, "Feminismus an der Hochschule: Erfahrungen und Überlegungen zur Arbeitsform in Frauenseminaren,"

in: *Frauenstudium: Zur alternativen Wissenschaftsaneignung von Frauen* Sigrid Metz-Göckel, ed. Hamburg: Arbeitsgemeinschaft für Hochschuldidaktik, 1979, pp. 47–62. Translated and reprinted with permission. Portions of this text are excerpted.

54. Towards a Methodology for Feminist Research*

Maria Mies

New wine must not be
poured into old vessels.

This article traces the roots of feminist innovations in research methodology to both earlier criticism within the social science community as well as the women's movement. The author sets feminist scholars the task of choosing topics and methods which help women who were formerly targets of research to appropriate that research so as to understand and change their situation.

Introduction

Criticism of the dominant quantitative social science research methodology started earlier than the women's movement. My first doubts about the scientific relevance and ethical justification of this methodology were raised when I was working as a teacher and researcher in a Third World country. Here I realized that the research situation as such, due to colonialism and neocolonialism, was a situation of clear dominance between research subject and research object, which tended to lead to distorted data.[1] In the United States, however, criticism of the established social science research came up in connection with the protest movement against American involvement in Latin America and Southeast Asia. Scholars like Horowitz (1974), Wolf and Jorgenson (1970), and Huizer (1973) raised their voices against this kind of research as a tactical tool in the "Counter-insurgency-and-containment-of-Communism" strategy of the United States. The emphasis of their criticism was on political and ethical questions.

In West Germany, at about the same time (1967–72), the positivist and functionalist theory of society, propagated throughout the Anglo-Saxon world, and the quantitative analytical research methodology were being attacked by the theoreticians of the so-called Frankfurt School: Horkheimer, Adorno, Fromm, Habermas, et al., who evolved the critical theory of society from a dialectical and historical point of view. The focus of their criticism was the claim of value neutrality and the structural separation between theory and practice of the

357

positivist approach. They attacked the scientific irrelevance, the elit-
ism, and inherent class bias of this approach and tried to revive the
emancipatory potential which social theory had in the eighteenth
century, the beginning of the bourgeois epoch. The criticism of
"critical theory," however, remained confined to the magic circle of
academic institutions. It did not reach the working masses and thus
reproduced the structural separation between theory and practice,
characteristic of the capitalist mode of production. In the mid-1970s,
an effort was made to bridge this gap by the proponents of action
research, first evolved by Lewin (1953).

The thoughts which follow on a methodology for feminist research
grew out of the debates on these three waves of criticism against
positivism as the dominant social science theory and its accompanying
methodology. On the other hand, they are the outcome of my
involvement in the women's movement and of my experience in
action research projects. They are not to be understood as prescrip-
tions to be followed dogmatically, but as an invitation for methodological experiment and innovation. The assumption underlying
these guidelines is the following: *There is a contradiction between the
prevalent theories of social science and methodology and the political
aims of the women's movement.* If Women's Studies is to be made
into an instrument of women's liberation, we cannot uncritically use
the positivist, quantitative research methodology. If Women's Studies
uses these old methodologies, it will again be turned into an instrument of repression. New wine should not be poured into old
vessels.[2]

Thesis: *When women begin to change their situation of exploitation and
oppression, then this change will have consequences for the research
areas, theories, concepts and methodology of studies that focus on women's
issues.*

If Women's Studies is to contribute to the cause of women's
emancipation, then women in the academic field have to use their
scholarship and knowledge towards this end. If they consciously do
so they will realize that their own existence as *women* and *scholars*
is a contradictory one. As women, they are affected by sexist oppression, together with other women, and as scholars they share the
privileges of the (male) academic elite.

The contradictory existential and ideological condition of women
scholars must become the starting point for a new methodological
approach. The postulate of objectivity itself makes it necessary that
those areas of the female existence which so far were repressed and
socially "invisible" be brought into the full daylight of scientific
analysis. In order to make this possible, feminist women must deliberately and courageously integrate their repressed, unconscious

female subjectivity, i.e., their own experience of oppression and discrimination into the research process. This means that committed women social scientists must learn to understand their own "double consciousness" as a methodological and political opportunity and not as an obstacle. Leavitt et al. (1975) wrote about this double consciousness that women have in common with other groups who have suffered from oppression.

In the following I shall try to lay down some methodological guidelines for feminist research. These will be followed by an account of an attempt to put these guidelines into practice in an action research project.

Methodological Guidelines for Feminist Research

1. The postulate of *value free research*, of neutrality and indifference towards the research objects, has to be replaced by conscious *partiality*, which is achieved through partial identification with the research "objects." For women who deliberately and actively integrate their double-consciousness into the research process, this partial identification will not be difficult. It is the opposite of the so-called "Spectator-Knowledge" (Maslow, 1966:50) which is achieved by showing an indifferent, disinterested, alienated and reified attitude towards the "research objects." Maslow calls the objectivity thus achieved scientistic, not scientific.

2. The vertical relationship between researcher and "research objects," the *view from above*, must be replaced by the *view from below*. This is the necessary consequence of the demand of conscious partiality and reciprocity. Research, which so far has been largely an instrument of dominance and legitimation of power elites, must be brought to serve the interests of dominated, exploited and oppressed groups, particularly women.

The demand for a systematic "view from below" has both a scientific and an ethical-political dimension. The scientific significance is related to the fact that despite the sophistication of the quantitative research tools, much data gathered by these methods is irrelevant or even invalid because the hierarchical research situation as such defeats the very purpose of research: It creates an acute distrust in the "research objects" who feel that they are being interrogated. This distrust can be found when women and other underprivileged groups are being interviewed by members of a socially higher stratum. It has been observed that the data thus gathered often reflect "expected behavior" rather than real behavior (Berger, 1974).

Women who are committed to the cause of women's liberation cannot stop at this result. They cannot be satisfied with giving the social sciences better, more authentic and more relevant data. The ethical-political significance of the view from below cannot be separated from the scientific one: This separation would again transform all methodological innovations in Women's Studies into instruments of dominance. Only if Women's Studies is deliberately made part of the struggle against women's oppression and exploitation, can women prevent the misuse of their theoretical and methodological innovations for the stabilization of the status quo and for crisis management.

3. The contemplative uninvolved "spectator knowledge" (Maslow) must be replaced by *active participation in actions, movements and struggles* for women's emancipation. Research must become an integral part of such struggles.

Max Weber's famous principle of separating science and politics (praxis) is not in the interests of women's liberation. Women scholars who want to do more than a mere paternalistic "something for their poorer sisters" (because they feel that, as a privileged group, they are already liberated) but who struggle against patriarchy as a system, must take their studies into the streets and take part in the social actions and struggles of the movement.

4. Participation in social actions and struggles, and the integration of research into these processes, further implies that the *change of the status quo* becomes the starting point for a scientific quest. The motto for this approach could be: "If you want to know a thing, you must change it." ("If you want to know the taste of a pear, you must change it; i.e., you must chew it in your mouth," Mao-Tse Tung, 1968). Most empirical research on women has concentrated so far on the study of superficial or surface phenomena such as women's attitudes towards housework, career, part-time work, etc. Such attitude or opinion surveys give very little information about women's true consciousness. Only when there is a rupture in the "normal" life of a woman: i.e., a crisis such as divorce, or the end of a relationship, is there a chance for her to become conscious of her true condition. In the "experience of crises" (H. Kramert, 1977) and rupture with normalcy, women are confronted with the real social relationships in which they had unconsciously been submerged as objects. As long as normalcy is not disrupted they are not able to admit even to themselves that these relationships are oppressive or exploitive. This is why in attitude surveys women so often are found to subscribe to the dominant sexist ideology of the submissive, self-sacrificing woman.

The motto of changing a situation in order to be able to understand it applies not only to the individual woman and her life crises, but also to collective processes. The very fact that today we are talking about a methodology for doing research in Women's Studies is the

result of a change in the status quo that was brought about by the women's movement and not by intellectual endeavors in universities.
5. *The research process must become a process of "conscientização,"* both for the so-called "research subjects" (social scientists) and for the "research objects" (women as target groups). The methodology of "conscientização" was first developed and applied by Paulo Freire in his problem-formulating method.* The decisive characteristic of the approach is that the study of an oppressive reality is not carried out by experts but by the objects of oppression. People who before were objects of research become subjects of their own research and action. This implies that scientists who participate in this study of the conditions of oppression must give their research tools to the people. They must inspire them to formulate the problems with which they struggle in order that they may plan their action. The women's movement so far has understood the process of conscientization largely as that of becoming conscious of one's individual suffering as a woman. The emphasis in consciousness-raising groups was on group dynamics, role-specific behavior and relationship problems rather than on the social relations that govern capitalist societies.
6. I would like to go a step further than Paulo Freire, however. The collective conscientization of women through a problem-formulating methodology *must be accompanied by the study of women's individual and social history.* Women have so far not been able to appropriate (i.e., make their own) the social changes to which they have been subjected passively in the course of history. Nor have they subjectively appropriated (i.e., integrated into their collective consciousness for themselves) those changes for which they have actively fought, such as the women's vote.

The theoretical analysis of such movements was usually done—if at all—after the event, and the results of these analyses were not fed back to the movements. This lack of historical documentation and analysis may be responsible for the fact that in subsequent waves of women's movements in the course of the last one hundred years, the same questions were raised, the same issues were taken up (i.e., the struggle for equal wages, or for the abolition of abortion laws).

The women were not aware of an historic continuity of their struggles; therefore, they could not learn from their successes or mistakes and these past struggles did not become part of their

*Note: By "conscientização," Freire means "learning to perceive social, political and economic contradictions and to take action against the oppressive elements of reality." In the following we will use the English version, "conscientization." (*Pedagogy of the Oppressed*, Freire, 1971).

collective consciousness. Thus, women do make history, but they do not *appropriate* their own history as subjects. Such subjective appropriation of their history, their past struggles, sufferings and dreams would lead to something like a collective women's consciousness (in analogy to class consciousness) without which no struggle for emancipation can be successful.

The appropriation of women's history can be promoted by feminist scholars who can inspire and help other women to document their campaigns and struggles. They can help them to analyze these struggles, so that they can learn from past mistakes and successes and, in the long run, may become able to move from mere spontaneous activism to long-term strategies. This presupposes, however, that women engaged in Women's Studies remain in close contact with the movement and maintain a continuous dialogue with other women. This in turn implies that they can no longer treat their research results as their private property, but that they must learn to collectivize and share them. This leads to the next postulate.

7. Women cannot appropriate their own history unless they *begin to collectivize their own experiences.* Women's Studies, therefore, must strive to overcome the individualism, the competitiveness, the careerism, prevalent among male scholars. This has relevance both for the individual woman scholar engaged in research and for her methodology. If she is committed to the cause of women's liberation, she cannot choose her area of research purely from a career point of view but must try to use her relative power to take up issues that are central to the movement.

An Attempt to Apply These Postulates by the Action Group: "Women Help Women," Cologne 1976–77

These methodological guidelines were not evolved merely through the study of social science literature but also through my participation in several field projects and the discussion of these experiences with women students and other colleagues. I had a first chance to try out some of these guidelines in an action research project which grew out of an initiative responding to violence against women in the family. This initiative was started by the women students of Social Pedagogy in Cologne in the Spring of 1976. They founded an association called "Women Help Women" and started a campaign to get a house where women who had been beaten by their husbands or friends could find shelter. Similar Women's Houses for battered women had already been established as projects of women's self-help in London, Amsterdam and Berlin.

1. A problem must be created (Postulate 4: In order to understand a thing, one has to change it.)

After an action group (fifteen young women) had been constituted, a position paper was drafted on its objectives, methods and organizational principles. The group then approached the Social Welfare Department of the Municipal Administration and asked for a house for battered women. The reply of the Social Welfare authorities, however, was that there was no need for such a house in Cologne.

The action group therefore organized a street action with posters, photos of battered wives, newspaper clippings and signatures collected from passersby, about the need for a Women's House for mistreated women. At the same time, people who came to their stand were interviewed about their experiences with and their views on wife beating. These interviews were recorded and provided firsthand data about the existence of this problem in Cologne. The whole action was reported in the press, including some of the statements made by the people. This public airing of a problem which so far had been considered a purely private affair mobilized many people to discuss the question of a Women's House.

The municipal authorities found it difficult to maintain their indifference and finally had to mobilize their own research cell to investigate the problem of wife beating.

With the aid of systematic publicity work in the press, on the radio and TV, the organization grew and became known in the city. Many women who had been mistreated by their husbands rang the number given in the press. Three months after the start of the project, women began to ask the group for help. At that time the group did not yet have a house, however, and its members therefore began to give shelter in their own homes to the women who asked for help.

This made the need for a Women's House all the more urgent. When the Social Welfare Department published the results of its own investigation, the action group stated that they had given shelter to about thirty women between June and September of 1976. It could no longer be said that the problem of private violence against women did not exist in Cologne. Eventually the members raised enough money to pay the rent of a suitable house, and later on the municipality provided a subsidy.

2. Partiality and egalitarian involvement in a social action (Postulates 1 and 3)

Members of the action group clearly stated in their position paper that they did not want to allow new hierarchies to grow or experts to dominate the organization. Therefore, they made it a precondition for membership that women who wanted to join "Women Help Women" had to do any type of work that came up. In the long run this proved to be a correct decision. The women social scientists who joined the organization had to give up their status of uninvolved, neutral, scientific observers or experts; they not only had to take sides with and for the mistreated women, but also to participate actively and on an equal footing with nonacademic women in all the work. This had the effect that all members had to feel actively responsible for the progress of the movement. There was no bureaucratic center of authority to which responsibility could be delegated.

This had the effect for the academic women that their horizon in day-to-day struggles was immensely broadened. In their discussions with women who sought shelter in the Women's House they learned more about the true social conditions of German families than from any number of quantitative surveys. For the women who had started the action group, the decision that there should be no hierarchy or bureaucracy meant that they had to learn many things that women usually do not know: From dealing with officials, lawyers, policemen, to speaking at press conferences; studying Social Welfare laws, to whitewashing and painting; driving alone at night to unknown places to meet women who sought their help, etc. The principle of action and egalitarian participation was also applied to the women who sought the help of "Women Help Women." After a time of rest and recovery in the Women's House, they were encouraged to participate in all the activities of the organization. This was not always easy, because the women who sought shelter had run away from an acute crisis situation. They expected help and looked upon the organization as an ordinary social welfare institution. It was difficult to get them to understand gradually that women's liberation rather than social welfare and charity was the aim of the action group. This understanding was furthered by the principle of active and egalitarian participation of all, including the academic women.

3. Discussion and "socialization" of life-histories as therapy, as basis for collective women's consciousness and as starting point for emancipatory action (Postulates 5, 6 and 7)

In the first phase of the action, intense individual and group discussions took place with women who had run away from their homes. It became necessary to help women to understand that their own experience of male violence was not just their individual bad luck or even their fault, but that there is an objective social basis for this private violence by men against women and children. This meant that they had to understand the sociological and historical dimensions of male violence if they were to get out of the masochistic tendency to attribute the failure of their marriage to their own failure as women.

The best method by which to make women in this crisis situation aware of the sociological and historical roots of their suffering appears to be the documentation and analysis of their life histories. This method, evolved as a technique of action research (Osterland, 1973), is not only an effective way by which to integrate the time dimension into social research; it is also an excellent method of conscientization. Only when women can use their own documented, analyzed, understood and *published* history as a weapon in the struggle for themselves and for all women will they become subjects of their own history. This implies that the documentation of their life histories, the video film, the book, the discussions, have to be integrated into the overall strategy of the women's movement. Although this mobilization of all women who so far have been passive victims of patriarchal structural and direct violence may transcend the scope of a small action-research project, the fact that the women who took part in it showed keen interest in starting a public campaign against private violence is an indicator that they are moving away from their status as mere objects of charity and social welfare and are on the way to becoming subjects of their own history.[3]

Notes

* To be published as, Maria Mies, "Towards a Methodology for Feminist Research," *Theories of Women's Studies II*, ed. Gloria Bowles and Renate Duelli-Klein London: Routledge and Kegan Paul, 1983. Reprinted with permission. German original: in *Beiträge zur feministischen Theorie und Praxis* no. 1 (1978). Portions of this text have been excerpted.

1. M. Mamdani's study of the *Myth of Population Control* describes the functioning of this kind of research. (See bibliography).

2. The present world-wide interest in Women's Studies, though a direct outcome of the women's movement, must also be understood as an effort to neutralize and co-opt the protest potential of the movement.

3. The results of this documentation have been published meanwhile in the book *Nachrichten aus dem Ghetto Liebe* (Reports from the Ghetto Love) edited by Frauenhause Köln. Frankfurt, 1981.

Bibliography

Berger, Hartwig. *Untersuchungsmethode und soziale Wirklichkeit*. (Research Methods and Social Reality). Frankfurt, 1974.

Freire, Paulo. *Pedagogy of the Oppressed*. Trans. Myra Bergman Ramos. New York: Seabury Press, 1970.

Horowitz, Irving L. *The Rise and Fall of the Project Camelot: Studies in the Relationship between Science and Practical Politics*. Cambridge: MIT Press, 1974.

Huizer, Gerrit. "The A-Social Role of Social Scientists in Underdeveloped Countries: Some Ethical Considerations." *Sociologus*, 23, No. 2 (1973), pp. 165–177.

Kramert, Helgard. "Wann wird die Selbstverständlichkeit der geschlechtlichen Arbeitsteilung in Frage gestellt? " ("When Will the Assumed Sexual Division of Labor Be Questioned? "). Paper delivered in Frankfurt, 1977.

Leavitt, Ruby, Barbara Sykes, and Elizabeth Weatherford. "Aboriginal Women: Male and Female Perspectives." In *Toward an Anthropology of Women*. Ed. Rayna Reiter. New York: Monthly Review Press, 1975, pp. 110–126.

Lewin, Kurt. *Feldtheorie in den Sozialwissenschaften*. *(Field Theory in Social Science)*. New York: Harper and Row, 1951.

―――. *Die Lösung Sozialer Konflikte*. (Resolving Social Conflicts). New York: Harper and Row, 1948.

Mamdani, Mahmood. *The Myth of Population Control: Family, Caste and Class in an Indian Village*. New York: Monthly Review Press, 1973.

Mao Tse Tung. *Über die Praxis, Über den Widerspruch. (On Practice. On Contradiction)*. Calcutta: National Book Agency, 1967.

Martin, Kay M., and Barbara Voorhies. *Female of the Species*. New York: Columbia University Press, 1975.

Maslow, Abraham H. *The Psychology of Science: A Renaissance*. New York: Harper and Row, 1966.

Nash, June. Report on the Conference on Feminine Perspectives in Social Science Research. Buenos Aires, March 1974.

Osterland, Martin. "Lebensgeschichtliche Erfahrung und gesellschaftliches Bewusstsein. Anmerkungen zur soziobiographischen Methode." ("Life History Experience and Social Consciousness: Notes on a Social-Biographical Method"). *Soziale Welt*, 24, No. 4 (1973), pp. 409–417.

Wolf, Eric, and J.G. Jorgenson. "Anthropology on the Warpath in Thailand." *New York Review of Books*, 15, No. 9 (1970), pp. 26–34.

A Critical Outlook

The German Women's Movement in 1982*

Dagmar Schultz

The "Summer University for Women" is a weeklong event in West Berlin that has been a tradition since 1976. Together with similar conferences in Hamburg, Bremen, and Dortmund, it can serve as an indicator of various trends in the Autonomous Women's Movement. Clearly, a change has taken place in the content and structure of the Summer University: under the thematic title of "Survival Strategies" a wide range of workshops and presentations was offered in 1982, yet the number of workshops addressing the newly found "spiritual" and body-related aspects of women's lives predominated. Hundreds of women attended sessions on treatment methods of Philippino healers and on meditation. Hundreds followed the call to trance sessions with sleeping bags under their arms. An even greater number, certainly including many of those who took part in the above workshops went to hear Alice Schwarzer talk on the subject "How Peaceful are Women?" Schwarzer, editor of the feminist magazine *Emma* and a controversial personality in the Women's Movement, attacked and ridiculed all those trends in the Movement supporting an idealized concept of motherhood or concentrating on developing their specifically female "magic" powers. How should we interpret the applause Schwarzer received by the very women implicated in her scathing and even unfair critique of spirituality? Was it a result of a personality cult, or did it indicate insecurity about political direction on the part of individuals and the Movement in general?

The tendency to retreat into contemplation of one's interior life and learning about positive energies women can (re)generate has definitely had its effects on the Movement, although I would not label such trends "neofascist", as did Ti-Grace Atkinson in a recent talk in Berlin. In the Berlin Feminist Women's Health Center for instance, of which I am a founder and have been a member since

* I thank Joan Reutershan for her helpful editorial comments.

1974, a controversy between two different factions has been waged for three years now. On the one side are the women who have been deeply involved in astrology, spirituality, meditation, etc. as philosophy of life. On the other side are those who are committed to struggling against the abuse of women and to establishing connections between women's health programs and other radical aspects of women's politics. The women who favor confronting the institutions of our oppression suggested that the group to move the Health Center to a house in a lower class district occupied by women "Squatters" who are participating in the Berlin Housing Movement. This experience, as well as the effects of the 1981 change from a Social Democratic to a Christian Democratic government did, ironically, help the group to find a balance between the two positions. The constant threat to the existence of the Health Center because of its mere location as well as the cutting of meager public funds allocated to the Center made toleration of differences in approach a necessity for survival. At the same time, several positive aspects of the spirituality wave could be seen in the women's health movement. The centers began with a major emphasis on gynecology, and have now broadened their perspective to a holistic approach to health. Techniques and interests include nutrition, using yoga and meditation in dealing with stress symptoms, trances and fantasy trips to help women address deep-seated attitudes and fears about disorders such as menstrual cramps, breast cancer, or dental problems. Because of these concrete experiences I believe that the health movement is in a particularly apt position to reach a more positive solution to the conflict over "spirituality" and "radical politics" than was expressed at the Summer University.

The changing political situation in the Federal Republic is playing its own role in altering the perspectives of the Autonomous Women's Movement. The threat which the government and the recent rise of the Right—specifically the Christian Democratic Party—pose to the Women's Movement has been driven home on several levels. To take the example of the Summer University again: For the first time, the Berlin city government refused to grant employed women an educational leave to attend the conference. A number of workshops were considered "unacceptable," among them a training session in resistance strategies. This was interpreted as an attack on the government's "monopoly over violence." Workshops on vaginal self-examination and various topics addressing lesbians were considered to be a danger to the morality of minors. The host institution, the Free University of Berlin, prohibited several sessions dealing with strategies in the struggle against increasing militarization and against government backlash.

Initially, the divide-and-conquer tactics implicit in attacking lesbians on the one hand, and "political" workshops on the other hand, seemed to be successful. Later, however, women were able to establish the connection between both repressions and to refuse to accept a concept of what is "political" imposed on them from above. The Summer University ended with a sit-in at the Berlin City Hall to protest the government's actions.

For me, these events at the Summer University reemphasized the importance of an open discussion on the *political* content of lesbianism. For too long, many lesbians have worked in the Movement without making their sexual preference an issue of political meaning. This attitude certainly reflects a more-or-less conscious recognition of the underlying homophobia in the Women's Movement and the overt homophobia in society at large. The danger of not introducing the politics of lesbianism in a continuous and open way became obvious at this conference. During a strategy session on the planned sit-in and confrontation with the official responsible for cancelling workshops, one woman said: "Let's emphasize the political aspects and not their opposition to lesbianism, because that only concerns a few of us." I couldn't help thinking of the autobiographies of heterosexual women who had been in concentration camps under Hitler, and their slanderous, homophobic talk about lesbian campmates. As long as heterosexual women in the Movement do not deal with their homophobia, the government does not need to put much effort into using the issue of lesbianism to divide us.

The government's reaction against a potentially radical Autonomous Women's Movement, is, of course, not all that recent. It has been particularly obvious over the past few years in the case of shelters for battered women. These institutions were established with government funding by women from the Autonomous Movement, who also successfully insisted that the program be run solely by women, that the victims be offered the chance for a prolonged stay, and that they receive help in setting up a new home, for example, in a communal living arrangement. After a number of houses had been established, the government attempted to place battered women in the grouping of "marginal, deviant persons" and to attach public funding to the acceptance of this legal definition. At the same time they used the shelters for their campaign purposes. More recently, the Christian Democrats have begun to replace the shelters of the Autonomous Women's Movement with institutions resembling safehouses or homes for "deviants". They will be run not by women, but by state-supported charitable organizations. What the Social Democrats could not carry through because of the opposition of at least part of the Coalition leadership, is now being completed with vigor by the Christian Democratic Union.

After thirteen years of a coalition government between the Social Democratic Party and the Free Democratic Party, women are asking themselves what the new CDU-FDP has in store for women. The previous government by no means left women much to be grateful for. The struggle for a revision of anti-abortion legislation was a hard one, and in the end brought disappointing results. No legal recourse was established for women who were raped by their husbands. The government passed an "Adjustment Law" to the legal code of the European Community for equal treatment of women. This is of no value to women, however, since it stipulated no specific requirements or sanctions for discriminatory or sexist employment. The campaign for an antidiscrimination law, modelled after those in the United States or Britain, ended with a benevolently granted hearing, in which even representatives of the Autonomous Women's Movement were permitted to testify! The SPD left office having established severly repressive laws against people of an oppositional, i.e., leftist political conviction. "Berufsverbote" (job bans) deny employment in civil service professions (teachers, professors, postal and railworkers, among many others) to individuals who are members of legal political organizations of which the government disapproves. Because so many Berufsverbote affect teachers, and 70 percent of all teachers in the Federal Republic are women, women are often inordinately affected by this measure. Military expenditures increased under the coalition of SPD and FDP. Energy policy favored the construction of nuclear power plants. Growing racism against so called "guest" workers was met with restrictions of immigration regulations and the right to political asylum. Unemployment has affected women to a greater extent than men, because their jobs are the ones most likely to be eliminated in crises. From its record so far, the Christian Democratic Union can only be expected to continue policies which are detrimental to the well-being of women.

The intentions of the CDU in dealing with women's issues become very clear in the position paper of the CDU entitled "The Gentle Force of the Family." Here women are once again relegated to their tasks as mothers and as unpaid social workers for family and neighborhood. The policy is reminiscent of attitudes towards women during the Third Reich, especially since it is clear that motherhood should be practiced to a greater extent only by white German women, not by foreign women, whose high birth-rate is viewed with alarm. The position paper states: "Many women give up employment when getting married or having their first child. This is not a sign of oppression. For women it means liberation." Employed mothers are blamed for all failures of children as well as other social problems. Women who give up all aspirations beyond marriage and motherhood are promised honor and reward. The CDU is dangling the promise of financial benefits in front of women, by talking about the possibility of a pension for housewives, while at the same time reducing child allowances because of the budget crisis. This political development runs parallel to those in the United States which are concretized in the Family Protection Act.

The specter of a broad government campaign for a motherhood ideology has, however, sharpened women's awareness about a serious danger. This is the potential cumulative effect of present government strategy coalescing with an ideology originating among women themselves, which is similar to its conception of women's role in society, even though it has very different intentions. Such analysis has become particularly pronounced in the discussion of women's role in the peace movement.

Women have organized against increasing militarization. They have been active leaders in the Green Party and regional alternative parties. Women in the autonomous women's movement have undertaken various actions to demonstrate their opposition to, e.g., the stationing of United States rockets in West Germany: they have visited rocket sites and subsequently publicized information on the locations and functions of the rockets. At numerous conferences woman have analyzed the politics which are considered to lead to a certain threat of a ("limited") nuclear war. Some women and women's organizations have, however, entered the Peace Movement proclaiming an ideology of women as peacemakers, because of their role as producers and preservers of life. This position has been criticized for reinforcing the ideology of women as having a "natural" vocation as mothers, and as reducing the purpose of our lives to being an incarnation of peacefulness and passivity, devoting our life to others in the name of love.

This criticism is not to denigrate the importance of the Peace Movement in German political life. This, as well as the ecology and antinuclear movements, represents the first grass roots civil libertarian resistance to government and industry since the antimilitarization movement of the Fifties. Women farmers were in fact the first to protest against nuclear power plants, and women have continued to play an essential role in these progressive efforts. Yet those women who expend all their political energies in the Peace Movement, arguing that women as (potential) mothers need to make the struggle for peace their priority and that without peace women's visions cannot be realized, are being challenged as to what kind of peace and whose peace they are fighting for. Dorothea Brockmann, herself an active participant in antimilitary activities, argues:

> For us women, no peace exists today. . . . The war against us is taking place every day. . . . My daily life as a woman is a constant war, a street war, a house war: Violence against my desire, denigration of my feelings, mutilation, rape of my children. . . . In the name of love generations of women have been annihilated. The war machinery and the peace apparatus are but the mystified superstructures of the same violence which fetters our bodies, benumbs our lives, suffocates our utopias.[1]

Brockmann argues for radical opposition on the basis of feminist politics and against a peace movement which struggles for pacifism and a peace mythology at any price. She maintains that the most intransigent tabu in the women's Movement is dealing with violence, power, anger and radicalism. She calls on women to muster their anger, because "resistance grows" with anger. I share the conviction that opening up to our anger is essential. If it is anger against men and male society, it is essential to feel it so that we can translate it into radical action. If it is anger against homophobia and/or racism in our sisters, it is crucial to express it so we can begin to initiate change. Expressing our anger may be our lifeline, the only way we can protect ourselves from being sucked up by lukewarm reforms, from being kept on the master's leash, from being reintegrated, coopted into the system which we have been trying to break away from. This is especially important at a time when male ideology is speaking through women. We can see this phenomenon of the current backlash against women's liberation on an international scale in, e.g., Betty Friedan's *The Second Stage* and Colette Dowling's *The Cinderella Complex* in the United States; Ireen Pizzey, *Prone to Violence* in England; and Frigga Haugg's *Victim and Perpetrator*, the latter being the work of a German left sociologist[2]. All present theories which seek the reasons for women's lack of power and for the violence waged by men against women in women themselves. Pizzey even maintains that women develop a psychological and physical addiction to being battered!

The political approach to our personal lives and the personal approach to our political surroundings can only be maintained and strengthened if we continue to review the developments of the women's movement. At this time, we need to learn to see where and why we were successful and when and why we failed, to understand how our own inability to act in radical ways has implications for the political and social context in which we live. In general, the great potential for intelligent strategy and for radical action has not yet been realized. Perhaps this is one reason why many (often younger) women are attracted to trance, meditation, and spirituality not in preparation for, but to the exclusion of, protest in the public area. The sense of movement history has not been adequately passed down to the coming generation of women. It is part of the responsibility of the older women with years of movement experience to help bridge the generation gap.

Improved communication has become a concern of women on various levels. More outreach and women outside the Movement and better coordination of information within the Movement were goals formulated at the last Berlin Summer University[3]. A recently formed organization called the "October Sixth Initiative" is planning to start a women's news service so as to improve the flow of information and communication about issues of interest to all women. The same group had called for a national conference in November 1982 to discuss the implications of the change in government for women. I am working with a group of women who got together to discuss ways of intensifying an international orientation in the women's movement. We are thinking of creating a journal utilizing translations of articles from women's journals in other countries, with an emphasis on women's activities in "Third World" countries (similar to *Connexions* in the United States).

While there is a definite need for improved communication structures, women in the German Women's Movement share the conviction that a national organization such as the National Organization for Women in the United States is not a suitable one for the Movement here. Past experiences, perhaps endemic to Germany, have created a deep mistrust of possible personality cults, hierarchies, stifling bureaucracies, and rigid programmatic lines. It is probably true that the German Autonomous Movement, with its small groups, with women's centers and independent projects, provides the best structure for action at the present time—though more initiative in the direction of coalitions among their own groups, as well as with certain "mixed" organizations would be desirable. Although there have been some severe personality and political conflicts among women within these organizational forms, paralyzing aspects of parliamentary procedures and hierarchical structures have been largely avoided. The autonomous groups have enabled women to focus on creative, cooperative work structures. They have also prevented women from getting caught up in the wheels of cooptation and compromise.

The projects, which have been central to the Movement, have helped concretize consciousness of our oppression and offered women alternatives, have proved, however, to be problematic in several ways. They have demanded so much time and effort from women, simply to keep them going, that the participants often have had no energy left to participate in more general activities, i.e., developing offensive reactions against government policy, or formulating women's strategies for the peace or ecological movements. Often the projects are incapable of maintaining an adequate procedure for evaluating their own work, largely because women are underpaid and overworked. If the projects are not self-supporting, such as cafes or stores, they usually suffer from financial problem. The discussion as to whether to attempt to get government funds has been waged since the women's shelters received grants, but had to deal with all the consequences involved in accepting money, including threats to their autonomy. There are far fewer possibilities of receiving foundation money in Germany than in the United States. At the same time, women here question voluntary work more than do their United States counterparts. In the States such voluntary work has a long tradition, and the country does not conceive of itself as a welfare state in the same way Germany does. Aside from the mere need to survive, women here feel they ought to be paid for their work, because women have been continuously exploited through unpaid labor. I agree with this position, though in a few cases I think it has become a stumbling block, for example, when a project did not want to accept unpaid services, and thereby exluded interested, capable women from an activity because they could not be paid. Women recently were able to create their own financial network in Berlin, called "Goldrush." An anonymous woman calling herself "Emma Goldnet" helped get it started, with a good-sized donation. The women intend to lend and give money to projects women want to start, as well as to coordinate counselling services on funding and finance questions. Hopefully, this effort will eventually enable certain projects to engage in research on and evaluation of their own work, as the Berlin Women's shelter was able to do with public funding.

Women in various professions have increased communication and exchange of experience among each other over the past few years. Women engaged in social work, in the media, in natural sciences, and architecture have been meeting regularly on a national basis. Within the Association of Social Science Research and Practice for Women, a section entitled "Women and Schools" held its first meeting in 1982. Teachers, high school students, and university women attended. Women's sections within the Teachers Union are working together with independent groups of teachers and with lesbian teachers to put pressure on publishing houses to eliminate sexism and homophobia from textbooks. Though the participants know a similar effort has been underway in the United States without much success, they still consider it important to try. Recently three hundred high school women from the German state Niedersachsen organized a conference to analyze their situation as younger women and plan strategy. Women of mixed professional backgrounds have set up a Communication Center in Berlin. They hold regular meetings and publish a newsletter to exchange experiences about their work situations and to develop ideas on how to improve them. All these efforts not only reduce women's sense of isolation, but they also encourage an intensified confrontation around women's issues in institutions.

Women in unions are also in the process of strengthening their positions. Recently a woman was elected as president of one of the largest unions in the Federal Republic, the Union of Public Employees. Closer ties to the Women's Movement are also being established. The next "Women's Week" in Hamburg, an event similar to the Berlin Summer University, will be organized with the support of union women.

Within the field of Women's Studies, some positive developments have taken place despite the severe cutbacks which here, as in the United States, have affected these programs more than any other university endeavor. Three German universities have now established centers to support and develop women's Studies and research on and by women, namely Berlin, Hamburg, and Bielefeld. The University of Dortmund is instituting the first Women's Studies Program for reentry women students. More women present talks about women's studies at the traditional professional conferences. Women involved in women's research are relating their findings to other questions of social, political, and economic policy on the national and international levels.

What is still lacking in the German Women's Movement is an intensified contact with women of foreign origin and a self-critical analysis and discussion of racism and antisemitism, such as is taking place in some sectors of the Women's Movement in the United States. The confrontation over racism between black German women, who are daughters of American soldiers, and white women, has been restricted to a small group. And there are very few Jewish women in Germany after the genocide this country committed forty years ago. Foreign women, of whom there are many more, live ghettoized by housing and work stratifications in German society, as well as by language and culture differences. Contact with German women in the Movement, who are for the most part of middle class life style if not origin, is restricted to a few projects (see article by Cornelia Mansfield). The discussion on racism and relations between women of different ethnic and national backgrounds is, however, beginning. Last year a group started meeting in Berlin to investigate ways to approach the problem. I am presently in the process of publishing a book of translations of Audre Lorde's and Adrienne Rich's work, which I hope will contribute a sense of urgency and importance to these themes here.

Readings of women's literature from Germany and other countries, women's drama and music, cafes and bars have become an integral part of our Movement. A recent event brought home some of the richness of earlier women's culture, and connected the younger and older women of today's movement with their sisters of a generation ago. Hundreds of women from all over the Federal Republic came to Berlin for three days to recreate and celebrate women's culture in the 1920s. The festival was held in a large turn-of-the-century hotel. Imaginatively dressed women were entertained by women's theater and music groups. Readings from a recently rediscovered book about Berlin's lesbian women in the 1920s, *Lilac Nights*, evoked a picture of the City when it had dozens of women's bars and several magazines as part of a large network of women's institutions.

The Autonomous Women's Movement in Germany today provides structures for mutual support and for action in our private lives, at the work place and in the public arena. Through our radical voices and activities we gain a sense of our unity and strength and reach out to other women. We encourage them and ourselves to fight back against our oppression, to dare not only to dream, but to think and act for our visions. In my opinion, it is not valid to declare the Women's Movement dead or a failure, as Ti-Grace Atkinson did for the United States, and as some women claim in the Federal Republic, although certainly much needs to be changed and improved. After fifteen years we have much more to lose, but it has also become harder to deprive us of what we have built. We are surely more aware of what we want and have a right to win.

Notes

1. Dorothee Brockman, "War and Peace", *Emma*, 1981, 10–13.
2. Betty Friedan, *The Second Stage*; Colette Dowling, The Cinderella Complex, 1981; Ireen Pizzey, Prone to Violence, 1982; Frigga Haugg, Victim and Perpetrator (Opfer und Täter), Argument Verlag, 1981.
3. These are results from a questionnaire handed out at the summer university and evaluated by Barbara Gröschke.
4. Adele Meyer (ed.), Lila Nächte (Lilac Nights), Zitronenprese, 1981.

Notes on Contributors

Elisabeth Alexander (born 1932), mother of three children and self-styled "original," has published poetry, stories, radio plays and novels. Her most recent work, with the startling title "She should have killed her children," deals with motherhood. Alexander lives in Heidelberg.

Edith Hoshino Altbach (born 1941, San Francisco) is the editor of *From Feminism to Liberation* (1971; 2nd, expanded edition, 1981) and the author of *Women in America* (1974). She has also written on Asian American culture. Married, with two children, she lives in Buffalo, New York.

Gisela Bock is Assistant Professor at the Free University of Berlin, teaching and doing research in European and American history, particularly of women, and participant in the women's movement.

Ulla Bock (born 1950) studied sociology of education and sociology and is working toward her doctorate at the University of Bielefeld in West Germany, concentrating on "the women's movement as a social movement."

Jo-Delphine Brox-Brochot (born 1935, Autun, France), after completing her studies in Lyon, moved to Germany as a language teacher. She has worked in citizens' initiatives and undogmatic women's groups. Married to a Catholic priest since 1968, she has two sons. Since 1979 she has been an independent representatives of the "Greens" in the Bremen state parliament.

Elfriede Brüning (born 1910), a member of the Communist Party since 1930, was imprisoned for anti-fascist activities in 1935. After WW II she briefly resumed her work as a journalist. A self-supporting writer since 1950, she has written novels, stories, TV plays, reportages and children's books. She lives in Berlin-GDR.

Brigitte Classen is a historian living in Berlin. Since October 1976 she has been an editor of the critical journal, *Die schwarze Botin.*

Jeanette Clausen (born 1940), teaches German and Women's Studies at Indiana U.—Purdue U., Fort Wayne. She edits the Women in German newsletter, and has presented papers and published articles on women and language. She has been working on this book off and on since 1977 and is looking forward to doing something else. She lives in struggle and solidarity with her daughter Erin.

Gabriele Goettle is a sculptor and germanist living in Berlin. Since Octobor 1976 she has been an editor of the critical journal *Die schwarze Botin*

Jutta Heinrich (born 1940) began writing for radio and magazines in 1970. Her most recent book records her "physical and mental reactions to life under a mushroom cloud." She works intermittently at various jobs to support herself while she writes. She lives in Hamburg.

Patricia Herminghouse teaches German and Women's Studies at Washington University. Beyond work on women as writers and 19th century German literature, she has edited two volumes on East German literature, an anthology of contemporary women writers, and a series of 19th century German-American texts. She has edited the *GDR-Bulletin* since 1975.

Marianne Herzog (born 1939, Mecklenburg, East Germany) moved to West Germany in 1957. It is her experiences as a factory pieceworker, the job at which she spent to longest time, that served as the basis for her book, *From Hand to Mouth*.

Elfriede Jelinek (born 1946, Murzzuschlag, Steiermark) grew up in Vienna and studied theater, art history and music. Her books are *Wir sind Lockvogel Baby!* (1970), *Michael. Ein Jugendbuch für Infantilgesellschaft* (1972), *Die Lieb-haberinnen* (1975), *Die Ausgesperrten* (1980).

Sarah Kirsch (born 1935) was one of several GDR artists to leave the country (in 1977) in the aftermath of the expatriation of singer Wolf Biermann. She is best known for her poetry, for which she recieved the Petrarch prize in 1976. She lives with her son in a rural area near Bremen.

Monika Kühn (born 1949, South Germany) was active in the Lesbian Action Center in Berlin, while completing her studies in the sociology of education. She now lives in the country and works in a lesbian carpentry workshop.

Hannelore Mabry (born 1930, Chemnitz) has long been active in the women's movement. She has a degree in the social sciences and is the author of *Unkraut ins Parlament* (1971) (a book on women's parliamentary work). She is a founder of the Frauenforum (1971) and of the Group to Promote the Establishment of a Feminist Party (1976). Twice married, one daughter.

Cornelia Mansfeld (born 1953) is a sociologist and engaged in the Berlin Women's Center (Abortion Group and Wages for Housework Group) and in the feminist anti-war movement. 1976–1981, community work with Turkish immigrant women. Now working as a journalist and teacher.

Angelika Mechtel (born 1943, Dresden) is a prolific writer of poetry, short stories and novels. She has been a member of the writers' organizations Gruppe 61 (since 1965), PEN and GEDOK.

Sigrid Metz-Göckel (born 1940) teaches at the University of Dortmund and is director of the Hochschuldidaktisches Zentrum. Active since 1976 in the women's movement, she is one of the founders of the group Sozialwissenschaftiche Forschung und Praxis für Frauen and has written extensively on curriculum and instruction and women.

Maria Mies is a Professor of Sociology at the Fachhochschule Köln (Cologne). She spent many years in India as a teacher and researcher. In the Hague, Holland she set up an MA program on women and development. A founding member of the German feminist Association for Social Science Research and Praxis, since 1982 she has been a co-editor of the *Beiträge zur feministischen Theorie und Praxis*.

Irmtraud Morgner (born 1933) has since 1968 focused her writings on the contradictions blocking women's personal and professional development. Especially since the publication of *Trobadora Beatriz* (1974), she has gained a reputation as one of the most inventive, witty feminist writers in the GDR. She lives with her son in Berlin-GDR.

Heike Mundzeck has studied law and political science. She lives in Hamburg and works as a free-lance journalist, dealing with legal, social and educational themes. Author of the 1973 book *Kinder lernen fernsehen* (Children Learn Television).

Helga Novak (born 1935, Berlin-Köpenick) studied journalism and philosophy at the University of Leipzig. In 1961 she married and moved to Iceland and (until 1965) worked in Icelandic factories. In 1966 she renounced her GDR citizenship and now lives in West Berlin.

Judith Offenbach (born 1943, in Bielefeld) is an instructor at a West German university. She worked for four years to write this "memorial" to her friend and lover, Sonja.

Ulrike Pallmert. I was born in 1950 in Karlsruhe and went to school there for twelve years. After finishing school I moved to Berlin to study, passing my final exams in 1977. Since 1979 I have worked in the shelter for battered women.

Claudia Pinl (born 1941) studied history and political science in Germany and the U.S. In 1964, Friedan's *The Feminine Mystique* put her vague discomfort about her role as a woman into words. Active in the German women's movement since 1971, she works as a journalist, mostly for radio stations.

Sibylle Plogstedt (born 1945) has degrees in sociology and political science— with emphasis on Eastern Europe. She is one of the founders and editors of the feminist monthly *Courage*. Her journalistic work has focused on internationalism, politics and labor unions.

Christa Reinig (born 1926), self-proclaimed "renegade" from patriarchy (since 1975), has published novels, stories, poetry and essays. Her most recent book *Mädchen ohne Uniform* (Girls Without Uniforms) explores homophobia from the time of Christa Winsloe to the present. Reinig lives with her lover Pauli in Munich.

Helke Sander (born 1937, Berlin) is a filmmaker. A participant in the student movement and, since 1968, in the women's movement, she started the Action Council for Women's Liberation (1968), the women's group Brot und Rosen (1972), and the journal *frauen und film* (1974). Her most recent films are *Redupers* (1977) and *der subjektive faktor* (1981).

Monika Savier (born 1952) has been active for years in the formation of feminist girls' groups and in streetwork with young prostitutes. Since 1980 she has been research associate at the Technical University of Berlin, in sociology of education. She is a founder of the "Flying Lesbians" and other women's bands.

Ingrid Schmidt-Harzbach (born 1941, East Prussia) studied politics, sociology, and history, was in the student movement, and, since 1973, in the women's movement. Since 1975 she has led women's forums at adult education schools and written on women's studies and women's history. She is a research associate at the Free University of Berlin.

Margot Schroeder (born 1937), divorced lesbian mother of two children, is a free-lance writer, "so free that even her emancipation is a double burden." Her most recent book is *Monolog einer Trinkerin* (Monologue of a Woman Alcoholic). She lives in Hamburg.

Dagmar Schultz (born 1941, Berlin) received her Ph.D. in 1972 from the University of Wisconsin. She has taught at Rust College, Mississippi, and, since 1974, at the Free University of Berlin, in American Studies. She is co-founder of the Berlin Feminist Women's Health Center and the publishing house sub rosa Frauenverlag. Books: *Ein Mädchen ist fast so gut wie ein Junge and Hexengeflüster.*

Jutta Schutting (born 1937) holds a Ph.D. in German and History and has taught at a technical institute in Vienna. She has published poetry and several collections of short prose as well as narrative fiction. She writes for people who expect individuality in the use of language.

Alice Schwarzer (born 1942) initiated the 1971 West German abortion rights campaign. Publications: *Frauen gegen den Paragraphen 218* (1971); *Frauenarbeit—Frauenbefreiung* (1973); *Der "kleine" Unterschied und seine grossen Folgen* (1975); *Das Emma-Buch* (1981); *So fing es an—10 Jahre Frauenbewegung* (1981); *Mit Leidenschaft—Texte 1968-1982* (1982); *Simone de Beauvoir heute— Gespräche aus 10 Jahren* (1983). Founder, in 1977, of the feminist monthly *Emma.*

Barbara Sichtermann (born 1943) studied economics and sociology. Her two books are *Leben mit einem Neugeborenen* and *Vorsicht Kind.* She works in broadcasting and publishing and lives in West Berlin.

Verena Stefan (born 1947) based her first book, *Häutungen* (1975) on her experiences in Berlin in the 60s and 70s. She has also published a volume of poetry (*Mit Füssen Mit Flügeln,* 1980) and, together with Gabriele Meixner, German translations of Adrienne Rich, *Dream of a Common Language* and Monique Wittig, *Lesbian Peoples.*

Naomi Stephan holds a Ph.D. in German literature from Indiana University. From 1967-1981 she taught Women's Studies, German language and literature at Valparaiso University. Currently she is director of Stephan/Moore Associates in Santa Monica (CA.), a training and development business specializing in creativity and growth workshops.

Ingrid Strobl (born 1952, Austria) worked on scientific projects and in Austrian television after completing her studies in German and art history. Active since 1972 in the Austrian women's movement, she became an editor of the journal *Emma* in 1979.

Ulla Terlinden (born 1945) is a sociologist and city planner and currently a Research Assistant at the Institute for Sociology at the Technical University of Berlin.

Maxie Wander, born in Vienna in 1953, lived in the GDR from 1958 until her death in 1977. She wrote for newspapers and film, and published short stories. Following *Guten Morgen, du Schöne* (1978) was a second posthumous publication, *Leben wäre eine prima Alternative* (1980), a diary-like chronicle of her struggle with cancer.

Brigitte Wartmann (born 1943) is a research associate in Social and Educational Studies, at the Technical University of Berlin. For four years she was an editor of the journal *Ästhetik und Kommunikation.* She edited *Weiblich-Männlich* (1980)—an anthology on the cultural history of femininity, and has written articles on female aesthetics.

Claudia von Werlhof (born 1943, Germany) is a sociologist at the University of Bielefeld and has lived in Latin-America, Africa and Asia. She has been active in the women's movement since the 1970s.

Barbara Witych (born 1955) studied German and history in the Department of Education, University of Bielefeld. Her examination topic was "Writing Women Today."

Christa Wolf (born 1929), one of the most respected and controversial authors writing in German today, continues to insist that her subjective authenticity is compatible with her country's ideology, despite difficulties there. Author of screenplays, novels, stories and literary criticism, including new editions of nineteenth-century German women authors, she lives with her husband in Berlin-GDR.

Christine Wolter (born 1939) worked as an editor and translator in Berlin-GDR and began publishing her own work in 1973. In her writing, she explores typical predicaments of women struggling to assert their independence. She is now living in Italy.

Index

F-TP

Altbach, E

GERMAN FEM

SUNY, 1984

389 pages